June, 2002

Frodo,

One more journey?
I would like to share this
adventure with you. My
own copy waits to be dog
eared just like yours. Just
say when!.

Distance may separate
us but your place as my
best friend will always be
in my heart.

Love Always
Sam (S)
wise

D0189170

Two Towns
in Provence

MAP OF
ANOTHER TOWN
and
A CONSIDERABLE
TOWN

Two Towns
in Provence

MAP OF
ANOTHER TOWN
and
A CONSIDERABLE
TOWN

M.F.K. Fisher

VINTAGE BOOKS
A DIVISION OF RANDOM HOUSE
NEW YORK

A Considerable Town

Part of Chapter 2 appeared in the Travel Section of
The New York Times on December 18, 1977.
Part of Chapter 7 appeared in *Gourmet* Magazine,
May 1978.
Part II of Chapter 11 was originally published as
"The Mahogony Tree" in *Woman's Day*. Reprinted by
permission of *Woman's Day* Magazine, a
Fawcett publication.

Library of Congress Cataloging in Publication Data
Fisher, M.F.K. (Mary Frances Kennedy), 1908-
Two towns in Provence.
Includes index.
Contents:
A map of another town—A considerable town.
1. Aix-en-Provence (France)—Description.
2. Marseille (France)—Description.
3. Fisher, M.F.K. (Mary Frances Kennedy), 1908-
I. Fisher, M.F.K. (Mary Frances Kennedy), 1908-
A map of another town. 1983.
II. Fisher, M.F.K. (Mary Frances Kennedy), 1908-
A considerable town. 1983.
III. Title.
DC801.A325F525 1983   944'.91   83-6901
ISBN 0-394-71631-0 (pbk.)

MAP
of
ANOTHER
TOWN

A Memoir of Provence

by

M. F. K. FISHER

with map and drawings by
Barbara Westman

For Nan Newton

Contents

MAP
of
ANOTHER
TOWN

> . . . it is very probable that if I had
> to draw the portrait of Paris, I would,
> one more time, draw it of myself.
>
> JEAN GIONO, 1961

OFTEN in the sketch for a portrait, the invisible lines that
bridge one stroke of the pencil or brush to another are
what really make it live. This is probably true in a word picture too. The myriad undrawn unwritten lines are the ones
that hold together what the painter and the writer have tried
to set down, their own visions of a thing: a town, one town,
this town.

Not everything can be told, nor need it be, just as the artist
himself need not and indeed cannot reveal every outline of his
vision.

There before us is what one human being has seen of something many others have viewed differently, and the lines held
back are perhaps the ones most vital to the whole.

Here before me now is my picture, my map, of a place and
therefore of myself, and much that can never be said adds to its
reality for me, just as much of its reality is based on my own
shadows, my inventions.

Over the years I have taught myself, and have been taught,
to be a stranger. A stranger usually has the normal five senses,
perhaps especially so, ready to protect and nourish him.

Then there are the extra senses that function only in subcon-
sciousness. These are perhaps a stranger's best allies, the ones

that stay on and grow stronger as time passes and immediacy dwindles.

It is with the invisible ink distilled from all these senses, then, that I have drawn this map of a town, a place real in stone and water, and in the spirit, which may also be realer.

Aix-en-Provence

. . . 177 meters above sea level; 52,217 inhabitants; former capital of Provence; seat of an archbishopric since the fifth century, and of the departmental law courts and prison, and the schools of Law and Letters of the University of Aix-Marseille; one of the most beautiful art centers of Europe.

The town was founded in 123 B.C. by the Roman consul Sextius Calvinus, and was made into a prosperous colony by Julius Caesar. Between the fifth and twelfth centuries it lost much of its political importance to the town of Arles, although it was once more made the capital in the twelfth century under the Counts of Provence.

During the fifteenth century, before joining France, it became the hub of European culture under the benevolent administration of King René and his two queens.

Le Guide Bleu: France, 1960

So HERE IS the town, founded more than two thousand years ago by the brash Roman invaders, on much older ruins which still stick up their stones and artifacts. I was as brash a newcomer to it, and yet when I first felt the rhythm of its streets and smelled its ancient smells, and listened at night to the music of its many fountains, I said, "Of course," for I was once more in my own place, an invader of what was already mine.

Depending upon one's vocabulary, it is facile enough to speak of *karma* or atavism or even extrasensory memory. For me, there was no need to draw on this well of casual semantics, to recognize Aix from my own invisible map of it. I already knew where I was.

I had been conditioned to this acceptance by a stay in another old town on the northward Roman road, when I was younger and perhaps more vulnerable. I lived for some time in Dijon in my twenties, and compulsively I return to it when I can, never with real gratification. And I dream occasionally of it, and while the dream-streets are not quite the same as in waking life (the Rue de la Liberté swings to the right toward the railroad yards instead of going fairly straight to the Place d'Armes and the Ducal Palace, for instance, but I always know exactly where *I* am going), still I am a remote but easy visitor, happier as such than as a visible one.

I do not, in my imagination, feel as easy there as in Aix. I have long since made my own map of Dijon, and it is intrinsic to my being, but the one of Aix is better, a refuge from any sounds but its own, a harbor from any streets but its own: great upheavals and riots and pillages and invasions and liberations and all the ageless turmoil of an old place.

I feel somewhat like a cobweb there. I do not bother anyone. I do not even wisp myself across a face, or catch in the hair of a passerby, because I have been there before, and will be again, on my own map.

I can walk the same streets, and make my own history from them, as I once did in a lesser but still structural way in Dijon, my first return to the past, forever present to me.

The town was put on its feet by a Roman whose elegant bathing place still splutters out waters, tepid to hot and slightly stinking, for a ceaseless genteel flow of ancient countesses and their consorts and a quiet dogged procession of arthritic postal clerks and Swiss bankers and English spinsters suffering from indefinable malaises usually attributed to either their native climates or their equally native diets. This spa, more ancient than anyone who could possibly stay in it except perhaps I myself, is at the edge of the Old Town, at the head of the Cours

Sextius, and more than one good writer has generated his own acid to etch its strange watery attraction.

Countless poems have been written too, in wine rather than acid, and countless pictures have been painted, about the healing waters and the ever-flowing fountains of the place. They will continue as long as does man, and the delicate iron balconies will cling to the rose-yellow walls, and if anyone else, from 200 B.C. to now, ever marked the same places on the map, in acid or wine or even tears, his reasons would not be mine. That is why Aix is what it is.

St. Sauveur

Almost thou persuadest me to be a
Christian.

The Acts of the Apostles, xxvi, 28

i *THE BEGINNING*

The structure of the baptistry of the Cathedral of St.
Sauveur (end of the fourth, beginning of the fifth centuries) is strongly influenced by the liturgy of primitive
baptism: immersion, conferred by a bishop upon adults once
yearly during the night before Easter. To this sacramental
rite of purification, performed behind curtains to protect
the naked participants, two symbolisms are added: the passing from shadow to light (the water flows from east to
west; two granite columns serve as entrance to the east,
facing six of green marble; steps descend into the pool from
the east . . .), and the resurrection and new life, symbolized
by the figure 8, the primitive symbol for Sunday, the eighth
day (the original baptistry was eight-sided, as was the mar-
ble-lined pool). In the sixteenth century the cupola was
heightened . . .

JEAN-PAUL COSTE, *Aix-en-Provence and Its Countryside*

MANY old towns like Aix in the Western world have grown
the way a pearl does, in micromillimeters of skin against
the world, around a germ, an alien seed, an itch, which in most
of them has been a Christian church, at once fortress and prison
and spiritual core.

Aix, however, grew around its baths, which still flow heal-
ingly behind the last of the old walls in the spa that is now run
by the government. Even the Cathedral that later became the

heart of the town was built over a temple bath, which in due time became its baptistry.

In St. Sauveur, the Cathedral of the Holy Savior, the pool is empty now in the octagonal room under the high vaulted ceiling, but beside it a cumbersome font still serves the parish, and from its walls local archeologists are still, discreetly between Masses, tumbling the bones of believers built into the niches.

Far above the stone ribs of the hushed room a small eye of open sky in the cupola looks down upon the empty basin that the first Christians found so conveniently ready for their baptismal rites, after decades of Roman ladies had bathed hopefully there to give themselves children. Perhaps, it is said, St. Maximin himself, one of Christ's disciples, stood beside that pool . . .

I remember it as about four feet deep, with crumbling steps down into it, and centuries dry. Once I was standing looking at it in the shadowy room, thinking of how long it and perhaps even I had been there, when I found myself a near-active party to a small christening that had suddenly shaped itself around the modern font.

There I was, and why would I be there for any other reason than to help make a new member of the parish? The parents and sponsors smiled at me with a polite preoccupied twitch, each probably thinking the other side of the family had asked me to come. I must not startle them, caught as they were in the hoarse whispers, the cold air, the irrevocability of the ritual.

I stood facing the fat careless priest, a man I saw often in the district of the Cathedral and never grew to accept as anything but obnoxious. His vestments were dirty, and he needed a shave and almost certainly a bath, whether Roman or Christian. He held the new child as if it were a distastefully cold omelet that might stick on his fingers.

The parents and sponsors were mute in their Sunday clothes, the convenient and almost essential uniform of black which will do for the next funeral, a vestment of respectability among poor people, who fortify themselves on what other poor people will think of them.

The new believer would most probably lead a long full life, although like many infants of its environment it looked moribund, a blue wax image faintly breathing, its eyes slits of world-weariness.

I prayed for myself that the lout of a priest would not ask me any direct questions about vouching for the little soul's well-being, and then, when the insultingly mechanical drone was plainly drawing toward a final benediction, I made myself disappear.

This is something that takes practice, and by the time I was standing there in St. Sauveur trying not to accept any responsibility for the sickly newborn baby I had become fairly good at it. It is mainly a question of withdrawing to the vanishing point from the consciousness of the people one is with, before one actually leaves. It is invaluable at parties, testimonial dinners, discussions of evacuation routes in California towns, and coffee-breaks held for electioneering congressmen . . .

As I flitted, almost invisible by now, across the baptistry, I nearly walked straight into the roughly paved pit where Roman ladies on vacation had splashed hopefully, where the first Christians had doused themselves, pressed down into the flowing water by the hands of disciples who had once heard the voice of Mary Magdalene praying in her cave.

I wondered as I righted my course around the dim room if anyone had ever fallen in. It would be only a bruise or two, perhaps a cracked bone . . . But why risk it? Why flee? Did I run from looking once more into the cynical eyes of the newest Christian, or did I escape from the more materialistic hazard of having to explain to the dismal young family that I was nobody at all, no cousin's cousin, an uninvited witness to the rites, not even real?

At the wide door into the comparative security of the nave
I felt safe again, and the air had a different weight and coldness. I could hear footsteps up toward the choir stalls: chairs
were being straightened between Masses on this Sunday morning. In the organ loft, Monsieur Gay flitted mockingly, tenderly, through two octaves of sound that came down to me as
pure silver, like hollow clean beads on a string. I could not
even hear the priest behind me. It was as if I had been bathed
again . . .

ii *AWAY, AWAY . . .*

We hear the wail of the remorseful wind
In their strange penance.

ALEXANDER SMITH, *Unrest and Childhood*

THE SECOND TIME we returned to Aix for more than a few
painfully nostalgic days, Anne and Mary and I made a point,
with some trouble, of being there during Holy Week so that
we could once again see the *reposoirs*.

They took place on Maundy Thursday, the day before Good
Friday. It was like a fiesta. People walked gaily from one open
church and chapel to another in a kind of jaunty quiet pilgrim-
age, part relief that Lent was almost over, part plain curiosity
to see what the Order of This, the Guild of That would
produce.

Chapels that were forever otherwise closed to the lay public
were open that day, and in each one an offering of money
could be left at the door. In the small convents and monas-
teries the whole main altar, with, as I remember it, no candle or
flame burning, was turned into a wall, a solid wall, of the most
beautiful flowers that could be found, which there near the
Côte d'Azur meant beautiful indeed. In the larger churches the

main altar was dim, and to the left of it, rising from floor to ceiling, sometimes perhaps thirty feet high, was the same solid mass of blossoms, now mixed all in a riotous jumble of spring, now austerely one kind of flower, one color.

It was a miracle that between the late night of Wednesday and the morning of the next day the old women and men could create such stormy pagan beauty, and then even more astounding that by dawn on Good Friday, or perhaps before, every sign of it would be gone, and the statues would be shrouded in black veils, and everything would be waiting for the recital of the Stations of the Cross.

When we saw the *reposoirs* in 1955 we decided that the most beautiful was in the Madeleine. It was, as I remember, mostly white tulips, with some scarlet.

Crowds filed into the great simple church with silent excitement, and gasped at its beauty, and as they left put money into the box to help pay for the flowers, and then went on to the next and the next churches, all over the town, which echoed to the sound of thousands of leisurely feet.

One of the prettiest walls was in the small chapel of a convent of Sisters of Charity behind the façades of the Rue Gaston-de-Saporta, a little below and behind Brondino's bookshop. It was never open to the public except on that Thursday of Holy Week. No nuns were in sight, of course, but a postulant stood by the coin box, pretending not to listen to the size of the sound of each bit of money hitting the rest. A little sign over another alms box said, *For the poor, the sick, and the ashamed*.

The most impressive *reposoir* was in the chapel of the Gray Penitents, or the Bourras, called that in Provençal because they wear sacks over their heads.

They are the last of the three active orders of Penitents in Aix, who devoted themselves, most strongly in the Middle Ages, to the burying of hanged criminals and abandoned victims of the plagues. The brotherhood today is a secret one, made up of businessmen and professionals who celebrate their rites and functions wearing over their regular clothes long tunics made of a gray sacking in much the shape of the Ku Klux Klan costumes, so that on the one time we saw them, silent and nightmarish in their chapel, their secular trousers and shoes showed absurdly beneath their grim disguises. They clanked with brutal-looking rosaries hanging from their waist-belts around their waists.

Their chapel is a plain room, without statues as I remember, but with the whole end an enormous carving, almost life-size, on tortured rocks, of the descent of Christ from the Cross, with the Act of Mercy of the Good Samaritan and perhaps a few others painted behind it. The carving is of gleaming gray-black wood. The altar, which of course was stripped the day we saw it, is in front of the carving and a part of it, so that the figures crouch and swoon and mourn above and behind it.

There were no flowers anywhere. A few of the Bourras stood clattering their rosaries and watching the silent fright-ened people, who filed in and then quickly went away. My children were scared.

And in a way I was too: it was a stern mercy that led those first hooded men to defy custom and disease, in the far days, and I wondered what bones and ashes they might rescue now, so silent behind their sackcloth maskings.

In the vestibule we bought some postcards of the altar, which I lost, and we left money in the coin box, beside which one last thin Penitent stood, perhaps listening to the size of the sound as if he had a real face with a real ear on either side.

We wanted to see all this with our older eyes when we were in Aix again in Holy Week. My sister and her three sons came too, earlier than they had meant, to see the pagan beauty of the flowers, perhaps the medieval fearsomeness of the Bourras. But the town looked the same on Maundy Thursday as it had on

Wednesday or Tuesday, and in St. Sauveur there was not a sign of the blossomed wall, and plainly one could not enter the little convents that are still everywhere behind the façades of Aix.

We went into the Madeleine, and there was nothing to show that once at least a mighty wall of white and scarlet blossoms had stood at the end of the south transept for some short hours, long enough for us to see forever.

I was perhaps a little drunk with being in the place again, and while my family stood gaping at a safe distance, I went up to a tall rounded young priest standing near the door and asked him where the *reposoirs* were.

That was the only time a man of the cloth has ever been discourteous to me, and later I saw this same one be quite rude to elderly women and very irascible with children, in a strangely sneering way. He sniffed, and stared down at me even farther than he needed, and asked in a high petulant voice, "Why would anyone ask that?"

"Father," I said with polite boldness bred of my joy at being home again, "we came back for the *reposoirs,* and I wonder where they are."

He looked me up and down, as the old novels would say, and then remarked in a disdainful way, "Anyone who is a believer knows, and therefore it is plain that Madame is not a believer, that the *reposoirs* have been discontinued in Provence as unfavorable to true Christianity."

I knew at once what he meant about the pagan element in them, but was sorry to detect his puritanical triumph. I thanked him.

"Where, if Madame is a believer, has she been? This is not a new edict," the priest stated suspiciously.

"Away, away," I answered in a half-deliberately fey manner, and I disappeared from his immediate vision and returned to my family and told them that the *reposoirs* had been forbidden.

We went away, away . . . in this case to the Cours Mirabeau, where we consumed sherbets and vermouth-gins according to our natures, and as returned amateurs seemed to grow like water-flowers under the greening buds of the plane trees, in the flowing tides of that street.

When the violet-man came along, we bought from him, and held the flowers in lieu of that older vision, ineradicable, of the walls of flowers, and perhaps of the painful sternness of the altar of the Bourras.

iii *THE ENDING*

Of a good beginning cometh a good end.

JOHN HEYWOOD, *Proverbes*

THE TWO BEST things for me, in St. Sauveur, were that I was able to know it full and know it empty, not of people but of the spirit.

Several times it was almost full when I went to concerts there, with an orchestra in the transept in front of the choir stalls, and then a full choir of men and of boys from the Maîtrise, and everything sacred delicately and firmly shut off. The organ was alive, with Monsieur Gay there at the console in his white cap and his wife beside him in a kind of choir robe to turn the pages, like two gallant old birds high above our heads, so knowing and so skilled in making near-celestial sounds.

Twice the Archbishop sat unobtrusively in one of the stalls to the right, in the big nave, and prelates and priests rustled beneath him and I sat close by, recognizing his spirit and looking, invisible and even more so than usual, at the hollows of his eye sockets.

The music sang out from in front of the dim altar, and I

knew it was a good thing to play it thus in the house of God.

Once I went into the Cathedral and it was a shell, waiting. It was by accident.

We walked up from the Hôtel de Provence on Easter Eve, I think, for no reason that I can remember, along Gaston-de-Saporta and across the Place de l'Archevêché, and there at the entrance to the cloister some priests and acolytes were bending above a bonfire.

It was startling to see. The flames lighted their intense faces. Around them were a few old women, the kind who are always present at such rituals.

I am sorry and a little ashamed to say that I forget now what they were burning. It had something to do with the purification by fire and then water of the vessels perhaps, and probably it was old candles and such-like, or the robes of Judas himself, but at the end a large candle was lighted, I think, and then from it each of us lit a long thin taper given to us by an acolyte or perhaps a lay brother.

Then we walked silently through the passage and through the side of the cloister, where I had been used to watching my children playing handball against the Roman tombs, and into the St. Maximin aisle of the church. From there we went into the nave, and found seats.

It was in one of the most impressive darknesses of my life. There was no sound except for the muted shuffling of our feet and the mouselike whisperings of people telling their beads, and the darkness in that great place was as palpable as flesh. It was oppressive. It pressed in upon my skin like the cold body of someone unloved. There was no help for it, no escape, and so it was not frightening.

I looked toward the dead altar, and out and up, and there was nothing anywhere except from the few feeble tapers that seemed to unlight rather than to light the intense worn hands and faces that nursed them.

A long and to me very pagan ceremony unfolded before the altar and then down into the chancel. It had to do with fire and water and rebirth. I wish that I could remember more of it, but all that stays clear is that it was ageless and real. And then gradually light seemed to come.

Of course it was partly mechanical, electrical. But that did not matter. I watched the magnificent conglomeration, perhaps two thousand years old, come alive, softly, subtly, and then like a mighty blare of trumpets, and seldom have I been so startled in my soul. I had for once known true hollow blackness, and then light. And it seems to me now that there was music too, a great triumphant blast of it from the organ, but perhaps it was only the return of light that I heard.

And then the time that I knew the Cathedral full, not empty, was almost as enriching, for I went to a concert there during the Festival, and listened to even that great place hold as much sound as an egg its meat, or the sea its waters.

It was as full as it could ever be with people too, of course, who had come from many lands to listen.

There was a symphony orchestra. The choir and the middle transept were filled with one large chorus of men and women, and one of boys, with the four soloists for the oratorio. Monsieur Gay was at the organ. The walls hummed with the colors of the Canterbury tapestries; the triptych of the Burning Bush was open and glowing; artful lights made the stones vibrate with subtle colors, as I had often watched them do at sunset with a kind of absorption rather than reflection of the colors outside in the town.

But the thing that was real was the sound. It was awesome, whether from a little flute as single as a pearl, or mighty as Judgment Day from the whole orchestra. Everything was a part of it, and the breath that went into and out of the mortals there, and into and out of the great organ, was in a mystical way the breath of the place itself, very old and ageless. I have seldom felt myself more identified with anything. It was perhaps as if I were the right grain of sand for me to be, on the right beach.

Afterwards we were quiet and tired, and that too was in the right way.

Main Street

Aix is nobility itself. It gives to the
least plane tree the grandeur of a cedar.
On the Cours Mirabeau, where the song
of the fountains mingles with Mozart's
music, its good taste comes so naturally
that not even the students can disturb
it. It was the last city of France to
give up its sedan chairs. Since then
(the beginning of the nineteenth century) the well-born people of the town
have gone on foot, not to economize
but instead to show their disdain for
money in its weightiest form, that of
time.

Marcel Renébon, *La Provence*

i *THE COURS*

Let the street be as wide as the height
of the houses.

Leonardo da Vinci

THE Cours Mirabeau is the main street of Aix-en-Provence.
It is less than half of a mile long (440 meters) and some
hundred and twenty feet wide. It is bordered on either side by
a double row of plane trees, growing in front of the straight
façades of seventeenth- and eighteenth-century town-houses,
most of them with shops or offices on the ground floor now.
There are four fountains down the middle of the Cours' length,
and . . .

. . . and it is impossible to continue writing of it in this
informative vein.

The Cours has teased poets and painters with its ineffable allure for more than three hundred years, but words and lines and colors do not capture the reasons why it is beautiful and not pretty, serene and not soothing, and dignified yet gladsome all the year, even in the stripped austerity of winter.

It is probable that almost every traveler who has ever passed through Aix has been moved in some positive way by the view from one end of the Cours or the other, by the sounds of its fountains in the early hours, by the melodious play of the pure clear sunlight of Provence through its summer cave of leaves. Some of them have tried to tell of their bemused rapture, on canvas and sketch pads and on scratch-pads and even postcards, but they have never been satisfied.

It is a man-made miracle, perhaps indescribable, compounded of stone and water and trees, and to the fortunate it is one of the world's chosen spots for their own sentient growth.

Myself, for too few years I crossed it many times a day, and sat under its trees, and walked up and down it on both sides alone and with my children and now and then with friends, in sunlight and moonlight and rain and fog, and every time it was the first time, and I felt a kind of prickling under my skin and a tightening in my chest and belly and a kind of dazzling in my head and a generally excited stimulated moved sensation, like being in love.

The street was made in 1651, after Marie de Médicis brought from Italy to France the aristocratic pleasure of taking the air in public, either in carriages or on foot or in sedan chairs, instead of walking quietly in one's own gardens. It became at once the center of life in Aix, and so it has remained.

Motor scooters and automobiles have replaced the chairs and open carriages that paraded during the cool of the evenings on the Cours of other days, but the delight of strolling its length at any time, in every season, has never ceased to charm, indeed almost to hypnotize whomever once sets foot on its majestic length and width.

The Cours is wider by some ten feet at its eastern end, for unknown reasons which have never marred the beauty of its perspective. It was built on the location of the ancient ramparts, which in one form or another had shielded the original town for almost two thousand years. Some Aixois say that a river flowed past these ramparts. Others say that the Cours covers the bed of an old canal. Whatever the reason, deep waters and long thirsty roots are why, everyone believes, the double rows of plantains on either side of the street have reached so high and withstood so long the ravages of wind and drought and gradual pollution of the city air.

The first trees were elms, and they too grew handsomely to shade the rich gentry in their carriages and the people of the upper class who strolled beneath their shade. They died in a plague that killed almost every elm tree in Provence, and beginning in 1830 they were quickly replaced by the plane trees which now thrive along the Cours and help make it what has often been called "the most beautiful Main Street in the world."

Perhaps one reason is that it was a deliberate conception of balance, one of those human plans which seemed to be realized most neatly in the seventeenth century, in that part of the world. It was planned from its beginning as a whole, balancing its three dimensions of width, length, and the prescribed height of the buildings which lined it on either side. These laws have always been obeyed except for a few off-set attics above the set height, and the result is one of the most reassuring of all civilized vistas.

ii *ITS FOUNTAINS*

In the hexameter rises the fountain's silvery column,
In the pentameter aye falling in melody back.

Samuel Taylor Coleridge,
The Ovidian Elegiac Metre

THERE ARE STILL four fountains, the length of the Cours, just as at its beginning.

The one at the west end was first reconstructed in 1728, and then again in 1778 to allow traffic from Paris and Marseille to flow near the edge of the city. There were sea horses splashing, with Neptune whipping them, with his face staring up the length of the Cours, and with jets of water spouting into the air.

By 1860 it was plain that the Cours must surrender again to progress and let down its bars to the wagons and stage coaches which were pushing out the genteel carriages that had for so long been almost its only traffic. Neptune vanished, and a monumental waterworks became the center of a wheel of important roads leading out like spokes to other parts of France. This fountain was named La Rotonde, and unless the mistral is blowing its spray too far up the Cours, it stops its spectacular splashings only once a year, when the Canal de Verdon shuts off its pipes for cleaning.

Compared to the other fountains of Aix, the Rotonde is melodramatic, overstated, brassy, a trumpet call with flutes.

The first sight of it, when a traveler approaches from Marseille, is exciting. One of them, Emile Henriot of the Académie Française, wrote it for everybody else in 1920: ". . . since I love fountains, especially when they sing sweetly, and this one pleased me so strongly, because of its long sprays of intertwined water which sprang from every direction into its pools,

I felt that through it I should salute the whole town of Aix in this one symbol, and I raised my hand to my hat brim."

In daylight La Rotonde tosses out its many plumes and jets of water like the breath of a hundred spirited horses. At night it glows, as do many great modern fountains, with white and colored lights which turn it into a kind of glorified wedding cake, audible if inedible.

It is crowned by three nobly sentimental white stone females representing Justice, Agriculture, and the Arts. The first faces up the Cours, toward the law courts and the prison. The second looks toward Marseille, for rapidly vanishing reasons. The third turns toward Avignon and its older and perhaps even greater culture.

Four jets spout from these figures' pedestal, into a wide basin from which many more mouths send out their waters. Far below an even wider basin catches them, and eight bronze cherubim astride frolicking dolphins send out double streams of water that curve like low rainbows and blow past the rim of the great bowl, sometimes, onto the wide circle of the Rotonde's paving. Big turtles along the edge of the basin spout back at the energetically fat little boys their counterstreams of water, weaving a kind of web, and to hold it all to solid earth enormous lions lie in pairs around the base, at ease but always wary, at the edge of the tent of interwoven crystal.

It is, in truth, a monument to nineteenth-century romanticism, and perhaps it escapes vulgarity simply by being in Aix. Certainly it is curiously satisfying, full of life and joy. It acts as a kind of noisy but melodious introduction to the other fountains of the street, which stretches eastward from it.

At the opposite end, always called the head of the Cours, stands the fine statue of King René, which has lent its serenity since about 1820, when it was sculpted to replace two fountains which had crumbled away or been removed.

As everywhere in Aix, water flows musically below the King's statue into the generous basin, and people fill their pitchers from its cool jets all day long, or perch on its wide rim to gaze about them tranquilly.

Traffic flows around the handsome King who made Aix known throughout Europe as a center of learning and beauty, and it seems right that he should hold in one hand a fat bunch of the grapes he helped develop, in his little kingdom, from its old Greek and Roman plantings.

Westward from René about three hundred feet is Old Moss-back, which steams like a theatrically inverted cauldron into the cold air of winter. It was built in 1737 to stay as it is now, over one of the fountainheads which first brought gouty Romans to Aix. Old people still dip their aching hands in its warmth, and many others drink its waters sparingly to "take the cure" for various human troubles, for it is credited with being a purge, a diuretic, an active solution of minerals, a fluid saturated with actinic rays, and almost every other possible remedy that one looks for with faith.

It has a faint but harsh smell, and it is one of those strange fountains of Provence which consist of a great lump of live stone on which thick lichens grow, with the water flowing up to the top and then down over the short furry mosses. Often generations of moss pile one upon another, feeding through all the rich fur under them to the stone. These monuments can become grotesque, but Old Mossback is merely comfortable to look at, like an elderly and benevolent dog, a little steamy and pungent.

Further down toward the Rotonde is the fountain of St. Lazarus, which is also thought to be healing and which is now the most popular on the Cours for drinking-water. People come for blocks, at noon and before supper, to fill their pitchers from the graceful curves of its basin, which is one of the most beautiful examples of Louis XV design in this town of flowing waters. It is known by everybody as the Nine Canons, instead of its saint's name, and it is an intrinsic part of many lives in the Old Town.

And then the Cours ends, after its harmony of light and color and sound and line, in the almost rollicking vigor of the Rotonde.

It is exciting, after the cool green cave of the street in summer, under the leaves, and then in winter the muted rose and yellow shadows on the old façades, to step into the penetrating brightness, never blinding, of its unshaded monument to the three Arts. It is like being a fish, up from the sweet depths to the surface for a different kind of air. Traffic flows around and around the great crossroads, but the sound of all the jets of water rises above it, and seems to drift always eastward, toward the Nine Canons and Old Mossback, to the feet of the tranquil King René with his fruits . . .

iii *ITS FAÇADES*

To blend in one tangible whole
The manifold features of change . . .
Gamaliel Bradford, *Soul*

THE HOUSES THAT face each other across the double width of the Cours Mirabeau, and then over the tops of the plane trees from their attics, are one of the few remaining entities of the seventeenth and eighteenth centuries in European architecture, unbombed and unburned in spite of the hazards and crimes of progress.

None of them still exists as the elegant town-house it was built to be. The families that flourished in the richest days of Aix, and built these palaces to prove their positions, have long since died out or retreated to their often crumbling country estates.

A few beautiful private apartments are still preserved, and the exquisite iron balconies of most of the houses, and then their staircases inside, are tenderly protected by their care-

Cours Mirabeau

takers and the city and the nation, so that students of all the arts may admire them.

From above the town one can see that many of the old houses now have artists living in their attics, with skylights that gleam like bloodied copper at sunset.

At street level, the tone of the Cours has changed almost completely since it was first built as an aristocratic promenade. For a long time not even a vendor of lemonades was allowed to endanger its gentility. Gradually its Left Bank let a few discreet merchants, all of them convenient purveyors to their social betters, open small shops. By now the Left Bank is an almost unbroken series of stores both great and small and mostly reputable, of open-air cafés for every class of people, of agencies for every need.

Occasionally a noble façade of delicate iron balconies and giant caryatids looms like a great jewel on the two firm straight lines of buildings. There are a few official residences, like the Sub-Prefecture, or like the Hôtel d'Espagnet, now owned by the University of Aix-Marseille which King René fostered, where the president of all the faculties lives and works.

Above the varied offices and shops, puny with silver and crystal and neckties or portentous with learning and crime, and especially on the Left Bank, the gracious old apartments, many of them looking back into gardens and courtyards, are rented to lawyers and doctors and strangers who are willing to fight their endless but beautiful stairways for what they find at the top, and a dwindling but dogged group of local people who still choose that rather than the modern houses of the flourishing new subdivisions that encircle the town like the tentacles of a bewildered octopus.

And it makes a mysterious whole, this generous vital stretch of trees and buildings and live waters. In any language, it cannot rightly be called street, thoroughfare, mall, road or roadway, route, boulevard, highway. It is the Cours.

The Two Havens

Fasten him as a nail in a sure place.

Isaiah, xxii, 23

i *THE 2 Gs*

Club: an assembly of good fellows
meeting under certain conditions.

Samuel Johnson, *Dictionary*

AT the turn of this century, a young Frenchman named Léo Larguier was stationed in Aix for part of his military service, and later he wrote a good little book about it called *Sunday with Cézanne*, for he knew the old painter as well as one could, so late and so shortly.

His view of the town, even from the dubious vantage point of middle age, was a quizzical one:

"We used to go sometimes, in good weather, to sit on the terrace of the Café Clément, which was at that time the best and most popular one in Aix, the place frequented by officers, rich students, and the dandies who were not afraid to lower themselves by being seen in a public drinking place.

"These last, not too numerous at that, belonged to old Provençal families, and their parents still lived in the rigidly private town-houses which I picture as crowded with beautiful furniture and dim cluttered group portraits . . .

"There was a piano at the Clément, on a low platform in front of the door, and the pianist, accompanied by a violin and a cello, was an exceedingly dark young woman who looked at nobody . . . she seemed like a schoolteacher . . .

"Under the giant plane trees of the Cours Mirabeau, the lazy and the aimless wandered, greeting their acquaintances often and ceremoniously. A few students could be seen on the balcony of their own club, across the street. At the Clément," Larguier added, "people joined their friends, or met them upon leaving, but I don't recall ever seeing a townsman nod to Cézanne. Nobody seemed to recognize him!"

My friend Georges, of Dijon, remembered the Clément from before the First World War. He evidently spent little time in it, having better things to do with his leisure in wild Marseille, where he split his life with the Boys' Lycée Mignet in tame Aix.

Now the Clément is the local showrooms and offices of an important dealer in antiques and paintings, and catty-corner from its noble façade, there at the corner of the Rue Frédéric-Mistral, is the 2 Gs.

I of course could have asked more questions and found out if it was indeed a students' club when Larguier sat looking at it "in good weather" at the Caf' Clem to the strains of the poker-faced female pianist. I seemed to be tongue-tied about such matters. Ghostlike, I listened instead, and sifted out whatever seemed appropriate to me, and applied it as I wished to the actualities of such places as the café where I was to spend many of the pleasantest waking hours of my so-called life.

In Aix, and I presume in every other respectable town of France, both great and small, cafés are known by the company they keep, and in one way or another the towns are known by their cafés. For most of this century Aix has been for itself and its visitors the Deux Garçons, the Café of the Two Waiters. About 1750 it was a chess and checkers club for gentlemen, The Guion, I was told, which they entered through the rear door on the Rue Fabrot to still any rumors of commercialism; and now respectable citizens, students who one day will be the same, and tourists both ordinary and extraordinary make it, still, their club in their various well-behaved ways.

It is two large rooms, elegant in a deliberately faded style.

The larger, which gives now onto the Cours Mirabeau through its door and two big windows, is long, with a looming old zinc bar across its far end, where the waiters fill their orders except for liqueurs and spirits, which are dispensed carefully at the high cashier's desk near the two public telephone booths.

The main part of this room is mirrored, with woodwork painted dimly in gold and black. Oblong tables of grayish marble go along the two sides in front of the leather benches, and then down the middle. People never sit in the middle unless the room is crowded.

There is a large fern in front of this third row of tables, on an obsolete circular radiator, and usually the philoprogenitive café cat is asleep there under its luxuriant leaves.

In the room to the left, which also gives onto the Cours, the elegant old décor is simpler, without any mirrors; and students sit there, as they always have, or rare tourists who do not know that they are intruding on the cabalistic rituals of beer and *Gauloises Bleues*.

Across the whole generous façade of the Deux Garçons stretches a terrace filled with little marble-topped tables, and dozens of green chairs. In summer it is deeply shaded by the double row of towering plane trees of the Left Bank of the Cours. In winter it catches all the thin pure sunlight that falls through their naked branches. In the spring the light is incredibly dappled and of the color of a fine greenish wine from the Moselle. Sometimes in late autumn after a rainy wind there are only a few eccentrics who still sit there, to watch the golden leaves plastered against the shining black pavement of the street.

The only time the 2 Gs, as the students call it, really spills

out to the edge of the wide sidewalk is during the Festival in July, when after a night performance hundreds of people stroll up and down the Cours in the soft air, with no automobiles anywhere. They murmur in a dozen tongues on the café terraces, and drink wine and beer and whiskey and hot chocolate and Coca-Cola and gin, and at the 2 Gs eat little lemon ices from silver cups.

Inside the main room, there is an ornate gaslight in each corner. They are kept in working order, and like everything else there they are well dusted. It is because of a city ordinance: every public gathering place must be prepared to illuminate itself adequately in case of no matter what kind of blackout of electricity. It could be a riot, a strike, an assassination, a prank, one is informed with a shrug. This tacit recognition of any good café's tinderbox subnature is generally ignored, except about twice a year when new students at the School of Arts, Professions, and Engineering serpentine through all the cafés on the Cours, bellowing in doggedly virile camaraderie and only momentarily interrupting the general conversation up and down the street.

Talk is as steady as the fountains themselves, in Aix. It goes on everywhere, sometimes noisy but seldom harsh. Of course there are many people, at least in the cafés like the Deux Garçons, who never speak more than a word or two to the waiters, or sometimes only make one face or lift one finger to get their accustomed *café* with *croissants*, their noontime *pastis*. But in general there is a good play of sound in the two rooms and on the vast dappled terrace, and certainly no need for a piano, especially one with violin and cello!

In the students' side the noise is loudest, of course, but seldom obnoxious, for the waiters can be as firm as any Mother Superior if they see that the other staider clients are displeased.

This is most probably one of the mysterious reasons why the 2 Gs remains through Invasions and Occupations and Liberations and even Insurrections the focal point of public life in Aix . . . along with its never flagging cleanliness, its skilled if basically emotional waiters, its imperturbable cat . . .

It is the first and last café of my visible and invisible life in that town.

I seemed to go there like a homing pigeon, the first day I was in Aix. I walked through dry bright August streets, along the Boulevard du Roi René and the Rue d'Italie from our hotel, with my two bewildered and curious children. I did not know what direction I was taking. We came upon the benign fountain of King René, with the green tunnel of the Cours stretching westward, and it was more like a flashing vision of promise than any I had yet seen.

There was a big café terrace on our right. We sank onto and into it. The little girls drank lemonade and I beer in complete and sudden ease: we were in the right place at the right moment, and we knew it would last.

For more than three years, on and off, this place nurtured various phases of our varied souls. It was a solace and refuge from everything: wind and blasting heat and rain, disasters, anxieties, too much noise or silence. It was protective of us, yet always aloof, able to do without us.

Once I ran from Madame Lanes' apartment at almost midnight to its telephone, to call a doctor for a suddenly sick child. The Rue Frédéric-Mistral was cold, dark, twice as long and quiet as usual. The owner took the coins from my fumbling hands and dialed for me and soothed me.

Often my girls went there for hot chocolate or a cool silver cup of lemon ice when they must wait for me and could not find me, and the waiters welcomed them gently. Often we hid there, singly or together, from things or people we could not cope with for the moment, and even more often we met people there whom we loved dearly, for that day or forever.

The last time we lived in Aix we walked up the Cours for

almost a year, often before winter daylight, to breakfast in the Deux Garçons' bright warmth, still smelling of hot suds and wax, before we went our ways to schools and work. Before and during and after market we would meet there on the terrace, and talk with whoever stopped beside us, and usually stay longer than we'd meant to, in a kind of daze of well-being and satisfaction about the rhythm and beauty of the town, the people, the fountain music.

We knew about Emile's Vespa repair costs, and Léon's termagant wife, and François' prostate trouble. We borrowed money now and then from the boss, and got advice about movies, elections, and even the National Lottery, without ever hearing or even being offered a word of local scandal, of which there was a great deal that even we strangers knew about.

The cat under the fern on the dead circular radiator became a friend during the school year we ate breakfast there, and came, except for an occasional day off for having kittens, to eat bits of *croissant* which we would put on the very edge of the table for her to take daintily between her teeth, from where she waited on one lap or another, and then to eat on the spotless floor. She had three and sometimes four large litters a year, and often that heavy plunge from lap to floor worried us, but unduly; she preferred that pattern no matter what her bulk.

The most surprising thing about our tacit acceptance as more than tourists, less than townspeople, was the way the old advocates and judges who were habitués of the 2 Gs when the Court of Appeals was in session began to nod very discreetly to us, after a few weeks of inspection over and around their papers. Inside the café, that is: outside on the terrace they never recognized us socially.

There was one famous old judge who breakfasted there every morning, Court or not; he was a heavy wheezing man with a gray face, who always put five lumps of sugar into the small cup of *espresso* the waiter set before him, and ate four of the round buns stuck with sugar crystals. Anne and Mary liked him, silently of course, and feared that he might be diabetic and lonely.

His wife had died, they decided. He lived in a fabulously beautiful apartment, early eighteenth-century of course, attended by a devoted but autocratic old woman who had been his wet-nurse. I, on the other hand, thought his wife had run away from him, because he apparently enjoyed belching at sonorous length after his breakfast, as he folded up *Le Temps* and *Figaro* and pushed them clumsily into the pocket of the huge shabby coat the waiter held for him. I was crass, Anne and Mary felt.

One of the strangest moments I can remember in the Deux Garçons was on the fourth day of the Insurrection, in April of 1961.

The café papers did not arrive. *No* papers arrived in Aix, when they always had before.

There was a kind of numbness on the faces of the usual customers in the café. They looked with apathy at the coffee in front of them and ate almost none of the *croissants* which generally were gone by eight o'clock. They sat silently on the benches along the walls under the mirrors. The actuality, the astonishment of the terrible fact that Aix was cut off from Marseille was like stone, a stone going into them instead of oxygen, or perhaps a kind of novocaine or liquid anesthetic that they were absorbing.

Finally a stubby unshaven man hurried in with a pile of papers under his arm, to leave the usual three copies at the cashier's desk; and before he had time to turn around, at least five usually staid habitués sprinted out to go to the tobacco shop up the street.

They brought back *Le Provençal*, and their faces were as innocent and shining as those of a prep-school football team.

They beamed like boys, indeed. They leaned over the shoulders of men they usually snubbed, and held up papers across the room in a recklessly sociable way. The Insurrection was, it seemed, broken . . . over . . . past bloody danger. The terrible four days had ended.

A student waved the front page toward his girl who came through the revolving door. "It's over," he called out, this time without being hushed or scowled at by the usually stiff lawyers and *antiquaires*.

Outside, the Cours had never looked more golden-green, more greenly gold.

The feeling grew in us, increasingly strong, that the café itself seemed to savor our ghostly faithfulness, although it was plain from the beginning that we must leave it sometime for our homeland.

Along with a few old-timers like the judge, and of course the boss and the waiters, most of whom had been there for years in spite of an occasional fugue owing to bad livers, unruly motor bikes, or extramarital furloughs, we sat out all the tides that washed through the old place.

We came to know when the American students would leave and the boys from Eton would arrive for their weeks of "language perfecting." We learned to look over the new customers before the plays at the municipal theater, to see what the artists on tour promised in Paris hairdos and mannerisms. We felt the growing excitement in June about the next month of Festival, and then sat out August happily alone, the only old-timers the waiters recognized in a storm, a mob, of Frenchmen on vacation from every place but Aix while the Aixois were on vacation everywhere but Aix, too. We knew the tension in the students during exams, especially for the dreadful "bac."

Carnaval was fun, with a kind of studied unruliness along the Cours and confetti on the clean floor of the elegant old café.

And the best was the Festival, of course: a high restrained excitement, as if everyone were a little drunk on the music of the long afternoons and the splendid nights.

And we were always there, not inquisitive, but very receptive in an almost invisible way.

ii *THE GLACIER*

> . . . my high-blown pride
> At length broke under me, and now has left me,
> Weary, and old with service . . .
>
> Shakespeare, *King Henry VIII*

FOR ABOUT A THIRD of the time we lived in Aix or near it we ate in our own home, and I cooked, but even then we went oftener than we would have in California to restaurants in and around the town.

There was always a good excuse: we were there *anyway*, in from the country for supplies; we must meet a late bus from Marseille with a friend or two on it; there was an important movie or concert that afternoon; the day was too beautiful for us to do anything but stay as long as possible on the Cours. In almost every case the weather was too beautiful to eat anywhere but at the Glacier.

It was at the other end of the Cours from the Deux Garçons, far back from the wheel of the Rotonde under fine plantains, in a little park called the Place Jeanne d'Arc, which it shared with buses, some handsome old houses, and the Police building. We went to its wide quiet terrace the first day we were in Aix, straight down the long green cave of trees from the café, led by the same blissful instinct that had made us choose that place instead of any of the others along the Cours.

All I remember about our first lunch at the Glacier is that

it was long and lovely. We ate well, and almost surely I drank
some white wine from Cassis, and Ange, impeccably suave,
observed us with a sudden strong sense of protection and sympathy, from all we could ever guess, so that from the moment
he first bowed us into our chairs that dappled August noon we
felt an easiness of spirit with him. We never had cause either
to use or to abuse it, but it was there, and he knew it as well
as we did.

From that day on, the Glacier was our main meeting place
after school.

Until the two girls got established at Ste. Catherine we
seemed to go there several afternoons a week after Mary and
I met Anne at the little door from the school into the alley
that turned off the Rue Mignet. All the children tumbling out
the door would smile and then whisper to their waiting
mothers, and everybody would stare more or less discreetly
at us, for until Mary got into classes there too, in a couple
more months, Anne was the only American girl who had gone
there in the memory of that epoch. It was a daily ordeal which
we savored in our own ways, and perhaps it is what added the
spice to our almost mechanical promenade toward the Glacier.

Once there, the pattern was firmly set: ham sandwiches for
the girls, a Cinzano and soda for me. The sandwiches were
perhaps ten inches long, a slender slit loaf of bread spread with
sweet butter and curtained limply with ham, and there was a
fancy "antiqued" thing of several pots of mustard fitted into
holes: pink, hot, cool, brown, yellow. Anne and Mary did not
like mustard, but it was amusing, each time without fail, to lift
all the lids and choose what one might eat if one wanted to.

Sometimes Anne, *petite voluptueuse*, ordered instead of the
ham sandwich a silver bowl of *crème Chantilly*, which the boss
was proud of because he actually ordered it fresh from Paris
twice a week instead of fabricating it himself. (How? Perhaps
with a machine it could be done, and the cunningly right

amounts of cream, egg white, vanilla — perhaps glycerin? The idea is nauseous.)

It was fortunate that common sense and Mary's entrance into Ste. Catherine combined to interrupt this gluttonous habit of ours, for gradually I was drinking two vermouths instead of one, and Mary too had switched to *crème Chantilly*, and the daily chit was using much more of my feebly kept allowance than it should.

And suddenly it was winter, and no fun any more to sit alone and shivering on the Glacier terrace: no more babies in their prams and dogs on leashes, no more sweet dusty sunshine, no more tourist buses to unload fifty-eight English people to visit the restrooms and drink tea in precisely twelve minutes and then head for Nice or Lourdes.

When the buses stopped, Ange took the afternoons off, and the woman in the toilets disappeared until Carnaval in February. She interested Anne and Mary because she had a face almost as flat as a Pekingese dog's, with prominent eyes and only two delicate little nostrils to show where her nose should be. She was very kind to them, and probably liked them because they looked at her with such obvious pleasure instead of the aversion she must have become used to, at least occasionally in her life.

When we returned to Aix some five years later, they saw her once on the street, for the Glacier had fallen on thinner times and did not keep anyone ever in the cloakrooms, and she suddenly kissed them both and then disappeared, perhaps forever this time. They were a little embarrassed, not because of her kind flat face, but because they were in their teens.

There were many other changes, of course, and it was plain to us, dedicated to Ange, that they all stemmed from the fact that he was no longer there. The old boss had died, it seemed; yes, that fat meticulous little man had simply dropped dead one day. His wife had too quickly remarried: she was an impossibly stylish and pretty woman, who wore tiny shoes and painted her dog's toenails to match her own, and who sat like a bright bird behind the cashier's desk, checking every tray and, we felt sure, giving every waiter her bright eye.

Then there were complications: contested wills, angry creditors, dishonest legatees. Result: the Glacier changed hands, and although I later came somewhat to admire the new boss, he was certainly a far cry from the old one. He did not, to put it charitably, know the business; for a small town like Besançon or even Montpellier yes, but Aix? Aix was unique, "a town of extreme elegance, of *tone*."

And Ange had been, it seemed, a desperate disciple of everything Aixois, and he had lost . . . too late to take up the first offer of the Vendôme to make him assistant headwaiter, which he had proudly refused . . . too late for him to start his own small restaurant of Aixois "elegance of tone."

He grew careless and bad-tempered. There was a row. *Pom, pan, paou*, as Spirou or Mickey Mouse would say . . . and Ange was flatfooting it in some fly-by-night new joint up on the Cours Sextius . . . and the Glacier, we saw and felt, was subtly shabbier and dirtier, and the service was far from subtly changed into a kind of slapdash who-cares fake of its old impeccable dash and sparkle.

One thing that may have affected it and all of us was the traffic, which roared around the Rotonde now in a flood five times as heavy and noisy as before, and much faster. It changed the air and assaulted our sensibilities.

Another was that the new boss had bowed to the times enough to take on a steady procession of chartered tours, for lunch, tea, dinner. Tired people staggered off the enormous buses like sleepwalkers, and were herded firmly into the back room, a dark unattractive cavern used mostly for piles of coats during Carnaval. They ate fast, and for the most part suspiciously. They fought sullenly for places in the two toilets, which perforce were far from tidy, without our flat-nosed friend to care for them.

Across the street at the Vendôme the more luxurious buses stopped, the ones with built-in plumbing and even little bars, but from what we could see, their passengers were just as tired and sullen, even though they were allowed to eat more slowly and off better plates. They all paid for their meals when they bought their tickets in Paris or Liverpool or Hamburg, it seemed, with the service included, so that the waiters showed small interest in either their wants or their gratitude.

All this gave us a dim view of bus tours, in the face of enthusiastic friends who would be tourists no other way . . .

. . . and we could understand why Ange had quit the Glacier: this hurried and basically tasteless serving was not in his tradition. He was a part of the "old way," his friends told us in quick asides as they dashed past us on the restaurant terrace; he could not endure anything else and would die rather than bow to it.

This was perhaps literally true, for once he "accepted" a very good job at the Deux Garçons, and quit in somewhat less than the two weeks his admirers had bet he would last. He could not, they explained almost proudly, adapt himself to *la limonade*, which was their trade slang for café service: the steady trotting with heavy trays, the tricks of remembering who wanted sherbet and who a vermouth-gin and who a *pastis*, the mind always ready to add up a bill, the hand always there to mop off a table, pick up a package, light a cigaret, empty an ash tray.

In five days Ange lost several pounds from his spare frame. In ten, his face was set in a pale mask of weariness and disgust. Then he was gone, and we saw him only about twice more. He wore rough clothes and carried what looked like a carpenter's kit. He was plainly sorry we had met, and we bowed distantly and refrained from the painful immodesty of asking more about him.

iii THE MEN

The sum is six pounds, and be pleased
to remember the Waiters.

English Inn-keeper, 1660

OF COURSE, because of our strangely permanent impermanence and our dependence upon restaurants and cafés, we got to know many other waiters in Aix. Some of the things we knew about them were even intimate, but it is interesting that with not one of them did we intrude upon their lives outside their work. If ever we saw parts of their families, about which we seemed to know something, it was when Anne might say that two of François' girls were in Third and Fourth at the Lycée with her, or we would meet Louis with a dashing Gypsy in Marseille and not nod. Indirectly we would know of Michel's jumping out of a second-floor bedroom window with a furious husband after him; directly we were blandly sympathetic with the hazards of his carrying heavy trays with a broken arm . . .

The nearest we ever came to personal intrusion on the extra-professional lives of our waiter-friends was when one of them got badly smashed on his Vespa. We sent a little note of real distress, through the boss at the Deux Garçons: Emile's back and feet had been hurt, and how could a good waiter surmount that? This one did, of course, for he had five children and a stupendous vanity about his work, and perhaps a month after he came slowly back into the café we received a formal recognition of our message, which none of us had ever referred to in person: "Monsieur Emile Joseph Gagnebin-Lenôtre expresses his sincere recognition of . . ."

Most waiters at the 2 Gs stayed there for several years at a time, for it was the "best" place to work and also one of the most demanding cafés in that part of the country. Sometimes, when they finally left, they bought small cafés of their own, near the markets, the bus terminals, the hospitals: they had made good money in *la limonade*. Others had spent it all and took lesser jobs, often in the new small restaurants that were opening and closing during our last stay in Aix, small pseudo-chic places featuring an open grill for steaks, water flowing down a wall of bad abstractionist tiles, imitation Provençal "specialties." We saw the men grow careless and flabby and sly, as they relaxed after the hard profitable years at the big café.

The few who returned to it could not bend again to its implacable perfection, and it was plain that the ones who had remained made it easy enough for them to quit. They had, in a way, been drummed out of the regiment . . . except for Ange when he tried to come back. As far as we ever could see or know, the men at the Deux Garçons did all they could to ease him into their unflagging pattern of speed and skill, but it was too late: he had been a maître d'hôtel for too long, even in such an unstarred and basically unstable restaurant as the old Glacier. Perhaps by now he is picking up a little work on Sundays at country restaurants where people play *boules* after Mass and then eat enormously. He is almost elderly, but I cannot see him as anything but slim, erect, and autocratic, no matter how shabby his jacket nor how outlandish his customers.

One afternoon, soon after we met him, Anne and Mary and I were sitting on the terrace after a good meal. It must have been a Thursday, because they did not have to go back to school. It seemed too foolish and difficult to leave that dusty golden air.

I ordered another *café-filtre*, and watched the great crazy fountain splashing and spouting in the Rotonde, while the children played a restrained form of hopscotch on the boxed paths of the little garden in the Place Jeanne d'Arc. I saw that a fat child, dressed much as they were in a kind of school uniform of pleated skirt and jacket, had joined them and was solemnly hopping behind them. Then they all sat on a stone bench and talked, in the absorbed way possible only to people their age who do not need written languages.

Ange spoke just over my left shoulder, bowing a little as I could see him sideways. "Madame does not mind the children's playing? I can interrupt it."

At first I thought that he meant the three little girls were being noisy, which they were not, and I started to protect them with a snub, but Ange went on, "They are having a good time. The other little foreigner is learning French too."

He bowed again as if that solved any possible problems, none of which I could imagine, and inside the closed glass part of the Glacier I saw him murmuring into the ears of several people at a big table. Plainly he was mentioning me or my girls, for the others looked out into the little garden and then at me.

I could see through the glass that they had degrees of color in their skins, from a soft non-shade whiter than white to a dark bluish brown. There was one woman with the intangible stamp of a teacher about her, and the other wore stylish clothes as if they were veils upon veils. The rest were five or six men of varying plumposity, in clothes that looked English, at least while they were sitting down.

So I looked again at the fat little girl, who sat by now entwined with my children on the stone bench: she was in a skin of soft ivory, and her eyes were ripe plums laid delicately into her face above the cheekbones. When she laughed they seemed to stretch out, two inches long at least.

Ange came back with the check. I was the only one left on the terrace, and he was the only waiter. He looked very swift and sure, with heavy green and gold epaulets on his apparently impervious white jacket. I asked him if I might stay on, while the children seemed so contented with their little friend. Her family agreed with me, I said, for through the wavy glass wall I could see fresh pots of tea being brought to the big table, and clouds of cigaret smoke blueing the air. There was a lull in the traffic. I could hear the fountain.

Ange brought another cup, and cleared off the cloth under it and flicked the table as he said, "Madame is not a racist."

I could not tell if he asked or stated this surprising sentence. It was very flat. I said as flat a no, without bothering to wonder.

"The little girl is an African princess," he said in an impersonal but urgent way. "She is here with her entourage. They live in Beaulieu on the Coast, until the trouble is over. It is quite different for her than for children from certain other countries. Today she is all right, though."

That was my first real conversation with Ange, and I hear it clearly, but with not the same insistence as his voice the night he would lean toward me, his status for once ruthlessly discarded, and look at me with his stern eyes, and say, "Reflect, Madame. Consider what you do."

The first time, the children told me of it: they loved the little girl, and thought it a waste that she must be royal. The second time, only I could know what Ange said . . .

The Gypsy Way

Steal! To be sure they may; and, egad,
serve your best thoughts as Gypsies do
stolen children: disguise them to make
'em pass for their own.

Richard Brinsley Sheridan, *The Critic*

AT the east end of the Cours Mirabeau, running between it and the Place du Palais de Justice, there is a narrow alley called the Passage Agard.

One enters it from the Cours, a few feet up from the Deux Garçons, through an arched doorway and then a dark kind of tunnel which even when it is crowded with bustling hurrying people seems to have an echo, like all such tunnels in the world.

Then the Passage widens and is uncovered, with old buildings on either side and a kind of intersection with another narrow alleyway which has a *pissoir* to the right, very smelly, and usually the sounds of music from the Conservatory which looks down on it. Then it is covered again and runs once more like a wider and more orderly tunnel to the Place, where a big arch and an iron gate open onto the bright air and the astonishing monument to Mirabeau.

This whole passage is an artery, or perhaps the cord that connects a mother to her child, feeding it air and blood. Unlike that cord it can be bypassed, but once its uneven, noisy, smelly crowded path has been learned, that is inconceivable.

In the early 1960s two or three new shops gave its dingy walls an unexpected elegance, and probably another few years will see it completely changed. In some ways I hope for that, for it could be a delightful surprise to come upon it unexpectedly if one did not know Aix, and to find it bright and welcoming. Meantime I liked its confusion and untidiness, and its steady flow, during the daytime, of preoccupied hurrying people.

There were several tiny shops, but nobody ever seemed to stop long in them. They were dim and for the most part shabby: a secondhand book dealer, not of good books but of old paperbacks and comics . . . a little shoeshop with some dusty handmade "opera pumps" in the window . . . a laundry where occasionally a beautiful old baptismal robe hung to be seen, washed and ironed for a new Christian. There was one foodshop with three or four boxes of fruit outside the door, a tub of black olives, and in the late spring a wire basket of snails hanging, very silent yet resentful, like all baskets of snails.

At the Palace end of the Passage, under the building that housed the Conservatory, there was one blank wall where posters of all the movies and concerts were plastered. The other wall had the dim but fascinating windows of Monsieur Colas, the antique dealer, and of the two elderly sisters who ran "Artistica," a shop filled with Provençal pottery and glass and cloth and junk and many other beautiful things.

There was also one small café in the Passage, where occasionally someone played a jukebox, always of Spanish or Italian dance music. I looked in as I passed: young restless men, perhaps workers in their town clothes, waiting for jobs. It was a pleasant little pub, but I never went in. I was sure there would be politeness while I was there, and then the normal sounds when I left . . . talking, the jukebox again.

The typewriter shop on the Rue Fabrot was remodeled, and when I was there one day to get my repaired Olivetti I was pleased by the new windows which opened onto the Passage. They gave an airy light feeling to the little shop, and made me hope that eventually the Passage might be modernized in ways to match the new shoeshop onto which the windows looked. It might be a project somewhat like the one that, over a period of a few years, changed Maiden Lane in San Francisco from a sordid alley to a stylish and even merry passageway between Union Square and the next street down.

There, of course, the general ill repute of the neighborhood had to be combatted, and it took persuasion and daring to get fashionable shops to install themselves. In Aix, however, I was unconscious of any such shabby connotations to the Passage.

I have been in Aix for several years, off and on, but I still do not know if there is any special part of it where prostitutes are lodged. Indeed, I have walked about at night, sometimes through the narrow streets which a few years ago were occupied mostly by the "Arabs," and only once have I seen a girl soliciting openly. That was not long before I left in 1961, and on the corner of perhaps the most stiff-necked and respectable part of the Old Town, Rue Cardinale and Rue du 4 Septembre. I saw her only because a friend was staying at the Roi René and I used to walk her back there at night.

The girl astonished me. She was like a still from an old German movie, one made by Emil Jannings or perhaps about the time of Dietrich's *Blue Angel* . . . thin, young, wearing the traditional tightly belted trench coat, leaning with wary grace and splayed blond hair against the wall under the street light.

Of course I saw tarts now and then, walking two by two on the Cours. They were almost certainly transient: Aix was not good grounds for them. Most were smartly dressed and rather old, perhaps there for a rest and the baths between Lyon and Nice.

But in the light and dark of the Passage Agard, in the life-stream between the big square and the Cours, everyone seemed in too much of a hurry to loiter for paid love.

Undoubtedly in such a town as Aix, where there have for

so long been students and young soldiers, there are girls work-ing for them. The only open reference to them that I can remember, for I have not read much about the place nor shall I ever be able to, is in the little book written by Léo Larguier.

He was a soldier at the barracks then, and he explained why so few of his comrades went into town on Sundays: "One had to count twenty-five or thirty sous for lunch and as much for dinner; six sous for an *apéritif*, ten sous for the bottle of beer one offered in the afternoon to a big dark-haired girl whom one met in a bar which was usually turned over to the military, and then two francs to buy the right to follow her to a tiny room where she was immediately naked on a dirty coverlet."

Of course all this still goes on, but even in a narrow passage-way like the Esquiche-Coude or the more vital Agard, there does not seem to be the slightest sign of a whisper, a dark wel-coming doorway, for any price at all.

Indeed, the only sinister thing I know about the Passage is what my children told me of it and the Gypsy, long after it had happened, as is part of youthful wisdom.

It of course was a form of soliciting that the Gypsy did, but of the spirit more than the body. And when it is a question of real Gypsies, perhaps it is best not to question at all?

They are real, in Aix. There are not many of them left. But in our own remote way Anne and Mary and I knew them: the feeling of the pieces of cloth they leave at their shrine at Les Saintes-Maries de la Mer, the children they have borne from one scant year to another, the ferocious bravado of them on the Cours, begging, whining, remaining always haughty. They go away and then return, in a wave that once known is always familiar, during the month of April. They gather. It is for the annual elections of chiefs and suchlike at the end of May, and for the worshiping and the dancing at Les Saintes-Maries.

When we first went to Aix, there were wiry, almost stunted

little girls scuttling along the edges of the Cours. The next April they were bigger, but not much, and with the same sly mocking manners. Then when we returned we were sitting at the Deux Garçons again, again pestered by the children but now complete, completely grown. They were women of maybe twelve or fourteen years, with the right swing to the haunches and the bolder gaze. And the next year they were back, but each with a little baby on her hip or in her arms. Most of the new ones were towheaded, and there was a boy, or rather a man of perhaps twenty years, with only one leg, who swung himself daringly alongside the most boldly begging girls, and he was without doubt the father of more than a few of the new Gypsies.

One day I went down a side street and a baby perhaps a year old stumbled laughingly up a stoop while its mother whispered under her breath to me the familiar "For the love of God give something to us and bring good luck upon yourself." The child was covered with sores, maybe impetigo, but was happy, and most astonishingly blond. I could see his father laughing too, the bold elated boy with one leg, one crutch, and several bright birds on his branch.

Neither he nor his covey, though, matched the Gypsy woman, The Gypsy, who once exerted her own tyranny over my children, in and at both ends of the umbilical Agard.

She was different from all the others in that she seemed more beautiful to me, the non-Gypsy. She was taller than most of the women in Aix, of both our races, and was lithe and slender in a way that I could understand, although still animal in a way that I could only recognize with some atavistic resentment and appreciation. She was dirty according to my own ways, of course, but not so much so as to blur her fine outlines. She was not dressed in the long swinging skirts that I remembered with a certain excitement from my childhood and the springtime encampments along the California riverbeds, but still she was not dressed like us, the non-Gypsy women: her heels were higher, her body was freer, her hair hung with a wilder swing from her small high skull.

She approached us on perhaps the first or second day that we were in Aix, and for almost a year she seemed a part of our daily life there, although I am sure that for weeks at a time we did not see her, while she went on Gypsy errands and pilgrimages.

We were sitting on the terrace of the café. My girls were drinking lemonades and I probably a beer, in the dusty green shade of the Cours on a fine August morning, and there was the Gypsy standing with silent abruptness by my side. She was smiling, in a sidelong sure way we came to know well, partly at us and partly toward the waiters who might chase her off, and partly up and down and all around to see if policemen were looking our way.

"I shall tell your fortunes, all of them," she said.

"No thank you," I said. I felt large and overfed and dull beside her sharp beauty, and I recognized this in myself at once: a kind of intuitive resentment and caution.

"You should let me tell yours at least," she said. "I can see many things about you. I can tell them to you."

"No thank you," I said, feeling even larger and more uncomfortable and wishing a waiter would flap his napkin at her.

The children watched me in a daze of newness. They did not yet speak French. They did not yet know where they were in this world, really, and perforce leaned upon my age and strength with trustfulness and perhaps some despair. I must stay strong and ageless to them, I thought, and I turned my shoulder to the Gypsy and she went away.

Not much later she was back. I felt astonished: I was sure she had been only a fleeting part of the first days in a new town, and not a fixture. The little girls recognized her from far down the Cours, and were disturbed a little because I had already been rude to her.

This time, or perhaps the next, she said, "I know much about you," insistently again. And when I said, "Perhaps. But no thank you," she showed anger for a minute and said sharply, "You have come over many waters, and you will sail on many more," and I laughed.

It was plain that we were Americans, or at least tourists, and so I did indeed laugh, glad to be able to prove her too foolishly obvious for my taste.

She stared boldly at me and then shrugged and walked up the Cours, one step before a waiter motioned to her to go away.

The children said, "You should not have made her angry," and I told them with an impression of futility of how silly she had been to tempt me to a session of fortune-telling by saying anything so banal as that I was a traveler. They looked uneasy.

From then on she never spoke to me, but we always knew when she strolled by. She would look daringly at me, pityingly at the little girls.

Sometimes in other parts of town she saw us and shrugged coldly.

It got so that Anne and Mary would feel she was coming, long before I could sort out her disdainful thin walk from the lesser people. The girls would look pinched, and I would know that somewhere they were seeing her.

Finally they told me that she made The Sign at them, behind my back.

I was astounded, and angry too, but I only told them that she could not possibly hurt them, by Sign or stares or sneers or any other instrument. She must earn her living, I said. She was like the rest of us, made of the same flesh if somewhat more beautifully, raised to eat and drink and sleep like us if somewhat more wildly. But she did not, I said firmly, know secrets or ways that would hurt us, just because I had spurned her foolish suggestion that she did . . . and her hints that she could . . .

Once, I told the children in an attempt at coziness, I had seen her sitting beside a man in an enormous army lorry left over from the Occupation, and she had nodded and smiled at me like any farm-wife . . .

"It could not have been she," they said in a dour flat way.

A little while before we had to leave Aix the first time, about a year after we met the Gypsy, we saw her do a most dramatic thing on the Cours. I have mentioned it two or three times since then, and Anne and Mary have remained silent as if under instructions, but when it happened they were as intense as bees and then hid their faces.

It was a bright twinkly day under the plantain leaves, and we sat as usual on the terrace of the café, I looking up to the head of the Cours at the statue of the Roi René. I saw the Gypsy walking down toward us, a gaunt Samothrace with her clothes fluttering against her and then back. She saw me clearly too, and her smile was more a sneer than ever.

Then it was as if she disappeared: she rolled sideways and onto the pavement and under a car, just like that. A serpent into the grass, she was gone. Two policemen walked by. When they had passed, she slipped in one almost invisible movement out on the other side of the car, and without a shake to her fluid garments or her long dark hair she was upright and scornful once more.

I have never seen anything faster or more pure than that swift casual hiding. I was moved by it, and I remarked to myself how pale the children were. They had already admitted to me that now and then they had seen the Gypsy as they came home from school and that she had made the Sign at them, but after I scoffed they said no more, and in spite of a few things like their obvious blanching at this fantastic roll under the car I was not really conscious of their fear of her.

It was not until years later that they told me about the Passage Agard.

It was when we returned to Aix, and they were almost full-grown. They said, in a reluctant way that meant they felt embarrassed and somewhat hopeless about my belief, that she had tormented them when they were little. She would be just outside the school when they left it at six by the side door that opened onto a little alley. She would stand boldly in the light from a shop, until she was sure that they had seen her, a few seconds, and make the Sign at them, and then go swiftly down across the Place du Palais and wait at the archway to the Passage Agard. By the time they got there, though, she would be gone. And then suddenly at the other end, there she would be.

They could not believe it, that she had run the long way around to be standing there; but although they never saw her go into the Passage, there she would be at the far end, smiling.

From what they told me I pieced together her whole scheme, and I believed it in spite of my wish to disbelieve. It was wrong to think evil of Gypsies because they were Gypsies. But I felt quite sure that this woman had been so rebuffed by me that she teased my children with all the nonchalance and skill and perhaps the detached amusement of a cat teasing two moths or two mice. It was fun for her.

Now and then, that first year, when she came up to me to tell me that she knew my future, she never made a sign that all the time she was tormenting Anne and Mary, and they never once betrayed to me that they saw her almost every day and were literally haunted by her. Perhaps if I had not been fighting my own tiny war of vanity, to keep my vow not to capitulate to her first demand, I would have been more conscious of what the little girls were enduring. I might have said, "Oh yes," just to get rid of her. Then she might have left the children alone. But I kept on resisting her, one woman against another, and she kept on appearing to them by the school and at one end and then the other of the Passage.

Of course they tried not going there, they told me finally. But it did not matter: she would be somewhere else in the town, and since they must go past one end or the other of Agard at least twice a day, no matter how they might avoid actually going through it, they seem to have made a kind of dare and gone right on using it, and seeing her in it, and watching her make the Sign at them . . . and not telling me.

Of course, if they had told me, I am not sure what I would have done. I think now that I would have accosted her, and asked her to leave my girls alone. I would perhaps have said, "Please tell my fortune now." I might even have said, "I am sorry that I laughed at you, for I know that you are a wise powerful Gypsy and that you have second sight and . . ."

As it was, I let this slow haunting go on for several months, and it was not until I saw Anne and Mary turn pale, a very short time before we left Aix in 1955, that I sensed something was wrong. And it was not until we returned in 1960 that I learned a little of what had once been happening to them, and then put together my own reasons for it.

We were sitting once more on the terrace of the Deux Garçons, dazed a little about being there, and suddenly one of the short plain little Gypsies we had known as importunate children was standing by our table. I am sure she recognized us, behind her skillful small whine for charity. I gave her some, and as in the other days she slid away before a waiter could come, and I said fatuously to Anne and Mary, "She has a new baby. She must be about thirteen by now."

It was then that I noticed their still stiff faces.

"What is wrong? Don't tell me you still think Gypsies are magic," I said loftily.

One of them said in a flat way, "That was a dead baby. I looked at it, and it was dead. She is in the power of the Other."

"What other?"

"You know, you know . . . The Gypsy. She must still be here."

"If she is here," one said, "I won't ever go through the Passage again. I swear I won't."

And it was then that they told me her teasing, not all of course but enough. I tried to be calm and wise and tolerant, but I felt sickened by what they revealed, of the months of trying not to see her, of running from her, of facing up to her at one end or the other of the narrow stinking old passageway. Most of all I was moved by their careful hiding of all this from me, the careless mother who had most probably caused it.

I flapped about in my bewilderment, and said something dull and senseless about how time passes and how I was sure it was not a dead baby the girl carried. The children looked in a kindly way at me.

"It was dead, all right," they said. "And it was The Gypsy who killed it and The Gypsy who told her to carry it in that shawl to us to ask for *our* charity. She is here."

They were wrong. The baby was not dead. Before we left again it was a strong blond little boy, and one morning I put two coins in its filthy hand while its mother, great again with child, smiled a radiant and rare smile at me. And although my girls and I looked both openly and sideways, we never saw even a shadow of that woman I had once laughed at. I watched Anne and Mary, and sensed her weight gradually lighten in their spirits, and while I always thought of her when I went into the Passage Agard, and knew that they did too, I felt little more than bewilderment, by then, at the unknown powers, the ancient secrets, of that beautiful woman and the race behind her.

Why did she bother with us? Surely other Christians had mocked or spurned her or even laughed at her approach? What made her use my children, *mine*, to point out our great differences? Or did she? Was it not perhaps an emotional gambit for two little strangers to pin their loneliness upon a shadow beckoning to them, making the Sign?

But what Sign? What did it say? Once I thought I knew. I have never asked. And by now I am not so sure . . .

The Foreigner

I do desire we may be better strangers.

Shakespeare, *As You Like It*

THERE are myriad facets to invisibility, and not all of them reflect comfort or security. Often I have been in pain, in my chosen role of The Stranger. Just as often I have counted on being so, and was not. Learning to be invisible has, of course, some moments worse than others. Perhaps I felt them most fiercely during the first months of my stay in Aix in 1954. I was alone in Europe for the first time in my life really; always before I had been the companion of someone well loved, who knew more than I did about everything, even things like tickets and monies. I had been younger, too, and full of confidence. Now I was single, with two small daughters, and a world war and some private battles had come between the two women of myself, so that I felt fumbling and occasionally even frightened.

Perhaps it was a little like learning to walk again: I must try hard to trust my weakened muscles, my halting tongue, and most of all the dulled wits in my graying head, so that my children would not suspect me and lose confidence. Once I got them into the dubious haven of "family life" with the Wytenhoves, I faced the unfamiliar prospect of long days which were my own responsibility. I went at it doggedly.

I could count on two or three walks across the Old Town to see Anne and Mary as they got out of school at noon, and then in the late afternoon. We would go to the Deux Garçons or the Glacier together for an ice or a sandwich: that would take two hours in almost every day.

Then coffee and reading in bed would use another half-hour or so each morning.

Slow roamings took another two hours or three . . . drifting along the streets to listen to the fountains and ruminate upon the proportions of the rose-yellow façades, three-to-six-to-nine, and the cornices, and the corner Madonnas, and the caryatids turning breasts and backs, male and sometimes female, to my gaze; and the open markets in three squares and occasionally along the narrow streets; and the libraries and museums: all these accustomed me to my invisibility.

Only occasionally did this pattern desert me, for a few moments of sharp loneliness which had nothing to do with my outer life, for I was received everywhere with the dispassionate courtesy of the French people. Friends of friends had sent introductions to me. Ladies of different levels were generous to me and helped me find lodgings and apples and knitting shops. I soon knew where to go for different kinds of books, and early learned the trick of roaming through the dime store, Monoprix, when I knew what something looked like but could not find the word. Paper clips, I learned from a delighted clerk, were called *trombones*, because that is the way they are.

All these warm details of my attempts to be independent of my own self were heartening, but could not ward off forever the flashes of complete aloneness, which I came to watch for as warily as any lost hunter. One danger for me, I soon found, was irritation, exasperation, impatience. I often felt them, not for myself in the main but for the people I was coming to know.

It sometimes seemed unbelievable to me that mature men and women who had withstood all the trials of wars and invasions, imprisonment, grief and hunger could continue to be stupid. Stupid they often were, no matter how tutored or naturally intelligent.

At times there seemed to me to be no order in their actions, but only a fumbling confusion quite separated from what they must surely know instinctively. Such waste of human spirit, I would groan, when I watched Fernande stumbling through ten hours of unthinking labor for what might possibly need one hour, just because that was the way her mother and grandmother had done . . . or Madame Lanes long after midnight, her face drawn with fatigue, secretly darning her white gloves for tea the next day because no lady had ever worn beige gloves or black gloves at four o'clock, in public, in Aix, winter or summer, cold or hot . . . or people hurriedly carrying one small pitcher to the fountain five times before lunch, instead of two small pitchers or even two large ones in one or two trips.

It hurt me to see this senseless extravagance of the strength that even some ten years after the last Occupation was plainly drained in all these sad wearied people. It was not brisk efficiency I wanted for them, but I could not help feeling a kind of cosmic exasperation at their stubborn clinging to patterns which had long since been improved upon. Sometimes it seemed to me that the women I came to know in Aix felt an apparently voluptuous pleasure in exhausting themselves with archaic ceremonies which taxed them almost past remedy.

The meals at Madame Lanes' were a good example of this, with their intolerable changing of plates and silverware and their dutiful chatter. Behind it, I knew of the dismal skullery kitchen with its inadequate dribble of cold water and its diminishing stock of chinaware, and its desperately thin larder. I knew of the frantic scribblings and figurings for each day's market list, and of the hurried scurryings through the town to find beans or even bread a few cents cheaper. I knew that the wine in the fine glasses was watered to its limit. I knew that the current slavey's eyes were swollen because the cook had hit her for having an epileptic seizure between the third and fourth laborious courses.

And always Madame Lanes was imperturbable and gracious, and did not push us genteelly out of the drawing room until ten at night, when she would firmly close the door, groan once or twice, and then sit down to the game table, to attend to her accounts until time to fall onto the little divan she kept half-hidden behind the well-polished grand piano (every other bed in the apartment was rented, to keep up this desperate gentility).

All this impinged upon my spirits in an occasional but dangerous thrust of world-pain, especially in the first and most solitary months of my new role of invisibility, and I must go raging out into the streets and walk with my own ghosts until we were amiable once more and safely isolated from the confusion of the others.

At first I felt lonely, now and then, because of the language. I soon got used to French again, although never with the elasticity of my younger years. Gradually I accustomed myself to the realization that I would never speak the language as I had always dreamed of doing, and that I must content myself with my blessed capacity to savor it when other people spoke or wrote it. My conversation was for the most part devoted to pleasant chitchat with market women and waiters, but my ears and eyes grew more and more attuned to words, and often I felt quietly complacent, to keep my solitude in hand so deftly with a lecture on the radio or a poem from *La Nouvelle Revue*.

A side result of this preoccupation with the language was my keener sensing of my own tongue. I read even the banalities of an American newsweekly with cleared eyes and ears. I re-read paperbacks like *Brave New World* and Swift's letters to his domestics with a fresh delight. Harmless drollery like

Cold Comfort Farm became almost unbearably funny to me. I was like a person giddy with a fever, amenable to every drift of meaning. It was a kind of ointment to my creaking spiritual muscles, in those first months of self-inflicted development as a ghost.

As I remember now, I was very conscious for quite a time of being hopelessly and irrevocably an outlander, and more especially an American outlander. This feeling had nothing to do with my own snobbishness. I have never felt any need to apologize for my mannerisms, my beliefs, my accent, or anythings else that betrays my Yankee birthright. Occasionally I have met people of older countries who have seemed patronizing about my less polished reactions than their own, but if they have been ill-bred enough to sneer a little, I have dismissed them as such.

In Aix I came in for a certain amount of the old patronizing surprise that I did not have an "American accent," which I do; that I did not talk through my nose, which I don't; that I knew how to bone a trout on my plate and drink a good wine (or even how to drink at all), which I do. I accepted all this without a quiver: it was based on both curiosity and envy.

What was harder to take calmly, especially on the days when my spiritual skin was abnormally thin, was the hopeless admission that the people I really liked would never accept me as a person of perception and sensitivity perhaps equal to their own. I was forever in their eyes the product of a naïve, undeveloped, and indeed infantile civilization, and therefore I was incapable of appreciating all the things that had shaped them into the complicated and deeply aware supermen of European culture that they firmly felt themselves to be.

It did not matter if I went four times to hear *The Marriage of Figaro* during the Festival: I was an American culture-seeker, doing the stylish thing, and I could not possibly hear in it what a Frenchman would hear. This is of course probable; but what occasionally depressed me was that I was assumed to have a deaf ear because I was a racially untutored American instead of simply another human being.

(Once my ten-year-old Anne came home from the Dominican day school greatly upset because a little girl whose father had been imprisoned when the Yanks occupied Aix said, "Ugh . . . I smell an American." Anne was the only American there, and when she told me of it she said seriously, "I probably do smell a little, because I haven't taken a bath in a tub for quite a while, but I don't smell because I am an American. Dirty American girls smell just like dirty French girls.")

Sometimes at Madame Lanes' I would be hard put to it not to ask to be excused from the table in a silent pet, when she would ask me blandly if I objected to some delicious dish which she had ordered to please one of the other boarders.

"I know you Americans don't care what you eat," she would state, and it was not until I knew her better that I could hear the friendliness in her teasing. "It always amazes me about how little you notice flavor and seasoning. You seem to have no definite tastes . . . only prejudices." And so on.

Then she would detail the gastronomical requirements of her other more demanding and therefore more sensitive and worldly boarders: the Swiss must have cream sauces with their meat; the Swedes would not tolerate garlic, olive oil or even tomatoes; the English wanted mustard always with meat; the Corsicans loathed cream sauce as well as mustard, but could not subsist without garlic, olive oil and tomatoes. Furthermore, Frenchmen from different regions must eat their native dishes and follow their set table-habits. All this was in exciting and glamorous contrast to the sterile monotony of American tastes: we apparently cared nothing at all for the niceties of palate.

And so on.

And so on.

No, I would rage silently. No, we crude Yanks are too polite, too well taught, to demand Boston baked beans or tamales from a French hostess. And I would smile politely, and curse the forthright boarders from Stockholm and Ajaccio, and enjoy what was set before me, for it was good.

Gradually I stopped my secret flashes of exasperation at the table, and knew with an increasing awareness that there were indeed many areas of perception where I would always remain innocent, at least more so than a person of an older wearier race could be. It became a strangely satisfying thing to know, on the other hand, that there were so many things I could and did appreciate, for which people like Madame would never credit me. It helped me to live alone from them, which I had to do anyway.

My outward blandness with Madame Lanes became increasingly sweetened with a real affection and an understanding of her veiled mockery, but occasionally in Aix I decided swiftly to wipe out this or that sneering person from my life and thoughts. It was as satisfying as discarding a rotten apricot from a bowl of fresh fruit, or lopping off a dead branch from a healthy tree. I had no personal feeling about either them or my ruthlessness; I did not care if they found me, the quiet perhaps colorless woman, unperceptive and oafish. I did care that I was thought to be so because I was an American . . . and when this was made plain in an ill-bred or stupid way, I simply eliminated the culprit.

Once, for instance, I was introduced through friends in Dijon to a very important and in some ways charming older woman. She gave me valuable advice about finding a good family for my children to stay with . . . things like that. Finally she asked me to have lunch with her and a few people who might be interested in helping me with my French, which, she assured me smoothly, was already past any real need for improvement.

The apartment above the Place des Prêcheurs was beautiful, one of the long airy waxed places that seem to exist only in old French towns, from Paris to Bordeaux to Strasbourg to Marseille. Tall windows looking into the green boughs, curtains drifting over the polished floors, books everywhere, noble armoires lined with padded Provençal cottons: it was a harmonious simplicity, where only man was vile.

My hostess was a short hearty woman, married late in years to a much older man, a retired colonel who mumbled distantly as he came into the drawing room, where a tiny fire burned in the marble hearth and the windows shook a little now and then from the great organ in the Church of the Madeleine next door, playing for a noon Mass.

There was a fire in the dining room too, made like the other one of the five-inch twigs I was soon to grow used to as the only heat in my room at Madame Lanes'.

There were three other guests, two near-mute assistant teachers from the Lycée who might possibly consent to exchange conversation with me once a week, and a red-headed tall thin Englishwoman with a deliberately throbbing bass voice and department store tweeds, who spoke nothing but schoolgirl French to me and often passed me later on the Cours without nodding, pretending not to see me.

At the table I sat next to the Colonel, who ate steadily. He was very senile, and unbelievably obscene in a quiet way which he knew nobody but I could hear. Now and then he would glance slyly at me through his crumbs and driblets, and murmur an invitation straight from the walls of Pompeii, and then chuckle as he popped a whole chestnut tart into his sagging mouth.

Gradually I came to believe, almost frantically, that my hostess had hated my old friends in Dijon since her first college days with them, and that now she was avenging herself, on me, for their greater worth, their brilliance, their strength and bounty. I was her victim. It shook me. She shook me. I could feel my inner head flapping back and forth on its neck like a rag doll's as she battered me with her merry little chuckles, her understanding glances.

"Tell me, dear lady," she would shriek down the table at me with a comradely twinkle, "tell me . . . explain to *all* of us, how one can dare to call herself a writer on gastronomy in the United States, where, from everything we hear, gastronomy does not yet exist? Explain to us, dear self-styled Gastronomer, to us poor people of this older world . . ." and so on.

And so on.

The other guests smiled or snorted genteelly, according to their natures, except for the Colonel, who stuffed more sweets into his toothless face. It seemed the longest meal I had ever endured, and its rich tedious courses bit like acid inside me, metamorphosed by anger and ennui.

"And now, dear lady," my hostess would sing out gaily, "now that we have eaten this little French luncheon, so simple but so typical of our national *cuisine*, tell us just how you managed to invent such profitable fiction about one of the sciences, when even Brillat-Savarin could not! We await your dictum!"

They would lean forward obediently at her signal, the two girls stunned with food and fear, the Englishwoman rigid with snobbish inferiority. The Colonel would belch and finger his fly under his spotted napkin. I would stiffen my mask and steady my voice behind it, firm in my ruthless decision: I would never speak anything but a civil good day to this person again.

The next day I sent her a huge box, shaped like a coffin woven of reeds and twigs, filled with the most beautiful flowers I could find in Aix, fresh from the gardens of Nice. It was my private funeral piece for her.

All this was good for me. It made me accustom myself to

acceptance of my slow evolution as an invisible thing, a ghost. The art of silent anger strengthened me, and as it changed to tolerance I felt even stronger.

The catharsis of pain, I reassured myself sententiously: it is purifying me with all this anger and exasperation, and it does not make loneliness intolerable, but rather betters it. Or maybe, I occasionally confessed, it simply diverts my attention?

Perhaps it was better not to try to remind myself that to the Aixois I was and would remain, no matter how well they might come to know me, an outlander, a tall, middle-aged well-bred American, just as irrevocably as I might have been a Swede or a German or an Italian, except that unlike older nationals I must face always a basic racial naïveté, rather as a callow young clerk in the diplomatic corps must face himself as such in the company of consul generals and ambassadors. I must remain impassive. Inside, my growing ability to be alone would protect me and keep me from being arrogant.

This certitude has, ever since, been of great comfort to me in thin moments.

17 Rue Cardinale

> . . . the empty perspective of the old
> street, austere and patrician, where a
> delicate little Virgin, high in a corner
> niche in the lacy leaves, bends her head
> to point out to her child the pictur-
> esque needle of the fountain of the
> Four Dolphins, like a musical toy to
> lighten the lazy hours and charm the
> stillness of this discreet and provincial
> neighborhood . . .
>
> Louis Gillet, *Treasures of the
> Provincial Museums: Aix*

i

IN most college towns in America there are widows of professors, and even retired female teachers, who hold on to
their emptying family homes by renting suitably discreet lodgings to other people in their own social and intellectual strata.
This is a blessing, sometimes dubious but basically essential, to
almost everyone concerned. Well-run faculty clubs are few,
and most people past thirty feel self-conscious in college
"unions," even in the thin disguise of graduate standing.

As far as I know, though, France has a much better climate
than the United States for people who must find lodgings with
another congenial family. On every social level board and
rooms are offered, usually with discrimination, to people who
inevitably gravitate to their own chosen patterns, whether
they be traveling salesmen or nuclear physicists.

In Albion, Michigan, or Whittier, California, Dr. Doke's relict courageously "takes in" one or two boarders to keep the taxes paid on her empty old house on College Street. In France, almost any empty room in no matter what kind of dwelling, from hovel to mansion, is put to use: it helps pay the taxes, of course, and it salves the instinctive guilt any good Gallic citizen feels about waste of food-space-energy, and waste most of all of what can be called the sense of humanity, or more plainly the basic and instinctive need of people for people.

I have lived with several families in France. More often than not while I was with them I fretted and even raged at the strictures of sharing my meals and my emotions and my most personal physical functions with people almost as strange to me as spiders or nesting egrets. In retrospect I understand that they shaped such strength as may be in me as surely as ever did my inherited genes and my environmental mores. Of course they had these to build on, for I did not meet my first landlady until I was in my early twenties.

She was a born Dijonnaise who lived down the street from the University because she liked to rent rooms to students, not because the house she rented was beautiful or otherwise desirable to them. She *liked* students. She liked to feed them and talk with them and play Chopin for them and occasionally sleep with ones who pleased her enough. She did all this with ferocious amusement. She was a kind of explosion in what had been until my first meeting with her a safe insular well-bred existence.

From then on I was aware.

She has been followed by decades of less robust but equally subtle relationships with French landladies. Now I know that I can live almost anywhere, with almost anyone, and be the better for it. This is a great comfort in contemplating the probabilities of the future . . .

First impressions are perhaps not as important as they are said to be, but they are good preparation for what may happen later, and I know that every landlady I ever met was part of preparing me for Madame Lanes, of Aix.

My mother would understand and accept my feeling that this old lady had almost as much to do with my development as did she, and would not ask for any explanation. It is at once an overt admission that I matured very slowly and a proof that people can grow at any stage in their lives. My mother would be pleased that I could still grow.

I was nearing fifty when I first met Madame Lanes, and well past it when last I saw her. It is improbable that I shall be with her again, for she is old and seven thousand miles away, but I feel serene and sure that if that happened I would be the better for it, and stronger to surmount the admiration, exasperation, impatience, ridicule, and frustration that she has always fermented in me.

The first landlady in my life happened as swiftly and irrevocably as a bullet's flight: I went to the students' office at the University of Dijon, the small elderly secretary gave me a list of boardinghouses, I walked two hundred feet down the first street on the right, rang a doorbell, and became part of a household for two shaking and making years of my life.

It was very different, the last time, in 1954.

I went to Aix for six weeks or at most three months. I stayed well over three years, in two or three periods, and partly it was because of Madame Lanes. I found her in a roundabout way, not at all bulletlike.

In my first interview with her she taught me the French meaning of the word "neurasthenic," which American friends in psychiatric circles frown upon, so that I am careful not to use it anywhere but in Aix.

I had not spoken French for several years when I sat in the autumn sunlight in her drawing room on the top floor of 17 rue Cardinale. I shaped my words carefully, listening to my rusty accent with dogged resignation.

"I have been told, Madame, that occasionally a room is available in your home," I said.

"Who told you, may I ask?" Her seeming question was politely direct as a police query: TALK, you!

I told her, and her firm rounded old face was as impassive as a Hindu postcard of Krishna.

"Why do you not stay in a hotel? There are many pleasant small hotels in Aix," she said, without any real interest but as if she were telling me to question myself, not asking me anything for her own information.

I took my first lesson, there in the thinning but still intense September sunlight, in speaking the kind of French that Madame Lanes expected of anyone who addressed her. It was a test I met intensely and even passionately whenever I saw her during the next seven or eight years, and even this long since, my accent in dreams is better when I am dreaming of her.

"Madame," I said, "I am very well installed in the Hôtel de France, where I was sent by Monsieur Bressan, the concierge of the Roi René . . ."

"I know him well," she interrupted. "A good man. A very reliable courageous man."

"He seems so. He saw that I did not like to keep my children in a hotel . . ."

"It is not the life for children. It is also expensive."

"Yes, Madame. So we went to the Hôtel de France until I got the children into Madame Wytenhove's . . ."

"Yes, I know her. Her sister-in-law's mother occasionally comes to my Afternoons. Your children will be subjected to a fairly good accent, vaguely Alsatian but better than Aixois in the correct sense of the word. Madame Wytenhove has had a sad experience; her husband died of cancer. Unfortunately her children speak like Spaniards after living in Spain while their father was an engineer there, but basically they are fairly well bred."

I felt desperate about my own way of shaping the half-forgotten sounds. "I do not like living alone in a hotel," I plowed on. "It is too impersonal. I miss my children. I hate the sound of the Vespas revving up in the garage on the Place des Augustins. I have no place to be except in bed. I hate to eat alone in restaurants. I feel unreal when I walk down the Cours at night from a movie where I have gone because otherwise I would have to go to bed."

All this suddenly sounded very voluble but logical and necessary to me, and my accent was forgotten in a relieving gush of words I had not used for too many years.

Madame looked dispassionately at me. We were sitting across from each other at a beautiful small chess table piled with her account books, bills, and correspondence, which I soon learned was cleared every night for cards or games. I do not know where she put all the papers, but they were out again in the morning.

"Madame," she said as coolly as any medical diagnostician but more frankly, "you are neurasthenic. Your surroundings are making you so."

I protested, for the English connotation of the word was not at all the way I thought I was. I thought I was bored and lonely but not at all neurasthenic in the dictionary sense: worried, disturbed in digestion and circulation, emotionally torn, tortured by feelings of inferiority.

"Oh no, Madame," I said. "I am very stable. I am very healthy."

"You are not mentally ill," she said. "You are simply moping. I have a small room, cold, ill heated, formerly for a maid, during the time when Madame de Sévigné's daughter used this as her town-house. I will show it to you. It is now occupied. But until it is free you may lunch and dine here."

I followed her across the tiles of the drawing room floor, and down the long dim corridor that split her apartment into halves, one sunny and spacious and elegant, the other small, with low ceilings and cramped dim space, made for servants and filled with people like me who lived there more happily, perhaps, than any varlets had.

ii

TEN YEARS AFTER the Liberation, French people were still steadying themselves. I became increasingly conscious of this the first time I lived in Aix. Anecdotes, some half-laughing and some apologetically tragic, came willy-nilly into almost every conversation, and little marble plaques saying things like *To the memory of six martyrs shot down by the invaders* still looked very new on the street walls. People were defeatist, and basically exhausted.

When I returned, some six years later, there was a feeling of comparative easiness of spirit, in spite of the mounting anxiety about the Algerian problem. Women who had seemed really harried to the point of masked hysteria in 1954, no matter what their social level, were relaxed and younger-looking.

This was true of Madame Lanes. She was on guard when I first knew her, wary but conscious of the fact that she had survived the Occupation (which was really three: German, then Italian, then American) and had escaped trouble in spite of being a staunch worker in the Underground for all its duration.

She was remote and hard. She fought jauntily a daily battle against poverty and rising prices and inefficient servants and inconscient boarders. She was like a tired aging professional dancer who would not dare stumble.

When I saw her next, in 1959, she was younger. A year later she was younger still.

Part of this, I think, was because her daughter Henriette had moved permanently to Paris. Most of it was because she had accepted the new stresses of postwar existence and recovered a little from the strains of war itself. She moved somewhat more slowly, for she may have been well into her seventies, and she used a graceful little silver-headed cane on the streets, but she still supervised the marketing and paid her calls on other ladies on their Afternoons, and went with composure and no apparent shortness of breath up the beautiful stone stairs with their wrought iron balustrades that rose from the street level of the Rue Cardinale to her top-floor apartment.

Generations of boarders had flowed in and out since first I met her, and instead of the cool acceptance, the remote calculation which I had first sensed in her, she seemed, the second time round, to feel a deep enjoyment in them. She was warm, and I could remember, with no regret and with real delight that she had changed, my early despair at ever having her like *me*, Mary Frances, the person who was me-Mary-Frances.

Often during that first stay there I would write home about this unaffrontable detachment. I would talk with my few friends in Aix about how I wanted Madame to accept me as another woman, and not as one more outlander who paid for her food and lodging and took as her due the dispassionate courtesy of the household which was forced to welcome her. Perhaps it is because I too was having to adapt my former ideas of the world to new necessities that I was oversensitive to this attitude of Madame Lanes and her like.

I knew that she approved of me as a person of some breeding, but there was always present an overt amazement that any American could really know how to hold a teacup, how to tell the difference between sixteenth- and seventeenth-century sideboards, how to say *Si* instead of *Oui* at the right places.

I would fight hard not to show my helpless hopeless rage when Madame would introduce me as the only American she had ever known who did not talk through her nose.

"Of course you must have taken many difficult lessons in voice placement," she would say blandly, and when I was fool enough to deny this and to say that both my parents were from Iowa but that I had never heard them speak with nasal voices, she would smile faintly and with heavy-handed tact change the subject. I would go to my room in a fury, and swear to leave the next morning.

This tumultuous resentment of my status lasted as long as I stayed with Madame. I never really accepted the plain truth that I myself could hold no interest, no appeal, for the cool gracious old lady. It was a kind of rebuff which perhaps Americans, very warm generous naïve people, are especially attuned to.

Spiritually we are fresh children, unable to realize that other peoples are infinitely older and wearier than we. We do not yet know much world-pain, except vicariously. Europeans who grow bored or exasperated with our enthusiasm are not feeling superior to us, any more than a group of "senior citizens" feel superior as they watch teen-agers rock-and-roll or do the twist. There may perhaps be a little muscular envy in the oldsters, but there is also tolerance and understanding which the young people are as yet incapable of recognizing.

Et cetera.

Et cetera.

This is the way I talked to myself, in an almost ceaseless monologue while I lived with Madame Lanes. It was good for me. Many things I should long since have known, about both outer and inner worlds, grew clearer to me as I learned that no matter how long I lived nor how many other lives I might be able to cram into my one span, I would never be as old as one of the children in the streets of Aix. I was the product of a young race of newcomers to a virgin land and must accept every aspect of my racial adolescence.

It was soon plain that I would stand a better chance of this with Madame Lanes than with any other of the people of her education and breeding who accepted boarders like me. They were more violently cynical and exhausted than she about the changes in their ways of living and the wounds of Occupation.

Some of them were openly resentful of my ambiguous state. I was too old to be a student, yet obviously not qualified to be a scholar or professor. I called myself a writer, but what did I write, and for whom, and even why? I was obviously middle-aged and yet the mother of two young girls whom I did not even live with. Neither fish nor fowl . . . and in spite of my appearance of respectability I was still an American, which basically meant that I must have been raised on De Mille spectacles, football and comic books.

iii

MADAME LANES, in spite of her deliberate detachment from her boarders as people and her overt acceptance of us as financial necessities, was unswervingly courteous and thoughtful. She remained unruffled through the maddest domestic upheavals, which occurred more frequently in her house than in any other place I have ever lived. She remained in full control of herself, a real lady, even at midnight with a maddened serving-girl whooping through the hall and down the corridor with her brain wild with nightmares of what the invaders had taught her. There was never any feeling of hidden frenzy in the old lady.

This was not true of other women I met, that first time in Aix.

Now and then, when I went back to Aix in 1959 to live again, I saw some of the people to whom I had been introduced just ten years after the Liberation, and I thanked God that I had made myself stay with Madame Lanes. She emerged from my memories as an unruffled monument of dignity and wisdom, whereas much that I had first felt about her fellow-landladies was plainer than ever on their ravaged proud old faces.

One, a Madame Perblantier, was their archetype. Her name was given to me by the head of the Girls' High School, a friend of an old friend from Dijon. Madame Perblantier would take two or three guests into her home. I should arrange an interview with her. I did.

Then I fled her, deep in sadness and depression about what had happened to a countless number of good French women.

She lived on the Avenue Ste. Victoire in a big house, non-descript from the outside, flush with the bleak street, very much like Spain. Inside, all the living rooms, the bedrooms, and the dining room faced toward the southwest onto a beautiful garden that descended gently to the edge of a little tributary of the Torse.

Inside, the house sparkled with that particular waxen clutter of the upper French bourgeoisie: varnished cabinets filled with Sèvres teacups; fans spread out in crystal cases; embroidered footstools from faraway military campaigns; a few minor etchings in recognizable styles from the eighteenth century, speckled in their heavy frames. There were flowers. The sunlight poured in through the beautiful windows, and stripped Madame's face like a scalpel, seeing viciously into the essence of her, the skin within the skin.

She was, like most of the other women of her class, used to a much easier life and was now accepting bitterly, bravely,

Fontaine d'Albertas

with muted noisiness, the new ways. Probably she was raised as the child of a high official of landed if discreetly small gentry. She had inherited or been given as dowry this large elegant undistinguished house, with fireplaces and back-stairs and all the other necessities of well-run domestic slavery; and now the rooms were almost empty of family, thanks to death and taxes, and there were no more slaves.

In a kind of insane denial of reality the women like her (many of them saddled with senile husbands or horribly mutilated sons or unfortunate grandchildren kept as much as possible out of sight), these exhausted women, in background very much like my own aunts and their friends, tried to keep their homes running for "paying guests." They tried, and doggedly, to pretend that it was really intimates they were sharing their homes with, and kept them bathed in an utterly false atmosphere of well-being and charm and interesting meals.

Madame Perblantier invited me to come to dinner, for a kind of mutual and of course unmentioned inspection: perhaps I would *do?* I arrived (Madame Lanes had approved my invitation in a discreetly noncommittal way in which I could sense a tinge of professional curiosity) bolstered by an armful of flowers which were accepted almost absentmindedly, as if of course anyone would have known enough to bring them.

The evening was ghastly, because Madame, like all the other women of this level whom I had met in Aix, was incredibly stubborn and brave and wasteful.

The dinner was in its way as elaborately presented as was every meal at Madame Lanes': plates changed from four to six times, with the gold fruit knife laid this way and not that way over the steel cheese knife and the pearl-handled fruit fork, even if it took some three hours, twice a day, for the retarded or deformed little maid-of-the-moment to stumble around behind us and then finally serve the beautiful artfully mended bowl of grapes and pears . . .

After the endless ritual of coffee, Madame Perblantier sat like a death's-head, her eyes frantic and her speech witty and stimulating, and she and I knew, but nobody else seemed to, that she had been up since before daylight dusting the countless opulent gimcracks and waxing the beautiful tiled floors; and that she had gone halfway across town to the open-air markets and carried home heavy baskets of carefully chosen and delicious fruits and vegetables, and flowers for the sparkling rooms; and that she had supervised the laundry and had done part of the cooking and all the planning.

She was dying, literally dying of fatigue, I thought . . . and years later she would still be dying of it, although much less plainly as the strain of the war faded.

Her pettish elderly husband, sneering with thinly veiled ferocity at something she twittered about Montaigne or Voltaire to the young American engineer . . . the two English girls tittering over their cigarets behind the Directoire writing table . . . the old poodle going desperately into the corner and making a mess on the tiles because always before that there had been a *valet de chambre* to trot him out before bedtime and now Madame was simply too bone-weary to do it (and dared not ask it of her embittered feeble old husband, who had never been himself since his legs had been broken in several places during an "interrogation" in the War) . . . the sound of the slavey's feet shuffling heavily between dining room and kitchen with piles of dirty dishes, down the long corridor toward the last-century sink . . . the beautiful flowers: there we all sat in the luster of this insane bright shell, and I felt a child's fear and dismay.

I was caught with a blind woman, fighting with courage and stupidity to hold on to shadows.

I returned with eagerness to the imperturbable remoteness of Madame Lanes and her pattern, which suddenly seemed less mad to me, although still criminally wasteful.

Instinct perhaps guided me, for surely when I saw her, years later, she had survived it with enrichment and was younger in spirit than before. She permitted herself to smile with a real gaiety, and to make mischievous but gently amusing comments which before had been only malicious.

iv

JUST AS THE waste of human energy in the upper-class land-ladies of Aix depressed me, so did their deliberate self-dramatization exasperate me. It made me feel like a bland phlegmatic "Northerner," I suppose, a cow caught in a flock of darting swallows. It seemed ineffectual, and actively stupid, to make such mountains and caverns out of trivia: screams, shrieks, vituperation, tears, passionate embraces of reconciliation were the daily music at Madame Lanes', over a broken cup, a few sous' cheating on the coal bill, a letter that did or did not arrive when expected.

Through all this hullabaloo Madame herself was the storm center, impassive and impregnable, and as I found myself growing fond of her in spite of her detachment toward me, I decided that she deliberately collected about her a group of near-maniacs which she used as tools: they would scream in substitution for her, and haggle in her place, and strike people she would like to punish with her own whip.

I also came to believe that one reason she kept me at a safe distance was that on the surface at least I too had been schooled to maintain something of her own calm and detachment.

All the time I lived there on the Rue Cardinale I floated on a hysterical flood of personal clashes which involved the boarders, the servants, the tradespeople, Madame's one child Henriette, and even the cats, who were perhaps the only creatures in the apartment with whom Madame permitted herself to be openly tender.

They slept with her on the couch in the salon, which she made up at night into her bed after we had all decorously left her: that way she could rent one more room. Sometimes I would hear her singing and murmuring to them when she thought she was alone, as she attended to her accounts on the card table by the windows.

They were very handsome big cats, always lazy except when Minet would yowl for a night or two of freedom. This always excited Henriette and the maids, who obviously felt more desirable in an atavistic way at the direct approach to sex of the tom. He would pace in front of the wide windows that opened onto the garden far below, and then, practiced as he was, he would station himself by the carved wooden door to the apartment and at the right moment evade every effort to catch or chase him, and streak down the great stone staircase and into the staid street. In a few days he would return, thin and weary, and revert to his cushions and his voluptuous naps.

This blatant maleness, a never-ending titillation to the younger females of the house, interested neither Madame nor Louloute the other cat, and they seemed oddly free and happy when Minet was on the tiles.

Often Louloute would care for Minet after one of his escapades, and wash him gently and play with him as if he were a kitten. He accepted this as his due, plainly.

Once he returned with a bronchitic cough, and everything in the apartment, conversation, bickering, dishwashing, would stop while he wheezed and hacked. Another time was the most dramatic, for all of us: Minet came home drenched and shivering, and that same night developed pneumonia. A doctor was called: for three weeks the tomcat must be confined to quarters, not just the apartment but one small cupboard that led off the seventeenth-century boudoir of Henriette's room.

It was straight melodrama, played to the hilt of course.

It involved elaborate and increasingly smelly arrangements about his functions, all of which had to be attended to several times a day with infinite labor, since the cupboard was at the farthest end of the hall from the front door, and the front door was perhaps sixty broad steps up from the street, and the street was where all the rubbish was left for the city scavenger service.

The little maid-of-all-work stumped up and down the staircase with her face set and her arms loaded with carefully folded newspapers. I held my breath as I passed Henriette's toilette to my room. Conversation at meals hinged largely upon Minet's temperature, his chest rattle, and his appetite. The three weeks seemed longer than usual.

But everyone was relieved to find that the big tom's illness acted as a kind of release for Henriette's neurotic world-anger; she became for that time as serene as a young mother with a puling infant.

v

THE HEAD OF the Lanes' household, after Madame herself, was Fernande, a tall, firmly stout woman of perhaps twenty-eight, who looked much older. She had a big stern face and a pasty skin that periodically turned bilious and yellow.

Her position was strange, as only that house could make it: she was the servant in charge of everything, and yet she was accomplice, personal maid, almost-governess to Henriette and almost-confidante of Madame. She was dictatorial about the continuous changing of charwomen, laundresses, and slaveys, and for the most part she was embarrassingly, mockingly servile with the boarders.

She and Henriette were violently jealous of their somewhat

similar dependence on Madame's tranquillity, and had dreadful rows, screaming and cursing each other behind ineffectually closed doors. Madame would speak nonchalantly of nothings, with not a wrinkle on her round noble little face, while the wild yells pierced the clear air of Aix. At the next meal both ferocious unhappy women would be bland and released, for a time at least, from their helpless rage.

A good custom in the Lanes' house was that breakfasts were always served in our bedrooms. This made it simpler for Fernande, even though it meant ten or twelve trips for her down the long corridor with trays, and I always thought that it gave Madame a fairer chance to turn her narrow little bed back into an elegant couch again, in the salon.

Now and then Fernande would talk with me, as she knelt in front of my minuscule tile stove to start a morning fire with the five-inch kindling it would hold. Once she was open, and with no real bitterness, but only resignation.

That was when she told me how she never went to church any more, because of the day of Cease Fire, when everyone flowed helplessly into the chapels and cathedrals of France to thank God, and she cursed Him instead.

"It was all a lie," she said without obvious emotion, "and now I am damned with all the rest of us. But I am not damned for being a hypocrite."

And that morning she told me that she had once had a real gift for music, and that she had been considered very advanced in piano when her town was invaded, early in the war. Her family was killed, but she was kept on in what must have been her well-appointed home by the commander of the invaders, who chose it because of the fine concert piano in the salon. He heard that Fernande missed her music, so with what she called "relish" he permitted her to sit for hours to listen to him play. Orders were given that if she even touched her piano she would be shot, but as one music-lover to another the officer let her silently enjoy his own technique.

I came to know Fernande as a person so far beyond normal despair that she was magnificent. She did not even walk through the town like other people; she strode with a kind of cosmic disgust from marketplace to meatshop to wine merchant, a fierce frown on her dark-browed face, and her firm breasts high. She got a certain amount of money each day from her mistress for all provisions for the table, and if she could buy what was ordered for less than her allotment she was allowed to keep it. She marketed honestly, and we always ate well, although with an insidious monotony after the first interest wore off.

Fernande had a good taste for style and often made Henriette's clothes when she made her own. She also saw to it, in a tactful way, that Madame on her Afternoons or on her formal calls to other old ladies' Afternoons was neatly turned out, in a way unique to places like Aix and perhaps Paris where such rituals are still followed.

Madame's was every third Thursday, and on those days Fernande was the perfect domestic, plainly reveling in her characterization. She was deft, silent, attentive, almost invisible in her correct black and white uniform, which was somewhat like seeing the Cyrene Venus in livery but not at all ridiculous. The little cakes were delicious. The tea, one of Madame's self-indulgences, was of the finest in all Europe or even China.

And usually the supper that followed an Afternoon was pure hell, with sulks, screams, and general bad temper from Henriette, Fernande, Minet, Louloute, and a few of the boarders. Madame remained aloof, a pleased little smile on her lips to remember that the old Countess de Chabot had taken two sandwiches, and that little Lucie de Troubillers was finally engaged to an elderly diplomat from Istanbul . . .

Now and then Fernande would cry out that she could not stand her life any longer, and that she would kill herself unless Madame let her run away. These were tense moments, no matter how often they arrived. Madame would become pale and stern. Henriette would hide in her room and clutch at passersby in the corridor, to whisper about how evil and dangerous Fernande could be in one of her crises, which were decorously referred to as "liver spells," but obviously came at monthly intervals and involved violent headaches, nausea, and tantrums. They grew very dull, in a noisy way, but I always felt ashamed of my ennui in the face of such overt fury, and stolid and undemonstrative and therefore unfeeling.

One time Fernande got so far in one of her threatened escapes as to dress for the street, which was very correctly in hat, gloves, high-heeled shoes. (She always looked more like a young astute madam than a respectable whore.) She was leaving. The household held its breath.

We all heard her come down the narrow stairs from her tiny room in the attic-above-the-attic, which she once showed me and which she had painted to match a postcard of Vincent van Gogh's room in Arles. We heard her go firmly down the corridor to the toilet, and then come back and stop at the salon, where Madame was waiting for her, at her accounts.

Henriette sent the maid-of-the-moment slipping into my room. The trembling little halfwit held a big stylish handbag under her apron. She motioned me to be silent, and without a by-your-leave hid it under some papers on my desk.

I felt like a hypnotized hen, too dazed to protest, and when the door opened after a perfunctory knock which I did not even bother to answer, and Fernande stood stonily inside the room, I sat numbly watching the little maid pretend to dust the top of a table with her apron, and observing that Fernande was puffed out like a maddened turkey hen, with a face as yellow-white as frozen butter. She was handsome.

"Where have you hidden my purse, you filthy sneak?" she asked the maid in a menacingly quiet way.

I felt that she was very dangerous, and was glad my girls were at school, for I did not think their presence would have stopped this, even though she showed them more affection than anything else. She was always gentle with them.

The little slavey lied too volubly, and Fernande turned to me and said flatly, "Perhaps you will help me. I must flee this. I am desperate. I will stop at nothing. If these beasts keep me from taking what is mine, my own money, my wages, I shall kill myself. Here. Now."

It is perhaps as well that I have forgotten what I said, but I know it was ambiguous and basically weak: something about not knowing enough of the true situation to permit myself to be involved in it . . .

Fernande shrugged, looked once at the maid as if she were a slug under a board, and went out. I gave the purse to the maid, for Madame Lanes.

By suppertime that night she was back in her black serving-dress, and she had cooked an omelet with fresh chopped mushrooms which was superlative, along with the rest of the evening ritual of soup and salad and a delicate pudding. I noticed a kind of awed constraint in Henriette and her mother. The little servant trembled more than usual as she changed the plates endlessly.

The next day Madame said, almost in an aside to me when I paid my monthly bill, that the household was quite used to Fernande's crises. They were the result of the Occupation, she said. They were frightening but unimportant, she said. Fernande was a courageous soul if one came to know her . . . "And I cannot go on alone," she added almost absentmindedly.

vi

IT IS UNDERSTANDABLE that a woman fiercely enough disillusioned to curse God, as was Fernande, would find the human
beings she must work with beneath her contempt. This complicated the extraordinary difficulties Madame Lanes faced in
trying to find domestic help in Aix in 1954.

Many people had died. Many more were maimed in one
way or another. The children born during the war years were
not yet old enough to go into service. Worst of all from an
employer's point of view, the few adolescents whose families
were willing to have them go into service as they had done
for decades were handicapped by malnutrition and worse, and
were unfit for anything demanding normal wits and muscles.
Many of them were Displaced Persons, who had been shipped
here and there to labor camps all over Europe, and who perhaps mercifully hardly remembered who they were or what
language they had first mumbled.

The procession of these human castoffs was steady, in the
beautiful enormous apartment on the Rue Cardinale.

Sometimes a maid would last for two or three days. Then
the orders of Madame about what plate to pick up and from
which side, or the ill temper and loud mocking of Henriette,
or the patent disgust of a boarder over a ruined dress or jacket
would send her with hysterics to the kitchen, and she would
vanish into her own swampland of country misery again.

Once there was a feeble old Polish woman. She spoke almost
no French. She crawled slowly up and down the great staircase, carrying buckets of ashes to the trash cans on the street
and loads of coke and kindling up from the cellars on the
ground floor. I had to set my teeth to pass her, but if I had
tried to help her she would have cowered against the wall in
a hideous fear of my motives or my madness. She did not

stay long. She was too feeble even to help dry the glasses without dropping them.

There were many Spanish refugees in Aix then, and one of them, Marie-Claude, lasted long enough for me to remember her as a person instead of a sick symbol.

She was sturdy and almost gay, and she and Fernande alternated laughter and passionate hatred in their relationship, for they must sleep together in the van Gogh attic, and eat together in the dark dank kitchen, and in general cope in the most primitive way with all the exigencies of living in an ancient house with several other people, archaic plumbing, and gigantesque rooms heated by drafty marble fireplaces or tiny porcelain stoves, which were set up like teapots every late autumn, after everyone was either in bed with severe colds or wrapped in all available shawls, sweaters, laprobes, and tippets. (For dinner, Madame often wore a finger-length cape of thick, long monkey fur which her husband had given her in Monaco in 1913.)

Marie-Claude was cursed with eyes so near blind that finally they were her undoing. She stumbled willingly about the apartment, knocking over little tables and leaving a thick film of dust and crumbs, which fortunately Madame herself was a little too nearsighted to notice. Fernande stormed after her, on the bad days, and yelled jokingly at her on the others, and between the two of them there seemed a general air of fellow-endurance, until on one of her days off the little Spanish maid ran her bicycle straight into a large truck, perhaps seeing it as an inviting continuation of the highway she felt fairly sure she was on, and a car in trying to avoid the zigzag truck hit it and then her, so that she was badly crushed. We felt sad. Her weak eyes were blamed on the hardships of her refugee childhood, and the motorists were dismissed as men whose driving undoubtedly had been influenced by the liberating Yanks and Tommies in '45.

There was one very strong coarse woman who for a time gave at least her physical makeup to the ménage, although Fernande shuddered often and volubly over her foul language. She was completely of the streets, not necessarily in her morals, which were undoubtedly as blunt and sturdy as she was herself, but in her skill at survival.

Every city evolves such people in its most evil districts. They are built in a special way, with bodies like brick walls, cruel eyes and mouths, stunted bowed arms and legs. They are as tenacious of life as it is possible to be in this world, and after plagues, famines, and wars they reappear from the holes in which they have managed to exist. They are not loyal or sincere, the way cats are not that. They are capable of unthinking devotion and tenderness, though. And unlike the more sensitive and highly organized people, they seem almost incapable of being hurt in their spirits. If they have not bred out their own spiritual nerves, they have at least developed through the centuries of travail a thick skin to protect them from weakness and above all from fear.

Louise was one of this breed.

I had never lived so closely with her kind, and I was glad to, for she was not at all unpleasing. Her manners were not uncouth with me, any more than a dog's would be, or a parrot's. Once she asked me if she might take my mending home, and I agreed gladly, but she would not let me pay her.

Like many charwomen in the world, she lived alone in a mean room in one of the ghettoes that every old town hides. Perhaps Aix could admit to more than its share of these sores, many of them sprawling behind some of the world's most elegant and beautiful façades, and I knew the quarter where Louise slept. It was miserable, with litter in the doorway and from far down its dank hall a sickening whiff that drifted out almost as tangible as sulphur gas into the street.

Louise admitted to being sixty-five, Fernande announced

mockingly, the morning there was nobody to help her serve the trays. Where was she? On her way to Spain with a man . . .

Fernande read the note harshly: "Cheerio, old girl . . . I'm off on a *voyage d'amour* . . . he's young and handsome . . . see you in Barcelona? Yoicks."

Madame reached automatically for her list of domestic last resorts, and said mildly, "Perhaps a proof that while there is life there is hope."

Fernande shrugged bitterly and closed the salon door without a sound behind her, but slammed the one into the kitchen with the report of a cannon.

The maid I remember most sadly in this procession of bedraggled broken women was the first I met there. Her name was Marie-Claire, and she walked with the shuffle of an old, weakened, exhausted person, although she could not yet have been twenty. Some of her teeth were gone.

Mostly she was unconscious of the world, so that she had to be told several times to pick up a dropped fork, or close a door. She used to exasperate Henriette to the explosion point, but Madame never allowed her daughter to scream at the little maid as she did at her own mother, and often Henriette would leap up from the table and run down to her room, sobbing frantically. The little maid never blinked at these outbursts, but they left the rest of us less interested in the amenities of the table, which were observed to their limits by anyone in Madame's presence.

One night, perhaps a few weeks after I had moved into my little *chambre de bonne* in the beautiful old house, I was propelled out of deep sleep and bed itself, and was into the dim hall before I knew that a most terrible scream had sent me there. It still seemed to writhe down toward me.

The two American girls who were staying for six weeks on their way to the Smith College course at the Sorbonne

came stumbling to their door. One was weeping and chatter-
ing with shock.

There was another long dreadful scream. It came from up
in the attic, where Fernande must share her bright décor with
the current slavey, and already I was so imbued with the sinister spirit of the big woman that a logical sequence of unutter-
able crimes, crises, attacks flicked through my mind as I stood
waiting.

The door to the salon opened, and Madame was there, calm
in a gray woolen dressing gown and the kind of lacy head-
gear I had not seen since my grandmother died in 1922. I
think it was called a boudoir cap.

There was a great crashing of heavy feet on the wooden
stairs to the maids' room, and Marie-Claire ran out into the
long tiled corridor. She was almost unrecognizable. Her eyes
were alive and blazing, her hair stood out wildly instead of
lying dull and flat, and she moved as fast as a hunted animal
down to where Madame stood. She threw herself on the floor
there, sobbing, "Save me, help me," and a long babble without
words except for the way they sounded in the air.

Both American girls were crying helplessly.

Madame frowned a little. "Tell them to calm themselves,"
she said to me. "Get up, Marie-Claire. Stop that noise. Fernande, come down at once."

Fernande was halfway down the stairs, pulling her hair up
with pins. She seemed as forbidding as ever, but not upset.
She looked at Madame with a bored shrug.

"Here we go again. This is the last time, you understand?"
she said, and gently picked up the half-conscious girl and carried her as firmly as any strong man could, up into her garish
room.

Madame sighed. "We must retire. Thank you for being
patient. That poor soul was cruelly tampered with when she
was a child during the Occupation, and she stopped growing.

Now and then she comes alive, and remembers, and it is terrible. Good night."

In spite of myself I reached out my hand to her arm. Perhaps it was because I was still hearing the first scream and then the second, and I too was shocked. Madame Lanes moved away from me with almost imperceptible reproof, and I turned from her with a polite good night and went along to my room, feeling chastened, reduced to clumsy childhood at my ripe age.

Marie-Claire was sent back to her farm: Madame respected her family as one sorely tried by the state of their daughter, but she knew that no patience from her could make the poor thing into even a slavey, and we started the long stream of nitwits, sick old whores, and dipsomaniacs again . . .

All this intimacy with the raw wounds of war was doubly intense with me, perhaps, because I was alone, and middle-aged, and scarred from my own battles since last I had lived in France. At times I felt myself almost disintegrating with the force of the incredible vitality of the people I was with. They were wasteful and mistaken and hysterically overt, and buffeted as I was by all the noise of their will to survive, I could not but admit, in my loneliest hours, that I was more alive with them than I was anyplace else in my known world. I was apart. I was accepted only as an inoffensive and boringly polite paying guest. But the people who blandly took what they needed from me, which was openly nothing but money, were teaching me extraordinary things about myself and my place in this new knowledge. I learned much from the warped malnourished drudges of Madame's household, that year.

vii

THE PHYSICAL CLIMATE of the Lanes' apartment was almost as erratic as the emotional, with dramatic fevers and chills from everyone and at unexpected times.

One night Minet the tom would let out a gurgle from his suppertime position on the dining room sideboard, and flip off onto the floor. Henriette would scream and rush to pick him up. Fernande would dash from the kitchen across the corridor and cry out, "No no, do not touch him, I implore you . . . He is plainly mad! He will bite you."

Madame would look in a mild way over her shoulder and say, "Leave him alone, both of you. He has perhaps a small stomachache. Fernande, you may serve the caramel custard."

Minet would lie on the floor, while Henriette gobbled viciously at her pudding, her eyes red with tears and anger. We all knew that after dinner she would slip out of the house to the Deux Garçons, the nearest public telephone, and call her vet. While she was thus secretly away, Madame would just as secretly carry Minet into her couch, give him half an aspirin . . .

Henriette herself was, inevitably, a mass of neurotic symptoms. They were of course unknown and inexplicable to any of the countless doctors she had consulted in her forty-odd years of world-sickness. They involved mysteries as yet unplumbed, at least by the medicos, and her fear of psychiatric help was almost frantic.

She had monumental hiccups now and then, which called for deep sedation. She had fits of dreadful weeping. She had dolorous shooting sensations in this or that part of her basically very strong body. All of these attacks were as close to the rest of us as this morning's coffee, and as inescapable, and her medical pattern added a kind of rhythm to our lives.

So did Fernande's periodic "liver crises." They usually meant that for at least one day we made short shrift in the dining room. This was basically agreeable: Henriette became helpful and almost pleasant, and Madame seemed to be less graciously remote.

The laborious and genteel clatter of changing plates and silverware diminished, and we lingered over two or three courses instead of five or six, which would be normal in the twentieth century, even in Aix, but which in the eighteenth-century manner still clung to on the Rue Cardinale was quaintly country-style.

Now and then Madame herself succumbed to human ills, and they always seemed especially poignant to me, for except in dire trouble she insisted upon continuing the serene pattern of her secretly frenzied efforts to keep the family head above water. She would walk slowly to the table at noon, her face suddenly small and vulnerable under her carefully combed white hair, and the conversation would lag a little in her general apathy, but when she finally walked away we would know that she most probably would be there again in the evening, ignoring boldly the fact that Dr. Vidal had told her to keep to her bed.

Once she had to stay there, with a bad pleurisy. For the first and only time the salon was openly admitted to be her bedroom, since there was no other place in the big apartment to put her. I wanted to offer her my room, and finally did so, but I was snubbed with exquisite tact for such presumption: it was a family problem, not to be shared with an outsider.

Any such illness was complicated by Madame's insistence that the household try to function as it would have done fifty or a hundred years before, with five servants or even ten. It was insane. But it served to bring all of Fernande's ferocious courage into full splendor, and we ate in muted satiety while in the beautiful room next to the long airy dining room with

the crests over the doors and mantelpiece Madame lay wheezing as quietly as possible.

Once she had a bad attack of sciatica. She hobbled gamely
about, but gave up her trips to market. My room was next
to the bathroom, and one day I heard her sitting there in a
steam tent made of old towels, trying to warm her poor aged
muscles, and she was groaning without restraint, although I
had seen her a half-hour earlier looking almost as always, if
somewhat preoccupied.

It is very hard to listen to an old woman groan, especially
when such is not her custom. I had to fight my instinctive
feeling that I was in some way her daughter and that I must
try to help her. I stood impotently in my little room. Finally
I went down the corridor and knocked at Henriette's door.

"Please excuse me," I said, "but Madame is in the bathroom
and she seems to be in considerable pain."

Henriette looked coldly at me. "Please do not worry yourself," she said. "She is quite all right. She is simply making a
little scene."

I went out for a dogged fast walk through the streets, and
stood listening to several fountains to get the sounds of the
old woman, and even more so of the young one, out of my
head.

One time Henry Montgomery and I, two boarders for the
time being, met a decrepit old nanny trying to push an empty
perambulator up to the first landing of the house, where the
Countess de Chabot was entertaining a niece with a recent
baby.

Henry insisted in the firm simple way of most Anglo-Saxon
men that he and I help carry the pram on up. The old woman
cringed and scuttled ahead, and for several weeks we were
somewhat testily teased by Madame about this breach of eti-
quette: a man of a certain class, and Henry was unmistakably

of the top level in his own country, does not assist in any way a man or woman of a lower class than his own.

This was a flat statement. Henry had betrayed his background. I on the other hand as a relatively uncouth American could not be blamed for my breach of breeding and manners, but I might perhaps have learned a lesson . . .

"But she was very old," Henry said flatly.

Madame's reply I can still hear. "I shall never forget one time I was about to cross the Cours Mirabeau. I felt very faint. I leaned against a tree. A kindly woman, very ordinary, came up to me and helped me across the street. It was most good of her, but it was rude."

We said, "But Madame . . . did you need her? Could you have crossed alone?"

"Yes, I did need help, and I could not possibly have crossed without collapsing, but she was not at all of my station, and it was basically forward and pushing of her to offer to help me. I would have preferred to fall where I was, unassisted by such a person."

Henry could appreciate this in his own inverted Scandinavian way, but I was, and I remain, somewhat baffled and very repelled by it. It was a conditioned reflex in the fine old lady, which was as natural to her as her need of a fish fork for fish and a game fork for game.

One more question we asked, before each in his own way pushed the matter into partial limbo: "Would you not have helped this woman if she had felt ill, just as we helped the old servant with her pram?"

"Never," Madame said simply, and we tackled the scallop of veal.

Letters from Madame between my two stays in Aix told of a series of ghastly operations, collapses, and maladies which afflicted Henriette in Paris, but never mentioned her own state of health, and when I saw her again in 1959 she did indeed look younger and less withdrawn.

She was perhaps encouraged by the fact that she of all her old friends was the one who had fought through the strange profession, come so late in life to her, of being a landlady. They, she told me mockingly, lived in their moldy shawls, playing bezique and bridge and tattling over their teacups. She alone supervised her household, her table, and her social life, and she did it with a late but appealing jauntiness.

Fernande was gone, in a cosmic huff. She finally ran away, convinced that Henriette had become the mistress of a man in Corsica for whom Fernande cooked during one of her summer vacations. If it was not that, it was something equally fantastic, Madame shrugged.

Life, she added, had been a dream of tranquillity since the big ferocious tyrant had disappeared, and now things progressed in seraphic perfection under the thumb of a sallow cricket of a woman, well-spoken and as sharp-eyed as a ferret, who "lived out."

It was she who hired the continuing but somewhat more palatable flow of maids-of-the-moment, and attended to the meals and the accounts. She coddled Madame. She put up with no nonsense from the boarders. One had the feeling that if it was her prescribed time of day to leave the apartment and return to her own home she would step neatly over any number of bleeding bodies and be deaf to no matter what cries for help, but that up until that moment she would do all she could to be a devoted and well-paid savior. I did not like her at all, and do not recall her name, but I felt thankful that at the end of Madame Lanes' troubled life she had fallen into the deft hands of this assistant.

I was glad for the look of relaxation in my friend's smooth old face, for by now I could freely call her friend. At last she had accepted me, perhaps for one of the rare times in her life, as a loyal and affectionate admirer in spite of my lack of ancestral permanency.

"Madame is originally from Ireland," she would say defensively, when I was the only American among her world-exhausted friends. "Her culture is obviously inherited."

At first this enraged me, but by the last time I saw Madame I was as unaffected by it as an ant by a fleeting shadow. I forgave her. She had accepted me for myself, in spite of any such linguistic protests.

We lunched together in a beautiful old converted château, the day before my last departure. She told me with laughing cynicism of how it had been declared a Historical Monument in order to reduce the taxes, and refurbished by a retired chef and his rich wife in order to profit by the armies of hungry tourists who wanted real French cooking in the proper Crane-fixtured setting. Meanwhile we ate slowly and delightedly, and drank with appreciative moderation, and savored the long reward of our relationship.

Never had there been any display of affection between us, beyond a cursory peck on each cheek, but no more did I feel pushed away, held at cautious distance because of my newness. At last with this adamant old woman I was me, Mary Frances . . .

She took my arm as we walked down the long stairway of the château-restaurant, and when she next wrote to me, in far California, she began, "Dear and faithful friend . . ."

Oath to Asclepius

> ... some patients, though conscious that their condition is perilous, recover their health simply through their contentment with the goodness of the physician.

> Hippocrates, *Precepts*

i   *THE PURE ONE*

> A well-trained sensible family doctor is one of the most valuable assets in a community, worth today, as in Homer's time, many another man.

> Sir William Osler, *Aequanimitas*

Some doctors are fine writers, and what they write is often read, even centuries later. Some doctors, on the other hand, are very fine doctors, and how they are so is usually written about by the other people.

Few write much more than aweful praise. It is considered a breach of human decency, really, to criticize or mock anything as essential as our healers, and the few good authors and artists who have dared bare the other side of the coin are classed forever as satirists, caricaturists, and worse.

It is of course easier to lampoon than to praise if one has the needed amount of scorn and hate in one's pen or ink-bottle. Even for me, it would be. That is why I think it a test of my powers to remember and to consider, over and past my moments of horror and fright, the few real God-sent healers I have known. They are as rare as hen's teeth, as are real God-sent men of God.

It is a curious thing that although I have lived more of my life in the United States than anywhere else, I have met only two or at most two and one-half real healers in my own country. I have of course met many doctors, mostly men who helped my parents and friends, and in spite of my need for them and my helpless desire to trust them, they have seldom come up to my inner standards. In the same way, I have met only two people who were true men of God, during my life in America.

In other countries I have known one woman of God, in Lugano, and I have sensed the Godly presence, as strong as wild thyme or a lion's roar, of an archbishop in Provence. I sat near him once, and once I watched impatiently as he swept up the aisle toward the altar of St. Sauveur, letting old women kiss his great ring. Then, even though I did not like him, I knew I was in the presence of a spiritual healer.

In the same way, for many years in Aix I had to recognize, at times grudgingly, that Dr. Vidal was, according to every severity of my preconceptions, the realest doctor of my life. This I resented having to do, for it displaced one other man, in California, who had saved my own and many other lives, and who had taught me in every way to know what both life and death could mean. I did not want to divide my allegiance, but it was impossible to ignore the purity of Vidal.

Much of what I know and sense about him is legendary, a myth, a dream, as is true of everything that has ever happened to people like me, the wanderers in space and time. His enemies, if ever they should read my own word-picture of him, would sneer and smile with pleasure at my ignorant betrayal. His friends would contradict much that I myself know, knowing their own versions more firmly.

The doctor, if ever he bothered to read my report on his

right to be called a healer, which in his case may be synonymous with man of God, would shrug and dismiss it as unessential.

I met him once in the hall at Madame Lanes' early in the 1950's. He had been called to look at a young Swede, Henry Montgomery, who felt worse than peculiar after a month in Spain.

Being passionately Nordic, Henry had detested the olive oil and garlic and hot peppers and strange fishy sauces of his travels, and once free of them had collapsed with a kind of nausea of relief, especially after he realized that Madame Lanes, in deference to his country and his own high position in it, would do her best to serve him the boiled pale potatoes and the poached livid fish and the bland puddings of Stockholm. He ran a fever, and tossed in his Louis Quinze bed, convinced that he had contracted dysentery, or typhoid, or Malta fever, or perhaps all three.

I went down the long corridor from my room. At the dim end, a tall strong young man came out of the Swede's room. He was dressed like an English country doctor, in gray slacks and a carelessly shaggy tweed jacket, which is to say that he looked utterly different from the professional men of Aix, who wore tight dark clothes, usually black, and hats always.

This man's hair was pale brown, and cut like an English schoolboy's, with a lock over his forehead. ("He is," Madame said tenderly, later, "a true Northerner, like myself.")

He spoke in a quiet resonant voice, looked keenly at me with large steady pale blue eyes, also so different from the dark hot gaze of the Aixois, and ran in an almost jaunty way down the wide stone stairs, the three deep floors of them with beautiful ironwork balustrades. I listened to the great carved doors bang behind him.

After I had asked politely for the diagnosis (and repose, a bland diet, aspirin for restlessness), I got Madame Lanes to tell me that Dr. Vidal was the best man she had ever known: so young, so strong, so sympathetic, so wise, so brave.

He had been a great hero of the Resistance, one of the youngest doctors to be able to practice, both in and out of the prisons he was held in. He had escaped a few times, to work underground, always as a surgeon and healer. He had been closest friend with the priest who became Archbishop, the youngest man ever to be named so by the Pope, and they still were like men born from the same father, even to their structure.

This I knew. The two times I came close to the man of God I saw Vidal in him, and when I talked later through the years with Vidal I saw the Archbishop; they might have been one man except that I think the priest had dark eyes. Both of them, though, looked with the same piercing quiet look at everything around them, with a kind of sensitive inner trust that has been rare in my life.

The second time I saw Dr. Vidal was about a year later. My two small daughters now lived with me, in the room where our bilious Swedish friend had lain in his final protest against Spanish gastronomy.

The younger girl, Mary, subjected to a regime of everything destructive to a human liver, especially a reputedly damaged one, had gone into a strange dream. It was increasingly hard to rouse her. She lay quietly, a remote half-smile on her face. At first I thought she was merely tired. Gradually I became painfully uneasy, and at last I ran through the town, to the Place de l'Archevêché where the children had lived for a few months, and asked my friend who had sheltered them to find me a doctor.

I remember being surprised that without hesitation she called Dr. Vidal, for she and Madame Lanes moved on different social planes, and in old towns like Aix they are as clear-cut as layers of bricks in a wall: lawyers and doctors and dentists and even hairdressers go always among the same groups in their various ministrations.

Vidal came within an hour or so, as I sat near Mary's bed. She lay without motion, and her breathing was faint and her face looked very remote and beautiful. I was taking nail polish off my hands, and repainting them, because I was inwardly frantic and must identify myself with inanity.

Vidal opened the door quietly. He was the same tall strong man, with deep eyes that regarded calmly whatever they chose. He sniffed. Then he came surely to the bed, and said in his resonant quiet voice, "Madame, do you recognize the smell of acetone?"

"Yes," I said, thinking he was talking of the strong hint of polish remover in the air. I felt clumsy: I should not have been doing such a vain silly thing while my child lay half-conscious and I sat waiting.

I started to apologize, but he went on firmly, "There is the unmistakable odor of an acetonic crisis in the air. The skin exudes it. The urine is undoubtedly heavy with it. We shall make tests at once. It could be diabetic but is more probably a slowing of the liver functions."

This was of course a hair-raising coincidence, but in spite of the open bottle of nail-polish remover I never questioned Dr. Vidal's judgment, and his treatment convinced me that he had known the odor under the odor, the body smell unmasked by the artificial one. It was slow and quiet, and as right to me as had always been the other doctor's I most admired: careful simple diet, almost no medication, rest, much lemon juice and pure water.

The little girl responded like any healthy trusting animal, and from then on she has known, as have I, how to avoid rich pastries, eggs, milk, ripe cheeses. Vidal also taught her how to recognize danger signals, and said in his almost hypnotically firm quiet way, "You must learn how to be rude politely, and say no."

Several months later Mary and Anne and I were living at Le Tholonet, and it came time to ready ourselves for the long journey back to California on an Italian freighter. Various shots and tests were necessary, and I was pleased to have an excuse to be with Dr. Vidal again: he satisfied me in a good but still subtle way, just as the Archbishop had done, the night I sat near him in St. Sauveur during a concert of Campra.

While Vidal was writing instructions for yellow fever shots, a small medicine kit for the ship, things like that, I permitted myself to enjoy him. I liked the way he sat easily, as all tall men do, at his desk. I liked his detached tenderness, his gift of making me feel reassured and yet held gently off from him, not held off as a female or even a person, but as an object of his care, toward which he must remain ever impersonal and clear-minded.

His offices were on the second floor of a tall noble town-house on the Cours Mirabeau. He lived there too, like most French doctors, with his wife and a growing family of hand-some children.

Madame Lanes, who literally worshiped him, dismissed his wife by saying that although she was charming she was "very simple." In Madame's language, that meant that Madame Vidal made no effort to be social and worldly, but was content to devote herself to her family. Over a period of several years I often looked at this "simple" person as she answered the door-bell when the idiotic little maid-of-all-work was busy else-where, and I found her tall, attractive, well dressed, and full of the same courteous detachment as her husband. I would have liked to know her more, but accepted the fact that I never could.

The waiting room at the head of the long corridor which was the family's apartment was furnished with discretion: Pro-

vençal cloth for the curtains and upholstery, gauzy curtains to mask the big window giving down onto the Cours, a few prints of *santons*, a rubber plant in a copper pot. The magazines were tattered and few. Most people who came into the room were really ill or in pain, and most of them looked poor.

Dr. Vidal's office, behind a door heavily curtained with a Provençal quilt like an old-fashioned American bedspread, was even narrower than the waiting room. His plain handsome desk was by the twin to the other window. They had balconies on them where in the eighteenth century the visiting grandees saluted the crowds below.

Toward the back of the office, on the corridor side, was a kind of cubicle. I never went into it, but assume it had some sort of table for people to be examined on. There was a low divan in the office, covered with green Provençal tissue. There was no sign of any medical paraphernalia except for a shabby stethoscope on the tidy desk-top. There were no framed diplomas on the walls.

Vidal looked up dispassionately at me with his steady eyes. "How do you like living with the peasants at Le Tholonet?" he asked me.

I told him we were happy there, living more simply than we ever had and perhaps than we ever would again. He asked me what we ate. I told him some of the intricacies of getting food for our meals, and he smiled with his eyes but no more. Then he asked if we ate any cheeses, especially the local ones rather like our cottage cheese but made with farm milk from cows and goats and sheep, and I said that now and then the shepherdess made us a *brousse*.

This is a delicate kind of bonny-clabber made from fresh ewe's milk left to "set," and sweetened and faintly spiced with nutmeg and perhaps ginger. It is as light and fresh as brook water, and leaves one feeling light and fresh too.

Dr. Vidal frowned a little, and shrugged. "How long do

you plan to be on this small ship through the Panama Canal, with no adequate medical facilities aboard?" he asked idly.

I told him about six or seven weeks.

"You are very foolish to risk getting Malta fever, then," he went on in the same remote way. He looked up from the directions he had been writing about yellow fever shots and urinalyses and so on. "I would surmise, Madame," he said in a way which from that moment on became part of our family-lingo, "that such a probability is *counterindicated.*"

That was all.

Perhaps I murmured agreement. Anything counterindicated to my hopes to help shepherd my two girls, two younger nephews, their mother and a sixteen-year-old French friend through the ordeal of life on a freighter did seem worth a fair warning.

I thought firmly about it, as I made plans to go in to Marseille with the children for the horrid yellow fever shots. I even read about Malta or undulant fever, which sounded damnably unpleasant, at sea or anywhere.

Then I looked at the five children, who had lived from sixteen to six years with plenty of freshly made cheeses and milks in their diets, and for the last few months the rare treat of the delicious *brousses,* and I decided that the die had been cast, and that we would not offend the shepherdess at this point.

She brought us one last bowl, the day we left, and her best plates because ours were packed. Never had it tasted better, nor had I felt more philosophical.

There was a long pause in my active relationship with Vidal because of distance, but I talked about him with my other important doctor, the American, and told him of the way Vidal would recommend fasting, bed-rest and (not a good book, as Dr. Lister once wrote) floods of hot herb teas . . . thyme, verbena, mint, sassafras. We agreed that such was an increasingly rare treatment.

At the end of the 1950s I went back to Europe with Anne and Mary. We stayed in Lugano about nine months, while they learned how to exist in Italian. We had a good life, when I could see them at Sant'Anna, which at first was seldom, and I coughed steadily all the time I was there. In the fine lake air I felt as if I were mildewing. It became a problem that remained unsolved by a series of doctors to whom I was referred by Swiss friends. I grew quietly despairing, but kept telling myself that a real illness was counterindicated.

A few months before we were to leave Lugano we came to the irrevocable decision that since we were already some seven thousand miles from home, we should stay a year longer and return to Aix, where we seemed to have left large parts of our human significance. As soon as we were sure of this, I began to think, most often against my sensible protests, my reason, my logic, that if I could last until I saw Dr. Vidal I would be well again.

I had spent several months in the hands of highly recommended and earnest specialists who swabbed, irrigated, sprayed, probed, and generally tortured me with a hundred medications, and who somewhat obviously considered me a neurotic, lonely, well-heeled tourist. I continued to cough like a sick cow, and to sweat and shiver at perfectly spaced intervals.

Let me get back to Aix, I prayed. Let me lie in a meadow, and drink herb teas, and know that Dr. Vidal's quiet voice will reassure me that all these humiliating pills and probes are silly.

This came about, by Providence. I did lie in the meadow in the penetrating Provençal sun, and I did drink teas brewed from herbs picked that morning by my children, and I even lay in baths redolent of branches of fresh thyme. I did find once more the serene dispassion of Vidal, and his deep calm eyes, and his fine voice, and the sureness of movement in his long frame.

The only change was that he had become a pill-man: he

prescribed intricate schedules of a dozen different kinds of capsules, troches, dragées, and pastilles. He was very firm about the rhythm of taking them. Gone were the simple teas and infusions. He was still loyal to his fasting and resting. Otherwise he had joined the pharmaceutical cabala.

I felt disillusioned but loyal, up to the same point where I had accepted his smelling the acetone and suspecting the *brousse*. I let the hot sun and the meadow smells soothe me, and I put the pills down the toilet drain, except for very rarely, when I knew he had prescribed a tranquilizer and I felt a fleeting need to dull the razor's edge.

During those first few months, sunny, coughless, and serene, I observed with astonishment the new intake of drugstore products by the general population.

The pharmacies were, as they always had been in France, almost like little outpatient hospitals; the owners were, as always, highly trained. They prescribed skillfully for aches and pains, and bandaged sudden cuts, and revived fainting old ladies and pregnant passersby. But most of them had streamlined their stores, and they did less free prescribing than straight prescription work, with not even a mortar and pestle in sight, and a stern list of what nostrums, placebos, and quackeries had been dispensed from hour to hour . . . to whom . . . why . . . on what physician's say-so.

I read, idly but with an increasing chill, that the daily, not the weekly-monthly-annual but the DAILY, consumption of pills in France was over 400 tons. I think it was 470, but must allow for time as well as natural shock.

Perhaps it was time that made me more tolerant of all this. Perhaps I felt that the air of Provence would protect me. When I needed Dr. Vidal to tell me that one of my children was losing too much weight and looking gray around the gills I trusted him, so wise and kind and remote, to tell me that she needed to stop trying to do three years of Latin in six months and go

lie on a rock on Porquerolles. I also trusted Nature and myself
to carry on from there, and I threw most of her pills down the
toilet drain again, for if I had tossed them into a rock pool the
fish might have turned up their tails, and I did not want that
to happen to them or to my girls . . .

The Aixois are very sensitive to things like the mistral, the
cold mean dusty wind that blows down the Rhone Valley at
odd moments. Indeed, if a crime can be proved to have been
committed during the mistral it is wiped off the slate, such is
the pernicious influence of this blustering devil. It is because it
comes from the north? In other countries people, usually
women, often complain about how a north wind makes them
nervous or peaked . . . Well, Vidal was prescribing what
Madame Lanes laughingly, affectionately called mistral drops!

Another thing the Aixois dislike intensely is drafts, although
most French people have somewhat the same aversion to any
fresh moving air. Anglo-Saxons notice this most keenly, especially in hotel dining rooms, buses, and, in the old days when
there was no so-called air-conditioning, in train compartments.
For every staunch British believer in fresh-air-and-be-damned-
to-the-cinders, there were a good half-dozen desperate Frenchmen who would have slammed down the windows in the face
of Queen Elizabeth herself, I or II. In Aix there are special
medicines against drafts — "draft-draughts"!

One more thing is a prime subject of commiseration and
medication, there: rheumatism. There is a great deal of it.

People have been going to the thermal places in Aix for more
than two thousand years, and the hot and warm and cool
waters have soothed and even cured Greeks and Romans and
Gauls and Saracens and Celts and in other words some two
millennia of aching crickety tourists. They arrive. They bathe
and rest. They leave beatific.

Meanwhile the Aixois themselves, forced to remain, are basically and incurably rheumatic. They ache. They hobble.

They creak. It is a locational hazard. They do not have time to dip themselves in the healing waters of the place, nor lie in the sun around the steaming glittering pools, nor take the Roman-esque massages and rubbings that go on all about them.

Often the simpler citizens take a pitcher to Old Mossback and let the steaming water spout into it, and then at home they cautiously sip a little of the water, to cure gout or swollen joints or plain misery.

Mostly they hobble about, especially in January and February.

I know, because I did.

I was amazed. I remembered how Madame Lanes had an occasional *crise de rhumatisme*. I looked about me. I admitted, now and then, that I could barely climb the five flights of stairs to my room, and that often I had to stop for a minute on the Cours and discreetly try to joggle my right hip into a firmer and less excruciating focus on the path ahead.

Finally I went to Dr. Vidal, in his tranquil austere rooms above the Cours. I could hear some of his children roughing it up a bit with the current nitwit maid. There were only a few patients in the discreetly Provençal waiting room, sitting like sick wilted birds on their chairs, all puffy with miserable feathers.

Two nights before, Dr. Vidal had been ambushed in a corridor of the Opera house by a hired band of ruffians from Marseille, during a political meeting in which he got up on the stage and denounced something that was very clear to me at the time but has now fled my mind. He was against something that most of the conservatives were for. Or perhaps he was for something all the radicals were against. I think it was the former, for although he was the most conformist of people in his behavior, albeit completely un-Provençal and of the "Northern" type, he seemed to like to express his social impatience by very overt behavior in politics. It was always surprising that people like Madame Lanes loved this rebellious streak in him, and deplored it voluptuously.

I had read about Vidal's latest entanglement with the Marseillais toughs with some dismay: he had been hospitalized, and I hated to think of it, for I plainly had a personal attachment to him, even if as distant as his own recognition of me.

Finally the last of the sick people pulled up the heavy quilt over his office door, and disappeared in a muffled murmur from behind it, and I could hobble in.

The room was very dim. He sat with his face toward the cubicle and the door into the corridor, firmly away from the light. Even then I could see that one eye was still swollen almost shut and surrounded by cruel smears of brown empurplement, and that his lower lip and his chin were nearly immobile with plastic bandages and stitches in the skin. He was a schoolboy mess.

For the first time in almost a decade of knowing him, I permitted myself something besides the banalities of bowel movements, temperatures, and other such data.

"I am very glad to see that you are still around," I said, looking at him as firmly as he always looked at me.

He almost smiled, and for an instant was one human to another, perhaps even one man to one woman. Then he withdrew again. "Yes, I was fortunate this time," he said formally. "And I see that you have become one of the Aix citizens at last: you are suffering from rheumatism."

His prescriptions involved my going twice a week to a beautiful convent, for most doctors in that part of France never give injections except at accidents. The treatment, which involved my bending over, bare up to the waist, before a kneeling nun armed with an enormous hypodermic, may not have been as efficacious as the passage of time and the return of spring, but during it I learned a lot about how the water flowing everywhere under Aix, but especially down the ancient canal on which the Cours Mirabeau is built, has affected the aches and pains of the citizens.

"Even the doctor himself," Sister Marie-Angeleine told me debonairly after we had become intimate, which of necessity was almost at once, "has to bow to an occasional injection."

When I had to go away again from Provence I thought with an actual pang, amongst many others perhaps even more severe, of whatever mysterious thing it was that Dr. Vidal had always given me, a kind of courage in the face of my own skepticism, indeed a jauntiness of spirit quite ill adjusted to his outward manners. I knew him to be brave, from hearsay and from my one sight of him after the beating. What I could not understand was how, and even why, he made me feel brave too.

I decided that I must thank him in some way for this. I composed a note. I even mailed it. Of course he never replied, for I did not put my American address on it, and one thing I like about him is that most probably he has never thought of it again, except perhaps when he goes to his confessor, who I was told is the Archbishop.

ii *THE UNKNOWN*

> The art of medicine consists of amusing the patient while Nature cures the disease.
>
> **Voltaire**

THERE WAS ONE doctor we saw for only a few minutes, whom I shall always remember for his strong charm over my girl Anne, in the Military Hospital in Marseille.

I reviewed the whole adventure exactly four days after it happened, when I sat feeling miserable about the mimeographed sheet of instructions which an officer had thrust at me. Perhaps if I had never read it I would have blamed my sensations on the weather, or a touch of liver. As it was, it acted like a delayed evil spell, and I huddled and shook where I sat.

Courbature, the sheet said I could expect between the fourth and seventh days, and *courbature* I definitely felt, if it meant aching bones. If it meant "bent over," I was. I was at least ninety-six years old.

It also said that I could expect *céphalée*.

This is a word not commonly used, in daily conversation at least, by the respectable middle-class people with whom my girls and I had been living in Aix, and I could only assume that its resemblance to "syphilis" was accidental, since it seemed improbable that even in a French military hospital a yellow fever shot would cover V.D. It probably had some connection with words like hydrocephalic. Perhaps it was merely a medical term for headache, which suddenly I had.

Neither *courbature* nor *céphalée* was in my paperback dictionary, but the third thing that the sleazy directions said I could expect was easy: *fièvre* . . . "light fever yielding easily to a dose of aspirin." I got out the little tin box, still holding almost its original dozen after a year in the traveling first-aid kit. Bent aching back and headache were already my lot, and with fever next on the witch's spell sheet, I would be prepared . . .

The whole business had been surprising, Anne and Mary and I agreed. A year before, we had come through the Canal to France without a thought of yellow fever. Now, doing the voyage in reverse, with perhaps a few more ports of call on the list, relatives in America were shouting sternly at us, and even the travel agent in Marseille said a firm "Of course" instead of his usual Belgian "Poof!" A little grimly I got the project under way.

By then we were living in Le Tholonet, northeast of Aix, and without either car or telephone except at the Relai de Cézanne.

I had a vague idea we should have urinalyses made, at least for the children: they had both caught the school-bug of sore throats a few weeks before, and analyses were made almost automatically for everything in that part of the country. Dr. Vidal agreed somewhat vaguely by telephone that it was "indicated," and I got the two little bottles onto the weekly market bus from the village and into the chemist's at Aix.

He said he would telephone the results to the doctor, who would in turn leave a message at the bar in the Relai. "No albumin" was the word when I walked down two days later for bread and cheese at the grocery which was the other half of the bar, so I engaged a taxi for seven the next morning, Friday.

It was a fine day, too fine to give a thought to the slight ordeal ahead: I hate things like vaccinations, but I knew this would be a little scratch with a quill on our upper arms, and then forgotten: "Absolutely no reaction," friends had assured me, and I said nothing at all to the children.

The salt air came in soft early summer puffs over the rolling hills as we neared Marseille. There was dark rain behind the city as we went down into it, and Notre Dame de le Garde was blurred on the far height.

Fernand, a dry skinny friend and one of the world's best drivers, drunk or sober, got us expertly to the enormous hulk of the hospital. He used to run a bar near it, and he knew an infinity of shortcuts. He parked deftly between the hospital and another bar run by a brother-in-law, and we agreed to meet him there in a half-hour.

At the gate a handsome officer with drooping eyelids and silvery hair asked for my certifications. I looked blank, or dull, or however it is that foreigners look to French people who are speaking clear correct plain words. He shrugged, and said firmly and loudly, "Urine . . . papers . . . *urine*." Anne looked embarrassed, and Mary tittered. He handed me a smudgy mimeographed sheet which I stuck in my handbag to read later. I had no papers at all, I told him. He smiled wearily and told us to go in anyway, to hurry up the line that was forming behind us.

The forecourt was packed with military ambulances on the ready. There was a long tunnel-like passage smelling of lye. Then we were in a great leafy pleasant square, with discreet signs pointing this way and that. Thin men in baggy pyjama suits walked in a gingerly fashion from bench to bench under the trees, and very short fat elderly women in white trotted briskly along the covered arcades at the sides, mostly carrying trays of tubes.

We got up to a third-floor room in a creaking stretcher-elevator marked *Forbidden to be operated by the gravely ill*. A boy in pyjamas and with no hair ran it for us. "Some tropical disease maybe," I murmured to Mary, who was plainly thrilled by this note in her mental book on how to become a doctor. Anne was discreetly withdrawn.

We were almost the first people in the ugly windowless waiting room, which had enough benches for perhaps twenty people along its walls. As it was to happen, we were also almost the last to leave it, and meanwhile it must have held four or five hundred of us.

Before it got too full, a very chubby woman in an old white tent formerly called a Mother Hubbard by American missionaries pounded gaily into the room. "All got your certifications?" she shouted in a smiley voice.

Instead of saying "No," which I did not yet realize I should have stated-screamed-even-wept everywhere from the very first, I said that the children had been "analyzed" three days before. She looked disturbed, and a sleepy young woman next to me on the bench said that albumin could form in twenty-four hours, and the fat attendant banged into the next room marked *Head Doctor for Dermatology and Anti-Amarile Vac-*

cinations and came out cheerily to say that it would be all right anyway.

For a couple of hours we sat, while the room got so full that we could not possibly have stood up to offer our seats to older tireder people. There were a lot of soldiers' wives, with many babies both inward and outward. There were a lot of colored men in uniform. There were a lot of teachers and nuns and so on, all going deep into Africa, Dakar, Djibouti . . . Everyone was polite, withdrawn, bored.

Gradually, from the murmurs, I understood that I too must have an analysis made. I pushed out into the hall and through the patient mob there to a room where a harried nurse agreed with me. In fact, she looked completely astonished at my stupidity, but forgiving. I pushed back to my pale children in the corner of the stifling room, advised them to stand in the hall where there was a little air, and said I would be back almost right away.

When I finally found the laboratory on the ground floor and across the leafy courtyard, the same fat merry woman in a Mother Hubbard was there to hand me an expertly designed little flask and point to the left. "Hah *hah*," she said as if she were glad to have one more routine task to do . . . which she did, of course, with the help of a tired mild young pharmacist, who flitted patiently up and down the rows of numbered tubes colored subtle numberless yellows. Fifteen minutes later I was handed a little paper saying *Albumin — None*, and I worked my long way back to the waiting room.

This time the elevator was run by a man in pyjamas with one arm in a big cast with dried blood on it, but he had a lot of curly hair on his head.

Anne and Mary looked smaller and paler, behind a solid wall of Moroccans, and I asserted myself and got them out into the almost equally crowded but less stifling hall, where they had been too polite to shove themselves at my first suggestion.

Once more and very gradually, from tired women and exasperated men, I learned that I should have signed up and paid, and then presented my certifications. I got into the necessary room somehow, and twenty minutes later came out feeling embarrassed and fatalistically frustrated: it would be impossible to vaccinate the two children unless they too had their correct new papers stating *Albumin — None.* The nurse in charge, with several shades of red, black and blonde hair and large beautiful eyes, looked patiently at me and shook her head. "This is over, closed up, at twelve noon, you know," she said with a kind of sadness about me.

I got the children down and across to the laboratory. The air in the big courtyard felt fine. The fat gay woman said, "Hah," and then, "Hah *hah,*" when she saw us. Anne and Mary were somewhat taken aback by the straightforward arrangements for procuring the necessary specimens. Nothing happened. The young pharmacist suggested running some water, loudly, which the attendant did with great amusement. Anne seemed desiccated with distaste and embarrassment, and even Mary could fill none of the basic requirements. I said firmly we would try again later, and was reminded with a reassuring guffaw that things closed at noon.

We straggled across the street to tell Fernand we were late and would be later.

It was hot in his brother-in-law's little bar. A woman from the hospital waiting room who by now seemed an old acquaintance was nursing her baby at the back table, and drinking a beer. Her husband, who had begun to turn purple in the hospital, looked almost normal behind a milky *pastis.* I would have liked one . . . or two. But I asked for a small blackish vermouth, and Fernand joined me, peering longingly at the *pastis* down the room. And I got the girls to drink almost two lemonades apiece, fast, before we hurried back across the street.

Everything proceeded smoothly; the fat woman congratu-

lated them with a reassuring bellow of approval laughter at
my strategy, and went right on hah hah HAH in a comfortable
way as we trotted off toward the third floor waiting room with
the correctly marked little slips.

The elevator was now run by a man in pyjamas and a large
white turban. "Head injury," Mary diagnosed professionally.
"Mohammedan," Anne said firmly, and I knew she was relieved to have everything behind her but the little scratch with
the quill.

The crowd had perhaps thinned a bit, and this time I could
pay the forty-five cents required for each of us and get through
the long joking interview with the rainbow-haired woman and
her young assistant, who were apparently very bored by hours
of ordinary French people of all colors and who found three
Americans as refreshing and delightfully heady as champagne.
Even the children cheered up completely at the fun the young
assistant had, a boy with an accent as thick as garlic mayon-
naise, pretending to stumble over the names Anne and Mary,
as if they were some new Yankee invention. It was entertaining, but the hands of the clock went on around toward noon.
It seemed to me that if I had to face Fernand with the news
that we must return on the next Tuesday or Friday and start
all over again with the analyses and the waiting, in order to
be able to flash our international vaccination cards at some
bored official in Trinidad or La-Union-Cutoco who had never
asked us for them before, I would need much more than one
of his brother-in-law's *pastis* to keep me from a good public
cry. My face was stiff from the joking, the cheerfulness . . .

It was four minutes to twelve when our names were called,
along with three blue-black soldiers and two young nuns, and
I heard fifty or so unfortunates stump glumly down the stairs
as the lock turned in the waiting room door.

The office was bright and efficient, and so was the nurse,
who must have swabbed alcohol on several hundred forearms

that morning. I myself felt smudged, shiny-nosed, and rumpled. The doctor reassured me by looking somewhat worn too, but unruffled, and he sent off the mysterious strength and calm that some men manage to do in his profession.

It was as well that he did, for Anne, who had once been brutalized with some penicillin shots by a "country doctor" who was the antithesis of our sentimental picture of such men, gave one look at the large tray of hypodermic needles and turned gray-green.

I was glad I had not deliberately lied to her about "a scratch with a quill." I prayed.

The nurse said, "Now don't be afraid, honey, because this . . ."

The doctor interrupted in a voice that was magnetically right for Anne, full of charm and sex and security. "*This* young lady is not bothered. I can *feel* it. We'll do her first . . ."

Anne looked fleetingly at me, and I knew she would not fly out the window in panic: we both recognized a fine man when we saw one. Then she smiled feebly with her large brown eyes straight into the tired smiling blue ones of the doctor, as he plunged a big needle into her skinny little arm, casually fastened a syringe to it, and pumped what looked like a half-cup of anti-amarile serum into her.

Later she was almost prostrated to realize that she had actually allowed anyone to give her an injection, something she had apparently vowed to prevent with her very life, if need be; but for time enough to get her out of the hospital and even back to Le Tholonet she seemed in a trance of happiness at having shared a moment of such intimacy with that wonderful man . . .

At exactly eight minutes past twelve we clattered down the suddenly echoing stairs, behind the hurrying black soldiers and well in front of the shy nuns. The leafy courtyard was empty.

Most of the ambulances were gone, and there was no handsome patient officer at the gate.

Across the street in the bar, when we pushed through the bead curtain, Fernand stood patiently in front of a *pastis* with the man whose face had once that morning turned purple and was now almost the same color again. At the back table the mother was still nursing her baby, with three other women who had not been able to make the noon deadline. Everyone tried to cheer up the few others who had been turned away, and congratulated the ones like us. Fernand stood the girls to a round of lemon soda. The air stung with the fine Marseillais perfume of licorice from the milky glasses and I felt so cheerful that one was plenty . . .

Lunch tasted better than usual, on the Vieux Port: there was something triumphal about us. Our favorite waiter dipped and dashed for us in a frenzy of silver platters and suggestions. Anne touched her arm softly now and then, and her eyes were starry.

And driving gracefully along the auto route and then the bumpier prettier route toward Aix, Fernand manipulated his car like a good horse and we chatted lazily, winily, about the new television towers far to the right on the Ridge of the Stars, the modern church steeple to the left with an angel something like Brancusi's *Bird in Flight,* the smell of the salt marshes of the Camargue as compared with the smell of the salty fjords around Cassis. In back, the two little girls sang a round, "White Sands and Gray Sands." Life was all right, indeed, and I felt like laughing hah HAH with the fat woman, behind her rows of yellow flasks with everything including death in them.

It was not for four days that I remembered to sort out the rubbish in my handbag. And there was the smudgy sheet the droop-lidded beau at the hospital gates had thrust at me. I read it with cool interest, still buoyed by the general well-being we had felt since that almost dim morning. It was clearly written, in spite of a few merely guessable words like *anti-paludique*, and I skimmed along casually through Precautions to take . . . Before presenting oneself at the vaccination-seance . . . Preceding the vaccination . . . After . . .

It was there I halted: ". . . it is useless to change one's diet, but dietary excesses and undue fatigue are strongly advised against, since a post-vaccination state can arise between the fourth and seventh days which it is best not to aggravate . . . *courbature, céphalée*, and a light fever yielding easily to a dose of aspirin . . ."

I counted back . . . four days! I thought of the delicious long luncheon on the Vieux Port. I thought of the afternoon spent climbing from bottom to top of all available parts of Notre Dame de la Garde. I thought of the two helpless little girls, pumped full of yellow fever serum and now out in the June mizzle with the shepherdess of Le Tholonet. My vision suddenly seemed less clear and my head was heavy. My back ached as if I were twice my years. That would make me more than senile, with a curved lumped spine: *courbature*! I felt sickish. I decided bravely not to mention all this to the children, but to watch them closely for the signs.

Outside, a little later, the early summer storm blew over. A friend drove up in her old Army truck. Creakingly I agreed to pile into it with all our children for a picnic: I would be silent about my misery, which disappeared almost at once. While we were gone, the mimeographed sheet must have blown off the table and into the meadow, for I never saw it again. I felt that my abrupt short reaction to it was normal, which is always a comfort, and as far as I could tell, the children never learned the words *céphalée, courbature*, even *fièvre*, although Anne perhaps learned a little bit more about *amour*.

iii *WHITE IS BLACK IS WHITE*

Evil and good are God's right hand
and left.
                Philip James Bailey, *Festus*

IN THE OTHER TOWN, Dijon, there was long ago a doctor who,
in the human sense, was definitely counterindicated. His name
was Blanc, and he lived in a new part of the town in a villa
with heavy lace curtains of a pale coffee color.

My landlady had sent me to him when I was about to go off
for a long vacation at Christmas and was nagged by a pain
which was plainly from an outraged appendix. I thought of
how unpleasant it would be to fall howling to the floor in a
hotel in Nuremberg, but then when I went into the villa I
thought how unpleasant it was to be there too. I seemed to be
alone with the youngish, tallish, blondish man in a black coat.
The light through the curtains was sickly. Upstairs I could
hear a piano playing a faint approximation of Chopin.

The doctor made some notes about my name and suchlike.
I wrapped myself in my innate innocence. He changed into
a white coat, unlike most European doctors. Later, when he
had examined me and confirmed my own diagnosis, he leaned
too easily against the table where I lay half-exposed, and I
knew even in my innocence that he would like to continue
another kind of examination of my helplessness. I arose, no
doubt with frigid dignity, paid him, and went away in a confused state of amazement and outrage.

When my landlady asked if all had gone well I was courteous. I stopped eating as much as I wanted of her delicious
sauces and puddings, and in Nuremberg I forgot to worry at
all about being caught by pain and gluttony, and sat gobbling
bratwurstglöckleinen and drinking beer to keep warm, where

perhaps Dürer had sat gobbling and drinking with the same hungry insouciance. But in the ghost-life I have led in Dijon since that far year and day, I have felt a certain regret that my one doctor there was such an unprincipled horny one. The only good thing about him was that when I met a second Blanc, I could exorcise that nasty one.

He was a young allergist Vidal sent me to. He was a shadowy man, with a feeling of dedication about him but in some indescribable way without Vidal's purity. He was most probably more intelligent, which was doubtless an asset in his ambitious path but quite unessential to Vidal's: a matter of training versus instinct, perhaps.

His offices were on the second floor of a moderately noble town-house on the Rue Eméric-David. He lived in Marseille, I think. The rooms were not shabby but were ugly and undistinguished. Most of his patients were very poor, and since he specialized in infections of the chest, there were many Algerians, who at that time were a menace to public health because of the tuberculous state they had fallen into in their French ghettoes.

I got to know several people there, well enough to salute reservedly. Most of them had alarming wheezes and coughs. There was a woman in a grubby overall who summoned us. I disliked her because she was very polite to me and barely civil to the Algerians.

They were of course something of a problem logistically in the small stuffy waiting room across the hall from Blanc's offices, because if one of them had an appointment, seven or eight came to keep him company and give him strength, like the Gypsies. They sat on the floor, and leaned against the walls, and overflowed silently into the cold ugly hallway. They were used to being shunned and did not seem to notice the surly woman's manner as much as I did.

Dr. Blanc was very efficient. He was the only Frenchman

I ever knew who used the archaic form of "Sit down," so that from him, in his detached light voice, it became "Pray have the goodness to be seated": *Assoyez-vous*. I liked it, and looked forward to it as a kind of sop, of solace for the long coughing, wheezing periods in the waiting room, where I seemed always to be the only well person there and perhaps in the whole world.

He used some rather elaborate equipment on me now and then, to see what clouds he could detect in my chest; but mainly his treatment consisted of an almost undetectable prick of a needle dipped in a Pasteur vaccine: he was riding his favorite horse, and fighting fire with fire.

Rarely, I could get him to talk. Usually he seemed on the edge of an exhausted collapse. Always he was detached, like Vidal but in a more personal way, somehow. Once when I knew that I must soon go away, I told him that I should always be glad to welcome him in California. There was a flash of first amazement and then warm pleasure behind his thin worn face, and then he was back in his prime role again, the detached young scientist struggling along in a provincial town.

When I left, he went to a lot of trouble to get names and sources and suchlike, so that when I got to my home I could continue with almost no break his treatment, which he believed was all-important to my future as a person and a writer. (Like many doctors, he was in awe of people who did anything with their thoughts.)

His past treatment and future prescriptions were reduced to scornful shreds by my American doctors, but I shall always be thankful that I met him, to lay the ghost of that other Blanc in the other town and to know that there are young men who seem to have *something* of Vidal's purity. They are not counterindicated in this world . . .

The Sound of the Place

... and the song of multiple fountains,
which one discovers with enchantment
in the fresh silent shade of the courtyards and gardens, where dolphins and
bearded gods blow water into their
deep beautiful basins.

Martial and Braive, *Aix-en-Provence*

A ix has been called "the city of fountains and music," and
the two are synonymous in it.

Summers, during the Festival, the whole town quivers to the
sounds, in the open air of cloisters and courtyards, of violins
and flutes and voices, and above them rises always the indescribable soft steady music from at least fourteen public fountains and uncounted murmuring basins hidden in gardens and
inner courts.

Late at night the year around, and even during the midday
hours in summer when all else sleeps, a person seeking it can
hear water flowing and falling somewhere nearby, and then
walk on a little to the magic radius of another and yet another
fountain, rather as in the Tivoli in Copenhagen one can stroll
from orchestra to orchestra without ever hearing the various
sounds conflict and snarl.

Each quarter in Aix has its main public fountain, to which it
is unquestioningly loyal. It is always the clearest, purest, most
beneficent water to its users, in this or that particular source,
which springs up through the subterrain as if through a miraculous filter, here warm and fumy, there icy-sweet.

When I lived on the Rue Cardinale I was caught between

two loyalties, for at the east end of the old quiet street spouted the wall fountain in front of the church of St. John of Malta, perhaps a hundred feet from my attic room, and further to the west there stood the beautiful basin and statue of the Four Dolphins.

St. John's basin is simple, a half-round with one jet of cold water pouring down into it, and a broad rim to hold the pitchers and buckets that are filled from it.

The Four Dolphins is its antithesis in elegance, and is in perfect balance with the small square of fine town-houses that frame it. Its sound steals always down the four streets that stem out from it, and in summer generous chestnut trees bend toward it. Four of the merriest dolphins ever carved by man spout into the graceful basin under its stone needle, topped by a stone pine cone, and it seems unlikely that anyone can pass by this exquisite whole without feeling reassured in some firm way.

The most beautiful private fountain in Aix, perhaps, is the one half-hidden in the garden of the Hôtel d'Espagnet, one of the prizes of all the great town-houses there. Now the official residence of the rector of the University, its garden, simplified by time and negligence to a few straggly beds of begonias and a graveled driveway for official cars, still bows to a monumental wall fountain of four diminishing shells, with water flowing down over them from the myth-figure at the summit, to the final low wide-lipped basin, with a most magical sound. I walked past this fountain hundreds of times, and when the wide shabby wooden doors were open, I went into the garden, and when they were closed I stood outside, long enough to wash other lesser sounds from my heart.

The doors were shameful, probably built temporarily a hundred years before, perhaps to replace forged iron gates that once stood there. A revolution, a war, a need for metal . . . I could never find out.

For a time I tried to interest the Rector in giving new ones to the city. I talked with Monsieur Colas the antiques-man, and he with enthusiasm enlisted the help of architects and a master iron-worker. But the University could not afford to help with the costs. And the costs would come to about a million francs. And the Algerian situation was precarious. And I did not know where I could find a million francs, even from lovers of Aix, who know the intense proprietary passion for it that has always been felt for real beauty. And then I had to leave. And the same scuffed barn-doors still mask the beauty of the noble wall fountain from people who should gaze at it through a beautiful Provençal grille, but the sound comes through always, and over, and around . . .

There are other fine fountains in Aix, simple and grandiose, amusing, lovely, even a little sad. Every street leads finally to one. They are made for man and often for beasts too, with generous stone troughs for muzzles and sturdy iron bars placed under the spouting water for pitchers and jugs, and often they are called for some loved native: Dumas, Marcel Provence, Cézanne . . .

Some are flat against the walls. Others stand free to the air in small squares and marketplaces. Almost always they are deeply shaded in the summers. Almost never do they cease their play of sound, and when once a year they must be silent for a day while the great canal is cleaned, everything around them seems uneasy and waiting.

Of them all, perhaps I feel most deeply about the Four Dolphins and the four-shelled one in the garden of the old town-house. It is impossible to say why, except that I have known them, in day and night, for much longer than any one person could ever be in Aix.

The University

In 1196 Alfonso of Aragon founded the chairs of Law and
Theology in Aix. In 1409 Louis II of Anjou added the
schools of Medicine and The Arts, eager to train and perfect
competent administrators. His son René, born that same
year and destined to reign until his death in 1480 as a painter,
musician, poet, and romantic writer as well as king, became
the protector of letters and arts, and built Aix into one of
the great cultural centers of Europe. By 1957 its students
made up one-third of its total population, and increasing
numbers of foreigners who enrolled in its schools of Law
and Letters, its normal schools, and its National School of
Arts and Professions strengthened the ties between it and
other hubs of learning.

Jean-Paul Coste, *Aix-en-Provence and Its Countryside*

Somewhere, I read once that Aix had more bookstores and
shops for students' supplies than any other town in France.
It is easy to believe. It was easy to believe, when we were
there, that people fed on the printed word as in other places
they feed on meat and bread . . . except of course that there
were plenty of places for eating food too.

On the Cours Mirabeau were a fat handful of stores, ranging from tobacco shops where a hundred different newspapers
and periodicals were sold, to venerable monuments, warren-
deep and with their high walls lined with carefully catalogued
books, where any scholar in the world would find his own
contentment.

On many of the squares, not one of which met the requirements in the true sense of being a space enclosed by four walls

of equal length, at least one bookstore supplied its own devotees with everything from Petrarch to Mickey Mouse.

One of the best, and perhaps the oldest in the town, was on the Place de la Madeleine, up the street from the Palace of Justice. Its floors went up and down, in many little rooms of what had once been a house. Its owner, who looked like an Italian tenor, short and rounded but with a sharp eye, would discuss seriously the merits of Latin dictionaries or prize novels, and knew a great deal about the history of French poetry. He sometimes appeared bored with people who were not students of any of his main subjects; and while he seemed always to be polite, it was for the girls from the Lycée across the Place, or the young men from the engineering school at Arts et Métier, or the professors from the Law School, or even the stuttering newcomers from the American University School that he laid out his real skill and kindliness.

He was typical of every book dealer in the town: they seemed to feel a kind of protective pride in the students who consulted them and bought their books. Some of them sold nothing but second-to-tenth-hand textbooks, and the others were apparently eager to pass along young men and women who could not afford the cleaner copies. Many of them specialized in books of a certain period, both new and old. A few, like the big stores on the Cours, sold nothing but new books. More than half of them, I would say, sold old and new prints and reproductions too, and there were several small galleries connected with them, upstairs or in the cellar, where good and bad artists gave shows of their canvases.

And besides the food for thought in this student town there were good places for them to eat for their stomachs' sake, and drink the wine advised for that.

Since the opening of the cafeteria in the New Faculties, which moved from the Rue Gaston-de-Saporta in 1950, most of the resident students for Law and Letters ate there: it was inexpensive; the food furnished in part by the government was simple and good; in spite of the fantastic overcrowding and noise it was amusing.

Then there were dozens, perhaps hundreds, of families who fed anywhere from two to twenty students, more or less well, and there were many hole-in-the-wall restaurants, often of short life, where students could eat well-prepared cheap food with their friends.

Both feeding and housing were a serious problem when I was last in Aix, because of the hordes of new students, but except during the dull years of the nineteenth century this must always have been so, for the town seemed to generate a kind of fever for learning, a fever for life, in almost everyone who came there.

As in any university town there were levels of endeavor, just as there were levels of behavior, appearance, ambition. The young officers did not mingle with the young engineers and architects. The future lawyers and teachers held off from all of them and even from each other. They all had their own rituals, which often brought life on the Cours to a patient standstill while two hundred graduating architects would serpentine in and out of the cafés braying happily, or groups of visiting German students solemnly serenaded the fountains.

There were favorite cafés where those with enough money could go, and of course the one or two that had long held favor on the Cours were always filled with a predictably changing crowd. There were seasonal currents, too, which soon became familiar: in Lent, for instance, there would always be dozens of fresh-faced lanky boys from England, wrapped in their long scarves. One boy we knew from Eton who lived in Aix almost a year said peevishly that he was thrown constantly, during the long vac, with everybody he had spent years avoiding at home . . .

Every autumn about sixty girls from Smith College spent six weeks in Aix, to get used to French life before their year at the Sorbonne. They lived two to a family, with people who were able to provide adequate bathing facilities, not easy in that seventeeth-century shabbiness, for what seemed a very generous fee. The girls were for the most part serious and attractive, even though they complained bitterly each October that French boys never lit their cigarets for them . . .

The American University School, as I think it was called, grew firmly while I was there. Several of my friends worked for it, in one way or another, and the reports I got from them were interesting. They said, for instance, that the boys were much softer and more spoiled than the girls, who seemed to adapt themselves quickly and with real enthusiasm to the lives they led with French families. The boys would languish, away from Mother's Cooking, and would often do childish things like going to Spain without their passports.

There were several Fulbright students there, both times I lived in Aix. They seemed to have very little wish to identify themselves with the life of the town, and small talent for it when they showed any at all. They lived apart from the ordinary students because of their comparative financial ease, and most of them were married to boot. They rented apartments as much like the ones at home as possible, and seemed to be made remote by the knowledge that they were birds of passage.

One Fulbright wife I knew grew openly depressed when her husband, after several months of eating in Aix restaurants and at the student cafeteria, requested that she learn how to make a decent soup without packaged "mixes." "What's the use?" she said despairingly. "I can't ever do it at home, so why learn here?"

"Oh yes you can," I said flatly. "There are bones at home, and carrots, and cabbage . . . things like that."

"But nobody does it, and I haven't time, and anyway he wouldn't eat it . . ."

It was a cultural quarrel, or perhaps only a gastronomical impasse!

In the early 1960s the New Faculties, with their dining rooms and lounges, were trying to assimilate all this into a vague approximation of an American campus imposed upon a European university cosmos, but the heart of the student life in Aix continued to be the Cours, whether or not the constant tides of young men and women had the inclination or the money to sit on the café terraces.

There was a never-ceasing flow, as in a streambed, of their intense living, their passionate interchange of thought and words. They would drift up and down the beautiful street, three or ten abreast, and salute one another with the local male handshake, a quick touching and thrust downward. They would exchange cigarets often. They would discuss politics of course, and the next examinations, and the New Wave films, and they would whisper scathing wittisms of Brondino or one of their other teachers and then go along shaking with knowledgeable laughter.

From the café terraces the foreign students would look casually at them, lost in their own intensities, their own poetry of the way they were living in the most perfect of student towns.

One of these young people, a Frenchman named Albert Aynaud, wrote many years after he had lived in Aix of the way of it: " . . . this hovel lost at the end of a nameless alley had lived in my memory as one of the most splendid places I have ever known, so much did the fervor of its host and the exaltation of his visitors ennoble it. We literally grew drunk with poetry there, and the lines listened to by their tireless devotees sometimes rolled on until dawn broke. Young poets (later to become the pride of France) brought their efforts there, and to a hundred other such garrets, and would murmur a marvelous sonnet, for example, which would in the next few days be recited, pale with admiration, the length of the leafy shadows of the Cours."

The Man and the Words

Ah! what avails the classic bent
And what the cultured word,
Against the undoctored incident
That actually occurred?

Rudyard Kipling,
The Benefactors

O<small>N</small> my invisible map of Aix, the Rue Gaston-de-Saporta
has two lines of sad and bloody ink in its printing that
should make it a distressing street for me, but that do not keep
me from walking often there with gratification. They are both
connected with the old Law School, and one is for a man and
both are for words.

Brondino is the man. He is indelibly alive for me, although
the last time I saw him he was dying, and later I read that he
had indeed snuffed out, like the final inch of a very slender
candle. For weeks before that, his bookshop was locked, with
a quickly dusty card stuck in the door saying *Closed because
of illness,* and the reprints of pictures which he used to clip
on cords strung across his small window were curling and
losing their colors in the dampness and the rare sun of the dark
narrow street.

That last time, he was climbing painfully out of a taxi to
go into his shop, with of course a pile of framed reproductions
on the sidewalk and under both his arms. I helped him with
them, and he told me that he had been very ill and had sub-
mitted to all kinds of tests, which proved at least that his heart
was a strong one.

He spoke somewhat hysterically of a miraculous cure that he was being given by a radical young doctor who was despised and feared by the established physicians of that most radically conforming of all towns, Aix. From there he went on to a poster of an exhibit he had sponsored several years before, when his choice of a Picasso sketch of bathers was banned by the City Fathers as lewd. And that reminded him of another case of provincial stupidity, and another, and all the time he was weaving with weakness against his table.

I left as soon as I could. In one direction or another it was Brondino's usual pattern, impossible to alter or arrest: a half-hour of agreeing and listening, mute in his feverish flow of scorn and erudition . . . I had an appointment I must keep, and I never saw him again.

The time before that, the next to the last one, I was walking down the Cours past the open-fronted flower shop on the Place Forbin, and there stood my poor little twisted friend leaning against the wall.

He was shocking to see, and I knew that although he actually looked much the same as always, he was in deep pain this time, so that his normally green-gray pallor and the normal suffering in his large sunken eyes were suddenly shocking. It seemed improbable that he would recognize me, so intense was the expression of agony in him; but he took his hand away from the wall when I spoke, and I shook it gently in the inescapable habit of the Midi.

I could not help asking him if he was all right, although the words were fatuous and almost insulting.

He replied with only a little less than his customary flow of impeccable angry French, but this time he was furious not at the government nor the art critics nor the publishers but at his own mortality. His breathing was shallow, and grew lesser with his railing at the pain he was being subjected to, which he considered a personal affront; and after I made sure that he would not let me help him and that he preferred to walk at his own creeping speed to the taxistand, I left him as fast as I could, to save for him some of the air for his diseased and martyred lungs.

I went to the shop a few more times, but it was always closed. I could tell by the occasional new reprints in the dirty window that he was still there occasionally. And I could tell from the withdrawal of my children when I mentioned getting Christmas presents there that they dreaded to see this little tortured man who had for so long been good to them.

When we first came to Aix, and they lived in the old Archbishop's Palace on the shady square to one side of the Rue Gaston-de-Saporta, perhaps the first or second shop they noticed in their neighborhood was Brondino's. They stopped always in front of his window, to look at reprints they recognized, or new ones they loved or hated, and he noticed them too with his lost feverish eyes.

One day we went in together and it was as if we had been there before, and when he saw that Anne and Mary knew how to open portfolios and let the pictures stand up or fall forward with hardly a touch, he was as delighted as an innocent child himself, and invited them to come whenever they wished, alone or together or even with me. They accepted gravely, and the invitation always stood and was often used.

When we went away the first time we had an agreement with him to send me posters whenever really good ones came along, for by then he knew my tastes. Of course he never did. I in turn knew him well enough not to expect him to. I never wrote to him, but often, especially when I looked at my favorite of all I had bought from him, the one Marc Chagall did for the town of Vence, I thought poignantly of him and of the murky legends I had half-heard, half-deduced, when I was in Aix.

He was, everyone agreed, eccentric, perhaps mad . . . not

dangerous, but often foolhardy, and as often ridiculous to the straitlaced Tories like Madame Lanes. They shunned him for a radical and perhaps even a Communist, and deplored what was felt to be his strange attraction for the young law students, the foreigners, the struggling artists, the intellectual mavericks of this rigid cultural hub.

Here is what I remember of his history, one person's vision, distorted, untrue, prejudiced, but which for unknown reasons I heard with my inner ear and saved from all things I did hear straight and not listen to:

He was a professor in the School of Law, and after the Liberation he was put on trial, having been accused of revolutionary activities or at least tendencies toward them. He was revered by many students, largely the hotheads and idealists and most vociferous and of course least acceptable in the stiff academic society of Aix. Because of the inexplicable esteem in which he seemed to be held, he was informed that he would be let free, but free from what I do not know except imprisonment itself, if he would take an oath that he believed in Divine Justice.

He shrugged.

In some embarrassment the Court then said, "Well, perhaps in Human Justice?"

At that he sneered openly, or laughed, or even spat. I do not know any truth at all about this except my own inner recognition of some such admirable follies.

He was allowed to go free, but never again as a teacher of Justice as it is meant in the governmental parlance. So he set himself up, almost next to the old Law School, and for several years sold books of every kind to the loyal and fascinated students.

Gradually he let his obsession for modern art take over most of his ponderously crowded little shop: he had a hundred theories, all passionate of course, about exposing children in schools, and their parents in bars and cafés, to the best of all paintings well but inexpensively reprinted, and he bought piles of good reproductions, so that this unbelievable clutter swelled upward and outward until going into his place was like being a pin pushed into a ripe fruit: it seemed as if a sweet juice of papers and prints and dusty books would spout out into the street through the door.

Almost always other people were there when we were . . . brave pins. They were elderly decisive nuns buying replicas of all his *Last Suppers* from Da Vinci to Dali, or bearded young *cinéastes* discussing Italian camera techniques, or, rarely, people like Picasso or Poulenc or Tailleux shaking Brondino's hand in a strangely conspiratorial way . . .

From his taxi drivers and other mutual acquaintances and our own eyes it became plain that at times he was more exalted than at others, and whether it was because of medication or alcohol or plain neurotic exhaustion none seemed to know. I myself would guess that now and then he deliberately over-dosed himself with any of a possible dozen modern tranquil-izers or mood-changers, from the way he acted, but I doubt that he drank much at all, for I have known people of his same feebly articulated build who reacted much as I think he would have done to alcohol: unrewardingly. However that may be, his absences from the shop became more frequent after we returned to Aix in 1960, and he forgot even more things that he had promised to remember . . . packages to be mailed, books to be ordered, prints to be laid aside.

Once, for instance, in early January of that year, Donald Friede uncovered a ripe pretty prize in Brondino's place, a clean and complete run of a series of satirical lithographs by a German artist whose name I forget. He snapped at them like a happy carp, paid for them, and got Brondino's firm word that they would be in New York within three weeks.

Then, that April, when the children and I returned to Aix

from Lugano, Donald asked me to remind Brondino that the prints had not yet arrived. It was our first view of the change in him, the one that seemed to make Anne and Mary unwilling, like most young animals sensing the touch of Death's finger, to return to the overcrowded excitement of his fat portfolios and all the quick conversation and the purchase of another print, a new Dufy, a forgotten poster . . .

He promised to send the lithographs to New York at once, and to my embarrassment climbed dangerously up over half-opened cartons of old papers and new books to show me that they were indeed there on a high dirty shelf, wrapped, ready to mail. I should have taken them and sent them. Instead, fearing to offend him, I left him a new copy of the address.

But several months passed, with occasional weary reminders to me from America and from me to Brondino when I could pin him down. Then in November the prints did arrive, in perfect shape, and were even more valuable than Donald had at first suspected. This pleased him because he liked them and had concluded a good bargain, and me because I felt quite sure that Brondino had known all along their real value and had not really cared about either selling or sending them.

Not long before we left Aix the first time, he had said that his only child, a remote handsome girl I had seen once or twice, was applying for a Fulbright to America. I told him that I would be glad to help if I could, but I felt that my suggestion was not of any importance to him and perhaps even a little unwelcome. Then, when we returned, five years later, I asked him about it and he became very sardonic, in a contained quiet way which was more disturbing than his usual furious blast of sarcasm. She had been turned down because of his reputation, he inferred bitterly. There was nothing more for me to say except ask where she was . . . teaching Greek and Latin in a small provincial high school . . .

I felt a curious satisfaction in him, behind his love and disappointment for his daughter. It was as if he had finally, conclusively, proved himself the scabrous and even destructive rebel he had always fought to be.

And then he was not at the shop for many weeks.

Since one final day when I stood looking passively at the dead flies under the fading pictures on the sagging piece of cord in his window I had not walked up the Rue Gaston-de-Saporta. I had had enough of it for a while. Or was I like my children, averse to feeling Death's finger? This kind of anesthesia was short-lived, of course. There was too much more there on my map, especially in the Place de l'Archevêché nearby, that was traced in less murky colors than his own . . .

Brondino died on April Fools' Day, 1961. I read many notices and heard much talk of him, largely good now that it was too late. On his door a black-bordered notice said that he had died suddenly, but I knew better. And I agreed with what one of the editors of *La Semaine à Aix* wrote:

"Our visitors to the next Festival of Music . . . how many musicians and amateurs, how many critics and writers, how many famous soloists frequented the literary meeting place led by Brondino . . . will be as lost as we are, robbed of an interpreter who was always for them the best guide to our regional painters and writers, just as Aix itself is robbed bruskly of a devoted and faithful lover and we are of a friend."

I can never think again of him without hearing in the back of my head the word *justice*, and then back of it, the dark bloody spot on my map, the word *assassin* as I am told it was said once, over and over, in a whisper that became a kind of scream, echoing now always in its syllables for me, in a classroom filled with young men, studying law in the old building past Brondino's and perhaps still in his shadow.

They were all between twenty-three or -four, a little past the Occupation which they had lived through as boys, and they were perforce hard and old for their ages. They were taking an advanced course in jurisprudence from a professor whose domestic concupiscence was even more noted than his legal knowledge. I do not know how these things become public property, but it was said openly, and apparently believed, that after the birth of his twelfth child he had been told that another confinement would kill his wife.

Nevertheless she conceived again, delivered the child, and died at once of an exhausted heart.

And as the professor returned to his class after her funeral, and stood to face the silent room of young-old men looking at him, a slow whisper began to beat into the air, never more than a whisper but endless, like a drumbeat, or like a cuckoo in a dream . . . "the snakelike sound of hissing," one great American criminal lawyer said of it, "which of all massed human noises is the most frightening."

"Assassin, assassin," the students whispered. "*Assssassssin, assssssassssin . . .*"

I do not know anything more about this day: how the man left the room, or if he paled or covered his ears. I was told that within a few months he married a young strong woman with eight children.

And willy-nilly the word is always a nightmare scream of whispering to me as I pass the old Law School in my ghostly wanderings, and Brondino's self-crucified face is a part of the meaning of Justice itself, but the Rue Gaston-de-Saporta is still a good street for me, because of the way it bends, and the places it leads to, and all the other inks it is printed with.

A Familiar

Angels may be familiar; those
Who err each other must respect.

Coventry Patmore,
Thoughts. V: "Courtesy"

ONE interesting and perhaps dangerous thing about the manufacture of inner maps is that sometimes they become two, as has happened with the one I made a long time ago for Dijon. My real one is there as plain as any ink, with all the streets named correctly and existent because they exist for *me*, but still conforming to the maps sold in bookstores. Then there is another one by now, which is printed only in my dream life and which, although it differs somewhat from the other, is immediately recognizable, so that even when I am awake I can remember its various aspects and when I sleep, and by chance go into it, I know immediately and always where I am.

These dreams of Dijon happen rarely, and I always savor them in a part of my consciousness which I keep deliberately awake, the better to enjoy the rare visit.

So far my map of Aix is completely conscious, and I have never to my knowledge used it or a facsimile of it for dream wanderings and revisitations. If I am fortunate, perhaps a few years from now when I am asleep in a place far from it, I can return and recognize it, even changed as is already the second one of Dijon.

Something of this recurring familiarity can happen, and just about as rarely, with people. One face, or one tone of voice, or the sound of one footstep and no other will recur like a chord in a long piece of music, always the same, even though sometimes heard a few seconds after it has merged with the other notes. It will sound without apparent reason, and linger on the inner ear or eye like the black image of the sun, perhaps, after an unmeant upward glance.

There are at least two of these faces in my life, as real as the maps that can be bought, or the inner maps I have printed for myself, shifting and merging like the one of Dijon that has made of itself a new but still recognizable plan followed only in dreams.

I saw one of these familiars in Aix, and several times, on the Cours Mirabeau. It gave me a strange and at first an almost frightened feeling, although I could not rightly say how or why: that town is a logical place in Europe for such people to come to.

It was the stylized, mawkishly handsome, almost pretty face of a boy about twenty — the kind that schoolgirls draw in their English Poetry notebooks when they are studying Byron and Shelley — with large slightly protruding dark eyes in hollow sockets, the small curling lips of a Greek hermaphrodite by Praxiteles, and abundant dark hair that framed it too luxuriantly and made it oversmall for the tall willowy body and the long white neck.

The boy moved with self-assurance, but also very consciously, and on the Cours or in the Deux Garçons his casual grace was painfully stiff and cautious to my old eye. To Anne he was beautiful, without stricture, and I could see that Mary too was drawn by his small perfect head at least. He wore an invisible cloak lined with cloth of silver.

Once we watched him for several minutes. He was waiting for someone, or pretending to, and he sat gracefully, very long of body but not fidgeting, at the little front table under the big fern in the middle of the café, where nobody ever sits unless he is a stranger. The friend never came, and finally he got up in a calm, rather disdainful way and went out onto the Cours.

Two or three other times I passed him, either strolling with a much younger less pretty boy, or leaning in an amused way against one of the big plantains that make the green vault of the Cours. His eyes always flickered over and past me, and it seemed to me that his lack of recognition was as exaggerated as was his whole appearance: too remote, too tall, too beautiful, with the head too small.

I felt a definite relief when several days went by and we did not see him. That was during the Festival, when everything is almost too much so. I had to admit to a slight obsession about him, for the first time I saw him was almost a nightmare in my life, and he carried the feeling with him, perhaps not to anyone else in Aix . . .

Sometime about a year before, perhaps in November for it was very cold, I had risked shaking Thomas Cook to its venerable foundations by being sold a ticket on a nonexistent train by one of its representatives in Switzerland. When I mentioned it in the station in Lucerne, the regular ticket seller was jubilant, and almost prayed me to make a fuss: it was plain he hated Cook's guts. I sympathized with his feeling of triumphant inferiority, but of course did nothing about it except wait for almost six hours in the great station for a train that did exist and that did run at a real hour, not imaginary, on the direct track between Lucerne and Lugano.

I had been in Lucerne a short time before with my children, and I recognized my sentimentality when I decided against walking across the bridge and getting a bed in the Hôtel Fédéral where we had stayed: I felt that it would be almost unbearable to lie there alone, with no living soul to know where I was or why. I contemplated telephoning or wiring to my landlady in Lugano, but it was past ten at night by the time the delighted government ticket seller and I had located a train that existed, and I feared to disturb my elderly friend.

It was the first time I had ever been stranded in a big station, even with people I knew, and there I was, completely alone, as if invisible except for the ticket-man, who dismissed me from his world as soon as he had told me that a train would leave at two minutes to four in the morning. I could feel his bitter regret, as I thanked him and disappeared: the chance of his lifetime to get even with Cook ruined by a foolish woman . . .

I considered leaving my suitcase in the checkroom and going out onto the wide terrace at the mouth of the river, where it flowed from the many-fingered Lake of the Four Cantons. I could go only a few steps to my right, past the beautiful bronze horses and into the new Kursaal: there was always some kind of exhibit on . . . or I could go to a late movie, or even the last half of a play or opera.

I recognized a core of old evil panic solidifying with this unexpected solitude, and in self-protection I deliberately turned my back on it, somewhat as I had done at the ticket seller's chance to shatter Cook's impregnability, and decided to spend all the time inside the station. It would be an experience in my life, most probably unique. I would continue my invisibility, perforce, until I got on the predawn train for Lugano. It was not childish, but instead wise of me, I said, to carry the little valise along instead of checking it. Inside it were the only identifications with my other existence: a hairbrush, lipstick, clean stockings, things like that.

First I went to the restroom, which I had visited on a few other trips. It was large and bustling, with pay toilets, and in the daytime a big rough-spoken but cheerful woman in a white pinafore to attend to things like towels and tidiness. At night, I found, a small frail old man was there.

He came out slowly from a little cubicle which I saw without real surprise had a kind of cot in it instead of a toilet and lavatory. I was afraid to permit myself to be depressed by this, and instead noticed that the air was fresh, indeed more so than out on the station platform.

He got me a towel and bowed me into one of the pay cubicles with a mirror and a chair, and then disappeared. I spent more time than I needed in the safe little locked space, and then felt ashamed of myself. I was not acting maturely enough to survive, at this rate, the creeping hours.

I went into the first-class buffet-restaurant from the corridor entrance of the station, instead of going out onto the very cold platform again. It was crowded. It was always crowded, for Lucerne was a focal place, and yet there seemed to be several groups of habitués, old men forever playing intricate Swiss card games on thick pieces of green carpeting unfolded on their tables. I found the last empty place, and put my suitcase on one of its two chairs.

The waitress took a long time to come. I studied the menu with resignation, and decided on a fairly expensive *plat du jour* which I knew would strengthen my aversion toward Lucerne dishes but at the same time strengthen me. I ordered a vermouth-gin with only the usual amount of difficulty, and when it came it was just what I wanted, except that as always in that part of Switzerland it was about the right size for a three-year-old midget on a spree. I would have liked to order at least two more, but although I had to laugh at myself I was afraid that the maid, already somewhat alarmed by my ordering such a potion . . . a woman alone . . . would report me to the police who must be somewhere handy in the enormous station.

After that I asked for, like a correct Swiss matron instead of a foreign sporting-lady, a small carafe of the Valais red, which helped me, when it finally arrived, to swallow the hideous *plat du jour*, which was exactly as I had expected, a real *Luzernerplatte* of old veal covered with a rich creamy sauce and piled heavily on a mound of pure glue called a *risotto*, with the rice grains almost homogeneous.

It was easy to eat some of this very slowly, and push it downward with my completely inadequate supply of the coarse cleansing wine. I would gladly have ordered another little carafe of it, but once more my prudish timidity denied the impulse, and I knew I had time ahead for more absorption.

I drank a coffee as slowly as I could, while I paid the bill. People were waiting for my little table, and I took my suitcase, the proof of my self-reality, and went out onto the platform.

Even with the ticket seller and the old man in the toilets and then the shy gluey supper I had covered only about a third of my wait.

I walked up and down resolutely a few times, with people laughing and pushing toward ski trains along the cold platform and around the lunch cart. I went with them to the edge of the crowd, and suddenly the woman who ran the little wagon looked straight at me and nodded and smiled, and I remembered that only two or three weeks before, my girls had amused her in a quiet moment by conversing at some length with her about the different kinds of hot sausages she sold. Her flash of recognition, of me there without them, was almost dangerous, and I hurried dazedly away, suddenly fearful and defenseless.

I stumbled into the small first-class waiting room, and sat on a bench along the wall, pulling myself roughly, angrily into cool focus again. There were less than four hours to wait, now, and I would do so with grace, I prayed.

It was the first time in my life I had ever spent more than a minute or two in such a room, and I knew very quickly that it would be a real test, for the air was almost tangible with human waste and pain and plain horror. My old panic was as heavy as a rod of black iron in my spirit, and I kicked at it with deliberate scorn for fear of anything softer in my actions.

I suppose all waiting rooms in big stations at night are much like that one in Lucerne in the winter of 1959 or '60: bright light and the occasional passing of a policeman outside the large windows onto the platform; the old man coughing blood into a rag behind his trembling newspaper; the occasional fidgety prim young women too correctly bred to sit alone anywhere but there while they waited for late trains; the drunken young man who might or might not vomit on the floor under his rumpled head that he rocked slowly between his hands as he bent in a kind of cramp, with his elbows on his knees; the whore so short and square that she was almost a dwarf, and so overpainted and underclothed that she was a caricature of a whore.

I looked at and through all these companions, determined not to feel despair for them or for myself, and just as I was about to leave or die, the boy I saw later in Aix came into the warm bright room with a girl.

He was extraordinary to look at. I soon felt that he was impervious to any stares, as if he moved in a kind of envelope of crystal, so I watched him easily. He saw me and knew what I was doing, but his large beautiful eyes flicked a half-smiling look over and past me, as if I were a natural part of the world outside his own.

At first I thought he was painted, but no, his skin was as pale and hairless as stone, except on his bright rosy cheek-bones; and his lips, fully modeled like the small almost pouting mouths of ancient Greek boys or Flemish cherubim, were moist and coral-colored. His dark eyes flashed and rolled in their noble sockets, and his extremely fine silky hair fell over his high white forehead and down almost to his collar, in soft black tendrils.

He was very tall, and wore high-heeled black leather boots which obviously had lifts inside them, so that he must have stood almost seven feet high. He wore very tight Italian-style brown velvet trousers with a line of black silk braid going down the sides, and a vast and tightly belted black leather trench coat, with the collar turned up to frame, as it were, the unusually small beautiful face on the long neck. His hands were gauntleted in black kid.

All his movements were floating and affectedly graceful, but apparently not rehearsed. He tossed his head and flashed his eyes and shrugged, as I watched him across the bright terrible room, as if he were on a stage just the size of himself, fitted in every curve to his body and yet still a stage, on which he pranced and simpered with constant self-attention. When he bent with exaggerated coquetry over his little companion, his eyes still flashed about him as if he were weighing the applause that roared and pressed up to him from the mighty audience beyond his footlights, and I felt that if ever he kissed anyone or took a human body onto the stage beside him, his magnificent eyes would still roll and weigh and accept.

Once he picked up in his black-gloved hands the bare paw of the tiny woman beside him, and kissed each fingertip as if he were turning it with the faint touch of his full perfect lips into a pearl or a moth.

She looked up at him with love and satisfaction on her small pert face. She was older than he, perhaps about twenty-five, and smartly dressed in the clothes that are pictured in popular magazines for women: high heels, pretty legs, a coat of thick green wool with a fur collar. She could be a doctor's secretary or a salesgirl in a middle-class shop, except for the man she was with: he was so fantastic in his beauty, his manners, his clothes, that he made her almost as unbelievable.

He knew that I was fascinated by him, and although he seemed to see me no more than he saw anything or anybody,

I felt that he was acting *toward* me and that he was passionately interested in his acting.

His silent miming with the girl became more active. He pretended to embrace her and then to chide her waggishly, to comfort her, to wipe away a tear on her dry cheek, to forgive her . . . she smiled and wriggled.

Once some young men outside peered in, and when they saw this freakish figure they rapped on the window and nudged one another and called something jeering and most probably lewd, in dialect. He heard it, but was impervious there in his crystal skin, on his immense stage the size of his body, and he went on acting toward the girl and, more and more plainly, toward me.

I felt that I must break away, at once at once, or lose all the careful control of myself and go out into shreds of horror. I walked as fast as I could toward the door onto the platform, and it seemed quite normal that in one lithe jump he was there to open it for me, with a disdainful remote non-look on his too small but exquisite face.

The air was as cold as Death, and I welcomed it and sucked it into my lungs, which seemed almost to have stopped moving for a few minutes.

There was no one at the lunch wagon, and I saw that the sausage-woman had high boots on her thick legs, and that she was beating her hands up and down her crossed arms, and stamping, the way people do in Russian movies. I half-smiled at her, so that if I had mistaken her first look of recognition she could ignore me, which she did.

I went into the third-class buffet. It was about one o'clock. The place was pleasantly crowded, mostly with men from the tracks and engines. There was a lot of rough warm noise, and laughing and shouting, for they all knew each other and were full of jokes. It was as if working in the night drew them closer together and made everything doubly important. It was their club.

It was hard to get the big breezy waitress to catch my eye, for she knew everyone but me. I wanted to get up and leave, but by then was involved politely, for I had sat down first at a table that was tacitly reserved, it seemed, for some trainmen due any minute for their regular steins of beer. I could barely follow the dialect of the man at the next table who told me this, but he was kindly, and when he picked up my suitcase and put it down beside still another table, I followed him meekly, feeling stupid and confused.

I asked for a coffee and brandy.

I did not want to drink it quickly, from shyness, for there was still a lot of time left; but in spite of myself I emptied the small cup and tiny glass fast, paid the waitress between her quips with the men at the big tables around me, and went out onto the platform again with my suitcase. I was beginning to feel a part of the place, like the trainmen and the little street-walker in the waiting room and the woman at the lunch wagon.

This time when I passed her I did not half-smile, for fear of her blankness again, but she unexpectedly beamed at me, still beating her wool-thickened arms around her shoulders and stamping her booted feet. She spoke cheerily to me in dialect, things like how cold it was and where was I from and oh what a mess to take a train that did not exist.

I hesitated about buying a roll and a sausage: I knew I could not even bite into them, and I feared that she might see me drop them into a dustbin. I lingered to the fatuous point, and then said good night to her.

The platform was impossibly cold for me, and I went back through the main hall of the enormous station, which seemed to look and sound and smell exactly as it would at three in the afternoon or at eight in the morning, and down the long corridor to the toilets.

The old man crept slowly from his improvised cot in the first cubicle by the door, and brought me another clean towel and let me into a pay booth. I wondered how many people had relieved themselves and put water on their faces since I was last there, and at the same time I wished that he had remembered me. His face was too small and gray for any kind of smile, at least in that place.

I could have bought the sausage after all, and brought it to him . . . but probably he had no teeth . . .

The first-class buffet was dark. I felt a kind of relief, but it was plain that I must stay off the icy platform; and between the third-class buffet which ran all day and night because of the trainmen and served as a kind of club, and the glassed-in bright warm room marked *First Class,* I finally chose the latter. I could not drink anything more, and with the trainmen I had not been as invisible as in the other place . . .

I felt that it was dangerous for me to ask myself any questions about the people; to observe them with compassion and detachment was my job for another hour or so. Then I would leave them forever.

There was still one decorous girl, sitting upright but with her head tilted in cautious sleep against the wall, her purse straps wound inextricably around and through her clasped hands, and her ankles firmly crossed.

The sick old man had gone.

Soon after I returned to this bright hell, the drunken young one lunged to his feet, both hands pressed desperately against his mouth, and ran by some miracle to and through the door, somewhere to rid himself of his painkiller and perhaps his pain too.

Then the shabby little whore stood up slowly, pretending that she had been there to meet someone by the way she looked at her watch and sketched a frown. She smoothed her clothes over her grotesque squat body. Her dirty white shoes were sizes too big for her and clacked on the marble floor as she simpered desolately out of the room, out of my life as far as I yet know.

A few men lay snoring on newspapers along the benches, but the truth was, finally, that I was alone with the unbelievable boy and his girl.

It was a test, I said to myself . . . a test of what . . . a test of my strength, my courage . . . but against what? I felt that if I could last through the next hour with them, I would know that I was brave. I was not yet sure if they were evil, but this was the chance to find out if I was good.

Nothing happened that was visible in the big room, until I stood up in a kind of disbelief and walked out to the track where my train was due in three minutes; and when I left I was not sure of anything except that I had grown a little inwardly.

The boy had been conscious of me all the time, and his gestures were almost daringly coquettish, not toward me but toward himself, with his girl as a receptive but unimportant audience.

He tossed his beautiful head so that the silky hair, so long and dark, fell this way and that over the startling white and rose of his face. His black-gloved hands moved lightly, flittingly, through the air and over the shoulders and arms of his companion, and occasionally he stood up with the lithe swaying of a cobra about to open its hood, and arranged the belt of his long voluminous trench coat. His feet in their highheeled boots were tiny and elegant. He studied them now and then with a pleased smile on his small soft mouth.

There seemed to be an understanding between us that my study of him was far from displeasing, and that I was neither impressed nor repelled by his increased show of mannerisms. That is, we were in our own ways enjoying one another.

From the way he acted, I decided for a time that he was a

female impersonator, really a very effeminate man who usually wore men's covering but who for a change, this night, was doubly masquerading in a completely feminine form of it. Then what of the girl? I watched her, speculating: perhaps she was a small solid pretty little man? Or was she a woman in love with another woman whom she had dressed in this travesty of manhood?

It became very complicated, plainly, and as soon as I felt sure of one surmise a gesture or look would weaken it. Once the girl opened her large stylish handbag and powdered her nose. With exaggerated tenderness the boy took her mirror and studied himself lovingly for several minutes, pursing his lips, arching his perfect black brows. Then they laughed silently together, with their heads touching, in a secret way, as if they were indeed playing some enormous joke. But on whom? What had they escaped from?

Perhaps he was a dancer, although he looked too frail and lightly built, and too tall for anything but perhaps miming.

She could easily be something in the theater, something healthy and fresh and dependable, a standby in a chorus line or perhaps a check girl in a respectable music hall. But she watched every move of her companion, every flutter of his white lids over his great flashing flickering eyes, with plain worship.

It seemed clear to me that no matter what he wanted her to do, she would do it without question and with unfailing passion. At the same time, although he seemed always to dictate her smiles and gestures, there was something protective about her. I wondered if she were shielding him from the world, so that perhaps after all he was not alone in his crystal self-sized stage, but had enlarged it to hold her, invisibly and blissfully his audience.

They never seemed to look at the time on the wall clock. Neither of them had a suitcase. Perhaps they had been more sensible than I, and had checked them. And they did not eat anything. Where were they going? What would they do when they got there?

The boy looked at me as I left. He was as blank and vivid as a cheaply colored postcard. He murmured something to the girl, and they laughed silently inside the crystal, but I knew it was not really about me.

Reflecting upon this extraordinary being helped me stay awake until I got to Lugano in time for breakfast, and afterwards when people asked me about my trip, I told them of the nonexistent train, and when they asked me what I did while I was waiting for a real one, I boasted about the hours I had spent alone in the big station, but I never mentioned the boy.

And a few months later, when I was running through the underground passage in Lucerne that leads to the train platforms, with my children, after a little vacation, I did not say anything when I saw him again. I hurried past him, but I know he saw me.

He was drifting, not walking, and he was alone. His very thin long body seemed supernaturally tall in the high-heeled boots, and his small beautiful head above the tight pants and the bulky black coat was like a perfect wax model, not quite life-size, floating through the clanging gritty tunnel.

When one of the children asked me curiously what was the matter, I said nothing: I must have looked startled, or amazed, or perhaps a little frightened. I do not remember now, but I know that when I saw him again, many months later on the Cours in Aix, I felt some of all that . . . and also an astonishing resentment, or perhaps horror, when both girls noticed him and exclaimed innocently about his beauty.

It is true that if he had been dressed as when I first saw him, they would have noticed his eccentricity first, being young. But he seemed, in what to my almost possessive eye was a supercilious way, to have tuned down everything for Aix. His hair was a little less Byronic; his coloring was muted by a pair of stylish dark glasses that hid the bright flash of his eyes and dulled the pink and white wax of his skin. His clothes were dandified to the extreme, but in Aix, especially during the Festival, there are fops and fairies everywhere.

I observed somewhat irritably, after three or four times of hearing the children remark upon him, that I thought his head was too small. They dismissed me with a smile: I was too old to know one end of a man from the other . . .

I wondered with a dread that I told myself was foolish if he would be there again the next winter, perhaps going to the University, or merely floating from the Deux Garçons to the Opera House to the Casino as some people seem to do indefinitely in Aix. But he disappeared.

And I hope very much, indeed I pray, that I never see him again. I cannot say why. I have tried to be clear about it, when I discuss it with myself, but I am really at a loss about him. I am not at all scared, as far as I know consciously, by sexual or physical anomalies, and I have always respected the right to be ambiguous in deed or thought. So why does this extraordinarily pretty and mysterious human being stay in my mind's eye, and why do I hope so deeply that I may never more see his face?

I reflect on all this now and then, and it did not surprise me, a little while ago, to recall that I very probably knew him when I was about nine years old. This seems to simplify things, for I was not bothered by him then, when he was called Lloyd Richardson Renfrew and went to school with me in Whittier for a few months.

His name is a part of my invisible book of inaudible sounds, and I can say it without thinking, every now and then, a string of remembered vocables without significance or necessity. They fade and swell again, with no warning, no invocation, and I think most people have them somewhere within. I am walking along the street, or lying await for sleep, or washing my hands, and suddenly my inside voice is saying rhythmically, "Es-ca-mi-llo-Escamillo-Escamillo," for no reason that I know. Or *"vomiteusement chocolateux."* Or "Lloyd Richardson Renfrew" . . .

Undoubtedly this name is scratched deeply into my subconscious sound track because the boy was always called Lloydrichardson at school, which is the only place I ever saw him. I think we must have been told by the teacher never never *never* to forget this exotic sound, almost like a title among the Bills and Harrys we knew. And he did seem like a prince or a count perhaps, so different from the rest of us: taller, with skin softer and whiter than a girl's, and long pale hands which he drew often across his large eyes and under the thick dark silky curls that seemed to float down his neck and above his wide high forehead. His cheeks were not pink, but exquisitely rose-colored, and his lips were like those of a prince in *The Blue Fairy Book.*

As I remember him, it would have seemed quite normal for him to stand aloof on the dusty playground in a dark velvet cape lined with silver, with gleaming buckles on his tiny pointed shoes. As it was, he did indeed wear clothes different from ours: dark and immaculate, always a jacket and a very white shirt.

Nobody ever played with him on the Boys' Side, at recess, and although he stood close to the fence of the Girls' Side, he never spoke to us unless we said nicely, "Lloydrichardson. Hello, Lloydrichardson." Then he would turn his eyes toward us, and smile dazzlingly and bow a little, as if we were applauding him. Sometimes we saw him shrug and make small graceful gestures with his hands, and we believed that he was saying poetry to himself.

He went away, and much later my mother told me somewhat ambiguously that his mother had been a peculiar lonely rich woman who had always longed to have a daughter, not a son.

And that and his name are all I know about him . . . except that now it seems to me that probably I met him after so many years, that long night in Lucerne, and then on the Cours. Yes, yes, of course it was he . . . exactly the same tall slender lost beauty, the same airy walk and gestures . . . Lloydrichardson! He has not grown old as fast as I, that is all. I would know him now, even in the dream-streets of Dijon.

The Unwritten Books

*. . . not the book returneth, but its
ghost!*

Andrew Lang, from *"Colletet"*

WHEN I first went to live in Aix, I felt that I wanted
to read everything anyone had written about it and
Provence.

I soon knew that this was a greedy impossibility: time was
against me, some two thousand years of it, long since caught
up with my half-century. In much the same way I came to
recognize that every book I must ignore had been written because of many of my own reactions to the compelling town.

"Oh no!" my old friend Georges from Dijon cried out when
he saw a writing-look in my eyes as we walked down the Rue
Cardinale toward the fountain of the Quatre Dauphins. "Not
you too! Not another tiny poetical masterpiece on the trees,
the flowing waters, the many-hued effluvia of Aix!"

And thus I closed my reading eyes, so that now I do not
know what has been written, really, since the commanders of
Caius Sextius Calvinus confirmed his directives to found, in
123 B.C., a military post near the abundant waters, part steaming
and part chill, of Aquae Sextiae. Except for guidebooks, to
verify some such detail as that one, I am innocent of conscious
research, and must follow my inner map to know what street
I am on, and even why.

One result of my possible frustration as a writer about the

shape and the shadow of this town is that I can think of several books about it that I would like to put into proper form.

The one on Balzac's view of Aix would, of course, demand a fair amount of research, at least quasi-erudite: even I knew that this fecund and romantic scribe had mentioned our town quite often and lovingly, but where? And why? It was too complicated for my limited patience . . .

I asked one or two people like Monsieur Colas the antique dealer about it. They got a delighted smile in their eyes, a kind of sly cautious sparkle.

"Have you said anything about this project?" they murmured as if discussing an indiscretion. "Does anyone know of this?"

When I assured them that it was simply a passing wish of mine to see some of Balzac's impressions of Aix collected in a little book which would interest some of the visitors, they almost pushed me out of their shops, with a last whispered warning never to mention it to *anyone*. I assumed that later one or another of them would then whisper a few juicy hints to a friend of a friend: the pipeline, it is called there with various significances . . .

Such a book could be entertaining, I still think . . . unless it became the sterile thesis of some pedagogic *docteur ès lettres*.

Another booklet which I approached with a kind of cautious languor, mainly as an excuse to visit the Musée Granet often, would also make a minor "item" for art collectors and gallery hounds. Egocentrically, I felt better qualified to attempt it than the one about the fat novelist, for it would be a kind of gastronomical tour of the fine town museum.

I went so far as to make a tentative list of the canvases that I, self-styled culinary *raconteuse*, would point out to my occasional reader.

There was the whole history of man's need for food in that beautiful old priory of the Knights of Malta, waiting for me to

unravel a silver thread from one to the next. It would begin
with the exquisite little Virgin suckling her child, I thought. It
would wind through the simplicity of country feasts to fatuous
wanton *soupers en ville*, and it would pick up the crumbs of
poverty and lonely old age. There would be still lifes of many
schools, and magnificent flowery "studies" of grapes and dead
birds. It would be amusing.

Of course I never wrote it, for want of my own hunger to
do anything but look and wonder.

And why was there not a little book, well edited of course,
a kind of anthology of everything good that could be gleaned
from other writers, poets, essayists, statesmen, diarists, even
worldly gossips, about the fountains of Aix? No visitor could
be there one hour or a dozen years without knowing their
harmony, their undying sound. Why not ease man's restlessness by letting him read what more vocal men had sung?

Perhaps Monsieur Colas would feel this too was a valuable
idea, to be guarded with jealous care from the ambitious, the
unscrupulous scholar . . .

Probably the luckiest creative carelessness on my part, professionally, was my almost compulsive shunning of what could
have been a very amusing and lucrative job of gastronomical
reportage.

Every year, oddly enough during Lent, there is a series of
luxurious dinners given weekly at the Casino, which is a gov-
ernment-subsidied institution throughout France and which in
Aix is called the Vendôme. Good and sometimes famous chefs
are installed for one week in its kitchens, according to a pattern which changes each year. The last time I was in Aix the
specialties were, with not too startling originality, of several
great regions of France. Once before the chefs had all brought
with them their best menus from well-known station restaurants like Dijon and Toulon.

The year I was asked by a magazine to write a series of

"portraits" which probably would have sold at a fairly fat price, the Vendôme had ensnared an impressive list of *"mères"* to prepare their most famous dishes for their respective seven days behind the pots and pipkins, and then produce one gastronomical blast in culmination.

There were of course several *mères* from Lyon, of one- to three-star renown. There was perforce one, *the* one, from Mont-Saint-Michel. A few other culinary centers produced their motherly quotas, and the redoubtable ladies brought off their Lenten tours de force with skill and poise, as far as anyone could judge by their series of expert menus.

I met a few of them, and found them brisk poised businesswomen, with decidedly less poundage and fewer gray hairs than their titles would lead one to expect. In more than one case I felt that the charming person I talked to could more possibly be a well-tutored granddaughter than the old omelet queen or fish-dumpling dowager whose name she bore. It reminded me a little of the letter of introduction I was asked to present to "one of Cézanne's most promising pupils," who turned out to have been a suckling babe when the old master died in 1906 . . .

The director of the Vendôme invited me to be his guest at any of the weekly orgies he planned for Lent, that year. He asked me to bring an escort. He asked me to write something nice about his ventures, present, past, and proposed.

All this seemed entertaining to me. I tossed a coin for Normandy or Périgord, and the truffles won. I asked Félix, less than half my age but the most available male, to escort me. We discussed clothes seriously: he would wear his new brocade cummerbund to the gala dinner. I outlined on invisible paper a series of interviews with all the famous *mères*.

Then the director of the Vendôme let it drop, too casually, that as guest of honor I would naturally be mistress of ceremonies and in full charge of the public address system, the giving of prizes and cotillion favors, and the general gay witty *ton* of the evening. I must, he said in a brotherly way, do everything but sing for my supper.

My throat closed as fast as a clam; my brain washed white. Of course my psychogenic nose dive was abrupt and complete. Félix put away his cummerbund, I spent the night of Mère Poularde's dinner in bed with a hot toddy, and the director of the Vendôme never again bowed over my hand when I crept in to his cozy bar to meet visiting firemen.

Most irrevocably of all, the invisible pages I had written about all the non-gray, non-old *mères* of France turned to ash in my head. It was a beautiful chance, forever gone, to write an unimportant, pleasant, and perhaps profitable little book about a unique gastronomical congress. Ah well and ho hum.

The other important near-miss in my literary approach to Aix was impelled less by my professional curiosity than by an aesthetic one. It itched at me enough to make me scratch my way through two interviews with a formidable tiny woman who ruled one of the great pastry shops of the town.

She was about half my size, which always affects my accent: it becomes lumpish and awkward, much as I myself do when I must be with Oriental women. Great white cow, I am with them; great Saxon oaf I am with some of the birdlike females of Provence.

There were at least three other pastry shops as good as hers, in a town perhaps more noted for them than any other in a country dedicated to the gastric hazards of almond paste, chestnuts soaked in sweet liqueurs, and chocolate in all its richest and most redolent forms. There were, in fact, two other famous stores on the same side of the Cours Mirabeau. Like hers, they served tea in the afternoon, in discreet side rooms where English and Swedish people hummed over the trays of goodies. And like hers, they seemed to follow a rigid pattern of production which from my first months in Aix interested me to the point where I grew brave enough to ask the woman about it.

By the time I did so, she recognized me as an inoffensive and fairly good customer: her cookies and wafers and cakes were plainly made of ingredients I approved of for my children, in spite of my responsibility to their livers, and the shop always smelled right, not confused and stuffy but delicately layered: fresh eggs, fresh sweet butter, grated nutmeg, vanilla beans, old kirsch, newly ground almonds . . .

Once my older daughter designed and ordered a birthday cake there for her sister. Madame looked openly shocked by the picture, and called the head chef. He came in with his hands rolled in his apron and a cigaret on his lower lip, which he dropped and stamped into the waxed floor when he saw the plan. Finally he looked sadly at us, and shrugged, and made the cake, but Madame told us coldly that it was the first time such a thing had ever been requested.

It was a large cake, big enough for ten people, made like a coiled green snake, to celebrate the birthday of the younger girl's pet fetish, a slim reptile of green beads brought once from Mexico, which she carried everywhere with her for many years and which her best friend finally stole. Freud rode roughshod through all the motivations of this strange gift of pastry from the older sibling, and it is no wonder that even the pastry chef blanched a little at her plan.

The result was a reptilian masterpiece, carefully carved in an artful sponge cake and then covered, coil by coil, in a thick layer of green almond paste. There were skin markings of glaze, I remember. A delicate pink fork of sugar protruded between tiny white teeth. The eyes were fierce. A miasma of Alsatian kirsch hovered over and around it.

We never saw the chef again, but guests at the birthday party screamed and then remained polite in our foreign presence, and the whole delicious monstrosity was eaten, and the next day my little girl succumbed to a semicomatose and vertinginous state called *crise d'acétone* in French and bilious attack in American. The episode was never mentioned by the wee lady, so smartly dressed and coiffed, who ran the pastry shop.

The first time I asked her about the beautiful rhythm of the cakes and fruits and bonbons that flowed through the one generous window of her store, she seemed remotely interested, but baffled by my own interest.

Why should I bother? What difference did it make? Of course, of course: reputable confectioners and pastry-makers always put candied fruits in their windows on such and such a date, and sugared almonds for the baptismal season and June brides, and strawberries made of fresh almond paste for this date and molded painted snails and shrimps for that. Of course; everyone knew that. If the right things did not appear in the good shopwindows at their proper time, where would Aix be? Where would life be? And as for the dates and seasons, everyone knew them.

I flapped oafishly, my accent in lumps and my spiritual bulk greater than my body's. I tried to explain that to a visitor the pageantry of the pastry shop windows was mysterious, exciting. It was plainly dictated by the supplies on hand, the new crop of almonds, the freshly preserved fruits like melons and cherries and figs, then the deep mysteries of all the different blends of chocolate at Christmastime, and the purity of Easter with white eggs and mimosa blossoms and sugar daffodils . . .

She looked firmly at me. "There are always the *calissons*," she said. "I see that you are a foreign writer. We shall make an appointment to show you the kitchens where we produce the *calissons* of Aix. The best *calissons* of Aix, naturally."

She offered me one, held in a little silver tong. I waved it respectfully aside, for we both knew that I had sent dozens of them, boxes of them, to unnumbered friends everywhere in the world. We both knew they always arrived. We knew too that they were delicious, and that I never ate them.

I assured her once more that the little pointed ovals of artfully blended almond paste were a superb confection, part pastry, part candy, light but rich, not cloying, haunting and delicate, old as the Romans or perhaps Jeanne the second queen of King René, a regal tidbit . . .

"Yes yes, and thank you again," I said in my stolid Saxon way, "but I should so much like to have you tell me about the calendar that you as the leading pastry shop follow here in Aix . . . the set days for producing all these other specialities for the town . . . "

She shrugged elegantly. "It is routine," she said. "We all do it. Everyone knows when it is time to start the chocolate fish for April Fools' day. But the *calissons* are a specialty unique to Aix. I shall arrange for an appointment with our kitchens."

The ugly truth is that I did not keep my date. I sent a note. From then on I sent my children or friends into the shop across from the Deux Garçons . . . there were two or three things there that I felt it almost to a duty to enjoy while I could, like the little oblong slabs, each made in its own pan, of a kind of thin solid sponge cake called something like "paving blocks." In the other town, Dijon, they had been round and called Genoa bread. In Aix the taste and smell of them crept into my private map, so that even now I can eat one on the terrace of the shadow-café, while I wait for six o'clock and the end of the children's schoolday and a drink with them . . .

Often, after I left Aix the first time, I thought of the book about the brilliant sights and smells of that rhythmic parade through the pastry shop windows. It was exciting. It was based on the main supplies of the strange rich dry land; the almonds, the colors of all the fruits and fishes, the spring floods of eggs and cream and syrups. Religion took it over, with pagan rituals behind the altars: spring, marriage, birth and re-birth, the miracles of Christmas and Easter. And through war and plague and near-starvation the pastry cooks and the candy-makers molded and melted what they had, into the right symbols always.

I decided to try again, and in 1960 I went back to the stylish tiny woman whose stronghold was on the Cours across from the Deux Garçons. She remembered me, with a small unsurprised smile, and offered me a *calisson* from silver tongs. I thanked her, and because of the passage of time I ate it while she watched.

My accent seemed somewhat less lumpy, thanks also to time and perhaps a vermouth-gin at the café, and I explained once more about my wish to write a kind of calendar, with reasons and dates, of the beautiful procession of sweetmeats in her fabulous windows and in those of all the other good pastry shops in Aix.

She bowed, and I bowed.

Then she tapped a bell beside the cash register, and informed the apprentice who popped in from the odorous rear of the shop, breathing with panic under her sugary smock, that I wished to see the *calisson* factory.

I was a foreign writer, Madame said. I wished to study the art of making the famous *calissons* of Aix.

An appointment was made for the next week.

As I went out, helplessly, to cross the Cours for another vermouth-gin, I arranged in my head to go to Marseille for three days, and I silently composed a regretful letter to Madame.

From the Deux Garçons I could see the windows of her shop. They were a blaze of brilliant fish shaped in replicas of all the mean, bright, fanged, horny, spikedy things that go into a real *bouillabaisse*, painted on artful molds of pure almond paste, spilling from nets and from reed baskets onto the wide window shelf. Seaweeds shaped from tinted sugar caught them. Tiny mussels and urchins tangled in the shadows. There was not a *calisson* in sight.

And back in the depths of the kitchens the next candies were being readied.

Was it for the Rites of Spring, the coming of the first strawberries, gleaming tiny *fraises des bois* looking more beautiful than possible in their little straw baskets, all made of sugar and vividly painted almond paste? Or was it time already for the cherries? Then there would be candied cherries as deep and translucent as the stained glass of a cathedral window, piled like symmetrical rubies upon silver platters. There would be one or two enormous willow-wand cornucopias, spilling out rich chocolate-covered cherries with their stems still sticking through to prove their race: cherries soaked and floating in the finest marc or kirsch, and then coated delicately with a fondant before the final imprisonment of the chocolate. And in Provençal pots and jugs among the glossy bonbons would be cherries of every possible hue and size, realer than life and artfully painted to out-mimic Bings, Royal Annes, and every other kind that ever grew in orchard. Cherries were ripe . . .

Or brides were. Or new babies were. Or it was time to be confirmed, and be given a little prayer book made of fine pastry frosted with white and gold. Or it was Carnaval, and hideous masks of frosted sponge cakes were dusted with edible confetti over their leers. Or perhaps it was simply the time when every pastry shop in Aix was filled with round high cakes covered with sugar made to look shockingly like ripe Gorgonzola or Roquefort cheese, with one slice cut out and two or three little sugar mice popping in and up mischievously. The more mice, the higher the cost, and for me there was never the real reason for this annual invasion, for I never got any kind of calendar of these tides and rhythms.

I followed them dumbly, perhaps as a fish follows the currents that push it here and there, and make it hungry one time and amorous the next and never more than protestingly wondering.

I sat in a kind of quiescent pet across from the shop on the Cours, mapping a revenge that always fizzled into another order of *calissons* to be mailed to Hong Kong or Pacific Palisades when I next went in for some apple tarts or *brioches*.

"When is Madame going to visit our *calisson* factory?" the tiny owner would ask me perkily now and then.

"Soon, soon," I would say with utterly false warmth.

Then she would offer me one of the bland little sweetmeats with her silver tongs. I would bow. She would too.

And here is the recipe, all positive that I have culled, so far, about the mysterious pattern of the pastry shop windows of Aix, which is apparently as irrevocable as the passage of time itself, and which does not deviate one day, one hour, for generations and even centuries, nor for war, pestilence, invasion, nor even peace.

CALISSONS OF AIX

Grind one pint of blanched almonds very fine in a mortar, with one pound of fine white sugar. Pass them through a sieve and put back into the mortar.

Mix into them a few tablespoonfuls of apricot or peach syrup, and then dry out over a slow fire in a heavy casserole. Spread sheets of sacramental paper-bread on a marble candy slab, and then spread the almond paste about one-quarter inch thick over it.

[This paper-bread is the kind that makes communion wafers in church and that is also fed to goldfish. I do not know where it can be bought except perhaps in pastry supply stores. MFKF]

Over the top of the *calisson* paste spread a Royal Glaze, which is made by mixing two whites of egg with one scant cup of powdered sugar with a wooden spoon until they form a smooth glossy syrup. Cut the whole into pointed ovals about an inch and a half long, and bake them in a moderate oven for a short time. They keep well.

This basic recipe, which is ageless, is varied by the pastry cooks of Aix to have a distinguishing taste of orange in one kitchen (probably the zest added to the almond paste), and hints of anise in another, but the flavor of fine fresh almonds must always predominate.

The Din

'Tis not enough no harshness gives offense;
The sound must seem an echo to the sense.

Alexander Pope, *Essay on Criticism*

THE second time, it lasted longer. For more than a week before the official opening of this extraordinary rout, called the Carnaval d'Aix, the Midway was open, and instead of fleeing its insane noise after a few days we stayed the whole ten, mainly because Anne and Mary were old enough to be in it for themselves, without me alongside.

The day it opened I sat in a kind of inner ague waiting to go down to the Cours for lunch, I remember. I was almost overcome with apprehension, not yet quite aware of how much my girls would like everything this time, which of course would make it tenable for me as well. At exactly eleven that morning the music had been turned on, and I knew that it would hardly cease until the fireworks had died down and the grand ball was in full swing, the night of Mardi Gras.

I could hear it at my desk, high in the Hôtel de Provence, and I knew that it would pour from every one of the dozens of large blue loudspeakers spiked onto the trees nearest the street, along the sidewalks of the Cours Mirabeau. I felt a little sick. I did not want to meet the children for lunch in that gross blare of piped music, which would never cease except when one of the innumerable local and visiting bands blew its way with bleary prancings down the street. A wave of foreign-ness chilled me, not the kind that would make me too

American in France, nor too much a ghost in reality, but something nightmarish that made the threat of too much noise a danger.

And it was more than the noise, I knew. Perhaps there was a Freudian timidity mixed in with it: one or two things that had happened the first time grew clearer suddenly to me. And meanwhile I must go to lunch, and try out the decibels of the hideous blue disks that were already rattling out their first day of canned gaiety.

A few days before, Mary and I, after a poor movie, walked down the muddy Midway, which was along the Avenue des Belges instead of Victor-Hugo as before. It looked more tawdry and sprawling, without the respectable façades of the apartment houses to contain it. There were several other changes, but even so I felt that I had seen some of the stall-keepers before, especially the short strong impassive women, the kind who seem to marry into that tough business.

There was the same big "ride," called something like "The Flying Snow," where a couple of long cars filled with people sped up and down on a track which was partly covered over, so that the passengers could snatch a quick pinch or kiss and emerge tittering, or perhaps even abashed, before the others waiting for the cars to stop.

There was a small ferris wheel, and there were several rinks, instead of only one, of the little padded cars whose drivers crash them loudly together at what seems fantastic speed, with screams and giggles.

Then there were endless booths that sold nougat, and the oblong waffles called *gauffres*, with or without a gob of imitation *crème Chantilly*, and of course fried potatoes. There seemed to be fewer of the sugared peanuts, purplish and brown, that men had made in big copper kettles with charcoal burning under them, but they were still making potato chips and twists

of fried batter in the kettles, so that the air smelled more of cheap hot fat than of the burning sugar of before.

A new thing this time was an electric gadget with a plastic container of hot frankfurters and then three or four deadly-looking spikes, apparently heated from within: the stall-man would cut off the end of a plump roll, stab it down over one of the spikes for a minute, and then dab a sausage into a dish of mustard and screw it into the hole in the bread. My girls ate these later, and reported that the sausage seemed to have been steamed to complete inanity and that the roll was sweetish and not crisp, obviously made by the same company that sold the gadgets. They were, they said, *deceived* . . .

There were of course a lot of shooting galleries. One, for a change, had a big crate of live beautiful pigeons to win, and another an impressive cage of all kinds of wild game like pheasants, exotic dappled guinea fowl, quail. It was sad to see them so pressed together.

Most of the shooting galleries that year had very tall staring dolls as their *Grands Prix*, all blank and blue-eyed but dressed as Spanish dancers or Brigitte Bardot, and everywhere the second prizes and below were dead-black Negresses in plaster bas-relief or in the round, with long necks and scarlet pouting mouths.

On the up side of the Midway were the merry-go-rounds for children, most of them with streamlined buses and sports cars instead of the old dromedaries and zebras and chamois. One had a queerly sentimental coach, pale blue and crested, with two fairy-tale horses pulling it, wearing plumes on their fore-heads. All the other things were sternly chromed, very 1961. There were only two children riding, that afternoon Mary and I watched, and one was inside the fairy coach for round after round, and one was riding the front horse that pulled it . . .

And there was one small drab ring with live donkeys in it.

It was doing the best business. It sported no blast of canned music, either. It could have been a hundred years ago.

Every other stall seemed to have its own loudspeaker and its own supply of worn records, with at least one tired blonde woman or poker-faced, gravelly-voiced man muttering into a little speaker fastened against their faces. It was bedlam, and I kept looking down desperately into the puddles with lottery tickets floating on them, as if to stop my ears with water.

On the children's side of the street there was one mirror house, of course, and across from it a single shoddy peepshow instead of the old row of them. A man in a strange striped coat promised hopelessly that a red-haired beauty would cut off, any minute now, the head of a black-haired beauty, both of whom stood there waiting for some tickets to be sold, as remote as cobras or plow horses, with fairly good bodies but venomously dead eyes.

So Mary and I saw all this, and I tried not to say much, for I could see that she dreamed passionately to return. And that was what she and Anne then did, all week, with or without other girls and boys. They brought back their prizes to me, mostly of bright dyed chicken feathers: one was a little paper heart, one a queer cutting from an old postcard of a man and woman about to kiss or be sick, encircled with fluffy lavender feathers and pasted for some reason to the end of a stick. I never questioned the allowances I kept advancing them. They were having fun.

I was not. It was probably not because I was so much older, either. Perhaps it was the new noise coming from all the loudspeakers at once? I used to like going to little fairs with my father in California, before there were radios. It was the onslaught of sound that made me afraid to go down to the Cours to lunch, I knew . . .

. . . and it was what had driven us away from Aix, six years before.

I had to walk through it and past it several times a day, and at night it seeped down the Rue Cardinale and up into our rooms at Madame Lanes', and I became inwardly fretted by it, worn by it.

The whole town seemed to be caught up in a kind of tarantella of sound, whirling faster and faster, and there were hundreds of Gypsies and carnies camped around the edges of their caravans and stalls, whipping the receptive townspeople into the nearest thing I have ever seen to a mass frenzy.

The staid Cours was decked out like a dignified brothel-keeper of advanced age and prestige, in colored lights and huge painted Mickey Mouse characters which hung across from one wide sidewalk to the other, and swung sickeningly in the wet winds that had blown since the Carnaval opened. The lesser streets along the route designated for the two grand parades were only slightly lesser madams.

Sword swallowers, trained poodles, and a handful of rather cautious or perhaps only tired belly-dancers performed in the stands along the Avenue Victor-Hugo and sometimes on the sidewalks of the Cours, and on corners big bubbling copper pots of sugared nuts and potato chips sent up almost unbearably fallacious fumes into the cold air. The carnies yelled and pounded drums and cymbals. Fifteen full bands and trumpet groups from every place from Arles to Bordighera banged and blew whenever they felt like it as well as for the official parades and athletic events and races. At seemingly inaudible signals like those heard by great flights of starlings, at least forty thousand of the fifty thousand Aixois shrieked and threw confetti, and popped guns at the clay pigeons and corks in all the cafés, and made noisy love everywhere.

It was to last twelve days.

The first four days were interesting and fun for my girls and me, who had never before been swept along in such a pagan sporting. We too popped both corks and guns, and rode on the latest thing in provincial roller coasters, and ate sugared nuts and potato chips and got lost in the Mysterious Maze of Mirrors and patted most of the trained poodles, and at night shook confetti from our clothes onto the dark sidewalks of the Rue Cardinale, before we tiptoed up the great staircase to Madame Lanes' apartment.

And suddenly the razzle-dazzle, which must have risen audibly a mile into the sky above the lovely old town, became too much.

On the first Sunday, about eleven, I went up to the top of the Cours with the children, and in some ways which I do not remember but which accumulated in my deafened spirit, I was pushed rudely and I was rebuked bruskly for starting to go through the wrong gate at the wrong time, or something harmless like that, and instead of forgetting it I felt weighed down by a listless loneliness. I found a Boy Scout selling tickets to go onto the fenced Cours later, and we went up through the Passage Agard to the Brasseie across from the Palace of Justice, where all the First Grand Parade was to form. We sat in the pale sunlight on the glassed *terrasse*, and I recovered from my depression, but can still evoke it.

The owner of the Madeleine gave us the table in the corner, the best one for seeing the whole assembling of the bands, the clowns, the floats. It was delightful. It was confused, in a way unique to Provence.

Several groups dressed in gawdy matching band costumes, young boys all in natty pearl-gray with scarlet satin capes, older men stuffed into maroon trousers and lavender jackets under their purple faces, everyone with an instrument bobbing alongside, searched nonchalantly, it seemed to us, for their prescribed meeting places.

Hundreds of children in cowboy costumes and frowzled tutus, all heavily made up by stage-struck mothers, ran past our window, and Anne shuddered with envy when two of her

classmates from Ste. Catherine teetered by in real satin opera
pumps to join the court of a midget Marie Antoinette on one
of the floats.

Then the floats themselves lunged and shook monstrously
down the Rue Peyresc from the Rue Rifle-Rafle, past the
Prison, to the first stop on their hazardous creep from the covered market, where they had been built and painted. They
blocked off the ominous Prison completely and stood almost
as tall, it seemed to us, as the Palace of Justice, where they
paused ponderously for the official start of the first parade.

The bands all tooted their own notes.

From where we sat, there seemed to emerge a kind of order.
From above, it must have looked like the concentric crowdings
of a thousand ants around a handful of scattered crumbs. And
then the first bands headed down the Rue Thiers toward the
head of the Cours, and the first great ugly float trundled after
it, like a swollen old dowager resolutely returning, edemic and
doughty, to the scenes of her early social triumphs.

We hurried the rest of our good lunch, and cut through the
middle of the seething paraders waiting to take their places
according to the order in the programs, and got through the
Passage Agard in time to see the head of the procession come
into view: the first of the fifteen bands, and then endless floats
top-heavy with costumed children. We had not bought places
on the ineffectual little camp chairs, but roamed at will up and
down the sidewalks, inside the fences. It was tiring and fun.

The day turned very cold, dark with unshed snow. We
worked our way into the Deux Garçons for a drink.

There were many more bands, and clowns with heads on
long necks swooping and miming, and always the bands of
costumed children waving from the tall floats to their happy
parents, and folklore groups dancing with their strange air of
patronizing enjoyment to flutes and drums, and then it was the
end of things with the grand float of his Majesty Carnaval

LVIII, and the real confetti fight started. Until that moment all that we had seen had been practice and unofficial, even though the streets had been snowed with it for at least four days.

A few genteel people we knew were somewhat timidly tossing little handfuls of confetti here and there near the *terrasse* of the café: Henriette Lanes and Lise, looking almost young in a deliberate way behind their masks, dodged in and out of the people at the tables and then seemed suddenly cross when Anne and Mary recognized them enough to throw a little confetti on their collars. And gradually things grew less well bred.

We went through the fence gates onto the Cours. It was beautiful there, without any cars, under the bare giant trees. Their branches reflected the garish lighting of the decorations overhead, and the people looked tiny on the black pavement, which gradually turned white. Confetti stands along the right side of the Cours sold at recklessly mounting prices, in spite of the official warnings against such profiteering in the program (which started out in red ink: *The Committee declines all responsibility for accidents or thefts which might occur during the festivities*).

Against one of the old trees a man with an enormous flat basket of lavender scooped up what was left of it into a flour sack, and went away, but I could stand there two days later and still smell the faint reminder.

We went back to the sidewalk, and a few little boys ran after Anne and Mary, some truly daring and some only drunk with bravado, and lifted the little black lace flaps of their masks and tossed confetti into their mouths. The girls dodged about, and screamed happily.

From Victor-Hugo I could hear the merry-go-rounds. We headed that way: I had seen enough of the increasingly weary gayety on the Cours. Boys were beginning to scoop up the filthy paper petals from the sidewalks, and throw them with brutality . . .

A slender tall man about my age, or perhaps younger, walked straight up to me, looked searchingly at my face, which was not masked, and threw straight into my eyes and not my nose or mouth a handful of confetti, with what I seemed to remember later as a small happy smile.

He disappeared while I gasped and then almost cried out, for the stuff was violently painful, and as I recovered from my first amazement and began to push it from around my eyes I saw that it was mixed with fine shreds of tobacco from an un-smoked cigaret. It had been carefully mixed. It was hard to get out.

My eyes cried, whether I wanted them to or not, to rid themselves of the cruel stuff. I stood there weeping, with black shapes running and screaming all around me and the music thumping up the Cours. The girls came back and I told them I had got some confetti in my eyes. They had wanted me to wear a mask all along, but it would not have made any difference.

We walked slowly through the thinning crowd to the Glacier. It was packed with people waiting for buses. Ange saw us and somehow he sat us at a tiny table, the kind such restaurants keep to squeeze into the aisles on fat days, and without my asking he brought hot tea for the children and a glass of brandy for me. He seemed to murmur, but it must have been a shout in that hubbub, "You should take the girls home now. Go on home."

My eyes kept crying, and I felt that nothing had ever been more painful to me in a surface way, and no confusion had ever been greater outwardly, nor no silence more complete within.

The people pushed and shouted and drank, released for a time, not happy but freed from all the strictures of ordinary conduct. But I myself did not seem to need or want this scheduled induced freedom. I felt invisible in a wrong way. The children looked happy as they sagged over their tea, their masks pushed back on their foreheads; the confetti caught in their dark hair was beautiful.

"You should go home and rinse out your eyes," Ange stated clearly over the din, and with a look it was understood that I would pay him the next day, and we shoved our way hastily out through the packed café and into the mob around the bus stop on the Rotonde. The noise was wild, and people bumped and pushed ferociously to get to their big cars marked Avignon, Pertuis, Berre, and they yelled in drunken time to a band that still thumped on its biggest drums and played an occasional tipsy fanfare all askew, by the grandstand built around the big fountain.

I lost Anne for a minute. Then she bobbed up like a small navy-blue cork frosted with confetti. Her eyes were enormous ripe plums behind the mask she had pulled down again, and until we could not find Mary I knew that she was really alive and in tune with this compulsive noise that to her was music.

We clutched hands and pushed this way and that as fast as we could, crying out Mary's name into an impossible noise. It was like weeping one salt tear into a sea . . .

Mary was taller than the Aix children of her age, but still she was living below the bleared eye level of almost everybody: it was impossible to see her. I had trust in her good sense, but still I could not swallow a sick fear for her as we called and shoved through the wild mob at the end of the Cours. Now Anne's face under the mask looked gray, and her hand in mine was a desperate claw.

We turned back to the Glacier finally, and found Ange, and I tried to keep fright out of my voice as I yelled at him that Mary was lost.

"But she is here," he said. "She had been here for at least a quarter-hour. Come back with me."

I felt my guts turn over with relief. We went back into the dark corridor between the kitchen and the toilets, and there on a pile of coats against the wall she slept, as comfortable as a fat little mole in its hole, as asleep as a bear in the deep winter. She had got separated from us, and gone back to Ange.

We almost ran home. The Rue Cardinale was empty and quiet. Mary staggered along in her own sleep-world, and Anne grew young again, and that night when she undressed there was some confetti in her panties, which I thought amusing, although she was delightedly prim about it.

At supper Henriette and Lise still seemed genteelly gay, and pretended to be incredulous that "two little rude demons" had thrown confetti at them. We smiled and jabbered, all part of the whirling sound and the foolish yet scheduled cruelty of Carnaval to my tired spirit. I felt dangerously lost, not strong enough to be a good bulwark anymore. And the next day I made plans to go away. We would stay until Lent began, and the confetti was all washed away, and the grotesqueries of the great swollen beckoning floats were hidden for another year behind the covered market. King Carnaval LVIII was dead . . .

. . . and then he was alive again, six years, six centuries older, like me. He was tracing new lines on my invisible map. The noise was more ferocious than ever, thanks to a municipal mal-investment of a modern loudspeaker system for the Cours, and to the little portable radiophones all the carnies wore. People seemed to walk faster, more nervously, along the streets, with all the ambling students gone to earth, and familiar faces absent as we once had made ourselves.

I could not help enjoying, still, the relentless strong squat bodies and faces, and the small hard eyes, of the people who ran the stalls on the Midway. Along the right side of the Cours, all the portable stands that sold confetti and nougat and imitation-felt cowboy hats were up . . . whistles with feathers at the end to tickle people . . . masks of girls for boys to wear, and ghastly imitations of men's faces for girls to wear above their tight blue jeans and their flimsy leather Russian boots . . .

Men were still testing the myriad bulbs on the giant stars strung across the two wide sidewalks and the grotesque bright "theme pieces" that swung at intervals over the Cours itself. This would be the brightest Carnaval ever, the city fathers had decreed . . .

All week holes were being filled in the pavement, so that the cumbersome floats would not topple into the crowds and crush people or break trees, and the electric current had been turned off to try out the possible and impossible capacity of the town's lighting system, and at night the light in our rooms at the hotel was too dim for reading, so that the Midway and the Cours could blaze correctly, and the merry-go-rounds could whirl, and all the loudspeakers could pour out their canned tunes and their commercials for washing machines, gingerbread, and aspirin, and their occasional official announcements.

And all of it, I thought sadistically, was for the last time, according to sour towny rumors. I was glad. Once it may have been delightful, when people were simpler and more truthful about preparing themselves for the long night of Lent by a light tonic of license. By now it had become a travesty, gawdy and not gay at all, nor any more essential to the exploding old/new town than a soporific to an already drowsy convalescent.

I could not envy my girls their fresh acceptance of Carnaval, but as I got ready to leave the hotel for the blasting Cours, I was thankful that I could stay invisible, not run away this time . . .

The Hôtel de Provence

Hotel: later form of hostel; an inn, especially one of a superior kind,
1765.

Shorter Oxford English Dictionary

THE Rue Espariat runs off at a mild tangent to the Cours, from their starting place at the Rotonde, so that by the time one is at its end, on the Place St. Honoré, the Cours itself is a long block to the south, instead of only a few feet.

Two of the most beautiful fountains in Aix divide it into three sections of small shops and an occasional old town-house of great nobility.

One is in the tiny Place des Augustins: a Roman column rescued from some mausoleum, surmounted by a copper star with six points. Once I slept for almost two weeks in a room just above it in the Hôtel de France, while I was waiting to enter Madame Lanes' sedate apartment as a boarder. I was glad to go, for the sound of the fountain was almost lost in the roar of two or three Vespa clubs, which met there in the Place at odd hours of the night, to start out on country rallies.

The other fountain, in a gracious cobbled courtyard open to the street, faces the town-house d'Albertas, which was built in 1707 by a great family of Aix. It is one of the most harmonious blendings I have ever seen, of form in its own high basin and in the ordered subtly ornamented façades of the buildings that enclose it lightly, and then of sound, and of light itself on the ever-flowing water which falls from the high basin into the one below and of more light on the soft rose-yellow stone of the buildings. Never did I pass this melodious little courtyard without veering irresistibly into it, off the street, to rest my eyes and ears from everything but its beauty.

Between the two fountains stand, on one side of the Rue Espariat the Church of the Holy Spirit, and facing it across the street the fifteenth-century Tour des Augustins. That is very worn now, and the fine ironwork belfry is silent, but the color of it in the sunset is deathless . . . or should I be surer and say only that as long as I myself live I shall see it?

Then there is a little wall statue in a niche, of St. Roch and his best dog, a coyote-faced animal but with trust in him as he leans against his protector. They look down the old Rue de la Masse, which like a few other streets was gradually being rescued and reformed when I was last in Aix. Beautiful old doors and archways were emerging from the boards and plaster of the last two hurried centuries, and the shape of the ancient courtyards and convents was returning to the intelligent owners and shopkeepers who were, it seemed, feeling a new custodianship. It was pleasant . . .

Espàriat climbs just enough to give it a special perspective, extremely beautiful at night when it is empty, or at sunset when the buildings glow with an almost audible vibration of golden light.

On the map of Aix it is straight, but on my private one it curves slowly south again at the Church of the Holy Spirit, so that from the edge of the terrace at the Glacier our hotel is out of sight. At least, I was never able to see it from there, but only to know where I would turn in, off the rough sidewalks, which like many in Aix are wide, narrow, high, nonexistent, with steps jutting out into them, potholes, cobbles one minute, slick old granite and marble slabs the next, now and then new cement. Tourists and a few elderly ladies complain, but after a time there it becomes second nature to know where to put one's feet without consciously watching.

The Hôtel de Provence is about two-thirds of the way up toward the end of the Rue Espariat, then, on the righthand side. It makes up most of an odd little triangle formed where the Rue Papassaudi loops off it to join the Rue Nazareth. We lived there for one school-year with the Segonds who owned it.

Anne's two windows gave onto Nazareth, and at night she could hear the beautiful fountain in the Place d'Albertas, a hundred feet or so farther east. Mary and I slept in a larger room which was the family center, and our three windows opened mostly onto rooftops. Across the narrow Papassaudi we looked down into the dim room of our only visible neighbors, although sometimes we could hear the little son of Monsieur François the tailor roaring in what seemed a life-rage, in their apartment above the shop across from Anne.

We were on the top floor of the hotel. Sometimes the stairs were longer and steeper than others, but our big room was always one of the most welcoming I have known. It had the right feeling to it.

We were too high for the radiator to work well, but in the little toilette at the end which had been made by squaring off the point where the hotel fitted into the triangle, so that it was itself a small agreeable triangle filled with cupboards, there was usually hot water in the basin and the bidet.

There were almost plenty of bookcases, and two beds that looked like couches, and two good tables for my work and for the children's homework and for countless picnics, feasts, and other ceremonies. On the marble mantel under a big dim mirror there was the perfect place for our record player and a changing parade of animals carved from olive wood, of *santons*, of shells from Porquerolles, and masks and fans from the Carnaval . . . immediate treasures. The floor was red tiles, and the wallpaper was bright pink and yellow, but we did not feel anything more than an affectionate disregard for them:

they seemed exactly right, if we had been questioned. Colors in Provence are not like any others . . .

I was never happy about Anne's room on the Rue Nazareth, which had a subtle gloom about it that probably contributed to one or two periods of strong depression in her. Dr. Vidal called them School Blues, and once we simply walked off from her work at the Lycée and Mary's classes at the Bon Départ, and went to Porquerolles. It worked well, but still I always wanted Anne to move, and always she resisted me fiercely. At least she could hear the fountain, I would try to reassure myself.

There were five rooms on each floor of the hotel, not counting the first where there were the offices and where once had been an elegant dining room. Its walls were covered with enormous dim panels of Provençal scenes, probably of little value except that they had been done long before auto routes and oil refineries changed the outlines of the land. Above the door was a large vignette of Frédéric Mistral: the owner's father had been a "Félibrige" member, one of the poet's disciples, and the good restaurant he ran there had long been a gathering place of their local enthusiasts, pledged to sing and write and speak the pure tongue of Provence.

There was one sign left of their ardor, a handsome shy boy who stayed overnight on the floor below us, every two weeks. He looked at us without a word, and Anne and Mary shuddered with a pleasure which I could still understand. Outside his door would stand his tall laced tambour. Inside by his bed, we were sure, lay his fife.

My girls called him Lou Tambourinaïre, and because of the *santons* and a few folklore celebrations we had seen, we knew that he would be the most beautiful one for at least a century. He would wear a broad-brimmed blue hat straight on his head, and a black coat and white canvas pants. The drum would hang from a thick strap over his left arm, and he would beat its slanted head with a little stick in his nimble right hand, and with his left play the thin short fife.

We always hoped, for our own reasons, that Madame Segond would introduce us, but she respected his dignity as the most famous *tambourinaire* of his age in all the Midi, and only told us once of a radio program we might listen to, if we but had a radio. For us he was the last of the Félibriges, and naturally the noblest.

Next to us on the top floor lived a dry silent man who for a long time had been a colleague of our friend Georges at the University of Dijon. He taught at the Law School or the Faculté des Lettres, I forget which. He was a good friend of the Segonds too, and she teased and pampered him with equal malice, and enjoyed forcing him to exchange more than a nod on the stairs: he plainly recoiled from so many females at once.

I wished that he would go away and let Anne have his room, but it was sacred to him, his home, although from what I could see when the maids were cleaning it with the door ajar, it could as well have been empty: he did not smoke, cough, even breathe, as far as we knew, although occasionally there was a book left precisely in the middle of the otherwise bare table.

Many people who came for a few nights to the hotel were old customers, and it sounded gay and smelled good when we went past the Segonds' low apartment back of the first landing and heard them all together: they still knew how to eat well, even though the breakfasts served at a few tables in the dismal back end of the old restaurant were perhaps the worst we had ever tasted.

The first morning there, I arranged to have it in our new room, which looked big and bright. It seemed a fine way to start the children off to school: hot milky coffee and fresh rolls and butter. But it was long in coming, and when it did get up to our level, I knew I must never try it again, for the old man who climbed trembling and wheezing up with the tray was, as far as I could tell, ready to die. It was dreadful.

The next morning we ate in the dim hideous screened-off part of the old restaurant, which had a few armchairs and two writing desks up front. I had thought that the breakfast was bad the first day because it was cold and mostly spilled, but it was simply *bad*. The coffee was thin and bitter. The butter was old. The milk was bluish, good only to make a thick skin on itself. The *croissants* were faintly rancid, and like wet felt inside. This is something that was always a puzzle to me, for we got to know the Segonds and to call them good friends, and knew of their gastronomical backgrounds as children of famous restauranteurs and brothers of great chefs.

I decided, fairly soon, that the best answer might be the old man who had first served us: it was he, the night watchman, who made the coffee and heated the milk on a two-burner stove in a tiny cupboard behind the desk where he sat up all night, copying out the accounts in a fine hand and opening the huge front door for a rare night owl among the staid clients. He was the most exhausted old man I have ever seen, and the frailest, although he did not seem to have a cough or to wince or limp. He was very small, and weighed perhaps sixty pounds.

Gradually we learned that when he finished his night's work at the Provence he went home and took care of a bedridden wife. At the hotel he also took care of the furnace. We never saw him anywhere but bent over his bookkeeping, at night, but hoped that in the small hours he might fold himself into one of the furiously uncomfortable chairs in the old restaurant.

Madame Segond was disappointed when after two breakfasts I told her that because of getting the girls off to school I felt it best to walk up the Cours with them for a quick *café au lait*. I could never tell her, of course, that in the hotel we seemed to be eating the old man, for that was what it amounted to: the dreadful coffee, the thin lukewarm milk, even the bread were a kind of summing-up, in cup and plate, of his infinite weariness.

Now and then people would stay for a week or two, waiting for a house to be painted or a job to be vacated, but in general we were the only regular lodgers, with the inaudible professor.

Once about fifteen English boys came for some courses at the University. They were very loud and dirty, and I was relieved that they were not Americans. (This was part of my conditioned pattern: I was hyperconscious of the fact that very often noisy people in restaurants and trains and so on were my compatriots, and that even if they weren't, many French people would scornfully assume them to be, from habit. This depressed me. Often it made me what Madame Lanes would call a little *neurasthénique* and defensive. I could not repress a triumphant pleasure when occasionally a Frenchman would outshout-outboast-outbully any Yank I had ever heard, even the occasional Western politicians who stamped through the Midi now and then wearing their loud-mouthed naïveté and their high-heeled boots.)

Next to our big room was the only bath in the hotel, so that by law we could not keep it to ourselves. A bath cost about ten cents, as I remember. The few people who used it evidently felt that this price included full maid service, but the two overworked slaveys in the hotel did not, so that I usually cleaned the tub in self-protection. I decided then that many people are latently swinish and that I would rather work anywhere than in a hotel.

Next to this little room, which I always wished I could paint and make into my own idea of how to enjoy a toilet and a tub, there was another of about the same size, shaped like it to fit into the triangle. At one end it was perhaps five feet wide, and at the other about seven, so that it was tight indeed for a narrow bed, some shelves, and the tiniest washbasin I have even seen except at the end of a third-class French train.

This room too made me want to pull down the dingy faded *tissu provençal* that tried to cover its shelves and spots, and slap some paint around, and make it mine. I could put Anne and Mary together in the big room, I thought. I could type and sleep in this little cupboard, fresh and clean and with the sound of the fountain at night.

But Madame Segond was almost aloof about it: she must keep the room for servants of her friends, sent in from the country on errands. Later I understood that she must keep it so that at least one room in the little hotel could honestly be rented, now and then, for the lowest price marked in the ratings in the guide books. As she knew us better she let our friends stay there now and then, especially if I told her they were poor artists, which often they were.

The lodger I remember most in that tiny room I saw only for a moment, the morning after I had listened all night to heartbroken sobs from it. He was a short strong man of about twenty-two, dressed in farm clothes. He looked angrily at me as he dashed down the stairs. His door was half-open, and as I went to wake Anne I saw that the bed had not been turned down, but was rumpled as if a child had played on it.

Toward the end of our stay at the Provence, the Segonds told us that they were in the process of selling it. He was far from well, a gray-faced man with a bad heart, and a very sensitive man, to make it worse. She was no longer young enough to cope with the whole strenuous business of maids-linens-repairs-taxes-correspondence. They were negotiating with "a blackfoot" from Algeria, a wealthy widow who would make the hotel her French residence and keep up its good reputation.

All this seemed wise, but we felt strangely distressed and knew that we would never return, even before we met the new owner. The moving was painful: Monsieur had another heart attack; Madame wept quietly for days; the two maids wept; Anne and Mary tried not to cry when they saw the heavy Provençal furniture being carried down from the Segonds' little apartment; I tried not to feel panicky, and resisted my usual impulse in such moments to snatch both girls from school and flee to Porquerolles.

The worst part was taking down the wall pictures in the old restaurant. I flapped around, helpless, while they were cut down and peeled from the walls: they belonged to the new owner, Monsieur said quietly. I asked if some of the Félibriges knew. He said that he had spoken with them, and with two or three of the art dealers, and that this had only made the new owner firmer in her wish to keep them.

They were of little value, but she would not know that. Why not ask to buy them for the canvas, I asked . . . young artists needed good old canvas, and that could be used as an excuse to keep the huge paintings . . . perhaps Monsieur Segond's brother who was making the Château de Meyrargues into a fine small restaurant-hotel could hide them, perhaps even use them?

It was hopeless: Segond was too weary, and he was not, he added delicately, used to dealing with people like the new owner.

The children and I went away like sick dogs for a weekend, and when we came back Mistral and all his countryside had gone, and striped wallpaper was being slapped over the scraped plaster. And although we stayed on for two or three more months, Lou Tambourinaïre never came back.

The new owner should be mentioned as little as possible, probably: life is too short. Two things were enough to fix her on the map for us: the maids and the ancient night watchman stormed off or vanished silently, according to their strengths; in one of our few conversations the woman told me that she had felt it in the wind to sell everything in Al-

geria and buy a hotel near the Coast, so that when her countrymen were forced to flee, she could charge them double in
their panic.

We stayed until time to leave, but the big room did not
seem so bright, and we were seldom in it unless it was the
time to be. It grew to feel like a chore to pass the low apartment at the first landing, where once good sounds and smells
had cheered us: now it was a bower of silver and pale blue
satin, half-filled by an enormous bed piled with tiny pillows,
on which lay the small fat woman who had kept the paintings.
She had perhaps been pretty once, and her hair bubbling from
under her lace "boudoir cap" was bright red, and her skin
was very white, and she was afraid of the whole world. She
was impossibly rude to almost everyone but us, which was
what sickened us the most.

We stayed away all we could, for I was determined to make
every minute that was left to us a good one, and so we did.

Men and Women Mendicants

> . . . at last, little by little, in battles, sieges, attacks, campaigns, yes, and in their winter quarters too, soldiers perish, they die, they rot and consume away, save but a few, who in their old age do furnish us with the best of all beggars and vagabonds.
>
> H. J. C. von Grimmelshausen,
> *The Adventurous Simplicissimus*

i

ONE cold twilight of mid-January, with no sunset but no real rain or snow, I heard over all other sounds, of cars and footsteps and an occasional child's calling, a thin accordion song. I knew who was playing it and I felt depressed. I had seen the man often before, with his two little dogs; one day he would be by the Little Market, then down on the Cours, then other days at the Big Saturday Market.

The first time, I felt guilty at not putting something in the little baskets his patient dogs held in their mouths as they sat on a soft pad of old carpeting he laid down for them. The second time I stopped, put down my own baskets and handbag, and got out an inadequate number of coins. I divided them, half for each basket. The man behind his dark glasses, even before I had put them in, thanked me, and continued wheezing a dull bass on his instrument. A few paces past him, I heard the sound stop. Vaguely I felt annoyed at him and the puny world.

Later, when I first heard his squeal of sound from my room at the Hôtel de Provence, with somewhat the same impatience at first, I did not think so much about him as about the newsvendor.

He was a man of the same indescribably malnourished twisted non-age of all such physical jetsam being helped by government benevolence, like the one who took tickets at the municipal theater and the one who sat waiting to polish shoes in the public toilet in the Herbs Market. He had a thin dark-eyed face, with several teeth lacking and the rest black and doomed.

I liked this man, at least as far as our current relationship went, and when we passed on the street we usually smiled. I forced him to meet my eyes, and then we smiled. It was a form of lovemaking which did not at all bother me, but of course it would be impossible to explain to my children.

In cafés and restaurants, when the newsvendor came in, I sometimes let my eyes meet his, and then we would salute each other thus, or I very consciously did not look at him and then would feel a slight jar of loss, of disappointment. It was a small connection, but good, like two rocks falling down a cliff together to join the sea.

Once in a restaurant Anne and Mary said, "Oh, here comes that man. I suppose you'll smile at him again. Why, why?"

I said, "I have only bought three newspapers from that man in six months, but we like to smile at each other, that is why."

And when they asked me, half-teasing half-frightened as such young females can be, why I enjoyed this occasional deep unquestioning fleeting communion I seemed to have with the instant of our eyes meeting, our lips grimacing, I said, "Perhaps it is because he has only two teeth and I have never before known anyone with only two teeth who could smile at me so sweetly, so unquestioningly."

"Oh God," they cried, and flapped sideways limply on walls, the way adolescents and great comedians do.

One day, then, I was going down the Cours, after having seen the little man and his two dogs at the Friday Market, and there he was standing by one of the benches with his blindman's black glasses pushed up on his forehead, and he was cutting neatly at the ends of a piece of rope.

Beside him stood the newsvendor, holding the two patient little dogs who always sat with the baskets in their mouths for pennies and their behinds on the piece of clean old carpet, but this time in the arms of a friend, and licking his face and shaking with joy. He looked very happy too.

I did not think it proper to intrude. But there for a flash it was the same as usual: his small black eyes met mine over the heads of the dogs and we all, I was certain, felt fine about things.

I went on down the Cours.

The little dogs undoubtedly went home sedately with their master, at the ends of the new rope leashes, and he was neither truly blind nor truly an accordion player, and later the newsvendor came into the place where we were eating lunch and I looked only at his back as he left. Perhaps in the same way he did not see me.

Late that afternoon I heard the first squeal from the street below our rooms, and I wondered if the little dogs could be there too, in the cold, but I did not look. And the next day he seemed to be settled there on his little folding stool, at the corner of Nazareth and Espariat.

I made myself lean out of our toilet window, to prove to myself that this sour music was as unmistakably his as I had first feared: it was indeed he, in the soft drizzle, with his helpers sitting on the small old rug beside him, holding the little Easter-egg baskets for chance coins.

His playing was dreadful, heard steadily and not in a quick

snatch. He seemed to know only one position in the left hand, so that although he could give out a strong and well timed if mistaken air with the right, there was always the same surly chord underneath. What was worse, the accordion had many exhausted flattened notes.

He played with what seemed almost enthusiasm, even at the end of a Saturday, when I knew he was always in the Big Market early and long. I wished he would go away from our corner: he had a strange tragic habit of wheezing through three old movie tunes, always using the same bass and quite often not remembering whether he was playing "Never on Sunday" or "Around the World in 80 Days," any suite of three such songs, and then, as if he were Larry Adler on the stage of the Alhambra, or Charles Trenet, a proud grand flourish.

Silence, except for the feet hurrying past.

Then he would play three more almost-tunes and end with another flourish, like a soprano hitting her high C and holding it.

Silence.

I did not want to look down from the toilet window. The dogs would be staring straight ahead over their little baskets. The man would be bent over his accordion. I dreamed vaguely about throwing down a handful of bills, ten francs, a hundred francs, everything I had. But the dogs would not know why I wanted them to be picked up, and the man perhaps could not see them . . . or even coins that none of them could pick up or see, or a note saying "Please go away" wrapped around a banknote and a stone. Who could read, who understand?

Certainly not I if I were the man or one of his gentle uncomplaining dogs . . . and how could I, if I were the man or the dogs, comprehend the tragedy in that evenly spaced finale?

It was always three tunes, played with the stolid dutiful concentration of a man who had probably never even whistled straight until they taught him to play an accordion in the Military Hospital when he lost his eyesight, and then, like a sugar cube to the deserving horse, he must always toss himself a suddenly professional one-two-three-hoop-la before the silent applause . . .

I felt sickish, so high above him, guilty for my dread at always having him end thus. I wished that he could at least not finish his dreadfully cheerfully hopeless meaningless almost musical din with this catastrophic smirk of self-approbation. I was ashamed of myself.

I wished it would rain harder, so that he would slowly fold the little soggy carpet and pour the pennies into his pocket from the baskets and tie the new ropes around his dogs' necks and go away.

Go where?

Away.

Surely it was a question of not knowing more than one chord in the bass?

ii

THERE WAS ONE old woman with an empty can, the kind that in America would have held salted peanuts. Someone had bent down the edge clumsily for her, so that it did not cut into her thin papery skin. She stood without a sound at the corner on the Rue Espariat and the Rue Nazareth, across from the beautiful Albertas town-house, and now and then she seemed to seep a little eastward as the sun sank and left her colder against the wall.

She was small, and like many women in her circumstances she may once have been beautiful, with fine withdrawn nose and mouth and eye sockets. She was always dressed in the shapeless coverings of the very old when they are poor and do not have proper shawls and bonnets.

The thing about her that got under our skins, and began to trouble us where, we all knew, we had earned the right to be troubled, was that she simply stood. She did not move in any way at all except now and then to edge toward the sun. She stood.

She stood in the rain . . . not the hard mean kind but the warm kind that was paid little heed in Aix. She stood in the heat of the first summer days when the street seemed to be ready to crack open.

And she never asked for anything. Her blind large eyes were half-closed as if in sleep. Her mouth was softly shut, and her nostrils did not seem to flutter with her invisible breath. Her hand, moreover, did not shake. But when we put something in that artfully arranged ugly little can in her unfaltering hand, we all, Anne and Mary and I and perhaps countless others, felt a terrible slow anger because it was so plain to us that she had been put there like a doll, placed there, shaped into the image of an almost invincible human being. The people who made the can fit her hand had fitted her also into the corner of the streets where Espariat met Nazareth, and we felt, without active rage but with sorrow, that she was left to stand there, blind and beautiful, until someone came to count the money and lead her back to wherever she lay until she went on stage again.

Now and then her lips would smile a little when the coins sounded like more than a penny. That was part of what she had been instructed to do and be.

She was not like the other one who used to come up the Rue Nazareth from the Cours. She was ferocious, not gentle. She fought every inch of her loud rhythmic way.

She was perhaps six feet tall, which in Provence is gigantic for a woman. Maybe she was from the North, or perhaps even from Burgundy where Rude made the heads of those magnificent women who scream down from the Arc de Triomphe in Paris. She had the same majestic stride and the same turn to her neck.

But she was the shambles, the ultimate wreck of a woman. She was diseased, so that her legs were grotesquely swollen and decaying under her. Her body too was grotesquely puffed out here, bitten into there. One of her eyes lay forever open on her cheek. Her mouth gapped with empty holes. She was a human mess.

She would start singing as she turned off the Cours. (Only once did I see her there, and she was not welcome because of her enormous female decadence. The waiters pushed her along with a kind of compassionate speed toward the corner where she would leave.)

In my room at the hotel I would hear her, and part of me would die off, because she was made as many of the women of my family were made, with long thighs, strong necks, small high-arched feet and wrists. I could look down at her from the toilet window, as I tried not to do, and see us there, all of us sisters . . .

The last time I heard her singing, a little girl went ahead with tutored patience and martyrdom and picked up the pennies that people threw onto the streets in front of her, for nobody wanted to risk touching her, and she was almost blind and too enormous to lunge and grope toward any café table. The girl was dressed in what seemed to be a neat blue school uniform, which showed up like a scream to the tawdry haphazard clothing of the magnificent wreck of a woman.

They came on up the Rue Nazareth, as usual. I could see from the little window where I knelt on the toilet that people were throwing coins down, rather than descend and touch this creature. The little girl from the school, going through who can tell what private hells of embarrassment and even dutiful boredom, skittered along before and behind, picking up pennies from the relatively clean street.

The woman strode on, and her head was thrown back, and she sang in a way that I have seldom heard in my life. It is called, I think, belting it. She sang from down where her belt might have been, once, when she was younger, and from where most of her breath used to come when she worked in the fields, and made love. Her voice suddenly rose to me, straight to me, as strong and clear as I have ever heard any voice in this world. She lifted her haggard monstrous face, and the sound came up like a bolt of lasting lightning. (The little girl looked up too, and her face was like a custard.)

It was a song for pennies, but I did not throw any down. I felt as if I had been sent some kind of message. Later I dropped some, wrapped in a sheet of typing paper, on the roof of a car, and the little girl in the uniform darted out and got it. She looked up at me and waved, and I liked her better, but I never saw her or the woman again. If she has not died, I am sure she is there in Provence somewhere, still singing her strange sweet triumph.

iii

A PERSONAL MAP, one like mine of Aix, has places on it which no printer could indicate, for they are clear only as a smell, or a sound, or a moment of light or dark.

My whole map has a special smell, of course, apart from a few localized ones like the firm delicate fishiness on Fridays as I walked past the open-fronted stalls piled with seaweed and all the animals of the Mediterranean . . . or like the dark brown greasy smell of the foot-doctor's corridor . . . or the one in the olive oil shop. There is the Aix smell, made up of the best air I have ever breathed, purified by all the foun-

tains and the tall trees and the stalls piled with sweet fresh vegetables in the open markets. I feel quite sure that if I could be teleported, blind, to a dozen places I have known, that smell would be the truest one to my inner nose . . .

It is the same about the whole sound of the place. Jean Cocteau has said that a blind man in Aix would think the city wept, but that is not my hearing of it. Instead, the music of the fountains lies under and in a mysterious way over every other, with a melodious gracious mirthfulness . . . on my own map, that is. And then I hear, always, the street sweeper of the Rue Cardinale, who in the dark of the night turned on the water from the little fountain of St. Jean de Malte and let it flood down the gutters, and then swept them with a broom made of long twigs which scratched forever into the unconscious listener in me. In full moon and dark, in the silent street, this sound became familiar, always almost frightening, always a strange reassurance of order and courage in the face of complete silent loneliness.

The light and dark of a secret map would of course be the most impossible to print. Even more than there is no ink for the smell of the Saturday Market or the sound of a broom in the dark gutter, there is none for some of the colors I shall always see clearly on my own cartography.

Perhaps one day was clearer than any other, for me. It happened about six o'clock. I was standing at the long point of the triangle on the Rue Espariat, in front of the Hôtel de Provence. The most golden sunlight I had seen that year lay suddenly on the old Church of the Holy Spirit, so rosy gold, so pure upon the stone, that I must turn my back on it and hurry up the long flights of stairs to our big room.

Once there I knew that the same light would be falling on all the walls facing the northwest, across from our windows. It caught the edges of the yellow and salmon tiles. It lay over blue pools in the tall shadows of the chimneys. It was, in all, a profound moment of light itself and its meaning, and perhaps I shall always know when it occurred, if not why.

It seemed to set, to jell, the whole pattern of that day, so that the lulling trivia fell into their sharp places in the pattern I must soon break by leaving for California. The moment of intense golden light fell on them in a way to keep them sharp always in their proper places for that one day, that one moment, and perhaps the sharpest of all was made at noon, when the flower-man came into the restaurant and without knowing it settled a point with my girls.

The settlement was as clear as the crash of a crystal bottle on a marble floor, as plain to their inner ears as the light was later on my own vision. It had started about seven years before, when we first went to Aix . . . Then there were more physically broken people, at least in public.

All, yes, all the newspaper vendors were badly crippled or maimed or diseased. They hopped and hobbled along the Cours from one café to another, and I always bought papers from them, and put coins in the hands and old sardine cans and laps of the sexless mounds that sat at the edges of the markets and in the Passage Agard, mounds that in a dreadful way seemed part of the families of the poor men who sold papers. It was like the Carnival of the Beggars in a book by Victor Hugo, so that the gray-blue swaddled baby in a filthy bitter Gypsy's arms seemed the child or perhaps the great-grandmother of any one of the newsvendors.

My girls were appalled by them all, not frightened of them as human beings but as spirits, emanations of war and evil.

I regretted this shock, but I could not hide either side of it, them from the human remnants, or the omnipresent population of life-in-death from them. So without searching for the chances I accepted the nightmare, and bought the papers and stopped to drop the coins.

There was one newsie who gave my girls an especial chill,

mostly because he always shook hands with me. I could not stop him from doing it. He headed straight for me, no matter where we were, and took my hand. Usually before he did so he wiped his dribbling nose with it, or ran it across his crusted eyes. He had only two or three teeth in his mouth, and they were snags, and he bared them at me in a truly horrible grin which was the best he could offer me, and which I recognized as such. But the children were still too young: how could they possibly know yet about the reasons for such ugliness? They were repelled actively as well as instinctively by the creature who saluted me as friend.

They became almost hysterical about it, and would run down dark side-streets to avoid all the quasi-beggars, but especially this most hideous one who never begged, but only touched my hand before he gave me the paper I had bought. Once they swore that they had seen him many miles away, in Avignon, in a café, hobbling along grinning and looking for us . . .

There was another one who sold flowers. He was very bent, as if every bone in him had been crushed beyond setting, and with a sideways walk that got better or worse, so that sometimes his head bobbled like a hunchback's on his crooked shoulders.

Occasionally he could speak and other days he only stuttered, and spit ran out of his very twisted mouth while his eyes, always the same large questioning ones, begged for patience. He was filthy too, and the girls could not bring themselves, even for politeness, to touch the flowers he pulled jerkily from his basket. And I always bought them.

Gradually he seemed, sometimes anyway, to be able to smile at me, and he often added a piece of mimosa or an extra leaf to the posy before he slid crablike out of our view.

Then we began to play a game which upset the children, but I told them why I thought it was a fine idea. The story in Aix was that he had no passport there, but was probably a Pole, escaped somehow from Nazi torture, and that he did no harm, and that although he never replied to questions, he seemed occasionally to speak almost any language a little bit, as if parts of him remembered one at a time what he had once had all in a whole.

He began to look at me, up sideways from his basket of flowers, and mutter a single teasing question at me: "Today are you . . ." and then he would put in any word like Swiss, Italian, Swedish, Dutch. I would say seriously to him, "Today I am Danish," or anything at all, and he would bow a little and hand me the flowers and I would hand him the coin, and if I had misunderstood and it was not enough . . . violets get dearer if it rains, and so on . . . he would stoop sideways a little more and dart reproach at me from his eyes, but now with a strange calmness behind the professional scolding. He seemed, at least to me, to accept me as an equal, a person one could joke with.

But of course all the time he did dribble and mutter, and his poor body looked impossibly warped as he sidled remotely from one café to another along the Cours, and my children hated it when he appeared, whether or not it helped him to try to speak to me. They felt sad and disturbed and repelled, and I understood all of it, but was able, because I had gone so much farther, to make a joke with him now and then and to sense, perhaps to see, surely to feel the look of amusement far behind his enormous glazed eyes.

When we came back, five years later, there were fewer shadowy beggars quavering songs on Market days, and the newsies were feeble but not crippled: dignified men who walked slowly from one café to another as if they had spent a long time in bed.

It was not until one of my girls mentioned casually that the paper-man who always shook hands with me was gone that

I realized that both children had been dreading, perhaps actively fearing, to see him again.

I felt sorry about this, that I had tortured them after my fashion. I still believed that it would have done them infinitely more harm if when the poor foul wretch touched my hand I recoiled from him outwardly. We talked of this, and they were older enough to agree with me and to accept my agreement with them that I too was glad the man no longer hobbled up and down the Cours.

About a few months after we came back, though, the flower seller was there. He looked much better, but was still a bad drawing of a cripple, all bent and fragile.

We were sitting on the terrace of the Deux Garçons with some friends who are impatient of any participation with sidewalk commerce: they consider themselves victimized, conspicuous, in some pernicious way emasculated if they give a Gypsy two pennies or even buy a paper or a flower for value received.

My girls moaned aloud when they saw the familiar flower seller creep toward us, and explained hastily that he was one of my pets, as if I were subnormal. I murmured to be careful, for he might understand English, and then added that he would most surely have forgotten us.

Of course he had not. He came in his painful zigzag to the large table where we sat, and looked up at me slyly and asked, "Are you American today? Or are you Norwegian?"

Perhaps because the children were there, and we were with the friends who could not accept such intercourse, or perhaps only because I was touched to make this strange encounter with a fellow-pilgrim after so long, I took his hand. It was a gray claw. I asked him without any preamble, for it was plain that he knew me, where he had been, and he murmured, "Sanitariums," and slid off, leaving a thin long posy of three cornflowers and some scraggly wallflower beside my glass.

Our friends asked gushingly about him and why he had not asked for money and why I had questioned him, and the children, sensing my wonder, replied gently that he was a man we'd once known.

Before we changed the subject back to genial café chatter, I said that he used not to be able to answer questions but today he'd done so. One of my daughters said, protecting me and not him from the uneasiness of the company, "He looks much better than before." Then we talked about *Le Nozze di Figaro*, I think, which would be given that night in the Archbishop's courtyard: the Music Festival was in its fullest swing.

We saw the little man often after that. Anne and Mary always spotted his painful crawling approach, and said *Again* and froze a little where they sat, and I would know that it could mean only the one hazard.

Yes, he would come gradually and inflexibly toward us. He looked much worse, almost as repulsive as five or six years before. He dribbled, and his eyes were most often unseeing, until he got to us and without smiling looked up sideways at me and mouthed, "Swedish?" or "Dutch?" I always bought flowers, of course, and when I could not get him to tell me the price of them and might hand him too little, he simply held out his hand for another coin, and then added an extra flower to the posy on the table.

I never told my children that once, when I was alone, I asked him bluntly, "Are you all right?"

He looked straight at me for the first time in our relationship, and said, "What do you think?"

"Can you go away again to the san?"

"It is too late," he said impassively, but more clearly than I had ever heard him speak.

He put down his basket, wiped his mouth on his sleeve, and to my astonishment kissed my hand. I was in a sudden daze, partly because I was glad the children were not there, and I do not remember watching him pick up his flower basket and go away. The next time we met, there was hardly a flicker in recognition in his great broken gaze, and he did not ask me what country I came from.

Then, the day of the golden light, while we were lunching at the Mazarin down at the other end of the Cours, he hobbled slowly in, with violets. The girls shuddered invisibly and hopelessly.

As he went past us to some farther tables, I said in what was perhaps a defensive way, "One thing I like about his flowers is that they are fresh and real, not doctored. Those violets, for instance; they smell. They are real, not perfumed."

"Yes yes," the children said with teasing compassion. "But remember that he may speak English."

"He could not have heard, and anyway," I said, "it was not bad, what I said. It was true."

"Yes yes," they soothed.

I got out two francs, which was the last price I'd paid for his flowers, and when he got to the table I said firmly in French, "Good morning. One bunch." I felt bored with my family, tired of the whole grim foolishness of things, things-in-general.

He looked at me and mumbled in his painful broken way, "One franc fifty."

I said firmly, "Thank you," and waved my hand for him to keep the extra coin.

And at that he grinned, a ghastly grin but one that was in his eyes warmly and well, and nimbly took from his pocket a little bottle of violet perfume and dabbed it on the flowers I held.

He did it so fast, and then hobbled off so quickly, that I hardly realized it until I heard my children laughing. They were completely pleased.

"Oh, how wonderful," they exclaimed, full of delight. "He

was teasing you. He heard every word. He is really a wonderful man."

They meant it. I do not know how next they might have reacted to his appearance if we had stayed longer in Aix and if he had existed too, but for that one time at least they felt a complete and indeed almost proprietary pleasure in his odd little mocking game with me. It was worth much.

For one thing, it made me feel respectful of the map of Aix which seemed to be drawing itself for me, somewhat as if my *being* at that spot of the world was in a way retracing, willy-nilly, exactly the same lines of streets and buildings and fountains that had already been drawn, but with a different ink . . .

The Outlook Across

Peep-Show: a small exhibition of pictures, etc., viewed through a magnifying lens inserted in a small orifice.

Shorter Oxford English Dictionary

i *THE WINDOW*

THE first time I ever looked across and into our neighbors' window was a Sunday morning, a day or two after we moved to the Hôtel de Provence from the country.

How nice, I thought, how typically French and simple, to put a rough table by the open airy window and on it place some grapes and some bread, four white eggs, and a bottle of wine with two tumblers! How fine to live near such companionship, I thought.

It was always impossible to ignore the window, from that day, for it was only a few feet down from the level of ours, and the lives of the two people who lived behind it were forever mixed with ours.

That first time I watched, they sat across from each other in the fine September sun, and slowly ate and drank, with finicky niceness. Then they finished eating, but they kept on at the big bottle of wine and by the end of the afternoon had drunk perhaps two more. Toward evening the man got out a sharp pocketknife and most fastidiously cut a slice of meat into tiny perfect cubes, on the windowsill.

Meanwhile they had grown very noisy. They shouted and banged the table, and leaned toward each other as if they had suddenly grown deaf. Often he made menacing gestures with his fists or the knife, and the woman cowered back, but they never touched each other.

We did not mean to snoop into this relationship, but it was very close to us physically, so that we could hear almost every word, even the slow expert clicking of the knife on the window ledge, which was stained dark from many such exhibitions of drunken precision, as we came to know. It was not pleasant at all, to be so near what at first had seemed a dreadful drama induced by too much Sunday wine . . . but all the windows in the town were as open as ours and theirs, and where else could we look, what else listen to?

Gradually our glances across the street became a habit, not inquisitive but fascinated, a morbid preoccupation. Soon I came to feel that I knew almost as much about the people as they did, in their behavior at least, and I regretted that we were always a little apprehensive: if I heard a cry or a crash I looked automatically to see if the woman had fallen, or had been struck . . .

Sometimes she leaned in a staggering heavy way out the window, her elbows askew on the greasy ledge, and I wondered impotently if she might overbalance her poor body and fall out, and split open like a ripe melon, as I had read of Modigliani's girl in Montparnasse long ago. Sometimes the man made such a rough gesture toward her that I was sure he would forget to cut back the speed in his arm and splash her eye out on her cheek, her teeth out on the floor. But nothing happened; they went on living in that one room, sleeping and washing and eating together, in an almost uninterrupted bath of the cheapest wine.

The room was perhaps fifteen feet each way, zigzag like all the attic rooms in the quarter. There was a kind of alcove at the back, with a skylight which I saw yellow at lonely hours in the night. I imagined a bed there. Facing me there was a Provençal chimney and hearth, where often a small fire flickered, and that and a little table burner heated by a can of Sterno or some such chemical were what the woman cooked with.

There was a straight chair by the hearth, where a black dog lay on cold days. I felt that the woman took care of him for one of the other people in the ancient building: I saw her now and then on the street with him on a leash, but I was fairly sure he did not live with her all the time.

There was the table, and then against the only wall I could see there was an ugly old chest of drawers with a gray marble top, on which a few pans and the day's food were put. There were always empty green bottles standing beside the door.

I thought that there was a washstand in the corner between this bureau and the window, for I saw the woman combing her hair there, but I knew that there was no piped water, for it was all dipped from a can underneath the window. I suppose there was some kind of toilet in the hall, or further downstairs.

Things like laundry in such a setting have always interested me, perhaps because for a time I lived in much the same lodgings in Dijon, except that I was young and clean and for the most part happy. Now and then the woman rinsed out a man's shirt and hung with it on the string across the window a pair of dingy pink panties. I imagined that both she and the man had strong smells, probably unnoticed by either of them.

He was bent and thin, with a hawklike face. Perhaps he was fifty, but worn. He was usually unshaven, and judging by his clothes he worked as a hod carrier or a porter. He had a sad fineness that was attractive to me, and although he talked in a helpless impatient way to the woman, in rough words that were limited and coarse, he seemed basically courteous, even gentle.

Sometimes he appeared to be in a kind of rage at the way he was living, the sordid clumsy hopeless filth of it, and he would heat water in a bucket over the hearth flames and splash it onto the floor and scrub with a broom and with dirty rags, all the time snarling at the woman but not touching her, only wrenching the water out of the cloths as if he were twisting a human neck, and kicking at the table leg or even the wall as if they were a body to bruise.

Once, late on a Sunday afternoon, there were cries, and I looked over as if I had been waiting for them, and the woman was leaning out over the foul ledge, half-undressed, her hair down, crying in a wambly voice, "Ah, he will kill me, he will kill me . . . he is taking me . . ."

The man stood close against her and behind, and as I looked, in a glance full of shame at my own peeping, he pulled her dirty hair back gently off her face and pecked once, twice, three times on her neck, in a gesture of passion and pity. I could not look anymore, but closed my window so as not to startle them. I felt somewhat moved sexually, somewhat unstrung with compassionate loneliness . . .

The woman was small, with a shapeless body that occasionally betrayed youth and even grace, as when she stood before a mirror that was invisible to me and pulled the dark hair straight up off her shoulders. There was the remainder of coquetry in her.

Even when, in a flat fumbling way, she slowly peeled a potato or cracked the shell off a boiled egg, her swollen fingers looked as if once they had moved lightly. Her skin was dull, and although I saw her only two or perhaps three times on the street I could guess that her legs were heavy, over inadequate feet, from the way she moved in the dim dingy room.

Once, not long after we got to the hotel, I must have been staring openly, for to my confusion the woman stepped to her window and looked across at me and asked the time, in a shy way. Almost at once I knew that she wanted to speak, to speak to anyone, to speak to anyone who would reply to her. So I replied.

I came to know that this speaking to me was extraordinary, for almost never after that was she able to focus her eyes far enough to see my window, much less the shape of me standing in it, and she never looked our way when the man was there.

That day she smiled in a feeble timid manner with her surprising question, and I was grateful to her to be able to cover my gaucherie at having been caught, no matter how unwittingly, in the act of peeping into her home. I told her what time it was.

She made a wandering gesture toward the back of the room, as if to indicate that she was alone, and leaned over the window ledge and talked to me. I am sorry that I did not conquer my own shyness and lead her on to more words, for I was never to hear her speak to me again except in mumblings once in the street. She said that she was very ill. Her back had been broken while she was in a labor camp during the war. She had been sent far off. When she returned, her kidneys were destroyed. She suffered constantly. It was necessary for a kind gentleman to assist her now and then, she said with a pathetic reaching for gentility, with her daily marketing and her chores . . .

We parted, turning away from each other shyly.

A little while later, perhaps a month, I was walking along the side of the hotel on the Rue Nazareth when I came upon her leaning in a daze against the wall, with the man standing helplessly beside her. She seemed about to lie down. I think she may have recognized me, for there we were, in communion of a kind, with people pushing curiously, impatiently, past us. She whimpered like a child that she had fallen twice in the street, twice, twice in the street. The man shrugged and looked sadly at me, with confusion and acceptance on his bristly face.

"Why don't you go to the hospital?" I asked.

"Yes," he said, and it was the only time he ever spoke to me, although once later he shook his fist at one of my girls from his window toward ours and said a foul word at her. "That's what I say too, Madame. A week maybe in hospital and she'd be all right."

I said, "Or two weeks. Why don't you do that?" I spoke toward the woman, but she was sliding down and down the wall.

"It's my poor poor back. They broke it," she whispered, but we all knew that she was nearly dead drunk too.

"Think of it, the hospital," I said urgently to the man, and I hurried away with what decent slowness I could muster, wondering why I should mix myself in something so obviously not my affair.

But it was hard not to, for the people were always there across the little street. There were times when as a point of honor I kept myself from the mechanical look, the automatic noting of a greasy casserole on the ledge, or a sad pink rayon nightgown hanging tipsily on one clothespin from the sagging string.

Sundays were the worst, of course. They always began fairly well, but the progression toward drunkenness, then quarreling, then copulation, then often a quiet standing side by side at the window in the darkening air, elbows on the ledge, occasionally the slow mincing and trimming of a piece of sausage or meat or even bread with the bright knife . . . all this made it hard not to watch with more than the inner eye. It changed the pleasure of our own picnic lunches in our big airy room, so that whenever we could we spent our Sundays away from there, away from the apprehension and the ugliness.

In the winter with windows closed, and usually with the light on in the room across from us, it was like an old silent film being run over and over. The first time it was fascinating: a realistic German movie, somewhere between *The Cabinet of Dr. Caligari* and Emil Jannings' *Le Dernier des Hommes.* Then it grew dull, like a habit of smoking cigarets or drinking gin, necessary but still boring. The taste was no longer even an unwilling taste, but only a need for one . .

The man would shout angrily, the woman would cower; they would drink and drink and then eat; finally he would try to take her bloated grimy body and she would run dully from him and then submit; afterwards they might get dressed and go out toward a low-class bar, they might simply sleep until early the next morning when he must go back to work: all this unrolled over and over, under our helpless eyes.

It was interesting that the man never missed getting up on Mondays. I too had to do it, to send Anne and Mary off to their schools, and I would see the light on across the street as I dressed, and would notice the man's shadow as he moved silently about the room. Often he would light a fire on the hearth, and fill the bucket with water from somewhere outside. He moved lightly and without fumbling. Mostly, I thought, he had slept in all his clothes except a cap and a thick jacket.

Much later the woman would get up, stumbling like a mole in the light. On warm days she often leaned for a long time on the ledge, her arms on a rag of cloth, and watched toward what she could hear on the street four floors below. She would brush back her dark hair with clumsy tender hands, and occasionally shake her head and talk to herself. Then toward noon she would straighten her back and stand by the stained table, painfully peeling vegetables or stitching string around a piece of meat.

It is a wonder that she never cut herself, nor burned her thickened fingers on the dirty pots which she put slowly off and on the one little burner on the table. When she would lift one off to make room for another, in a dreamlike way, the flame would shoot up almost to her face, but she never blinked or drew back.

She was, indeed, dexterous in her quiet evasion of disaster, and watching it was one sure reason for my inability to stop. I hated this peeping, but I could not deny my horrified curiosity about if and when she would burst into slow bright bleeding, or flame up like an oily rag. It is not that I spent hours looking across the street at her and her man, but I did live in the hotel attic with three wide windows a few feet from theirs, and I did move back and forth, and in my moving I did bow to this occasionally worrisome absorption. How could I have known, anytime in my life, that I would have this strange bird's-view of behavior so different from any I had known? I was not hurting them. I was perhaps learning something from them.

I speculated freely, if only now and then, upon such things as what her thick soups and fried meats tasted like, rather than upon what had made her what she was. They really ate well and decently, those people, with salads and fresh peaches and melons and oranges according to the seasons. And I wondered how they made love and if they thought much about it . . . and how old the woman had been when she was sent to the labor camps . . . and if she was Polish perhaps . . . her accent had not been French . . .

There was detachment in my attitude, and acceptance, as well as compulsive curiosity. There was almost an element of fear, for I knew exactly what was being said for all of us one day when Mary remarked, "He's cutting a piece of sausage on the ledge again!"

We were sitting thinking of quite other things, eating and talking, but this side issue seemed natural. Anne said, "He's practicing."

Mary said, "Some day he'll do *her* in neat little pieces."

"Probably," Anne said without any apparent horror.

I started to tell them about a cook we once had who did indeed cut her mother into little pieces, or rather into strips, with her famous French knife, but I thought better of it, and we went on with what we were doing, which was enjoying our Sunday selves.

Later I noticed that the man had closed the windows and turned off the light, and I felt a slight erotic question, and the next morning was relieved, in a curiously remote part of my daily awareness, to see that he had taken in a piece of washing and gone off to work as if all were well.

Then, in an early spring, the windows of all the town were open wide again, and although I did not hear the woman I was more conscious than I had been for a while of her occasional tottering path across my line of vision. She seemed even less sure than before, but her puffed hands still had a delicate feminine turn to them as they moved mazedly about the table or her own face and shoulders.

She talked to herself. I wondered if she argued with the invisible and distant man, or with all men, or perhaps with a grandmother she knew when she was fresh and unbroken.

Once more I watched her with an open view, working with her strange dexterity, never cutting or burning herself, to make two meals every day for the hawklike man who protected her, and I wondered about the meaning of devotion, and about the limits of it.

ii *THE TROUBLE*

ONE THING THAT indicated boldly the morbidity of our unwilling interest in those two people who lived across the Rue Papassaudi from our big room in the hotel was that when their window was not open at least once a day we watched it with an obvious fear, not of how and when it would open but of why it might not.

Once toward the end of April, 1961, it stayed closed for three or four days, with only a faint light showing from the skylight at night, and we grew conscious of the occasional sound of a dog crying.

The dog might not be the black one I had sometimes seen with the woman. But the sound came from there, there in the closed room, and suddenly I began to wonder, not putting it into words to Anne and Mary, if perhaps instead of the poor dog's having been shut into the empty room while the man and woman were away or in prison or in hospital, the sound came from her, shut there.

I tried not to think this way. But the window stayed shut and the dog howled at night and even in the daytime.

I wrote letters to New York and California, trying not to listen.

I explained that I could not send a birthday box to Norah's children, because they would not be accepted at the post office without being opened to look for bombs, *les plastics*. There was quiet steady terrorism in France, especially in Paris.

On the 23rd of April the news was very bad. Everything seemed stopped, waiting, holding its breath, and my own breath came grudgingly as I read the papers. I tried not to be short and morose with Anne and Mary, at breakfast in the Deux Garçons. I parted from them with vague muted feelings of pain.

On the way home Monsieur François the tailor stopped me. I thought at first it was to ask if I had decided from the samples he had loaned me what kind of suit I would want him to make. Instead, he wondered what results there had been from my somewhat hysterical and fruitless visit to the Police Commissariat three days before, about the continued howling of what might be a little black dog and what, as I had decided to my horror, might be the woman behind the window.

It had been Saturday I decided that; and the shutters had been closed since the Tuesday before, when the sound of the long feeble howls began. Any speculation was dreadful, whether for beast or human, and Saturday I could not stand it longer and on my impulsive but determined path to the police I had met Monsieur François and asked his opinion of whom to call, where to go: he was of the neighborhood and we were friends.

And so on Monday he asked me what had been done, and I had to tell him that I failed completely. I did not tell him that I felt helplessly annoyed with him for not doing more than advise me, even though I knew that like most Frenchmen he preferred not to interfere with anything that might prove distasteful.

Yes, the howling was indeed somewhat worse, he agreed . . . and Sunday night had I noticed a light which showed for perhaps five minutes through the shutters?

I told him that the police had sent me, at first gently and then with patent boredom, from one man and one office to another, until finally I was in the presence of the Commissaire himself, except that he was not there. Every available policeman was patrolling the town, as I remembered when I walked past the two sentinels at the door to the big building. They stood carefully behind their steel boxes, submachine guns on the alert. So a pudgy civilian clerk spoke wearily, insolently to me behind the chief's desk: What was I doing there? Had I gone through this and that formality? Exactly what did I want? What was I trying to stir up in this time of trouble?

All his implications were that I was a gossipy interfering unbalanced neighborhood nuisance as well as a non-French-woman, and by then I was so unnerved that I became pretty much what this lout had implied, and was so helpless with worry and anger that I lost my voice, and shook, and in every way proved his points.

An officer came in, and I tried, apologizing for my shaky state, to tell him what I had by now repeated seven or eight times. He said nicely to me to come back some other day, perhaps on Tuesday.

"And meanwhile she dies?" I asked very tremblingly.

"Who dies?" he asked coolly. "Whom do you really imagine to be dying, Madame? What proof have you of any of this fantasy? Here in France we must have proof before we violate the privacy of a man's home."

Ah hell and damnation, I wanted to cry out. I managed to say a thank you, to the officer and not the clerk, and I fled, sobbing and red-nosed behind my dark glasses. I was in pieces, and all the time I had to ask myself if the police had been right and if I were indeed nothing but a neurotic annoyance in this time of riots and *plastics* and suspicions.

And a couple of days later I managed to tell some of this to Monsieur François (I had told Anne and Mary late Saturday of my ordeal, and then when the dog would howl they would put out various feeble suppositions: the sound did not really come from that closed room, the people must be on a little vacation, and so on), and the tailor and I both agreed to increased alarm and he grudgingly said he would speak to a neighbor who was a member of the SPCA. Otherwise, he agreed with the police, there was no way to enter a dwelling to investigate, unless I wished foolishly to swear out a formal complaint. We worried the subject cautiously and politely; it was a dead rat.

Then I said that I would come across from the hotel later to show him the sample the children and I had chosen for my new suit. He was disturbed, he said, because he had ordered several pieces of cloth and of course no packages were allowed through the mails now . . . and suddenly he was shaking and leaning against his counter and saying, "I've had it, Madame. I've had it, all I can stand. I fought the whole war here. Then I was deported. I was two years in Germany, in Hamburg. I was in Hamburg from the first bomb that was dropped to the last one, the very last one. And now I swear if they tell me to fight again, I'll tell them. Pardon me, Madame, but I'll tell them WHERE TO PUT IT."

"Ah, but will you? You can't choose, can you? Can anyone?"

He seemed to look smaller all the time. He shrugged tiredly. "It's civil war we're all afraid of," he said. "It's what they want. French against French."

Abruptly he bowed to me and I left.

I went up to the room with my heart and head at war. I fought down panicky imaginings, and in spite of myself recalled the faces of my sister and brother as they were evacuated from Berne, on M-Day of the war, while I stayed behind. That time it was because my husband was pinned to a bed. This time, if we were ordered to leave, I would want to stay again, to get through whatever must come, with the French people. But I would go because of Anne and Mary, because we would have no right to take up the space and food and energy needed for French women and children . . .

I looked dully out of my window, and for almost the first time in Aix I saw three, not two, Algerian women dressed in very bright soft robes, walking at their never-hastening speed up the Rue Nazareth. Then there were four more. Did I imagine it because of my inflamed emotions, or were the Arabs more brightly dressed than usual? Did they feel a new confidence in that city where they were a troubled minority? Had they perhaps been instructed to walk thus bravely together down the streets, instead of going out silently two by two to market?

I read the front page of the *Provençal*, and the loud stern words of De Gaulle: yes, barricades were being set up in Paris, especially in the St. Cloud quarters, and yes Paris was alerted to probable insurrection directed from Alger and Oran, and yes the airdromes of France were on guard for possible attempt at seizure, and yes the people were begged to resist propaganda and to obey all and any orders for the government and its loyal soldiers and not from the rebels and their mad henchmen . . .

I had not dreamed all this, nor how we had tried four times at the newsstand before some papers came in from Marseille. Across the street the dog still howled.

The men who for several days had been treading cautiously over the roof next to the empty room with new tiles and plaster called roughly down, in voices that echoed enormously in the street, "Shut up, you! Quiet! Silence!" But it did no good.

I could not say honestly that I hoped it was a dog and not a woman, for atavistically I could not condone the realization that a human being had been chained like a beast in a room, but death would be preferable to any life that I had seen her living, that far. Perhaps she should die, rather than an animal? Either way, the confused surmising was dreadful, and just as I knew that the Insurrection must and would be either better or worse, so I knew that I must do something more to find out where the sounds really came from and what was making them and who caused it all. If I could determine those three things, I thought, I might possibly feel more real.

Meanwhile many other things were taking shape around us, as irrevocably but at the same time as fleetingly as deciding to drop a thousand men by parachute on the airfield at Marignane, or shut up a dog, or tie a woman to a bed leg in a dark room.

On April 20, for instance, a great flight of what I called swallows but what English Humphrey stated were swifts had arrived from Africa.

Perhaps the rumor was right, that they were the vanguard of the invasion? They were larger than swallows, I admitted, and they flew almost like bats in astonishing swoops speedier than my eye could really follow, and always making a high thin scream, also like bats but a scream and not a squeaking sound. They circled early in the morning and then at dusk, most surely to catch insects. They made me know, as I half-saw them against the paling sky, the darkening one, how van Gogh knew about the crows that flocked past his eyes and then into his soul and out upon the mad canvases he painted in the fields near his last asylum. Humphrey said they flew at perhaps two hundred miles an hour. Their cry was almost as inaudible as they were almost invisible.

They had come before the Germans too, we were told . . .

iii *THE RETURN*

TOWARD DUSK of the 23rd of April I looked down into the Rue Papassaudi and there by his door the man was standing uncertainly, with the little black dog, which looked silky and plump from our fifth floor. Later the shutters were opened for a few hours, on the dim window across from us, but no light showed, and before morning I heard again the feeble sound of something howling.

About five o'clock of the next afternoon I awoke from a half-sleep on the bed where I had lain quasi-helpless in an escapist doze, with the sound of the whimpering in my head, but this time leaving a nightmare imprint of words, as if the howl had turned into a call, a call to *me*. I tried impotently to recapture what I thought I had heard, what I had perhaps and perhaps not dreamed . . .

I went to the window, but there was nothing new to see, and with the same hopeless feeling I let fade from the first place of recollection the horrible suggestion of syllables in my dulled brain, in the clear air of the afternoon in springtime.

At about half-past five, when there came the sound of the *Marseillaise* half-sung and half-shouted, the window across from ours did not open, but I hung out of mine with my heart beating and with a kind of desperate human pride surging in me, as perhaps three thousand people flowed like a quiet river down the Rue Nazareth.

They were led by two policemen on bicycles, chatting and skidding one foot along the street to keep at the right speed. Behind them came what seemed like an endless stream of people, not straggling, but not really marching in the orderly sense of that word. There were many women with children. Sometimes they had put the smallest ones on their bikes or *vélos* and walked alongside. Men and youths and enlaced students came in groups, or beside their women. An occasional band of youths would be calling out in ageless unison *"Sa-LAN aux po-TEAUX, Sa-LAN aux po-TEAUX,"* but without much more real threat and hate than a band of parrakeets.

I was interested to note that during all this slow procession, neither as dour as a funeral nor gay as a picnic, I was seized by the shivers. It was an animal reaction, and I observed it with detachment. It was a kind of funk. It was pure emotion. Quite possibly it acted as a purge, an antidote.

What moved me the most, and at the same time soothed my perhaps neurotic and partly unrecognized apprehensions, was the quiet steadiness of everything. The parade had been called all over France for five o'clock that afternoon, and ten million workers, wage earners, salaried people marched as these Aixois did, from their town halls to their Prefectures if they had them, up their own Cours Mirabeau, to stand calling for the Prefect and then when he did not appear to disband and be absorbed once more into myriad alleys, innumerable rooms. It was unforgettable, that silent strong relentless walking . . .

The next day the air was different, because of the quiet show of strength.

People on the streets looked less harried. In town the café waiters were wary, especially along the Cours, and ready for possible trouble from small gangs of nonchalantly strolling bullyboys, dressed as students but organized in Marseille. There were many more Algerian women, even young pretty ones who before were never seen on the streets. They moved with easiness along the Cours, in their bright soft-flowing dresses, instead of stalking mutely through the open markets and then into their unofficial ghettoes. There was a general air of relaxed but still acute tension.

It was in a strange way like comparing two onions, one of which was without its first layer of skin: we all seemed to have been peeled, that day after the parade, of a layer, no matter how thin, of suspicion and prejudice. I saw this clearly in Anne and Mary. They were looking with new eyes, thinking with unsuspected brain cells . . .

I would like to say that as I stood shuddering and ennobled by the quiet parade flowing down the Rue Nazareth, I saw the poor woman from behind the closed window opposite our room staggering along, supported by her man, a look of rebirth on her puffed face. But it is not so. That night the dog still howled. The next morning the masons who had been working on the roof piled rubble into a wooden trough with an enormous clatter and thud, perhaps with the rumble of a small *plastic*, and along with several others of us on the Rue Papassaudi the man in the closed room slid open his shutters a few inches, and leaned out cautiously to see. He wore his beret, but no coat. He did not look up. He closed the shutters again after a few seconds.

I began to think that he was not at work because he was taking care of the woman, that perhaps she was in a crisis which was familiar to him, and that with his innate tenderness, which

I had long sensed, he was with sad accustomedness protecting her and keeping her caged until it passed. I hoped something like that was true.

That night there was no light on, but the dog did not howl again, and the next Sunday the man and woman sat once more in the window, with the tall bottle between them, and the scene was played again, but this time we were free from it. We had learned how, during the Insurrection, to disengage ourselves, to wear our new skins perhaps. It seemed almost good to know that the woman was well again, returned from whatever voyage she had made.

The Almond Blossoms

Is it so small a thing
To have enjoyed the sun,
To have lived light in the spring,
To have loved, to have thought, to have done;
To have advanced true friends, and beat down baffling foes?

Matthew Arnold, *Empedocles on Etna*

THERE was one old chambermaid at the hotel, not five feet tall, with a cynical merry grin and rather gruff reassuring manners, the kind of woman I would not mind being tyrannized by, domestically: she would scrub and sweep and scold, in my dream, and there would be mutual amusement. I have met one other such ancient troll, many years ago in Mexico. I forget her name. This one was called Rachelle, but I had great difficulty in ever thinking of her as anything but Babushka, for some reason I can't know.

One day we came in from the country with some sprays of almond blossoms, and she was standing by the hotel desk talking with Madame Segond. We gave them each a branch, with much talk about the unseasonable warmth, the danger of frosts to come, the great freeze of February 2, 1956 . . . ah, the dead olive trees, the almonds, the live oaks . . . and then the freeze of last April 30, which took two-thirds or three-quarters or five-eighths of the wine this year . . .

Then we went on up the winding stairs. Madame disappeared into her apartment.

I looked down from the third floor, into the dark well, and at the bottom Babushka was brushing vigorously at the carpet

by the desk, with her branch of almond blossoms held up toward the end of the broom handle, so that it and her white
head were the only lighted things, swooping minutely in a
little tidy dance. It was perhaps the best thing of a delightful
day, which we did not wish at all.

There were some people who lived in Marseille but had a
mas out toward Vauvenargues. My sister Norah met them the
summer before we were in the hotel, when she lived near them,
and introduced us first to the daughter Hélène and then gradually to all the rest of the family, before she must leave for
California.

Mary and Hélène enjoyed each other. Anne on the contrary, or perhaps because of this, found her pedantic and dull.
It is true that Hélène had a way of contradicting or correcting
all of us, a kind of supercilious amusement which I think was
mostly assumed owing to a hidden jealousy of the girls' greater
travels and so on and so on. Whatever the reason, Mary saw
much more of Hélène than Anne did.

Even so we lunched together a few times in Marseille, and
I kept a very straight face when Hélène asked some outrageously superior question about the pronunciation of an American slang word or something like that. I really enjoyed her,
because she had beautiful eyes and hair and skin, and she
amused me in an innocent way.

Norah had told me about the excellent cooking in the family,
and the droll father, the pretty older sister, the tiny old grandmother who occasionally gave out a chirruping but extremely
pointed comment.

I wanted to know all this, but at the same time I did find
Madame, even more so than her daughter, rather painfully
instructive, in a way that is tedious even to try to explain.

It always seemed as if she stood ready to make a hundred
corrections, to teach me all sorts of facts about whatever we
were discussing, from the weather to the French school sys-

tem. She explained patiently to me things I had known for decades, like the origin of the Provençal *santons* or the significance of hallmarks on solid silver. I felt that it was unbelievable to her, or at least inexplicable, that plain Americans like us had ever heard of such things as good silver, or would give a damn about such local phenomena as the *santons* . . . and of course as I tried to fight this suspicion of her basic disdain and ignorance of us as a people, I became at once ruffled and clumsy, so that my poor pronunciation grew worse and I made laughable mistakes in grammar.

I had to give myself something of a talking-to, especially when I realized that I was relying upon Anne's overt boredom and Mary's shyness, to get out of the kind invitations that this extremely well read and pleasant family kept making to us, perhaps to teach us more about their country, but really not as patronizingly as I occasionally felt.

That was why, in the face of real annoyance and dismay from both my children, I accepted Madame's suggestion that we go that Sunday, to lunch with them at the *mas*. I was rather blandly pragmatical, I suppose: the prospect bored me, but the weather was supernacular, to put it mildly, and I knew the food would be delicious. I would be polite and would try to be charming, and in return I would take everything I could of this most beautiful of sunny days.

I did, in every sense, and I was rewarded for my basically insolent attitude by feeling almost free from, or at last past, the somewhat similar attitude I had sensed in the French family.

They were open, generous of themselves, very amusing to listen to. We laughed a lot. There was a minimum of the in-and-out complicated manner of After you . . . No I beg of you . . . No I insist . . . After you . . . Please serve yourself . . . No, after you.

The grandmother was just as Norah had told me. She must have been very old. Everyone was thoughtful and affectionate with her. She ate nicely, which is rare at her state of senility, and apparently she heard when she wanted to, for suddenly she would say something in her ancient voice which was sharp and funny, or she would laugh with a fragile heartiness at one of Monsieur's many silly and melodramatic grumblings and growlings.

He too was as I forethought: a tall heavy man, basically neurotic and hypochondriac I'd guess, with a finished way of sneering and mocking everything, absolutely everything. He professed loudly and wittily to detest everything from De Gaulle to poodles; and from the spontaneous pleasure of his family I surmised that he was too good an actor to ruin even a brilliant quip by repeating it once too often.

The whole family was good at laughing, and with real enjoyment, and I liked the way they encouraged one another in it. It is a subtle thing, and rare, the way a thread, sometimes a very thin one too, is kept spinning through one bit of teasing, then an anecdote, then a quick play on words, then another story. I do like that, and they did it.

The older sister, Anne-Marie, was probably the most open and simple of the family . . . pleasant, attractive, impersonal. She talked easily with Mary, I noticed. A friend of hers was there, a plainer girl, perhaps not very sweet tempered, who was a trained nurse in Salon. Anne-Marie worked in a factory as an analyst of soils.

Hélène would be an interesting woman later. Then she was unsure and affected, but also generous of herself.

Yes, it was a good day, and I ended it with a kind of affection, and a fairly unashamed dismissal of my first acceptance of it for nothing but the spring weather and the good meal. As for them, they were both of the best.

All the windows of the simple pleasant house were wide open, a wonderful feeling for us after the winter in a hotel, and the walls were white plaster and the good furniture was dark with age and shining with wax, and the floors were of red square tiles. In other words, it was the kind of Provençal *mas* that I most love. And on the hearth a leg of lamb turned on an old spit: Anne-Marie was the family roaster (and salad maker), and she sent Hélène and my girls out for the first sprigs of wild thyme for it.

In front of the house, about fifty feet away, was an old table made of two solid slabs of stone with a piece of marble laid across them. It must have been almost as old as the great bare oak tree above it. Then there was a thick row of lilacs, their buds swollen and waiting. There was a field sown with oats, now up some four or five inches. It was too early yet to hear birds, and we saw only one ant walking drunkenly across the stone floor of the terrace, but there was the family cat, with a thick blue-gray coat, stalking nothings, and there was also the family dog Bobèche, more or less a gray poodle.

It is almost always the case that poodles bring out the most amusing side of their owners, and this family was delightful to listen to, once started on his subject while we drank coffee.

Among dozens of other things, Madame said that once Bobèche escaped from the apartment in Marseille and ran down the Rue Sylvabelle, nonchalantly turning over every garbage pail as he went, and she ran after him in her house slippers, more and more helpless and furious. Finally she caught him, and just then a man asked her in a very admiring and polished way, after many compliments about the dog, "Is he perhaps a *Griffon d'Autriche* or on the other hand a *pur-sang Tolèdain?*" And Madame was so furious at Bobèche that she said loudly, "*Non, mon cher monsieur, ce chien est un* INFIME BÂTARD." Then Monsieur added, "But the worst was when we took him to the vet . . . another client asked delicately, 'Is this dog perhaps a crossing of races?' and the vet said seriously, '*Monsieur, je dirais plûtot un carrefour qu'un croisement . . .*'"

I don't know if this is very funny in English, but it sounded fine there in the thinning warmth of the February afternoon, after the good lunch.

Before it, I sat in the sun with Monsieur, and we drank a *pastis*. Madame came out and with great finickiness her husband made her a small iced vermouth-gin. She said she loved gin and when I said I did too but for its effect rather than its taste, she said that she really loved the smell of it the best, and that she could hardly tell the difference between it and a good toilet water, so that when she got older she might well confuse them and drink up all her eau de cologne.

That is the way it was, casual and pleasant. The sun was almost hot. The younger girls were here and there, picking thyme, picking violets from a neglected flower bed that was like a mattress, unexpectedly, with deep purple and enormous blossoms which should be almost odorless but instead were heady with perfume. The older girls basted the *gigot*, carried plates and tumblers out to the table . . .

Lunch was long and simple, the way I like it.

We ate Anne-Marie's salad of endives, the white Belgian ones so good that time of year, cut in pieces with a dressing made of plenty of mustard, no salt, and plenty of olive oil . . . very little vinegar. It was delicious.

The lamb was the way I like it, very rare. There were brown crisp cubes of potato, and artichoke bottoms cooked with sliced mushrooms and bits of bacon.

Then there was a good mild but ripe Camembert and a good Bleu de Bresse, the way I like them, and then a rather tasteless *crème* with little sweet *brioches* . . . and fruit . . . and coffee.

We drank a *blanc-de-blanc* from near Arbois . . . it was nice. Monsieur was a little annoyed because he had forgotten to warm up a Gigondas to drink with the meat . . . it had been in the cellar all winter. It did not matter. In the warm sunshine the white wine was the way I like it. I looked about me and missed Norah.

I had lied to Madame in accepting her invitation, and said I had an appointment in Aix at three, but even with my changed feelings about the family it was a good time to leave. Monsieur drove us into town. We walked along the Cours with the almond branches, and I felt a little sheepish, for there in Aix only city slickers picked even twigs from trees that could bear nuts or fruits or olives.

And then we went into the hotel and divided our five branches with Madame Segond and Babushka. Anne put one branch in her room, and I stuck the other two in a jar of deep blue anemones by my desk. In the last bright light coming over the yellow and rose tiles of the rooftops, it seemed probably the most beautiful posy of my life.

I thought I should mention this in my invisible notes on the secret map, but before I could get to it I had to tell myself again about the strange feeling of affection and mystery that came over me as I looked down the dark stairwell and saw the white blossoms sweeping stiffly in the dark, on the top of Babushka's broom.

There was nothing more to *tell*, really.

Correction on the Map

O the moon shone bright on Mrs. Porter
And on her daughter
They wash their feet in soda water.

T. S. Eliot, *The Waste Land*

THE second time we left Aix was at once easier and more prolonged: I knew what I was doing, at least somewhat more clearly, and I could salve myself with the knowledge that I had returned once, and therefore might again.

In between these two leave-takings was one which does not count as such, for it was at the end of a short Christmas vacation there from Lugano, in 1959 I think, when after about ten minutes in Aix, I knew without even looking at my girls' faces that we must come back, leave Switzerland, change every schedule, seize this moment of being at least on the same side of the oceans as Aix then was to us, for as long as I dared make it last.

By then I knew more how to be a good ghost.

As I remember it now, I had remained in pain and bewilderment for a long time before we first left Aix. I wrote about it to a few confidants. I was not sure why I felt I must leave, I said, except that I wanted the girls to stay American. Then I gave reasons like their need to continue the orthodontia that had been skillfully interrupted to last one year, no more, of absence from San Francisco. I mentioned my need to earn money, which of course was a lie, at least in my implying that it was impossible for me to do so in France: I was a writer and could work anywhere, and I need not feel guilty about accepting another country's hospitality, for I paid fat taxes as a foreigner and at the same time kept up equally fat ones at home. No, there was an uneasy ambiguity about my compulsion to quit Aix, the first time, and in many ways it still puzzles me, for mostly it seems ridiculous now.

Should I? Why? I would moan, and a friend would look straight at me and ask gently, "Yes, why should you?" and I would have no intelligent answer.

Now and then someone in America would write sternly, admitting vicarious pleasure in my being in Aix. "Stay. California is far from there. Stay while you are there to begin with." And so on.

And I continued with my plainly masochistic and grudging pattern of return, withdrawal, escape, whatever it was.

A night or two before Anne and Mary and I left Aix that time, we ate dinner at the Glacier. We ordered, I think, a favorite dish of one girl's and then a favorite of the other's, and I drank my favorite wine there: fresh asparagus, tepid and not chilled, with a vinaigrette made at the table; plain boiled chicken with rice and a good sauce, all called Poulet Suprême or something like that; a bottle of *blanc-de-blanc* from back of Cassis . . .

It was a good night, under the leaves beginning to grow heavy with their summer dust.

While the children went in to the toilets I said in a willfully calm way to our friend Ange that we would not be back for a time, that we must go home.

He expressed some trite but real regrets: we both knew that he liked the children and me too, and that we in turn felt reassured by everything we knew about him and by the way he looked, as slim and silvery and histrionic as the oldest trout in a well-fished stream.

He glanced around, his professional eye checking all the terrace before he let down the mask to me. His face was lean and sad, like a saint's. "Madame," he said in a stern quiet insistent way, his dark eyes linked with mine, "Madame, consider what you are doing. *Consider*."

I stammered hopelessly to him, "I have. I have. I feel I must go home with them. I have, Ange."

He was the priest, I the penitent. I was young and tossed, he the rock.

He looked deeply at me for an instant more, and said again, "Reflect, Madame," and then he flicked his napkin at a coffee-filter and was Ange again.

I felt infinitely disturbed. Everything I had been pushing away from me in a kind of protective bewilderment rose with the good wine in my throat. I said to one of the other waiters to tell Anne and Mary that I would return at once, and I ducked across the circle of endless cars around the Rotonde and walked into the noise and mist of the great garish fountain, hearing those quiet doomful words *reflect, reflect* . . .

Nobody could see me there, I knew, and for the only time in Aix I cried hopelessly, the uncouth sobs of a resigned child, alone, not terrified but puzzled. I walked furiously, perhaps three times around, or five. Ange's face bent toward my inner eyes, and above the sound of traffic and the spouting waters my inner ears were etched relentlessly by the diamond needle of his voice: *Reflect*.

Never before had I abandoned myself so trustingly, so shamelessly, to the impersonal view of a public place. I could have screamed safely there in the turmoil of the waters and the cars. I circled the fountain as fast as if I were fleeing, until it was safe for me again to cross to the Glacier, and there I got the children into the dappled night shadows, and we went homeward, each of us in a daze of our own pain of imminent removal.

Ange of course did not reappear on the terrace, and when we came back again years later and I wanted to show him that we had indeed returned, he had been fired for arrogance, we were told, and was picking up pennies doing wedding suppers and even mop-up work after athletic club reunions in some of the lesser cafés. We nodded on the street now and then with a kind of nonchalant regret, but behind his cynical weary face, puffier than before, I saw his stern eyes and heard him say, as I shall for as long as I live, "Reflect, reflect . . . "

But the second time it was easier, mostly, as I have often told myself, because I had done it once and then got back to it. And I was much older, and more patient of the improbable.

I could reflect with an almost supercilious compassion upon the old bewilderment of my first flight, and when people still asked me occasionally, "But why did you leave and then return, instead of staying and sparing your children all the confused schooling and so on?" and so on and so *on*, I could shrug and admit honestly, "I do not rightly know." At least I had matured enough for candor.

The second time we must flee I was able, with what might be called either resignation or masochism, to go deliberately from one important place to another in my private city, the invisible one, putting it all into final order on the map.

Tomorrow, I would plan to myself, I must go alone to the olive oil shop near the shady little Place des Trois Ormeaux, and smell it to my own satisfaction, and perhaps buy three or four kinds of olives from the open kegs, just to stir up the cool air toward my greedy inner nostrils . . . And the next morning I would walk up the Cours Sextius and into the gardens of the hotel spa behind the remnants of the Roman walls . . .

For many days and nights, once we knew definitely when we were to leave for home, a word which by then had been shaped into its most essential usage on all our tongues, past any need of explanation, I wandered like this in a kind of trance through my own streets and looked with the most seeing eyes of my whole life, and in the same way heard and smelled, and without question I knew that Anne and Mary were doing it too, wittingly or not.

Perhaps because I was older I knew more clearly than they that for many things it was too late. There was not enough time left in the world to find Brondino alive again, nor even to wait for the night when the priests would stand over the flames outside the cloister of St. Sauveur, to light the holy lamp again for Easter morn.

Never again would any of us watch the five law students teetering on the rooftop across from our windows in the Hôtel de Provence, whispering as the sun went into total eclipse and then in the unearthly dark crying out with cracked bravado, "Encore, encore!"

But there were some small lines I could trace more firmly or even rectify on my map, I thought . . . tidily I could attend to a few small bits of unfinished detail, for my own satisfaction: a measurement here, a dingbat there. One ghost in search of several others, I trotted dreamily about, proving to myself that things were in order: the corners must be sharp and clear, the lines incisive for my future contemplation.

A morning not far before the end of June and the end of the stay, I was sitting alone on the terrace of the 2 Gs, resting my feet from a full morning of this secret ferreting, before Anne and Mary could come from school. I thought of feet in general, and of the Provençal feet, short and high arched and well treated, and of how our longer less solid ones could suffer there on the cobbled streets and the rough stony land.

When we first moved into the country at Le Tholonet, before we left Provence the first time, it had been unbelievable how our feet hurt, after a week or so of going without shoes or with only rope-soled espadrilles.

Mine ached like hollow teeth when I went to bed at night, and burned like hell-fire. I would sit in the middle of my big bed, feeling like a self-indulgent ninny, and rub them voluptuously with mentholated salves squeezed from tubes marked *La Baume du Docteur Smythe-Schmidt* or *Pied-Magique, Analgésique Miraculeuse*.

Anne despised such nostrums because of their texture, and seemed to solve the problem of walking by dancing instead, along the ground.

Mary, about nine then, was the worst: she literally hobbled like a crone. It was pain to watch her. At night I would rub her like a little pony, up as far as she went, with the balms and with watered brandy. She would purr. And in the morning she would start up the path to the shepherd's house hamstrung and hobbling again . . .

After perhaps a week of this I could not stand it any more for her, and decided to go in to Aix for more help than I had found at the pharmacy.

I felt many reservations. I knew from what waiters had told me, as perhaps the worst sufferers from their feet in modern life, that quasi-doctors and even quasi-quacks fattened everywhere on their torture. I did not want to expose my girl to such a risk. But it would have taken Dr. Vidal a courteous three or eight weeks of injections, x-rays, pills, tests, analyses, to tell me the obvious: Mary's good little feet, overprotected for some years by leather, were not yet tough enough for the ancient trails and streambeds . . .

. . . and meanwhile, wincing but dogged, she stumbled slowly after the shepherd of Le Tholonet, and along the streets of Aix.

So one day I collected a local friend called SaSa Tailleux, one of those cultural hybrids with eyes forever to be called drowned violets, a fine sensitive dangerous child if ever I knew two or three, and we all caught the market bus for Aix. I felt braver with more of an audience.

There was a woman on the bus with two bumptious young dogs she planned to leave at the pound unless some of the passengers wanted them, while she went on to pick fruit near Avignon. We all helped her on and then off, uncommitted to fosterhood, and when one of the pups threw up on a Gypsy's shoe he laughed and took care of it. SaSa focused her great flower-eyes at me, and if I had looked even vaguely fastidious she would have thrown up too, and then my girls would have, in sympathy.

As it was, I looked as much like an amused Gypsy as possible and we got to Aix all right and started things off by veering a little to the left of the bus stop to one of our several "favorite" cafés, where we downed the necessary tipples for our ages.

We then fused into one, SaSa clutching Anne clutching me on one side and Mary clutching and wincing along on my other, to go up the left side of the Cours Mirabeau, which for anyone who has not done it in early summer can be described as swimming languidly, happily upstream if one is a languid happy fish. The impossibly high plane trees bend over like reeds, like river weeds. The air moves with a mysterious tidal current.

Of course no real fish people could possibly swim up the Cours Mirabeau the way the little girls and I did that day, under the curving haughty gracious weeds, with the many fountains spouting and splashing as if their waters were a part of the air, or the air we breathed was really green-gold water.

An old friend, Armenian like most of the street photographers in Provence then, motioned to us with his camera to his eye and hunger back of his face, and at my nod he snapped us, and later we did look almost but not quite real on the film, with four feet stepping forward, four behind. But the only real thing to me as it happened was that poor old Mary could hardly put one foot or another down at all. In the picture I was smiling, but I remember how sick I felt; she was so courteous about it.

Near the Deux Garçons I'd often seen a badly lettered sign

about foot care. While I located it more carefully in my thoughts, we sat down and had an almost unprecedented second drink. SaSa looked tipsy, sucking away at a tall glass of chocolate milk, and my girls eyed me silently over theirs, sure something was up. I let the false fire of a vermouth-gin warm my timorous insides, and then said, "Come on. I know now where we are going." By that I was committed.

The three tender helpless children stood up, with docility their masks. We left our packages there with the waiter, and a few paces to the north of the café terrace I started up the dirtiest smelliest flight of stairs I had ever climbed in the town. It was next to the shop where Cézanne's father once sold his felt hats, near the mouth of the Passage Agard. Behind me I could feel the children's expressions without looking at them; they were quiescent and repelled.

The building was late seventeenth century perhaps, and the air in it seemed to have been there for most of the time lapse, so that it had a color and texture, both bad. The walls were very oily to touch as we climbed. The newest stains on them were square clumsily lettered posters vaunting the foot doctor's amazing successes, and as I went on and around I read their strange boasts and began to bow to my uneasiness.

What kind of man would quote some other man's word that he was a master, a superhuman healer, God-sent? What hungry miserable egocentric would pay someone to hand paint his marvels? What deity could keep on breathing and performing in this greasy dank heaven?

Behind me Mary thudded, as heavily as an exhausted waitress.

We came to a half-glassed door, well covered with small lettered signs about the doctor, and finally an old woman opened to my ringing, with a relatively fresh puff of air reeling with onions and hot fat.

I asked if we were late, thinking it might be her early dinner hour, but she assured me no, and went into a long palaver about appointments, while SaSa and Anne stood on this foot and that and Mary stood on as little of either as she could. The old woman rapidly closed in on me as a possible new convert to her faith, and gabbled hysterically about her son as she led us down a dim corridor to a room no bigger than a generous bath mat, with two chairs hunched into it and the dark plastered walls covered with framed clippings and photographs. The ceiling was low enough to make me stoop a little.

The mother padded on down the hall toward the sound of fumy sizzlings, the girls looked politely at me, sideways, and I smiled overtly and falsely at them.

"We'll get Mary's feet adjusted and then simply *run*," I said.

We sat for quite a while. I wished I had drunk two gins, and the children's faces looked sunken. A man limped up the stairs and past the door. The old woman yelled out at him from the kitchen about how busy the doctor was. He groaned. She said feet were feet and his were not the only ones, and he went limping back down the stairs, to return for an appointment in nine days.

Mary looked at me impassively, but her eyes said *Nine days!*

We studied the framed clippings, and the pictures of deformed human feet with clumsily typed quotations under them. This is a club-thrombo-disk malformation, or something like that, it would say in French, and the little girls would read it glibly and then say, "Oooh. Ugh. Aach. Look at the knob on the bone." Then they would inspect a picture of what flat feet could do to the posture, and Anne would say that any time now Mary would get that bulge on her spine and never get married, and SaSa would laugh a wild half-French half-Irish laugh and Mary would shrug amiably and read another caption: the doctor we waited for was miraculous, no less, in his healing of all ills, not just plain old bunions and broken arches; he was incredibly gifted; he was, to speak bluntly, Messiah, and so on.

We all grew pale and fidgety, and I wondered if SaSa and Anne might fall over or be sick, in the ancient dank fog of cookery and pain. Mary sat staring at her culprit feet.

Suddenly the old woman crashed into the cupboard of a room, almost over our legs and into our laps: her son, she told me with high hysterical laughing speed, was impossibly busy but might possibly arrange to see us in three weeks to the day hour minute.

The children stared at me, and then Mary looked away, and I thought furiously of how I could not, I would not let her hobble out again to the poppy fields, down to the brook, on her poor little feet, and No, I made it clear, *NO*.

The old woman glared at me with what may have been admiration, and dashed back down the hall and slammed her door on the continued sizzlings.

Somebody else limped up the stairs, banged, and then clopped slowly down again.

We did not look any more at the pictures of bulging growths and deformations on the dark streaky walls. The smell of greasy onions seemed to grow thicker around us, like our silence.

Then in a kind of jubilance the old mother slammed in, to tell us that as a special favor the doctor would see Mary, and soon, that very hour. Ah, no people and certainly no passing strangers, no foreigners, had ever before been so fortunate as to be treated immediately by such a proven master. Ah, what fortune!

And then, as in a nightmare which we could not stop, we listened to her read almost every quotation under the pictures, in her high laughing voice. They were from magazine articles, letters from patients, medical dictionaries, professors in schools of chiropody and divine healing. She read and read, while plates clattered and cutlery clanked against china revoltingly in the kitchen and the little girls nodded politely to her litany.

There was a crash, as if someone had fallen off his chair and pulled the tablecloth down with him. The mother put her hand over her weary adoring face, and then pulled it down past a new smile and excused herself as she ran out toward fearful silence.

The air was now almost too thick to breathe through, as if it were dirty flannel pressed over our faces. The low walls seemed to swell in and out and touch us with swollen toes, broken arches, twisted bodies.

I stood up as straight as I could in the low room. The children wheeled from their hynotized crouches before the pictures of troubles which I had until then considered structural or bacterial rather than of the soul. I whispered, "Help me now. We are going to do something bad. We are going to run away before the doctor comes."

There was no question from them. We flowed down those dank stinking stairs like one shadow, not four. We fled silently out onto the Cours. There was not a word in us as we ran from the sick air and the mad old mother.

I felt a kind of panic that her laughing voice would shriek down at us from a window high in the ancient building. Run, run, I cried silently to the children, but by the time we got to the 2 Gs we were seemly enough on the outside.

We got the packages from the table behind the big room, where the waiters always left them, and then outside we all seemed to want to hurry again without talking. It was not until we passed the last brimming fountain, and were almost at the bus stop on the Rotonde, that I noticed that Mary was prancing along like a little pony. Her fine strong feet were almost twinkling on the pavement.

And years later I thought of all this, one of the last mornings of my own secret verification of the inner map.

It was about the same time, in season and day, with the leaves firm in their new ceiling high above the Cours. Girls walked by in fresh cotton skirts high too on their young legs, high themselves on stilt heels made only for the Cours in that town of cobbles and rough pavements. Youth and vanity, I thought: my own feet were past either, and I knew with rueful resignation that I should treat them better than I had done lately, in the survey I was making of my own streets before we must leave.

In a half-hour Anne would come from the Lycée and Mary from her classes at the other end of the Cours. I would ask Monsieur Barthélémy, the pharmacist, for the name of a good chiropodist.

I must have been dazzled, in my haze of effort to fix things forever with my own ink on the paper, to find myself so surprised when the pharmacist said with professional caution that of course there was a foot-man just a few doors down, who had a certain reputation . . . Somehow I had let myself assume, when I remembered the time we went with SaSa up those fumey stairs, that by now the man must have vanished, if ever he did exist except in the mind of his wildly loving mother. Or perhaps it had not happened at all.

But while Monsieur Barthélémy spoke to me, and gave me the names of one or two other doctors, I knew I must go back at once to the messianic healer we had once read and heard about so intimately. There was still time. There was a place that suddenly seemed blurred on my map, and I must repair it.

I hurried onto the Cours, and then started up the narrow twisting stairs toward the top apartment, and gradually as I mounted and turned, the greasy air seemed to clear my head instead of further clouding it, and I felt a dreadful apprehension.

Above me I saw the half-glassed door, with the same badly lettered signs on it.

If the old woman came again to open it, I would follow her down the reeking corridor, and then sit in the low little room with the pictures of toes and tumorous spines and drawn pain-twisted faces, and from the kitchen I would hear food cooking in rancid fat and then a crash as if someone had fallen heavily from his chair, with all the soiled china crashing down around him. Then . . . what then? Who would come down the hall to the room where I was waiting?

I stood for a moment in front of the door. I could push a button, I saw, or I could knock.

Instead, before anyone could come to open for me, I turned and went down the stairs again toward the pure air, as fast and silently as I could, and then I hurried down the Cours, past the Deux Garçons where Anne and Mary were not yet sitting on the terrace. I tried not to feel real panic that perhaps the old woman would scream at me from her high window with her wild laughing voice . . . Madame, Madame . . . you have not kept your appointment . . . Dishonest, coward, cheat. . . . The fountains would stop to listen . . . the life of the Cours would stop to look . . .

I went into a pharmacy at the corner of the Cours and the Rue de la Mosse and bought a tube of some kind of magic mentholated salve.

I felt quite shaken, but by the time I got back to the café all was well again: the ink had dried, only a little smeary, on my correction to the map, and the sun lay green-gold on the faces of my children. For some reason they had decided to order chocolate milk, which I thought they had long since outgrown. As a ghost, I was free again.

The Royal Game of Tennis

At the beginning of the eighteenth century, the municipal
theater of Aix settled permanently into the royal tennis hall,
built in 1660. In 1756 the Duc de Villars had it remodeled,
and it was decorated again in 1786. At this date it supported
two troupes, one for opera and ballet, and the other for
tragedy and comedy. There were also two concert societies
in Aix, one functioning at the Town Hall and the other at
the municipal theater . . .

Jean-Paul Coste, *Aix-en-Provence and Its Countryside*

FROM somewhere in my life I remember the smell, the feel
even, of a very old jewel box lined in fat tufts with faded
dusty velvet. Or perhaps it was a pincushion, set in a chased
band of silver.

This seems vague, but is strong enough in my past for me
to have recognized the interior of the Opera of Aix at once:
it was the same feeling of dust, of elegance, that I got. I was
at home there, rather like a forgotten earring or brooch caught
in the frayed lining of the jewel box, or an invisible pin stuck
into the fat dingy little trinket that may once have sat upon
my grandmother's dressing table.

Over the next years after my first comfortable recognition
of the place, I sat everywhere I could in it, depending on how
quickly I had got to the ticket office in the Parfumerie Truphème, what seats I had been able to buy for the seasonal
"Gala d'Art Dramatique," and the general state of my purse.

Once I sat in the second box, right stage, to watch the long
afternoon of *La Pastorale* at Christmas. For a whole season
I sat in the fourth row center of the second balcony, for the

plays that sifted down from Paris. Once I sat front row center, first balcony, to listen to Presti and Lagoya, who had been rained out of the Cloister of St. Louis during the summer Festival. Once I left at the intermission, a variety show too loud and dull to tolerate, with a "public address system" pure torture there where the sound was so undistorted. And once I went to a political meeting which I did not quite agree with but which was exciting. A few times troupes of dancers did not turn up, and after some bored stampings and boos the thin audience left, to get back their money the next day at the Parfumerie.

The acoustics of the theater were very good, especially perhaps for orchestra, although the proportions of the small building were such that a provincial opera troupe could sound as swiftly mellow as if it were from the Métropole itself. The man who ran the downstairs bar told me that the best seat for listening to tenors was three rows under the first balcony, behind the pillar, but I never tried it. For full orchestra, which ranged from mediocre to very fine according to the available musicians from the Conservatory and "around," I liked to sit in as near the center of the theater as I could get, or else very high.

There were two bars, both of them bleak rooms that had once been fairly elegant.

The one that looked down upon the Rue de l'Opéra had no doubt been built for the genteel occupants of the boxes and the first balcony, and was not always open. I liked the one behind the ground floor seats much better. It had sawdust on the floor, and a good smell to it, and it was run by the frail-looking man who advised me about acoustics. I always wondered how and why he knew so well. But he was too reserved to question, and I never saw him except there, between the acts.

Now and then, for something like the official balls of the

Carnaval, a floor would be laid out from the stage over the pit and the seats, and surprisingly the first row of boxes would be almost at its level, with the dance bands playing at the back of the stage, against one of the familiar shabby old drops showing something like a Venetian canal or a formal park.

I went to one of the children's costume parties, which was held an afternoon during the Carnaval, with a runway for the little Pierrettes and Mickey Mice to walk down for the judges, who sat in the panoplied Mayor's box and kept notes. It was a touching spectacle, complete with essential tears and topplings. Already, over the sound of the bored jazzmen dressed in white trousers and bright blue jackets, there was hammering, and a general bustle for the main ball of the Carnaval that night, and baskets of confetti were being stacked in the corridors, and extra ice in sacks for the champagne, and the children sobbed in the corners and trembled with pleasure.

The best concert I ever heard in the Opera was given by the municipal orchestra in celebration of the 300th anniversary of André Campra's birth in Aix. It was all Provençal music: Campra of course, Henri Tomasi, and then Darius Milhaud's *Le Tombeau de Mireille*, and the *Arlésienne Suite* by Georges Bizet, but played as I had never heard them before, with solos by an old man with bagpipes from the Camargue, I think, and beautiful saxaphone-flute-harp in the Bizet, and the young boy who sometimes stayed on our floor at the Hôtel de Provence doing a long intricate kind of sonata in the Milhaud on his little drum and his tambour. I was put under a spell by it, and so was everyone in the crowded place. I have never felt more real delight come almost visibly from so many people at once.

I was very sorry Anne and Mary had not come with me, but they must study . . .

On looking back, it seems impossible that those two young girls managed to go so often to the theater and still keep up their schoolwork, which of course was all in French and already twice as demanding as it would have been at home in their mother tongue. Their teachers did not approve of seeing them with me so often, late at night, but they could not say that it seemed to affect the children's work wrongly, and I myself believed that as long as they stayed healthy it was an experience that could never happen again and therefore should be seized and savored.

While we lived at the Provence we were within ten minutes' walk of everything we wanted to see and hear, whether it was Josephine Baker doing another "farewell tour" at the Casino down past the Rotonde, or *Zazie Dans le Métro* at the Cézanne, the new movie house two blocks down from the Cours on the Rue Mazarine.

Up the Cours was the dingy old Rex, which showed everything from prizefights to second-run pictures, with now and then an exciting troupe of actors too poor or too late to book into the Opera . . . like one from Paris, most probably starving but gifted and well costumed, which gave a beautiful performance of a Greek tragedy written by Kazantzakis.

And then at the top of the Cours and past the little restaurant, and across from two noble old town-houses called Lestang-Parade and Grimaldi, was the theater, the Opera.

It was squeezed into a comparatively undistinguished block of lesser buildings, and before we left there was increasing talk of the need to build a big municipal auditorium which would do for all such present and future problems as legal congresses, international lunch club conventions, and even the Music Festival. Friends tried to quiet us by saying that such rumors had been thriving for at least one hundred of the two hundred and fifty years since the old royal tennis courts had been officially made the town's theater, but it could not but be worrisome.

The Opera was plainly in a state of alarming if still functional disrepair, and local squabbles and scandals about responsibility (Should Monsieur Truphème act without municipal consent? Would he answer for the bills?) kept any activity at a minimum.

The theater was surprisingly clean, probably thanks to the frail barman who may well have been janitor too. The toilets were hopeless except in dreadful emergencies, and I was told that the dressing rooms were shockingly drab and ill lighted. There was of course no real ventilation at all. The gilt of the proscenium was dim and peeling. The carpeting was in tatters, and the upholstery on even the few rows of new seats in the orchestra was stained and shabby. The stairs and high stools in the boxes creaked and rattled, and the box doors banged loudly because all the padding had worn off.

But it was a little jewel box, that theater.

It had been remodeled from the tennis courts in the style of the mid-eighteenth century, like La Scala, like the Paris Opera, with tiers of boxes rising straight up its sides to right and left of the deep stage, and with three balconies curving around to meet them, steeply, facing the proscenium.

The young and limber, the students, sat mostly in the top balcony, and it needed a clear steady head to lean without dizziness over the rails, to listen and of course to flirt. The balcony below it was deeper, and the boxes were a little fatter, and it was made for the middle classes in age and station, who could stand hard uncomfortable seats at a middle price, and would take a middle view of things. The first balcony was somewhat more sumptuous, and the orchestra seats were the most comfortable, the most costly, often the best every way . . .

As always, the boxes were more to be seen in than to see from, and we avoided them except for *La Pastorale*, when the audience, dressed mostly in Provençal clothes and speaking the language of Mistral, was almost as much fun as the play. It lasted almost six hours, during at least two-thirds of which we were sure we could not stand to stay another minute, but which were unforgettable for the devout way the story was unfolded, of the birth of Jesus in a little Provençal village.

And here, partly to pamper my own amazed nostalgia, is a little of what we saw one single winter at the theater, not counting four operas given by the regional company, two or three evenings of ballet presented by my girls' old ballet teacher, and about six other evenings of dance, one unusually good by the small American Ballet company . . . and of course several concerts like the one in honor of Campra:

The Choutes Sisters, by Barillet and Grèdy
The Year of the Final Exams, by José-André Lacour
The Diary of Anne Frank, by Goodrich and Hackett
Léocadia, by Jean Anouilh
Inquisition, by Diego Fabbri
Hard-Tack Inn, by Marcel Achard
The Doors Slam Shut, by Michel Fermaud
The King's Filly, by Jean Canolle
Electra, by Jean Giraudoux
The Dressen Collection, by Marc-Gilbert Sauvajon
The Nitwit, by Jean Anouilh
Andromachus, by Jean Racine
The Tidings Brought to Mary, by P. Claudel
Rhinocérus, by Eugène Ionesco
The Prisoners of Altona, by Jean-Paul Sartre

The Ionesco was done by the Odéon-Théâtre of Paris, and *Electra* by the Comédie Française, and almost every play used the talents and occasionally the genius of the best actors and directors and designers in France. It was an exciting example of what touring repertory can do to keep the stage one of the great human expressions.

The Opera is said to have been made the official stage of Aix in about 1765 at the passionate request of a group of graduates of the College, who with a high percentage of the population of the snobbish little city found their greatest pleasure in amateur dramatics. In the schools it was taught, according to the dictum of André Campra himself, that opera, ballet, and tragedy would keep the body supple and light, and breed ease and "stage presence" in even the youngest thespians. Private theaters flourished in many of the Provençal country houses, as well as in town, and when the Aixois were not themselves on the boards they were cheering the performances of traveling troupes from Marseille and Avignon and Toulon, in what had for so long been the royal tennis courts.

There is still a little stone plaque in the corridor of the theater that leads up to the first balcony, stating in thin shallow letters that in 1660 this cramped building did indeed house the royal courts, and it is there that visiting actors played out their comedies and tragedies. Once I watched a real game in just such a place, on the grounds of Hampton Court Palace, and it was easy to see how the net-protected gallery for the ladies could turn into one for noble spectators of a drama, with the groundling let onto what would be the court itself, and then a kind of stage at the opposite end of the gallery for the actors. It had the accidental logic of all good public places.

By the time we got to it, the Aix Opera was still in much the form it had been given by the Duc de Villars, with nineteenth-century incrustations of course, and in spite of its cramped size and its general decay, it was a strong and perhaps final proof that the town was still provincial, and passionately loyal to its own troupes and musicians as well as to the steady flow of talent from everywhere in Europe.

In the theater as in many other things, Aix seemed to be on the world's path: Paris and Lyon to the north, for musicians and companies coming up from Rome and Barcelona and Lisbon and even Malaga and Morocco; Italy and Germany and Spain and Africa, for everything traveling south from the Métropole and even from England and Scandinavia.

At the Opera itself, the performances were most either local concerts and galas or plays from the North.

Most of the chamber music went to the Casino, an elegant and larger room with fine acoustics, and decorated with fairly uncompromising finesse in pale blue and white, with crimson velvet . . . as in the Vienna State Opera, I believe, and Carnegie Hall. Often in the afternoons there were somewhat elegant gatherings for fine chamber music sponsored by little groups like the Dante Alighieri Society, with duos and quatuors up from Florence, Bologna, Rome. . . .And once a month there was, in two performances (at six and nine) in one day, which must have been gruelling for the arts, a meeting of the Jeunesses Musicales.

When we first were in Aix, I could go into the "J.M." with a regular ticket, because Mary was kindly accredited with needing an attendant. The next time I had to get my own card as a member auditor, since I was past thirty and she was past eight . . . but I was given a free and fairly good phonograph record for my dollar subscription, and it was amusing to have to show my card with the little passport picture on it when I bought tickets.

The young audience was vital, teeming, pulsating with life and curiosity: it made me feel more invisible than ever, in a good way. I usually went to the first performance, with my smaller girl, and toward the end of our stay Anne went to the later one with members of her *bande*.

It was lucky for us that the "J.M." was very strong in those days, and I hope it will stay so. Its aim was to "enrich the general culture of young men and women by acquainting them with music" . . . and one winter, for instance, we listened to

and saw the following concerts, all with erudite and witty
lectures alongside:

> Romance and Laughter in the French Operetta, with
> four soloists and piano.
>
> The Paillard Chamber Orchestra, with twelve musi-
> cians and violin soloist.
>
> The Beautiful History of the Dance, with four danc-
> ers and pianist.
>
> The Jamet Quintet, with harp, violin, flute, alto and
> cello.
>
> Campra and His Contemporaries, with the Provençal
> Ensemble and soprano.
>
> Chopin and Schumann, Their Tone and Imagery,
> pianist.
>
> Panorama of Jazz, with Claude Bolling and his group.

And besides a gala presentation of Molière's *L'Avare* at the
theater, for the "J.M.," there was a fine rowdy performance,
that same winter, of the Comédie de Provence' *Taming of the
Shrew*, and best of all there was the Comédie itself, always
there in Aix.

It worked out of the Archbishop's Palace. There was a
steady titillating come-and-go, with loads of costumes being
carried in, or screams and slashing sounds in the courtyard,
from the rehearsals. Once Mary helped unload an old truck
filled with props, when she was very little, and later Anne
studied diction with the fine old coach Monsieur Rèbe. We
got to know some of the young actors, at least enough to
smile shyly at them across the café terrace. It was a good
feeling, to have a troupe of real actors there in the town . . .

And of course there were concerts a few times a year in
the Cathedral. They were always especially impressive, with

artful lights focused on things like a great illuminated book on the edge of the pulpit, and the tapestries glowing with night color, and the altar masked. There was a worldly hum in the aisles. It would fall and then rise again with veiled excitement as the Archbishop came quietly into a seat in the side stalls, or the Mayor or an Air Force general walked toward the transept to be nearer the music, in fuller view. . . . It seemed like one of the rightest ways in the world for such a great prayerful structure to be kept alive, by the music that rose from the choirs and the orchestras and always from the organ with Monsieur Gay's white head bent over the console . . . a double satisfaction it was.

And then there was the Festival . . .

The Velvet Tunnel

The Music Festival of Aix-en-Provence, formerly called the Mozart Festival, is held in that city from the 9th through the 31st of July, during which time five operas are usually given some thirteen times, some ten concerts are given by five or six orchestras and chamber-music groups, and three recitals are given by famous musicians. The operas are presented in the courtyard of the Archbishop's Palace, the soloists and large groups perform in the Cloister of Saint Louis, and smaller instrumental groups play in the courtyard of the Maynier d'Oppède town-house. One concert is given each season in the Cathedral of the Holy Savior.

Official publicity folder

Part way up Gaston-de-Saporta, past Brondino's window full of reprints of Cézanne and Modigliano and Botticelli on the left, and across from it the even smaller window where in 1954 there were still a few dried *cigales* painstakingly dressed in Provençal costumes, the Place de l'Archevêché seemed to open suddenly like a window itself, wide into tranquillity.

There was a pastry shop on its farther corner, toward the Cathedral, and now and then in the basement floor of the house where my children first lived was a drowsy collection of modern ceramics for sale. The rest of the façades were closed and quiet and very shabby, with a few beautiful doors ill kempt and cracking in the sun. The tall trees flourish there, and make a fine shade.

The second time we lived in Aix cars were beginning to park there in the Place, where even six years before it was all space or, on Market days, the donkeys were standing, their little carts empty of farm produce, waiting for noon and the quick trot home.

There was also quite often one horse, with a sagging carriage, the last one in Aix. The driver was a fat drunken old man who cursed at Anne and Mary and Henri when their kick-ball rolled under his nag's patient belly. And then he was dead, and so was the horse, and the children in the little Square were gone: my own girls were too old for kick-ball anywhere, even in Aix, and the little boy Henri was a sober grind at the Lycée Mignet, a spoiled prig for all we could tell, planning to be a diplomat. And Chantal and Mireille, the rough kindly girls who sometimes played with them, were married and mothers . . .

On the left side of the Square is a narrow alley, which leads into the Cloister, and where once we watched half-mystified and half-exalted as the priests burned a bright fire (Were they burning the robes of Judas, as in Crete?) in the dark night before Easter morning, and lit our tapers from it, and then led us into the unbelievably black hollow terrifying church.

From the alley to the end of the Square is the house Anne and Mary lived in, on the top floor, with Henri and his mother and two older sisters. It had once been a wing of the Archbishop's Palace, which forms the end of the Square. I suppose it was used by visiting prelates, for the rooms were large and gracious but without the grandeur of the Palace itself.

It must have been adequately elegant in the eighteenth century, but by the time we knew it the walls were cracked and sagging, and the tiled floors went up and down, and the only noble things left were the fine curving stairway with its delicate forged iron balustrade, and the beautiful carved wooden door.

Madame Wytenhove's apartment, the top one in this fairly low three-storied building, was a dazzle of sunlight, a delight.

As I remember it, the kitchen, a short hall, the salon which was also the dining room, and two large bedrooms looked down onto the square through tall generous windows, and for them alone I would love to live there, even with the whole dismal state of disrepair and shabbiness, and the ridiculous plumbing.

My girls slept in a small dark room next to Henri's sisters' room, in a short wing which branched out in back to form one wall of the Cloister. The sexton slept just below them, to keep an eye on his domain, and now and then when he did not feel like going down to the Cathedral to ring a little bell for some religious or touristic purpose he would simply lean from his window and jangle it toward the main building of the church. He was the official guide, to show to visitors the famous triptych of the Burning Bush and the tapestries made for Canterbury in 1511, and the bell they were requested to ring for his services often rang all day in his room while he slept beside it. Occasionally it would sound out with obvious irritation, and the children above his room would hear him chuckle . . .

Mary was about eight then. After a few weeks of living with the family and studying with Madame Wytenhove the older Anne started to go to school with the Dominicans, so gentle with little strangers, and Mary stayed on for a time by herself, the only child in the big apartment.

She would go before every meal for a pitcher of fresh spring water from the Fontaine d'Espéluque which spouts from a remnant of Roman wall between the Cloister alley and the pastry shop, and she began to speak enough words to buy bread and cakes there for Madame, and then for herself. The fat old woman who lived behind the shop with her husband and helped him ice his pastries was kind and smiling with her, as everyone seemed to be.

One time when she was roaming about in the Cathedral, listening to the organ and peering into the side chapels, the sexton scared her by pushing her roughly down behind an altar, until she saw that he was smiling and holding his finger to his lips: she had got mixed up in a wedding somehow. She crouched there until the long service was over and everyone gone, and then the old man came for her and led her across the great silent nave to the door into the familiar Cloister, where she and Henri played every afternoon among the broken Roman and Gothic carvings, when he got home from school.

And another time she saw men unloading beautiful dresses, and fantastic wigs held up delicately on sticks, from an old truck in front of the arched passageway that led into the Archbishop's Palace next door, and being a straightforward child she went as close as she could, to watch. Men ran back and forth with what seemed an endless supply of glittering capes and pantaloons and robes, taking them deep into the great courtyard, for all she could see or know.

She went nearer and nearer, and finally a man smiled and said something to her which she could not understand, and thrust a pile of gauzy bright silk into her arms.

It was natural and right to follow him, through the open gates of exquisite forged iron and around the first corner and then into the dim storeroom where other excited people were hanging the clothes on crowded racks. She made several trips, mute but willing, and when the van was empty she ran up the stairs next door, to tell as best she could the morning's adventure.

That afternoon, well primed by Madame, I could explain to her that she had been helping the famous Comédie de Provence unload its props after a tour through France, and we made plans to see a play sometime in that beautiful courtyard. It took almost six years . . .

In the summer of 1960 we stood again where the Place opened like a window from the dark twisted walls of the Rue Gaston-de-Saporta. It was at night, and soft full lights masked high in the trees made them somehow more than ever like tall sea ferns, with us the fish at the bottom of the gold and green water. Hundreds of other people murmured all around us, and we flowed with their currents about the open gates of the Archbishop's Palace, where the long tunnel of the entryway was lined now with velvet and rich silk.

No light came from the windows where once my girls had lived, but I could see the shapes of women leaning silently on their crossed arms, watching.

We put our empty champagne glasses on the long white-covered bar, and the waiter from the Casino smiled and motioned us to hurry. It was the end of the entr'acte of *Don Giovanni*.

The dry shabby courtyard we had first known was now a most beautiful theater, with rows of seats rising halfway to the eaves, before the enormous proscenium that seemed to disappear when the music started and the singers opened their lips. We knew, as perhaps did few other people there, that under the rich velvet of the entry was the door where Mary had helped carry up costumes into the storerooms with two other offices now, oddly juxtaposed in such a once-revered building, the Bureau of Mental Health and the Aix branch of the Communist Party. And behind the heavy steel bleachers at the far end of the courtyard were the high windows which often Anne and Mary had watched with horror and then murderous delight while silhouetted against a curtain two of the young *Comédiens* would rehearse a violent stabbing, and fine strangulation . . . And then underneath and behind the huge temporary stage, we knew, were the basins of the old fountain, that must once have sounded almost as beautiful as the music the orchestra now played in front of it.

We could remember when a bedraggled tall palm tree (or were there two?) still grew beside the empty pools . . . and the music was telling us that soon we would be not there in the strange theater under the soft sky in the old Palace courtyard, but in front of the village inn where Donna Elvire waited so foolishly, so helplessly, to let love trick her again . . .

That was the first night of almost a month of music, in other places of Aix but mostly there.

The Festival seemed to generate a kind of haze, an enchantment, so that going to the concerts and the operas, and waiting for the music to start and stop and start again, and then walking through the streets empty of any people but others in the same dream, and the moon rising over the proscenium in the courtyard, and the slow glasses of champagne before the music started and the slow walking away again and sleeping in strange deeply purified sleep, wrapped that month with timelessness forever, and made it hard to recall and yet part of our spiritual marrow.

The first night, as if to try to escape before it was too late from this magic, we broke off from the main current of people pushing in a bemused way out through the velvety corridor, and instead of flowing with them on down Gaston-de-Saporta past Brondino's dark shop, we almost ran down the one little street that leads directly into the Place de l'Archevêché, Rue Adanson I think, to the crooked passageway called Esquiche-Coude in Provençal because a big man can scratch his two elbows at once on the sides of it.

It was empty. We staggered, drunk with the music, touching this side and then that of the cool walls, and veering fast around the gentle corners, and laughing in a stifled way. We tiptoed, even at that silly speed. Suddenly we burst into the Rue Gibelin, and then zig and zag and we were in the world again, with the street lights soft and mysterious under the trees of the Cours Mirabeau, and the café tables set far out onto the pavement for the crowds. All of us . . . everyone from *Don Giovanni* . . . felt and looked elegant, weary, exalted, perhaps reborn, with no more half-felt urge to escape.

And then, months later, I went alone to the courtyard of

the old Palace. It was dead, and everything was gone: the bleachers, the orchestra pit, the proscenium. The walls looked shabbier than ever. The entryway, stripped of its false velvet skin, was a drab tunnel, with the handsome carved door at the street end, on the Square, and the delicate iron grille at the other, and leading off it the offices to help the Communists, the mentally unwell, and the stage-struck. The one remaining tree, which the summer before had obviously felt sickly and about to lose its prematurely yellow leaves, had been severely trimmed, and would obviously survive another year or two of partial suffocation in the bleachers, which rose each season to its first branches.

I knew that I must turn my eyes, both inward and outward ones, from the notices that had begun to appear everywhere in Aix about the next Festival. If I could stay for even one night of it, I would be lost, never able to leave again. I knew that.

It was inconceivable that sometime I might do as many others do, and be there just for that month, or even a part of it. I must have the whole, and I must have what comes before and then remains, the slow growing excitement everywhere and the repeated climaxes of all the concerts and operas, and afterwards the voluptuous and bemazed exhaustion and fulfillment. It was all as clear-cut in its preparation, achievement, satisfaction as a perfect sexual experience, but lengthened by the necromancy of great music to weeks instead of hours and minutes . . .

I wanted to be able to go again into the bare courtyard of the old Palace, and stand in the thin February sunshine which was still rich and warm from the color of the walls. Two men that morning were slowly lifting old stone vases onto the edges of the ancient basin of the fountain, which had emerged again, noble and silent, on the south wall. In a few more months the same men would drag the vases out of sight once more, and the fountain would disappear in the gradual monotonous rebuilding of the great stage, and the stone basin would again become a part of the orchestra pit. By the first of June rehearsals would start . . .

For a long minute or perhaps second I knew that I must flee while I could, while I was still a ghost, still free.

Some of the lines of my map were still blurred, too, and there seemed neither time nor space, right then, to strengthen them.

The notes, though, the music: they were not blurred at all.

The sudden sure acknowledgment of this as I stood looking at the courtyard made me feel ready again. I would forever hear the little mandolin, plucked in the orchestra pit while onstage Don Giovanni pretended to play to the silent mockery of an inn where his mock-love listened. And I knew in a fine positive way that I could nevermore walk any street in the whole real world without hearing, somewhere up from the immediate sounds, the quiet music of the fountains of Aix.

The map was made, and there was no place to flee from it, if I might ever again walk any street, listen to any melody of strings or water. The outlines might gradually twist themselves, as they had done with that map of yet another town, Dijon, but I would always know where I was there, in dream or waking life.

I was a ghost, most fortunately, for ghosts can be wherever they *must* be.

I rolled the invisible map carefully so as not to crease it, and walked out through the open lacy iron gates of the Archbishop's Palace, and through the cool stone tunnel, soon to be velvety again. The thin light of spring lay like gold seen through water on the wall of the house where Anne and Mary had once lived. The mouth of the short alleyway to the cloister of St. Sauveur was open and silent. Down the street Brondino's shop was as blankly dusty as a dead moth.

When I turned onto Espariat toward the Hôtel de Provence I stopped, listening with my sharp ghost-ears to the sound of the water dropping serenely from basin to basin in the Albertas fountain. This time my children would be waiting for me under the faint returning green of the trees on the Cours. The next time, I knew by now, might be any time at all, whether or not the map was exactly true to scale, and plumb, and legible to other eyes than mine. I need not worry about coming back, for I was there anyway.

A
Considerable
Town

M. F. K. FISHER

For my girls and my sister

MARSEILLE: 13 B. du Rh., Provence; 893 771 h.

Voir: Basilique N.D. de-la-Garde; La Canebière; Vieux Port; Corniche Président J. F. Kennedy; Port moderne; Palais Longchamps; Basilique St.-Victor; Cathédrale de la Major et anc. Cathédrale de la Major; Parc du Pharo.

Musees: 4

Excursions: Bateau, autobus, chemin de fer, avion (Office de Tourisme, Acceuil de France, T.C.F., etc.)

Paris 777 km, Lyons 315, Nice 187, Toulon 64, Toulouse 400, Turin 370

Hotels: 28, de 'grand luxe' à 'simple mais convenable'

Restaurants agréables: 20 en ville, 5 sur la Corniche

—1976 Michelin Guide to *France*

MARSEILLE: Bouches du Rhone, Provence: postal zone, 13

To see: Basilica of Notre Dame de la Garde; The Canebière; Old Port; Cliff-highway J. F. Kennedy; Modern Port; Longchamps Palace; Basilica of St. Victor; Cathedral of La Major and ancient Cathedral; the Pharo Park.

Museums: four main ones listed.

Transportation and **Excursions** by water, railway, bus, and air. **Information:** Tourism Office, French Welcome Center, etc.

Paris, 777 km. from Marseille; Lyons, 315; Nice, 187; Toulon, 64; Toulouse, 400; Turin, 370.

Hotels: 28 listed, ranging from luxurious to "plain but decent."

Restaurants: in the same categories, 20 listed in the city, and 5 on the Kennedy Corniche.

—A simplified version of the several pages
devoted to Marseille in the 1976 Michelin
Guide to *France*

ICI
VERS L'AN 600 AVANT J.C.
DES MARINS GRECS ONT ABORDES
VENANT DE PHOCEE
ILS FONDERENT MARSEILLE
D'OU RAYONNA EN OCCIDENT
LA CIVILISATION

[Here,
in about 600 B.C.,
Greek sailors of Phocea came ashore.
They founded Marseille,
from which civilization spread
throughout the
Western world.]

—Bronze plate sunk in pavement of
the Quai des Belges on the Vieux Port,
at the foot of the Canebière

Alphonse de Lamartine   en 1832
Frédéric Chopin   en 1839
George Sand
       séjournèrent en cet hôtel

[Lamartine,
and Chopin with George Sand,
stayed in this hotel]

—Plaque outside the entrance of
the Hotel Beauvau

PLAN

DE

MARSEILLE

Ville considérable de Provence
Fameux Port sur la Mer Méditerranée
par
Nicolas de Fer
Graveur et Géographe
1702

[Map of Marseille,
a considerable town of Provence
and famous Mediterranean port . . . by Nicolas de Fer,
engraver and geographer,
1702]

CONTENTS

A CONSIDERABLE TOWN

Chapter 1

THE PLACE
WHERE
I LOOKED

One of the many tantalizing things about Marseille is that most people who describe it, whether or not they know much about either the place or the languages they are supposedly using, write the same things. For centuries this has been so, and a typically modern opinion could have been given in 1550 as well as 1977.

Not long ago I read one, mercifully unsigned, in a San Francisco paper. It was full of logistical errors, faulty syntax, misspelled French words, but it hewed true to the familiar line that Marseille is doing its best to live up to a legendary reputation as world capital for "dope, whores, and street violence." It then went on to discuss, often erroneously, the essential ingredients of a true bouillabaisse! The familiar pitch had been made, and idle readers dreaming of a great seaport dedicated to heroin, prostitution, and rioting could easily skip the clumsy details of marketing for fresh fish. . . .

"Feature articles" like this one make it seem probable that many big newspapers, especially in English-reading countries, keep a few such mild shockers on hand in a back drawer, in case a few columns need filling on a rainy Sunday. Apparently people like to glance one more time at the same old words: evil, filthy, dangerous.

Sometimes such journalese is almost worth reading for its precociously obsolete views of a society too easy to forget. In 1929, for instance, shortly before the Wall Street Crash, a popular travel writer named Basil Woon published *A Guide to the Gay World of France: From Deauville to Monte Carlo* (Horace Liveright, New York). (By now even his use of word "gay" is quaintly naïve enough for a small chuckle. . . .)

Of course Mr. Woon was most interested in the Côte d'Azur, in those far days teeming and staggering with rich English and even richer Americans, but while he could not actively recommend staying in Marseille, he did remain true to his journalistic background with an expectedly titillating mention of it:

> If you are interested in how the other side of the world lives, a trip through old Marseilles—by daylight—cannot fail to thrill, but it is not wise to venture into this district at night unless dressed like a stevedore and well armed. Thieves, cutthroats, and other undesirables throng the narrow alleys, and sisters of scarlet sit in the doorways of their places of business, catching you by the sleeve as you pass by. The dregs of the world are here, unsifted. It is Port Said, Shanghai, Barcelona, and Sidney combined. Now that San Francisco has reformed, Marseilles is the world's wickedest port.

(Mr. Woon's last sentence, written some fifty years ago, is more provocative today than it was then, to anyone interested in the shifting politics of the West Coast of America. . . .)

While I either accept or deplore what other people report about the French town, and even feel that I understand why they are obliged to use the words they do (Give the public what it wants, etc., etc. . . .), I myself have a different definition of the place, which is as indefinable as Marseille itself: *Insolite*.

There seems to be no proper twin for this word in English; one simply has to sense or feel what it means. Larousse says that it is somewhat like "contrary to what is usual and normal." Dictionaries such as the Shorter Oxford and Webster's Third International try words like *apart, unique, unusual*. This is not enough, though . . . not quite right. Inwardly I know that it means *mysterious, unknowable*, and in plain fact, *indefinable*.

And that is Marseille: indefinable, and therefore *insolite*. And the strange word is as good as any to explain why the place haunts me and draws me, with its phoenixlike vitality, its implacably realistic beauty and brutality. The formula is plain: Marseille = *insolite*, therefore *insolite* = Marseille.

This semantical conclusion on my part may sound quibbling, but it seems to help me try to explain what connection there could possibly, logically, be between the town and me . . . why I have returned there for so long: a night, ten nights, many weeks or months.

Of course it is necessary to recognize that there is a special karma about Marseille, a karmic force that is mostly translated as wicked, to be avoided by all clean and righteous people. Travellers have long been advised to shun it like the pesthole it has occasionally been, or at best to stay there as short a time as possible before their next ship sets sail.

A true karmic force is supposed to build up its strength through centuries of both evil and good, in order to prevent its transmigration into another and lesser form, and this may well explain why Marseille has always risen anew from the ashes of history. There seems to be no possible way to stamp it out. Julius Caesar tried to, and for a time felt almost sure that he had succeeded. Calamities caused by man's folly and the gods' wrath, from the plagues ending in 1720 to the invasions ending in the 1940s, have piled it with rotting bodies and blasted rubble, and the place has blanched and staggered, and then risen again. It has survived every kind of weapon known to European warfare, from the ax and arrow to sophisticated derivatives of old Chinese gunpowder, and it is hard not to surmise that if a nuclear blast finally leveled the place, some short dark-browed men and women might eventually emerge from a few deep places, to breed in the salt marshes that would gradually have revivified the dead waters around the Old Port. . . .

Meanwhile, Marseille lives, with a unique strength that plainly scares less virile breeds. Its people are proud of being "apart," and critics mock them for trying to sound even more Italianate than they are, trying to play roles for the tourists: fishermen ape Marcel Pagnol's *Marius* robustly; every fishwife is her own Honorine. The Pinball Boys are thinner and more viperous there than anywhere in Europe, they assume as true Marseillais, and the tarts are tarter and the old hags older and more haggish than anywhere in the world. . . .

Behind this almost infantile enjoyment of playing their parts on a superb stage with changing backdrops that are certainly *insolite*, and a full orchestration of every sound effect from the ringings of great bells to the whine of the tramontane and the vicious howl of the mistral, held together by sirens from ambulances and ships, and the pinpricks of complaining seagulls . . . behind this endlessly entertaining and absorbing melodrama, a secret life-source provides its inner nourishment to the citizens.

There is a strong religious blood flowing in that corporate body. Catholics and other Christians, Communists, Free-thinkers, Arabs, Gypsies, all admit to an acceptance of powers beyond their questionings, whether or not they admit to *being* "believers." The gigantic bell Marie-Joséphine, at the top of Notre Dame de la Garde, rings for every soul that has ever lived there, no matter how much a race-bound parishioner of St. Victor might deny the right of a Moslem in the Panier across the Old Port to understand its reassuring voice.

Naturally, in a place as old and *insolite* as Marseille, there is a strong dependence on forces that are loosely called occult, or mystical, or perhaps demonic. There are many fortune-tellers, usually thriving in their chosen ways of neighborhood help or prestigious social acclaim. The best known of the Tarot cards were adapted to a special ritual that evolved there, and are called by the town's name. Cabalistic signs are often in or on graffiti, political or otherwise, and it is plain that the right people will see and understand them. Why not? After all, the churches build their altars over early Christian sepulchers laid in turn upon the stones of temples built to Artemis and Adonis, who in turn . . .

There is a good description of the withdrawn side of the noisy, rough-talking Marseillais in one of Simenon's books about Inspector Maigret. It was written about another French town, but it is Marseille to me:

> . . . a stone jungle, where you can disappear for months; where often you do not hear of a crime until weeks after it has been committed; where thousands of human beings . . . live on the fringes of the Law, in a world where they can find as many accomplices and hideouts as they need, and

where the police put out their bait now and then and pull in a fish they were waiting for, all the while depending more for such luck on a telephone call from a jealous girl or an informer. . . .

This quasi-occult mutism is what has helped defeat the invaders of Marseille, I think. Certainly it baffled the last militant "occupants" in the 1940s. Many different stories are told about how and why a large part of the ancient Greco-Roman bank of the Old Port was destroyed by the Germans, but the basic reason for this move was probably that they simply could not keep track of what was going on in the deep warrens that went up from the Quai du Port past Les Accoules toward La Vieille Charité and the Place des Moulins. What was worse, they could not tell from the flat black eyes, the blank unmoved faces of occupants of this filthy old neighborhood, the pimps and bawds and small-time gangsters who went there as a natural refuge when their other ways of life were interrupted by war, which of them were working with what appointed or subterranean leaders, and even which of them might be town fathers in false beards rather than black marketeers dealing indirectly with the invaders.

The answer was to get rid of the whole infamous district, and it was easy to have the German-appointed city council approve a plan to blow up the mess from underground. It was done neatly, with complete evacuation of the helpless residents and full warning to the numberless unknown invisibles who were using the old tunnels for their special version of the Liberation. (Some other destruction during that dubious time was less circumspect, of course, and a few foul tricks were blamed on the invaders when an orphanage, or a clinic, say, was without notice shattered from above and not below ground. . . .)

Soon after the dirty tunnels and gutters above the Quai

du Port were mined and hopefully wiped out, they were once more in full swing, of course: rats and moles know how to dig again. A lot of the diggers were summarily lined up and shot, but that did not seem to impress the strange breed called Marseillais for so many centuries. Some thirty-five years later, the whole quarter is threatened with a new demolition, to make way for high-rise housing projects, but the people who live there, as elsewhere in the big town, remain impassive and tough and sardonic . . . that is to say, *insolite.*

This cannot be a guidebook, the kind that tells how, with a chart to be got free from the driver of the tour, to follow a green line from A to G and then switch to either the red or the yellow lines to Z, depending on how weary or hungry one may feel. I am not meant to tell anyone where to go in Marseille, nor even why I myself went where I did there, and saw and smelled and felt as I did. All I can do in this explanation about my being there is to write something about the town itself, through my own senses.

I first spent a night there in late 1929, and since then I have returned even oftener than seems reasonable. Beginning in 1940, there were wars, both worldwide and intramural, and then I managed to regain my old rhythm. Each time I went back, I felt younger: a chronological miracle, certainly!

One reason I now try to explain all this is that when I cannot return, for physical or perhaps financial reasons, I will stay so enriched and heartened by what I have known there that I should be the envy of every crowned head of several worlds. I boast, and rightly. Nobody who has lived as deeply for as long as I have in Marseille-Insolite can be anything but blessed.

There is an almost impossible lot of things to see there, and for one reason or another I know many of them, and have been part of them with people I loved (another proud boast!). If I started to tell why I wished everybody in the world could do the same, it would make a whole book, a personal guide tour, and that is not what I am meant to write, according to my secret directives. I would say words like Longchamps, Borély, Cantini, Les Accoules, St. Victor, St. Nicolas, La Place des Moulins, La Vieille Charité, Notre Dame de la Garde, La Rue de Rome . . . and it would be for every unexpected reason known to human beings, from the smell of a sick lion in a zoo behind Longchamps to an obviously necrophilic guardian of the tombs in Borély to the cut of an exquisite tweed skirt in a Paris boutique on the Rome. Each reason I gave for wanting some people to know why I've been there would make the guide a long hymn, hopefully shot through with practical asides about how far Borély is from town, and how steep the walk is up through the Panier to the Vieille Charité, and how much to tip the elderly patient men at places like the Musée des Docks Romains . . . and yes, why did I not mention it before? Other places, other sounds: they tumble in my head like pebbles under a waterfall, and all I know is that I must try to understand why I myself go back to this strange beautiful town.

If I could be in only one part of it, I would go directly to the Old Port, and stay there. I know that a lot of people consider it hopelessly touristic or noisy or vulgar. I feel at ease there, perhaps more so than in any other populous place I have ever known. Most of the reasons for this escape me or were never even guessed, but the fact remains that if I could within the next three minutes go by teleportation to the Quai des Belges on the Vieux Port, I would know exactly what to do and say and eat, and would feel as welcome as any shadow. It is very nice to feel like this.

The Vieux Port has a narrow entrance, past the Pharo Palace that Napoleon III built for his Empress, so that from almost any part of its three quays it looks landlocked. Every Marseillais, though, and almost every stranger there, knows that out through the tumultuous inlet and past the jetties of the new port of La Joliette lie several little bleak harsh islands, one of them crowned with the tomblike Château d'If that Dumas peopled with his noble ghosts.

Coming back from the Château, sometimes a very rough trip indeed, the Rive Neuve is on one's right, with the Abbey of St. Victor and then La Garde towering over it, and on the waterfront the façade of the Criée, the public auction house for fish. It looks something like a fragment of the Gare de Lyon in Paris, tall and with grimed glassy walls. It is said to be doomed, now that so much transportation is done by trucks and rail from all over Europe, with their mounting traffic problems, but I first heard this as an imminent fact some ten years ago, and it still hums and screams from late night until predawn, and then is as quiet as a church, except for the men who hose down the walls and trestle tables and floors for the next night's biddings. There are usually a few trawlers docked alongside to unload big catches or wait for cleanups.

The Rive Neuve is patchy and beautiful, architecturally, with some fine blocks of buildings that went up at the town end of the Port after the galleys stopped being built in the middle of the eighteenth century, a surprisingly short time ago. There is a dwindling number of good restaurants either on or just off the Quai, and the little fishhouses tacked onto the massive old blocks are tacky indeed to look at, and mostly evanescent. Portside there are private moorings for pleasure boats and larger yachts, a couple of clubs, generous moorings for small professional fishing boats. The feeling is lively, expert, no-nonsense, with several little cafés and chandleries and so on across the Quai.

Auto traffic is heavy and fast there, because of the cars that tear through the tunnel under the mouth of the Old Port from inland. Until the late 1940s, that end of the Port was hurdled by a strange thin loop of steel, referred to locally by several names, the most respectful being the "shore-to-shore hustler." Once Simenon wrote of it as a "gigantesque metal carcass, cutting across the horizon, on which one can make out, from a distance, tiny human beings." Raoul Dufy said it even better, with paint.

It seems odd to me that I never noticed the obtrusive "*pont transbordeur*," until it was gone when I went back after the Occupation, in about 1951. It had always been there when I was, but since I had never seen the horizon any way but barred, I accepted it without question as part of the magic. It was no more gigantesque than any other man-made edifice: Notre Dame de la Garde, ugly but inspiring; St. Victor, ugly but reassuring; the aerial bridge, ugly but practical. Then when I returned to Marseille with my two small girls, I stood in a window in the old Hotel Beauvau on the Quai des Belges and felt a shock that made me gasp: the bridge was gone! The sky was free! Our eyes could look out over the boats, past the Pharo, which from the harbor always seemed more like a hospital than a palace, and then bend down as surely as any seagull's onto the tumble of rough water into La Joliette and our own Port! Perhaps it was the way a young sheep feels after its first shearing, very lightsome and cool suddenly.

The Quai des Belges is the shortest of the Port's three shores, at the head, the land end, of the little harbor. Like all centers of life past and present, it is concentrated, so that it has fine-to-sad restaurants and brasseries and commerce and mad traffic and a church and a bus terminal cramped onto the land side, with a subway station to open shortly, and then on the Port side docks for all the excursion boats to the Château d'If, and so on, with careful room for the fishermen to chug in six or seven mornings a week to set up their rickety tables in the casual market that strings out along the wide sidewalk.

For a long time in my Marseille life, the Quai des Belges had a sloping place where boats could be drawn up onto the pavement. When the wind was wild, water came onto the street, over the big plaque that tells how the Phoceans landed there. Then in perhaps the early sixties, some time after the *pont transbordeur* was taken down, the sloping pebbly pavement was made level with the rest of the Quai, and the edge went sharply down into the water so that it was uniformly convenient for the fishermen to put in with their catches for their wives to sell. Who dragged his craft up on shore, anymore, for a rest or some quick repairs? What fine ladies waited there to be rowed into mid-Port and then handed up to their sailing vessels?

One time, before the old beaching place was changed, I watched a small grey vessel of the American Navy swing delicately down the middle of the harbor, ease itself sideways within a few feet of the slope, and unload . . . disgorge . . . explode . . . what seemed like hundreds of sailors. I stood upstairs in my window, on that Christmas Eve, and it looked as if the young men flew onto the wet sloping pavement from their deck, without even touching the little boat alongside that was meant as a bridge. They gathered in knots on the windy Quai, and then melted fast in three directions, but mostly up the Can o' Beer.

Later a few strings of Christmas lights went on, looking pretty, but the next day there was almost no sign of life on the grim little vessel, and before the second dawn she slipped out of the harbor, presumably with her full crew. She was the last overtly military vessel I ever saw in the Vieux Port, although I suspect derring-do of international proportions in a few superpowerful-elegant-sleek-rich yachts I have watched there. (The whole district is more James Bond than Henry Kissinger!)

Around the north corner of the Quai des Belges, past the old church that is sinking slowly into the mouth of the Lacydon River (poetic justice, some infidels say!), the church that still shelters a few of the last of Marseille's infamous army of public beggars, there is the long ancient unequivocal stretch of wide street and wider portside pavement called the Quai du Port. Boats stretch from the Quai des Belges out to the Harbor Master's Quarters just before the Fort St. Jean and the entrance to the harbor. Near town they are small plain craft with oars, outboard motors and no masts, often scruffy, but looking as familiar as housecats. Until a few years ago, retired fishermen used to wait there to snag visitors, and take them jerking and bouncing on "tours" of La Joliette.

These self-styled tours were never the same, never dull. There were two or three little boats with awnings, I remember. They cost more, but were reassuring to visiting friends when we went over the bumps between the Vieux Port and the breakwater of the new port. One time in La Joliette we were putt-putting along under the prows of gigantic ships loading for Africa and Indo-China, and suddenly looked up into a beautiful Spanish or Italian vessel and its elegant Captain's Quarters, with mullioned windows and rich brocade curtains! It was a facsimile of one of Christopher Columbus's little toys, that had been made for movies and international fairs, and was being taken under motor power to Naples or Barcelona or some such coincidental port. The clean brutal outlines of a diesel freighter to Djakarta were almost a relief.

Farther along the Quai du Port, and especially in front of the little Town Hall that was saved from explosion by mutual agreement with the Invaders in 1943, there are dreamily beautiful yachts of every club and country. They come in and out. Usually they are in fine condition, at least to the eye, and now and then a lithe crewman polishes brass, but in general they are empty when we loiterers glance or stare at them. One time a "tall ship" with three masts, all painted a dull coal black, lay alongside the Town Hall for several weeks, and nobody seemed to know why, or what it was. It flew the French flag. And once in 1976 the ugliest hull I ever saw lay there, not attracting much notice.

It had faky anchors painted here and there near its prow, and was plainly some sort of mockery of everything beautiful about an ocean-going vessel, with almost no superstructure and yet without a single porthole that could be seen. It too was a flat ugly black, and was lettered minutely, *Club Méditerranée*. I knew about that so-called social corporation, of course, and asked a couple of Quai-watchers if it was going to be turned into a party ship. There was no answer, more than a shrug. It seemed strange, to look over from the Beauvau, too, and see that uncouth thing in front of the dainty little Town Hall.

Within a day or so, of course, when I was back in Aix and reading local interpretations of Marseille news instead of being there to garner the real truth of such matters (!), I learned that the ship was already famous, and would compete for the Atlantic International Cup on a solo volage. It would be piloted mostly by electronics, and by a single Marseillais, alone in that dreadful carcass. I felt sick and fascinated and strangely embarrassed at my own unawareness, and I followed the log of the *Club Med* the whole way, and felt triumphant when it joined the "tall ships" in the great bicentennial parade on the Hudson River, July 4, 1976. I felt proud.

On the harbor water, which is somewhat cleaner as one goes along the Quai seaward, are docked the trawlers, the *chalutiers*, the vessels needing a deep draft for their enormous nets and, in port, their full hulls. They come into port to discharge their big fish across the harbor at the Criée, and then dock at the Quai du Port to keep their papers in order with the Harbor Master, and perhaps rest a few hours or days for the sakes of their crews. Drydocks mean going up the coast, although the smaller crafts have their own simple lifts along the Quai.

Most of the organizations of Vieux boat owners, professional and social, are housed portside on the ancient shore, and they are called Nautical Societies or Syndicates or Friendly Rowing Clubs or Lacydonian Brotherhoods or suchlike. They have simple clubhouses, firmly fenced off from the wide walk where people stroll and where nets are mended. Usually on weekends young couples chip at a small dangling hull, or paint seriously while the family dog or baby watches from the cobbles. Now and then a Sunday crowd on the Quai looks amiably over the fence as a group of amateur fishermen grill their catch of sardines and cool their fingers on plentiful bottles. The whole thing smells good: fish, wine, smoke from the burning driftwood; fresh paint from the next Société des Canotiers to the east; westward a whiff of tar from a modest drydock. On weekdays professionals take over the Quai, and watchers are fewer as men work hard on their boats or nets, and the air can be very salty.

Landside there are somber arcades almost hysterically lighted by countless thin deep espresso joints, and a few excellent restaurants that in fine weather flood their tables as far as possible out across the sidewalks toward the traffic, which is not quite as lethal as on the Rive Neuve. There seems no need for music, although now and then in summer a flameblower or a tumbler will pick up a few coins from the more sated diners.

As one moves back toward the Quai des Belges along the port, the gastronomy swings from pasta to bouillabaisse, and from Chianti to white house-wine, and the restaurants are more filled with tourists and with locals on a little weekend spree than they are with vacationing decorators and actors from "up North." It is pleasant, a good way to eat and talk, and behind, the pinball machines throb on, and the tiny espresso cups sit half-empty everywhere in the long bright bars.

And then behind the arcades and the pinball joints rise the graceful hills, where the Greeks and then the Romans built temples and theatres on the sites of older altars. Now the clock tower of Les Accoules rises sturdily, if off-time, as it did for other purposes in the thirteenth century, and leads up to the old Place des Moulins through streets that are cleaner than they have sometimes been, but still suspect to tidy travellers and even some City Fathers, who would like to get rid of them for high-rise condominiums.

And at the land's-end of the Port, high and straight behind the Quai des Belges to the west, new but lightsomely majestic, rises Longchamps, which cannot be suspected except from hilltops or out at sea. It is an astonishing public building, one that could never have been erected in France except in the mid-nineteenth century, when Napoleon III's taste was rampant. It spouts water in controlled extravagance from great carved mouths, down many churning basins toward the thirsty town, and on out along the course of the ancient Lacydon toward the open sea. It sweeps the Vieux Port cleaner than it has been since men started to pollute it some two thousand years ago, and then clogged it foully when they built over the mouth of the old river. Around this majestic waterworks that spews its blessings from the wicked river of the Durance, first curbed in 1838, is built a garishly wonderful palace that houses natural and manmade history, and that hides a relatively tiny little botanical garden and zoo. It is all almost nightmarish at close range, like being lost in a fetal Disneyland, but from afar, Longchamps is beautiful.

It is one of the reasons I want to say why I must return to its town. When I have tried to tell natives that I need to write about it, they are courteous in their own sardonic way. They do not mock too openly, but they manage to imply flatly that I am presumptuous: "Ah? You think that after a few visits here you can explain this place? Good luck!" Once a man who was repairing a typewriter for me lost some of his remoteness and said almost angrily that he was astounded at the effrontery of people who felt they could understand a subject or a race or a cult in a few minutes. I told him I felt humble about it, but undaunted, and we talked about how a model can sit in a room with ten painters and have ten different pictures of herself result. "Yes, your picture will not be mine," he said. I said, "I don't want to explain Marseille. I want to try to tell what it does about explaining myself," and we parted amicably, and not for the last time. Now and then taxi drivers have asked me why I stayed in Marseille, and I have told them that I did not want to leave until I had to, and they have either said I was a misguided sentimentalist or have indicated plainly that I should shut up.

The whole implication has been that nobody can understand anything about Marseille except the Massiliotes, as they used to be called. It is almost like the mystique of being a Gypsy. Either you are or you are damned, condemned, blasphemed, as *not*.

This is doubtless true, and in ways too mysterious to probe. But there is no reason why I cannot write about how I, an obvious Anglo-Saxon of American citizenship and birth, must accept the realization that I feel at ease in Marseille. Just as I can shrug off or laugh at the conditioned reactions of many of "us" to the place and its seething movement of people, all held in focus by the phoenix-race bred there since pre-Ségobridgian times, so I can enjoy an occasional soft voice, a reassuring pat on the shoulder. I felt pleased to have a wise old citizen of the town write directly to me in his *Evocations du Vieux Marseille*: "It is like no other town on earth." That is what I need to have him say, because I can never know as well as he does what we both still know.

And it is nice to read, in a letter Mme. de Sévigné wrote to her daughter in 1672,

> I am ecstatic about the peculiar beauty of this town. Yesterday, the weather was heavenly, and the place where I looked over the sea, the fortresses, the mountains, and the city is astonishing . . . I must apologize to Aix, but Marseille is lovelier and livelier than it, in proportion to Paris itself! There are at least a hundred thousand people here; and I cannot even try to count how many of them are beauties: the whole atmosphere makes me somewhat untrustworthy!

Chapter 2

THE CANEBIÈRE

I

The Can o' Beer, as countless English-speaking sailors have long called it, is by now a wide, ugly twentieth-century street that lives in their memories more for what its neighboring alleys offer them than for its own merits. It rises in a gigantic phallic thrust from the Vieux Port eastward toward the hard white hills that much of Marseille is built on, and in spite of its almost bleak lack of beauty, it throbs with vitality drawn from the body of the sea, the ancient riverbed it follows, the people who throng its wide sidewalks and race between its stoplights in every kind of mechanical transportation.

The Canebière has stretched along the path of the ancient sacred stream, the Lacydon, since before A.D. 909, when it was mentioned in a document of the Abbey of St. Victor, or perhaps since 1667 when King Louis XIV ordered new buildings along the path ropemakers had traced to gather hemp from its marshy banks. The whole length, of about a mile, was until 1928 called by three different names as it rose from the Old Port to the high hill where Longchamps now spouts out its beneficent waters, to replace the clogged and dwindling Lacydon in its ancient fight to cleanse an almost landlocked little harbor on the salty but nearly tideless Mediterranean.

The Lacydon was revered for its purity, by priests and people, long before Protis landed near its mouth in about 600 B.C., and even now its name has a watery magic in Marseille. Little fishing boats and sleek yachts and stylish clubs and marinas are called for it, and erudite diggers still probe its fresh-water springs, its banks and prehistoric camp-sites under concrete and stone and plaster, for artifacts to fix its dates firmly in history and not fable.

And over the ancient river a flood of traffic now flows, for many hours of every day. Past midnight a few signs still glare above the empty sidewalks, but except for the width of them and the street itself, it looks like any sleepy, small-town Broadway in Kansas or California.

It comes awake early, with people catching buses or hurrying toward the big railroad station of St. Charles on its northern hill. By eight it is bustling with shopkeepers heading for business or buyers for the enormous Marché des Capucins just to the south, or down to the Quai des Belges to get the pick of the fresh fish. By nine most of the shops are open: a mixed bag of elegant jewelry stores and cheap bazaars with tables out on the sidewalk piled with sleazy pants and cardboard shoes; big chain stores like Monoprix, and a famous cake shop, and an almost stylish depot catering to "Ladies of Unusual Build" (i.e., Fat, Skinny); a dozen places to buy perfumes. There are several small "exchanges," where for a barely honest fee, money from any nation in the world can be bought or sold. There are pharmacies, usually with one old well-dressed lady sitting on a chair as if waiting for her prescription to be filled, to add respectability to the age-less trade in miracle cures for everything from warts to tertiary syphilis. There are stylish shoe stores and slick travel agencies, busy snack bars, and at the top of the long street, a few movie houses.

Once, about twenty-five years ago, my little girls and I were rambling up the Canebière, pleasantly full of breakfast and already thinking almost subliminally of ordering fresh grilled sardines for lunch, when a nicely dressed young American came from behind us and said, "Excuse me, but I was listening to you folks talk. And I need help."

We were used to a certain amount of panhandling, although not in good Chicagoese, and Mary (my direct one) asked, "Are you hungry?"

"Yes," he said. "Yes, I'm really starved. Do you mind if I tell you why?" I readied myself for an old pitch: lost passport, got rolled, cable from sick mother.

He walked along beside us, and his story was too good to be anything but true. He had been chosen as Most Promising American Undergraduate by an international "luncheon" club, and for almost two weeks he had been escorted from one French town to another to give a set speech of goodwill ("It mentions Lafayette," he said listlessly) and to sit through endless noonday banquets served in his honor. Every local specialty was produced for his pleasure. In Burgundy, he said, he ate snails four days running and coq au vin, three. In two Alsatian towns he was served *choucroûte garnie* on platters several feet long. Once there was a pig with a glazed apple in its mouth. Somewhere along the line he ate truffles in everything, "even in plain scrambled eggs," he went on as if he were talking to himself.

"I'd be bilious," Mary said, and he said, "No, I really feel

O.K." Then he stopped in his tracks, and said loudly, "But what I want to find out *is*, do you folks know where I can get a hamburger? If I could just eat a hamburger, I'd be all right. Five more days to go . . ."

We went into a huddle on the wide sidewalk, with people skirting us as if we might be contagious or tetched. The children told him that Surcouf made a really fine *boeuf tartare*, if he had enough money, and he said desperately, "That I've got! *Plenty!* But I have to eat a big banquet this noon, and I'll be in some important fellow's house tonight, and all I need is a kind of snack, something to get me through." Then he said, "Would you care to join me, you ladies?"

Anne and Mary loved this overall designation, but grilled sardines lurked somewhere behind the pleasure on their faces. We hated to tell our gastronomical fugitive that we did not know of a single hamburger spot in Marseille, even in Provence; we asked him if he would settle for a fairly good excuse for a hot dog. His face fell and then cheered. We told him how to get to a snack stand near St. Charles. He thanked us with real emotion, and hurried up the Canebière, his head high. The children chided me when I laughed about his problem, and Anne (my hungry one) said she felt quite faint and in fact more so for *food.* . . .

From across the street we read the big signs for porno movies. This was part of the Marseille routine, with my translation of a few words the girls had not yet learned in their convent. Later at lunch we talked again about the boy from Chicago, and decided his trouble might have been worse, if the luncheon clubs had tried to serve him American delicacies like pumpkin pie and fried oysters . . . even hamburgers. . . .

That morning we had stopped for breakfast about a quarter

of the way up the Canebière. We came onto it from our hotel
on the first short street to the right, Rue Beauvau, which runs
from the big main street three blocks to the Opera. In another
short block we passed the monolithic Bourse to the left, and
the little Place across from it, bleak and quiet then, with
plane trees around it but not showing themselves near the
long perspective of the Canebière.

On the west corner of the Place, for a few years into the
fifties, one of the last of the street's famous brasseries looked
almost like an elegant tearoom, or the solarium of an upper-
class English hotel, with comfortable wicker armchairs
painted white. It was patronized, however, by firmly French
gentlemen of all ages past fifty, respectable but not stodgy.
They came in the morning to read their favorite newspapers,
before lunch to meet their peers for a mild drink or two, in
the afternoon to doze or talk or play cards. There were genteel
older ladies at teatime, and attractive younger ones then and
perhaps at night, not all of them on the prowl, but apparently
meeting people like aunts and lovers. And we went there
for breakfast on sunny mornings because it was a fine place
to watch the street, and the croissants and café au lait were
the best we had yet tasted, indeed the best of our whole lives.

(This paragon of cafés is by now a streamlined publicity
office for airplanes, and the only big cafés left on the Canebière are up across from the sad old Hotel de Noailles. They
have a dogged air about them: elderly waiters walk tenderly
on their hopeless feet; the once grand hotel has a Polynesian
cocktail bar, a snack lounge. The few patrons of the café
look as if they would rather be in a tiny narrow pinball joint
than in spacious dinginess. But across the street under the
trees of the Allées de Meilhan, there is the ineffable sight
and smell of the Flower Market, three times a week. . . .)

I I

One block up the Can from the Quai des Belges, there is a strange "tourist" shop on the corner of the Rue Beauvau. I knew at first sight that it was not what it seemed, but what it really was I cannot even guess. For years I was aware of the dust on the windowshelves, which thoroughly hid the interior. The little painted clay figures of the Nativity called *santons*, set up in every local household for Christmas and in every gift shop all year 'round for tourists, were uninteresting. The postcards faded irrevocably. The lampshades made of translucent shells lost any dubious allure they might once have had. But there was always a steady come-and-go of thin young men, certainly not dressed for the fishing boats a few dozen feet away.

Once in about 1960 my children wanted to buy a Christmas present for a dear friend who was sitting in a high window at that moment in the Hotel Beauvau, watching the Port. After long study from the sidewalk of the dirty windowshelves, they discovered a tiny silver icebucket with a bottle of champagne packed in cubes of crystal. That was the predestined offering, and it was Christmas, and we went in for it.

The man behind the rear counter looked at us with what I charitably adjudged to be amazement, and his few dapper customers slid away. He assured us grudgingly that the wee trinket was costly, but my children had saved some money, and put it out grandly for what was later called at Tiffany's in New York a very valuable *fantaisie*, indeed silver, indeed crystal, and worth fifty times what they had paid. (The adored friend was appreciative but uninterested, although his wife liked it.) Both the shady boss and I were glad when we left, but the little girls were prancing with pleasure, and the trinket, dusty as it was, promised well.

I vowed silently to the puzzled uneasy boss, "I'll never come back to interrupt you," and I never did. But years later when I rounded that corner again, people were dragging a safe and cartons from the little shop, and I felt a pang about the dusty *santons*, the obsolete postcards. I longed suddenly for a little gondola made of polished shells that we had often laughed at: it had a light in it that went on and off, to show a geisha doll lying suggestively in a nest of erect coral spikes. It was marked Hong Kong, of course.

Why had I not bought it? There were two reasons: it was so hellishly quaint as to make me seem affected, especially if I carried it in my limited luggage past the mean-eyed customs inspectors in some place like Los Angeles. And I did not want to go into the strange secret shop again. The man behind the counter had not wanted me to come, and especially not to buy anything. He was pretending to sell tourist stuff, but what was he really selling? Whatever it was, I did not want it. My girls' little silver and crystal toy could have been a password, part of a code? Was he a fence or supplier? What was he really selling?

Certainly we got our money's worth, and judging by the low price we paid, although it seemed like a lot to Anne and Mary, he was glad to get rid of the bit of jewelry and us. The shell gondola, so lewd, still amuses me to regret, but I did not care what new front would occupy that corner on the Canebière, and felt nothing but detachment when, not long ago, I went past the little shop and saw the familiar clutter of trash and possible treasures beyond the dusty windows.

The man was back, I thought without curiosity. And my children were safe, by now.

I I I

Two little blocks up from the Vieux Port, on the right-hand side of the wide street and opposite the gigantic but strange appealing monolith called the Bourse, which can be reached by a blood-curdling pattern of pedestrian crossings, is a pleasant small square currently named for Charles de Gaulle.

The Marseillais, at least the kind I have met during the last couple of decades, plainly do not waste much love on their historical Grey Eminence, and when I would say to a taxi driver, "Place de Gaulle, please," I was unfailingly rebuked with a sardonic correction, "The Place du Gé-né-ra-l de Gaulle, perhaps?" Of course I would agree, sometimes with a weakly muttered, "Sorry," and the rest of the ride would be mutually amicable, or at least not hostile politically.

During the Revolution in the late eighteenth century, there was of course a busy guillotine in the little square, then called Liberté, perforce, but I have never received any cruel vibrations there. Once I lived on a small square in Dijon that had held the public guillotine during the worst years of the Revolution, and the gradual presence of its fear and rage became too strong, and I fled after three months. Nothing ugly ever happened to me on the little Place in Marseille, though, unless one counts human contacts: a Gypsy tapping hopelessly on a taxi window, a terrified tipsy Parisian. People have met there in the sunshine and rain for a long time, for good reasons as well as bad, and by now old women call the benches their own, and knit and watch over their new descendants. Many of them look as if they have sold fish or balloons or hot peanuts along the Quai des Belges in their lustier days, and its sounds still roll up to them, over all the noise of traffic, birds, babies.

The Place de Gaulle has been there since it was laid out in 1784, after the Grand Pavilion of the Arsenal of Galleys was torn down. It was called Place de la Tour, for an important man and not a tower. Later it was Necker, again for politically judicious reasons, and while the guillotine took over, it was logically renamed Liberté, and just as reasonably Impérial during the Empire, and then Royale. After the bulky grandeur of the Bourse rose in the 1860s, it gradually and almost grudgingly became known as the Place de la Bourse by the Marseillais, who liked more glamour in their civic vocabulary. It is interesting to speculate on how they will shake off the present unwelcome name, and for what substitute. . . .

Meanwhile the tidy little square is no longer anything it has ever been before, except that it is everything, with a definitely growing karma about it. It is an easy amble from the Vieux Port, and a short block or two from the Opera and its immediately outlying attractions, ranging from the Cozy-à-Go-Go, with rooms by the hour, day, or week, to the comparatively respectable Hotel Beauvau. Not far away in opposite directions are two of the big covered but open markets that feed the town. There is a glass kiosk like a birdcage on one corner of the Place, bulging with courteous fatherly old cops who help bewildered strangers, of which we are many. There are almost always taxis, with their little cafés across the street from the stand, fumy with *pastis* and with disinfectants from the obligatory toilets.

I have roamed around through the square whenever I was near it, for almost fifty years. I keep an eye on things, like what wars do to little shops. Some are empty now that once looked smart and thriving: a place that sold elegant leather gloves and belts and purses is a snack bar, as I remember . . . something fleeting like that. There used to be an English pub, but War and the Exchange and perhaps the Common Market closed it, as happened to a lot of British pharmacies and bars all along the Côte d'Azur, and now it is bleak and boarded up. Some noble old buildings are "modernized" into one-room studio apartments, and a once-stylish café is now an airline agency.

And one time when the Place was hastily being transformed into a little park for a Christmas present to Marseille, I watched the tall plane trees that ring three sides of it being pruned in what seemed a crazily brutal way. It was painful. They were butchered. Some of us stood outside the barricades and watched with real dismay as the fine trees endured this punishment. Then, magically, for Christmas Eve and the formal opening with its speeches and music, the tall trees turned into *arbres de Noël*, twinkling with thousands of little lights the color of champagne. By now they are still Christmas trees every winter, but lend cool green beauty to everything around them in the summertime, like fashion models, artificially tall and graceful.

After World War II, there seemed to be an extra lot of thin tumblers and jugglers doing shaky handstands on old carpets rolled out on the pavement of what was still the Place de la Bourse, but since about 1971 when the Old Girl got her face lifted again and wore a new if somewhat unwelcome name, she has become a charming if comparatively colorless little square, and it is rather difficult to think of it screaming with furious citizens, running with blood, blazing with firebrands.

Parts of it are a little sunken, but not so much as to be hard on oldsters and toddlers. The modern benches are many, and artfully comfortable. There is water waving musically up from shallow basins. The shrewdly planted shrubbery is low enough to discourage satyrs and agile muggers. (There

are few of the latter in a port town dedicated to more serious crime, but no doubt the tidy little park has its fair share
of licentious dreamers, even in broad daylight. . . .)

It is a nice place now, very nice, very pretty, and a few
years after its latest rebirth it has a pleasant feeling of *being*
there, of being accepted . . . at least until another leader can
lend his political, emotional, and usually posthumous name
to it. It will surely be called less cynically than by its present
one. And underneath the new pavements and fountains and
perhaps pre-Martian and probably post-hydrogen artifacts
called monuments, there will always lie very old bones.

I V

There have been rich invaders in Marseille since the first
men found its salty swamps, and it has always made good
money for them. That is why its Chamber of Commerce,
oldest in France and perhaps the world, is powerful and
canny, controlling airports, canals, harbors, tunnels, gov-
erned by a constantly renewed body of local merchants with
a real doge as their leader, some of them already as subtly
Arabian by now as they have been Corsican, Sicilian, Roman,
back through the Greeks to the Ségobridgians themselves . . .

After the all-powerful body was formed in 1599, it func-
tioned in several places on the Quai du Port until it moved
into the new Town Hall in 1673. It continued to grow,
along with the city, and shifted to temporary quarters near
where it is now, until Prince Louis Napoleon laid the first
stone in 1852 for the present heavy enormous rectangle called
La Bourse. In 1860, when he was an emperor at least pro tem,
he inaugurated this temple to Man's studiously regulated

cupidity, and it still stands, facing what is for a time called the Place de Gaulle.

There is a majestic anchor of great *machismo* in front of the impressive bulk of the temple. Inside, there are hidden delights. On the main floor, in what was meant as a kind of atrium, there is a quite fascinating maritime history of the Old and New Ports, with good maps and models; higher is an excellent public library of the town's past, to be reached and enjoyed at certain times on specified days, and worth every frustrating assault, through long corridors and up endless staircases at the back of the palace; there is even a post office on one side, where I once watched a girl stamp and mail a large flimsy straw hat with a ribbon on it saying "Souvenir de Nice." (This may sound trivial, but her insouciance and the clerk's sardonic acceptance were part of the town.)

Of course ports are places of traffic, in and out, and Marseille has been trafficking in most of our human commodities since before Protis, the Phocean, went there in about 600 B.C.

The Greeks had been stopping along the Mediterranean coast a long time, usually to buy salt before putting out for England and its valuable metals, or perhaps to head directly home again with a full load of the precious stuff. Undoubtedly there was other traffic with the illiterate but canny Ségobridgians: a few coins for a night with a lady, a small amphora of wheat or wine for a night with a girl. Protis was apparently the first sailor to stop in the marshy little harbor and then be paid for *his* favors: the night he anchored his galley, he was offered the King's daughter Gyptis by her own impetuous choice, if he would stay and rule with her. Who could refuse? How could he lose?

This forthright bartering is as intrinsic now as it was then, in the young captain's powerful new kingdom, and is probably why the first Chamber of Commerce was established in Marseille almost four hundred years ago. The control has always been rigidly honorable and cautious, but under its almost imperial nose a dozen other international markets have continued to flourish. Not one of them is new. Now and then, and thanks perhaps to social pressures, some rare woman can be worth more than olive oil or salt, but at this moment heroin and cocaine are much more profitable to handle than "white slaves" ever were. . . .

Marseille is noted, as well as notorious, for its drug traffic. It is, as it always has been, a perfect center for any such trading, on the Mediterranean with three ancient continents at hand, and therefore close to depthless sources of raw material. It has a perfect Old Port, and an impressively efficient new one, easy of access and therefore of quick exit, with convenient depots in outmoded big villas scattered over the hills. It is very old, and so it is accustomed and amenable to every kind of trafficking, neither with open welcome nor with disapproval and punishment, but with ageless disinterest. It is also new and alert, and can offer the most modern laboratories and processing plants for uncountable amounts of opium and other raw drugs that are reduced, cut, tricked, distributed, mostly to the West and perhaps most of all to the Americas.

Of course some opiates are used in Marseille, as they have long been on this planet, wherever there is either sated abundance or intolerable misery. (Even the word Canebière is derived from the Latin one for hemp!) I myself have never watched any "pushing" there, although I have openly been offered a fix on Geary Street in San Francisco, and more than once in women's toilets in luxury hotels from there to New York and back.

In Marseille, I have never noticed what I would identify as a user or addict in need of his help, although I am sure this cannot be literally so: various forms of human sadness become part of any great scene, and do not stand out. Here at home I have often been depressed or frightened by obvious highs-and-lows of people I have watched or known. But as Joseph Conrad once wrote, the Marseillais are an abstemious race, so that just as he never saw any very fat or very thin townspeople, so have I never been conscious of a badly drugged state in anyone I've seen there. (In this same vein, I have rarely seen a Marseillais more than happily tiddly from wine or *pastis*, although I am sure that alcoholism and drug addiction are commoner than they may have been one or two thousand years ago.)

Of course trade, illicit or straight, breeds its own form of subtle inebriation, and I have watched well-dressed burghers leaving the new Chamber of Commerce, or the great banks near the Place Castellane and the Rond-Point, whose clothes were only a shade more impeccably conservative, whose careful steps were only a shade steadier, than those of their henchmen around the Vieux Port. All of them have the same faces, carefully controlled in public, cold as hawks, with well-massaged jowls and a subtly Caesarean look that means heady power in the old town, as it has since the General himself reduced it to comparative serfdom in a deadly squabble with Pompey in 49 B.C.

These men all possess an intoxicating strength, and are affably courteous when they meet one another at lunch in stylish restaurants. At night it is different, and the so-called leaders of the town, escorting women obviously their wives, never recognize their shadier counterparts, as obviously dining with beautiful Scandinavian ski bunnies down from Davos or costly-looking Paris mannequins "resting" in Nice. The traders' faces are different with sundown: more socially cautious on the one hand, on the other more arrogantly relaxed. The next morning, though, masks fit on again, and barter in international oil stocks as well as heroin, race horses, and girls will go on addictively, as it has for almost too long to recall.

According to local and even worldwide reports, traditional mob control has lost its power in Marseille crime levels. There are apparently no solid leaders; worse yet, a single one is missing, the *capo*, the *chef*. Instead, many small groups, their goons inept spratlings in an ancient shark-infested sea, fumble through petty holdups and car thefts and riots, mostly in neighboring provincial towns, or simply "wait around," as the Pinball Boys seemed doomed to do, pandering a little, betting punily, snoozing off the caffein shakes.

Meanwhile, the vulpine traders and their henchmen keep an eye on the general state of things, perhaps waiting like many other earthlings for another Capone or Hitler. Business is good, although in flux: cocaine, hash, and heroin sell well in the West, but sexual permissiveness has hurt the flesh market.

Local Catholics are bitter against Protestants about their apparent tolerance of this new promiscuity. Protestants are equally bitter about Romish "charity" toward the insane acceptance of "Arab" citizens since the Algerian troubles in the early 1960s. Both religious groups in turn are openly hostile and even vicious about denouncing the Communists for all this. Trade suffers, but continues.

And the honored Marseillais who carry on their long supervision of the many-colored commerce of the city know almost atavistically that ideological strife has never much hurt the market. They have been appointed to four-year terms in the Chamber to "guard and defend their fellow-citizens on land and sea," and since 1599 have done so. If they must share their fashionable tailors with the traders they smile to at lunch at the Jambon de Parme or the Pescadou and then cut dead at dinner in the New York, they act with one eye on their city's honor and the other on its prosperity. Their mystical fortress, the Bourse, is behind them.

The palatial Bourse itself has had its whole face washed, slowly, side after side. It has been scrubbed and scraped, a gigantic and tedious cosmetic process all round, and especially on the Canebière façade, with its heroic statues stonily enduring most intimate explorations for soot, bird lice, mildew, and related grime. For a few decades now it may look somewhat friendlier and less austere than when it sulks behind city dirt, but never more ponderously important. The little square across the street remains subject to frequent changes of names, depending upon the times, but it seems inconceivable that the enormous fortress of the old-young Bourse will not signify commercial security for several centuries more, to the canny citizens who trust in it as a potent symbol.

V

A little farther up the Canebière from the Bourse is the Cours St. Louis, a pretty leafy Place that in good weather teams with snack stands and with people eating at them, eating on the *café-terrasses,* eating on the curbs. It all smells good and stays tidy, because who buys food and then throws it away? And across the Canebière is the Cours Belsunce, with the noble Port d'Aix at its far north and a big fish stand down at the hectic entrance. Traffic lights there turn red and green, cars stop or screech ahead in the inimitably hellish music of any such intersection in France, and people go right on choosing their squid or scallops from the cool seaweedy piles of them on the corner. In summer, when the stand is closed, it seems strange to turn into the Cours Belsunce without its whiff of clean subtle brininess.

All the crossings along the Canebière are hair-raising to a stranger, because of the astonishing speed the cars can attain in a few feet from a dead stop, and although there are zones marked for pedestrians in several places, it is recommended (by me as well as any other visitor claiming average intelligence and survival wishes) to spot the traffic lights and use them. There are three or four, and they are worth the extra footage to reach them. And once across the wide Canebière and safely onto the sidewalk again, one feels mystically *younger*. . . .

A good place to cross, except perhaps during the meal hours, is up in front of the vaguely drab old Noailles café, where the Boulevards Dugommier and Garibaldi meet at the Canebière. The Noailles is a fine place to sit, after a late morning survey of the Flower Market, which is always crowded, even in any rain but a downpour. People look dazed by its fresh beauty. They buy whatever flowers are in season, and every kind of nursery planting in the spring, every kind of dry root bush or tree in the fall. They buy things in pots. They take their own containers and supervise the skillful gardeners who fill them. They gather around a collection of succulents, and then drift on to look speculatively at some rare hideous begonias.

On about June 24, there used to be a Garlic Fair along the enchanted Allées, and dealers came from all over France to choose their year's supply of the virile herb. Famous restaurateurs were there, and unknown housewives, and if the wind was right, the wonderful light whiff of all the ivory ropes of the stuff could be caught as soon as one turned up from the Quai des Belges. By now the Fair has been moved a little south of the Canebière, but it can still be smelled out, and it still is exciting.

And from the first Sunday in December, there is the Foire des Santons. It is unique, which means normal in Marseille. Dozens of booths are lined up under the bare trees of Les Allées. There are beautiful *santons* from human size to one-half inch, by local *santonniers* as well as any other reputable artists in the country or in the world, and there are many clumsy, undistinguished kinds alongside, painted garishly or left plainly in the baked "red earth of Provence stained with the Saracens' blood."

Weekends are liveliest as Christmas approaches, of course, with families choosing additions to their own crêches or buying new characters of the Nativity story for their friends, but perhaps the best (or strangest) time to go along Les Allées is after the holidays. Many of the stands have closed and moved away for another year. A few old women in layers of wool and thick felt boots stand hopefully behind their little counters. At first they seem to have almost nothing to sell. Then they begin to pull out broken shoeboxes and grimy paper sacks filled with flawed tiny images. Some of them are pitiful, or plainly prankish. Once I bought a two-inch *santon* of a famous character in the Nativity play, the village simpleton. When he looks up at the Star blazing in the sky, his jaw drops, his eyes roll, and he raises his hands mutely toward Heaven. This time, though, a mischievous *santonnier* had neatly turned his arms downward, at the elbows, so that his ecstatic upward gaze and his earthy gesture were shockingly at odds. At first I thought this heathenish little joke was funny. But before I took the *santon* home, I let it fall onto a tile floor and be shattered.

There were other small tricks that had been pulled, perhaps by naughty apprentices, and gradually the old women brought them out, looking casual but with a sharp eye on my reactions. Most of the dolls were unpainted. There were wee dogs with five legs, and some shepherds with only one. A sow a few inches long lay on a pancake of clay suckling ten piglets that were really kittens. I bought a rooster with his head on backward. With a little patience it would be easy to assemble a small-scale Nativity worthy of Hieronymus Bosch, or perhaps Salvador Dali . . . and it was interesting that the crowds of jolly, pushing Christmas shoppers had intuitively rejected all these mistakes. I took several back to California to give to people, but by the time I got home, their first strange humor had vanished, and they seemed almost evil.

And, as always, the windows of the dim old Café de Noailles are the best place to watch the Foire . . . warm and lively in the winter holidays, even at night. People come in with their children, and compare their *santons* over orange sodas and *pastis*, according to their ages. Thin "Arabs" drink tea silently. The elderly waiters move slightly faster, and the fat cashier is almost pretty in her best clothes. Down the winding stairs, the mysterious subterranean toilets rumble and shudder as usual, under the traffic of the big intersection.

The Noailles is most familiar to me at noon, though, in winter or any other season. Then the people run wildly homeward for their two-hour meals, and on Flower Market days they carry big bunches of tulips, say, or a flat of pansies. Once I saw a very short Oriental girl totter toward the café and then across the Canebière onto the Boulevard Garibaldi, under an enormous pot with a rubber plant in it, taller than she was. I watched her with amazement and alarm, but under her black silk trousers her knees were not even buckling.

This corner café is a prime place to look for a peculiar

color of hair dye that was popular in 1973 but almost rare three years later. I call it Canebière Red, and like to assume that it is the same "henna" that was used two thousand and more years ago. It is almost purple in its shadows, and is more orange than scarlet. It seems to make female hair stiff and coarse, like the stuffing in a very old mattress. Many middle-aged women used it in '73, even elderly fishwives from the Quai des Belges. Mostly it was seen, though, on tough girls of twenty or so, the kind that made no bones about being what they were . . . mixed blood, African, Gypsy, Indo-Chinese, candles burning bright and fast. By now this unique color has grown out, faded, perhaps even been shaved off to help cheap wigs fit better. The few women one spots from the old Noailles who still wear it are otherwise like others of their general class, short heavy sensible people, who would have their hair dyed black again if they had not invested too much in 1973 for Canebière Red.

And past Les Allées and their elegant old bandstand, now a publicity office run by the city, the Canebière seems to end logically with a huge church, set obliquely on the rising ground, called St. Vincent de Paul or "Les Réformés" or its more correct name of Les Augustins-Réformés. It is typically Marseillais, in its tongue-in-cheek bravura, for although it looks pure Northern Gothic of about the thirteenth century, it was built just in time to be dedicated in 1867. It still remains impressive: plainly an ecclesiastical joke, but not a shoddy one . . . perhaps a trick, but not a lie! Like the *santons* of the wintry fair below it in the Allées, it is noble as well as subtly prankish, a fitting comment on the street it dominates.

Chapter 3

PORT AND QUAYS

I

The Old Port of Marseille has always been an ideal small harbor, which of course used to seem much bigger than it does now. It is a neat oblong, going in from the Mediterranean Sea to what was once the mouth of the Lacydon and is now the Quai des Belges, with the Quai du Port on its left, and the Rive Neuve to the right.

When Protis landed somewhere along the swampy shores in about 600 B.C., the settlement of fishermen and saltmakers was relatively simple. By now, of course, the city is commonly dubbed tough and evil, which I doubt that he found it.

Marseille is tough, all right, the way all big ports must be. The people who have stayed there for so long are uncompromising in the way they face the sea for their livelihood. And Marseille is evil, the way all big ports have always been, for lonely sailors must put in there for a few hours or a night or two, and they need women and other kinds of warmth, and know or are quickly told where to get it. But the toughness and the evil, so-called, have never scared me, because they are intrinsic to the strength and dignity I have always felt there. This respect is difficult to transfer to anyone, and sometimes impossible.

People say, "Oh, don't go to Marseille. Don't bother." People from as close to this mysterious city as Aix-en-Provence say, "Don't go there! It is a dreadful place." People, mostly from England or New York, say, *Marseille! Nobody* goes there!" (The English say Marsales.)

But I do go there. I have been returning almost helplessly to the Old Port since my first stay there in 1929, and have always felt the same inner acceptance and exhilaration. When I lived in Aix for a few years with my two young girls, we went on the bus to Marseille as eagerly as if it were a kind of escape hatch from the requisite gentility of the old Royalist town, and its convents and bells and fountains and schools. And when I finally stayed near the Port for several months instead of a few days or weeks, and could ask people to meet me there, I was astounded by their responses to the invitation itself, and then to what they found if they dared come that far (everything from a few kilometers to several thousand, not counting the hovercraft over the Channel and dock strikes in New York and suchlike modern gimmicks).

In general what they felt was good-to-fine, with mutual easiness and communion. In one case, though, a long friendship may well have drifted brutally onto the rocks. Marseille was too powerful for the tenuously strong relationship that had been kept alive through rare exchanges of letters and parcels and even visits through World War II and before and after. Ropes snapped almost visibly while our Scottish friends were in the town, and they cut themselves free in near-panic, a few days ahead of the scheduled end of their visit, and headed toward Paris like rescued sailors, breathing hard and glancing behind them now and then.

My sister and I were living in a two-room flat, the kind with a gas-plate for cooking in the bathroom and a superb view over most of the Vieux Port, so we got a room for our friends at the Beauvau on the Quai des Belges at the land end of the Port. They could see the whole thing a few floors below them: the constant movement of the fishing boats, the morning market of everything that swims or creeps or sits underwater along the Mediterranean shores, the people, the two sides of the Port: that is, the most exciting view in the world, or one of them.

They were plainly not quite comfortable. We thought it was because they were tired. Then we thought it was because they really mistrusted French food and were not used to drinking much wine and were constitutionally (historically) averse to "the French" as such. Soon, though, it was plain that they were actually timid about being in Marseille, center of the White Trade to South America, Arab terrorists, smuggling, and now heroin. They had heard of what was going on, they finally told us, and it seemed fairly clear that they had come to persuade us to leave this place, if not for our own sakes for those of our departed parents, whom they had both known.

My sister and I are chronologically mature people, I at least to the point of overripeness, but I know that these two dear friends were persuading us, urging us, to leave, to escape with them in their comfortable car, to get out of this peculiarly wicked place while we could. It was as if we were two runaway teenagers, and we both felt some of their loyal concern for our safety, but went blandly walking home at night from the Opera or filthy movies like *The Last Tango in Paris* (along well-lighted streets and purposefully of course, and together!), and sitting in cafés drinking degenerate apéritifs before lunch, and prowling around the piles of rescued stones at the government reconstructions going on at the Abbey of St. Victor and Paul Puget's great building of the municipal poorhouse, La Vieille Charité. How could these two nice young girls have become so careless and so blind? they wondered in balloons over their uneasy heads.

They told us that several friends had said jokingly before they left England, when they admitted they were going to Marseille, "How mad! *Nobody* goes to Marseille! But be sure to bring us back a pocketful of Big H, if the bullets miss you! . . . some top-quality fixes, old boy!" And they told us more than once how when one returns to England, if there is any mention of having been in or near Marseille, one is held in Customs, for drastic investigation.

We tried to be gentle and thoughtful about it, and planned little picnics and nice meals at places they would like, preferably with no view at all except at a safe minor mural from Italy to reassure them. The lusty little fish places along the Rive Neuve were very upsetting to them, in a completely discreet way, and we knew that both of them had been suffering at the Beauvau from expected and awaited gastric distress after our two or three such sorties. . . . We decided that the main trouble on the quays was that people walked along the sidewalks and looked in to see what everybody was eating and then read the menu and then either came in or walked farther along, while a trained female barker at the door cajoled and insulted them. We were used to this, after so many years and months, but it was too embarrassing to the visitors, and we settled for upper-level somewhat elegant restaurants with muted lights and soft views of Venice in the sunlight or the moonlight or at dawn, and *no windows.* . . .

One day, though, my sister and I proposed to show them

the ruins of the Vieille Charité, which are gradually being put together again according to Puget's golden dream. It will take another twelve years, perhaps, and when it is done, with the strange chapel in the middle of the galleried court, it will be a school for students of the communications media . . . film, television, radio, printing, everything. It is another fine plan, and we knew our friends were aware and educated about ecclesiastical architecture, and we wanted them to see the gradually revivifying core, the chapel. It was a reassurance of the human spirit, to Norah and me, and perhaps it would be to them too.

It was a bright day, and we walked up to the Place des Moulins at the top of the hill, past things like the Maison Diamantée and of course the exquisite Town Hall, and the Scots were lively and interested. Naturally we had to climb through quite a lot of sordid crooked streets, in the quarter that is now mostly Arab because it is old and ill-furnished with what human beings are supposed to require for modern life. But up at the top, on the austere little square, there was the sound of children playing in the grammar school, and we looked pleasurably at the remnants of the two or three remaining stone mills and then headed down toward the old poorhouse.

It is a big hollow block, with small windows now toothy with broken glass on the outside walls, and a medieval-looking tipped grating over the sidewalks to keep stones from falling on the passersby, that hangs out, strangely hostile and evil. One can't help looking up at it, and my sister, who hates rats dead or alive, was sickened to see three withered bodies of them lying on the coarse wires. They could have been there for a week or ten years, and could have been tossed out by tenants or simply been suicidal.

There is only one entrance to the Charité, I think . . . that is, the kind a carriage could go through, to bring a doctor or a municipal officer. And immediately one sees the chapel in the center of the enormous courtyard, and the lacework of all the galleries running around it. The usual mournful guard was not there, and we poked around the piles of numbered and labeled stones that had been pulled down by Beaux Arts students working on the reconstruction, and I think that our friends were for a time happy and easy in their skins. She toyed with the possibility of taking perhaps one tiny stone home with her, an idea we all discouraged firmly, and then we encouraged him when he said he planned to read about Paul Puget, once home again. We left unwillingly.

We walked down the crooked steep streets, sometimes only staircases, and there were wispy good smells of hot couscous and fish in the air. We turned toward the sea, and came out below the Cathedral and then went to a café called something funny like Le San Francisco and drank an *apéro* in a mild gale: orange squash for them, and my sister and I ordered dry vermouth.

We were very hungry, and with prearrangement we headed our tired friends toward a place under the arcades along the Quai du Port, where the old quarter used to be that was detonated during the war. The blocks of new buildings are hideous, but arcades are always good, and it was satisfying to be in the shade after our windy drink out at the end of the Port. My sister walked ahead with the lady, and I loitered a little with her husband, because I had known him a long time and wanted to reestablish a connection that had suddenly, after all the years of student exchanges, war, bombings, stress, fellowships, all that, perhaps been cut off by an accident in place rather than in time.

He leaned toward me confidentially, although the two others were at least a hundred yards ahead of us, and said,

"You know, my dear, I . . . we . . . really don't mind too dreadfully the dirty gutters in these old slums, and the piles of fruit skins in corners and the washing hung out of the windows. We know that the underprivileged are always somewhere." He chuckled a little. "I must say your poor sister was a bit startled by those dead rats hanging over our heads though!"

"She has a slight phobia about them in general, dead or live," I said.

"Of course, of course," he went on firmly. "But I do think these people down here where things are nicer should wash the blood off the pavements."

It was plain to me that I was already somewhat defensive, and for a flash I dismissed this criticism as part of the whole fiasco and decided not to look down. Then I remembered what a brave man our friend had always been, and what he saw during all the bombings in England when he was one of the chief fire wardens, and I knew at once that the dry brown splatters under my feet were indeed old blood, and then that they came from one of the dozens of narrow cafés under the arcades, and I made myself say casually, "Oh, yes . . . there was a bad shooting there a few days ago, but you'd think they'd swab down the sidewalk before now. Perhaps it's for publicity. Ghoulish . . ."

I knew that I was putting my foot in my mouth . . . one more proof that my sister and I had lost all our good middleclass standards of behavior, to be able to stroll past a gory den without a visible shudder!

"I suppose it was connected with the drug traffic," our friend said, trying in a subtly disapproving way to match my nonchalance, and a little triumphant that at last he had proof of what everybody at home had warned him about. He took my arm after we got past the stains, and murmured, "Let's not say anything about this to the others. . . ."

We did not, but he was right, and as if meant by the gods I had taken him straight to the proof of everything he knew in his bones about Marseille.

We had passed the Tanagra, one of the countless deep bars that have emerged as naturally as mushrooms from dung, along the Quai du Port, under the new/old arcades. About four days before we went by, two men had come in and gunned down, in what was generally referred to in the press as "American-style," the barmaid-owner named something like Rita, a goodlooking and apparently innocent young man drinking his first or tenth espresso, and two known informers or henchmen in one of the many small gangs that seem to have supplanted any firm organization of crime in Marseille. The gunsels then left, calmly. I forget whether they were later arrested. Nobody seemed to be much annoyed by anything except the fact that the act was one of petty revenge carried out by amateurs. Where was the old spit and polish in crime? lamented the editorials in everything from *Le Meridional* to *L'Express*. Marseille might be the great center for the American drug market, but it was sadly lacking in local solidarity, and panache.

Well, what with *la patronne* shot dead beside her coffee machine, and all the fuss about fingerprints and so on, the sidewalk never got washed, and the little sad café was closed and dark as we hurried past it toward the ladies, my sister and our friend. It seemed odd that I had not thought much about the Tanagra. I knew about the almost nonchalant gunning, and I understood why it was called "American-style," with chauvinistic regret that it could not have been labeled Sicilian or Sardinian or Algerian, or . . . And the little bar and its hapless owner and customer were just across the Old Port from where we lived. But we had never thought about going there or *not* going there to see about the blood, and suddenly we had done so!

All this was too complicated to explain to my plainly troubled friend. He said hastily before we went into the restaurant and joined the two women, "You know, my dear, we do worry dreadfully about you, here in all this," and I said urgently, "Please don't worry!" and we sat down.to what turned out to be the best meal of their stay there. He and I had a secret, valiantly kept, and his wife and my sister were as blandly ignorant as well-fed geese about it. But all the time I was thinking of the Pinball Boys, and petty crime that can turn vile, and the mystery of what I clumsily call the karma of a place.

I I

Now, when you read about the Occupation, or the blastings done with municipal consent by the Invaders in 1944, or the takeover of the American-style gangsters since then, with perhaps a municipal wink, it is all revolvers, submachine guns, hands-up-face-to-wall, who ratted on whom, and an unborn resistance of some 2,500 years, at least in certain parts of Marseille like the section back of the Quai du Port.

One Sunday in 1973, down on the wide and active Quai, and in toward the city from the Tanagra where my shaken Scottish friend and I had stepped firmly over the dried blood in front of the narrow little bar, there were the usual crowds of a bright spring holiday . . . clots of people watching a man trying to sell watches, a woman twisting peanuts into an odorous bowl of boiling caramel for people watching her and already munching. There were wild posies of balloons, and stands selling dreadful nougat and fried Algerian sweets. Certainly there would be a shell game going on, set up with a couple of big empty paper cartons and involving three little paper cups or empty tomato-paste cans, and a thick crowd of men watching some fellow gull being robbed. It seemed part of an almost innocent *voyeurisme*: "He is dumber than I am! I would have known where the peanut, or the two-franc piece, or the old dice was. I would have known all the time. . . ."

My sister Norah and I liked to dawdle and watch, as did anyone who went to the long buzzy Quai on a Sunday. We stopped now and then. There was one young man with a rather exhausted-looking woman, a dramatically thick bandage over her eyes, who would intone magic numbers when they were "thought" by the quiet but cynical audience. (Drifters like us are tough, except for our basic gullibility and friendliness!)

Norah expressed real or at least conditioned pleasure at seeing this kind of cheating encouraged and permitted so openly; it was one of the few lasting pleasures, one of the rare liberties left to us, she said firmly.

Farther along the Quai, about across from the rosy perfection of the old Town Hall, there was the usual crowd of silent watchers in their Sunday clothes, around the usual man manipulating his usual shell game on top of his pile of paper cartons. We went toward his back, where there was a thinned ring of people, so that we could hear him con, or try to con, all of us.

Surprisingly, he seemed to have a helper, a burly but slick-looking man in a light coat. The two stood close together, murmuring to each other and to a third fellow facing us, with his sharply cut suit turned backside to the noncommittal watchers. I thought in an almost hilarious way that never had I seen such perfect casting and lighting for a low-grade gangster movie. The back of the shell-game man, and then the two profiles muttering to him, were heavy, clean, dangerous, with an acute wariness about them. One man wore the sensitive but thick carving of a Roman, a pip-squeak Mussolini, with arching lips and cold veiled eyes.

Down the Quai, past the toylike Town Hall, was the one-of-a-hundred tiny bars where the four people had died lately, and still I continued to feel amused and silly about how trite the casting was for any and all such underworld melodrama, so wasted here on the Quai for a meaningless shell game. My sister continued to explain the beauties of such legal freedom, where men could drink or not, get bellyaches on sugared peanuts if they wished, bet on which nutshell has a pea under it, all along the lapping waters of the Old Port, the bounds of the ageless Lacydon. Moral freedom, she said.

The two new men leaned close to the shell man, whispering, their eyes darting every way over the silent ring of watchers. For a second I thought with a strange dismay that they were smarter than the average lot of the gulls, and as such were challenging him about some money he had not repaid them on their one lucky guess. (They were two-to-one, and bigger—)

Suddenly the quiet crowd stepped back, right in front of us, and the three men went past us so fast that I did not really see them, until they were across the wide street and into the paddy wagon, the shell man pushed politely into the back and the two plainclothesmen with their cold Italianate faces pinched into the front part.

As they slipped past us in the crowd, a small thin rat of a man whispered to me with an emanation of glee, and with his long wrists crossed suddenly in front of him, "The cops! He's manacled!" This seemed to delight him. And sure enough, the quiet crook or victim or whatever he was, the nondescript man we had often seen moving three small tin cans or paper cups around on top of his old cartons, had his short arms helplessly locked behind him, so that he had to be boosted up into the police wagon before the door was slammed on him.

The silent crowd seemed to have a gigantic word written above it in another comic-strip balloon. It looked vacantly, impersonally, at the old cartons. Then it straggled this way and that along the Quai, and the top box blew off toward the water. My sister and I went along toward the sea, not talking about human freedom or anything else. We felt as mute, inwardly, as everyone else had seemed to be.

Later, on the last ferry across the Vieux Port to our side, we talked with a certain awe of the perfect casting of the two plainclothesmen . . . except for their eyes, we said, those cold eyes suddenly unveiled, no longer looking stupid enough to play the shell game, trained to watch for the trick that inevitably would be tried, open in the crowd of watching sheep. Until those two chosen men had lifted their reptilian lids, narrow and quick, they looked like the rest of the Marseillais on Sundays on the Quai du Port: sharp clothes, the kind that will do for weddings and then for funerals with a different tie, a close holiday shave and some pomade on the hair, too much noon dinner. But once they moved in, they showed their snake-eyes, and did not hide them again, even though their backs were calmly turned on the thick crowd around the two cartons, the three cups, the lonely gambler.

In some other place (what more likely one than there?), at some time (although when as well as then, with crowds around on a brisk day of celebration?), we might have had a rattle of bullets, bigger than the one at the little Tanagra where only four people died with a lot of blood, or there might have been knives drawn and women scuttling for shelter with their babies, as happens everywhere every day. But this was all very calm, and the back of the middle-aged shell man looked silent and resigned, as he sped almost expertly between the two detectives toward the safe wagon.

Probably he served in the great game of Liberty and Freedom, as my sister saw it, as a kind of catalyst. As I myself prefer to use it in my own self-dramatization, he was front man, helpless, a patsy for passing signals and so on to at least one organized band along the Quai du Port. His crowds, many of them well paid to stand there stolidly and draw other goons, made easy go-betweens for messages and signals and small packets of drugs. Perhaps he even made a little honest shell money on the side, from his own game, that is.

There was a general feeling that he was hardly more permanent a character there than we were—at least on that quay so much older than all of us.

III

Some of the many small bars along the Quai du Port have been there ever since the monotonously matching apartment houses were built after that area was blown up to cleanse the planet of one of its most thriving and pestilential sores. (Success, if any, was temporary.)

The new buildings, designed heavily but to the same height as the exquisite old City Hall in their center, and with arcades running along the street level and with decent-sized balconies, seem to be occupied by every type of tenant, judging by the furnishings of the port side of the apartments.

Some of them are discreet exercises in static symmetry, at least seen from fifty feet below, with four potted dwarf cypress, two imitation Roman tubs filled with whatever beauties the florist can supply and the beating summer sun and occasional cruel mistral will let survive, and even an occasional head of a faun or fragment of a neo-Pompeian mosaic, depending on the purse and proclivities of the flats' occupants, who could be local retired soap manufacturers or Parisian decorators. And some of the balconies are hung continually with bright laundry, as in the enormous *"cités"* on the outskirts of Marseille and every other big town of France, and that means that the people who live there are fairly poor as well as clean. On the Vieux Port it also means, most often, that they are Algerians, some Arabs as they are called with varying shades of meaning, and some repatriated *pieds noirs*, or Viet refugees.

These newcomers, when they can house themselves decently in such apartments as line the Quai du Port, are fastidiously clean, and they are usually very poor indeed. And many of their sons go downstairs to the tiny crowded bars, as they would probably be doing in North Africa or Saigon if they could still be there. . . .

The bars look as alike as houses in a low-income American suburb, so that one wonders how their occupants or habitués know Bide-a-Wee from Dunrovin in East Colusa, Idaho, or La Lune Bleue from Bébé-à-Go-Go under the arcades along the Quai. They are a new phenomenon, much smaller than those prewar pubs that always had steamy windows and the quiet clickings from a billiard table toward the back, and men playing long slow card games on tables with thick cloth covers. These new espresso joints are almost pinched in size, and stuffy with cigarette smoke, and very noisy.

They smell alike, of bitter coffee from the innumerable tiny cups that are their standard drink, of strong tobacco, occasionally of disinfectant from the toilet at the back end. And they sound alike, because of the jukebox music that seems to pick itself up from one café to the next, in a broken blaring rhythm that is not unpleasant if one can move along outside, and not be in with the immediate beat and the urgent stench and the look of chromium and rigid nearness that is dictated by the space the cafés are crowded into. They all have a long very narrow bar, running from the sidewalk to the back, where there is a legally required sign saying Telephone-Toilets, although trying to use either of them is inadvisable. There are usually two or three minuscule tables along the other side of the room; again a legal order? There must always be a cigarette vendor. And there are two or even several wildly lighted pinball machines.

There are of course countless native-born men in an old port the size of Marseille, with a current population of about one million, and they are of every size and shape and color. There is, however, a strongly *typical* size-shape-color of some Marseillais, and it is easy and strangely heartening to recognize one immediately. He is short, broadly built, with very strong arms and legs on a long torso, and he has black eyes and hair and often a nutlike shade of skin. His voice is deep. He emanates a feeling of male power, quiet but unquestioning. When he is not working at the intense and almost unceasing job of being a fisherman or perhaps a mason, he is with a woman built almost exactly like him, and although their children are skinny in their first years, they soon grow into the same adult mold as their parents and their forebears for more than two thousand years.

That is why it is puzzling about the Pinball Boys, the slender hollow-chested dandies who seem to spend twenty hours a day in the small smoky cafés under the arcades, and perhaps in other quarters of Marseille. Where did they come from? They are often tall, with white fingers, and silky hair worn to their narrow shoulders. It seems improbable that they are the sons of the tough blunt men and women who are intrinsically Marseillais, and it is true that in smaller towns in Provence, and perhaps everywhere in France, their pale twins lean against the same bars and drink the same endless tiny cups of espresso, and pull languidly at the pinball buttons. They are too young to be a ghastly result of wartime spawnings. They are too frail to have been bred by working people or real peasants, and most of all, they are too much *alike*, in their long bones and cavernous and sometimes pretty faces, to be a local phenomenon, something unique to one part of this or any other town.

As French youths, they are supposed to have been subjected to some kind of vocational training after their enforced years of primary education, so that they can say they know the rudiments of truck driving or baking or hairdressing. On the streets near the technical schools in Marseille, for instance, it is easy to recognize young people who are preparing for this or that kind of trade: they are busy or preoccupied or worried, and they are in a hurry, and they look as if they will turn into solidly built sane adults, no matter how slow they may be mentally. The Pinball Boys, though, are another breed, and besides wondering where they came from, from what and whence they sprang, one ponders on how they manage to survive now, putting endless coins into all the machines, and what will possibly and probably become of them. Certainly they look eminently susceptible to the dangers of fresh air . . . or of steady employment.

Fortunately the customers who can fit into the tiny cafés are as thin as skeletons, and young and restless enough to prefer standing or leaning to sitting. They move with accomplished deftness from bar to jukebox and back, leaving their little cups here and there. If they have their girls with them, they share an occasional cigarette as a grudging sign of possession, I suppose, and since there are no ashtrays, the floors become almost stylishly filthy by midafternoon of a swinging Sunday. The girls never seem to stand up by "les pinballs," as they are called in Franglais, or show any interest in them or the players: it is probably something about the unwritten laws of local *machismo?* They sit at the puny tables, or in good weather out on the sidewalk terraces, with one or two other chicks dressed exactly like them, whose men are inside gaming. The girls usually drink cokes or bottled fruit pop; they always pay for this debauchery, but never for their cigarettes . . . *machismo* again.

Their boyfriends dress alike, too, in light-colored suits with pinched waists. In the seventies their shirts are dark and their ties exaggeratedly wide and soft, boldly striped. Their hair is more long than short, with elaborate sideburns, and few of them wear either beards or handlebars, probably because the times and they are not yet ripe enough. They have narrow closed faces, and it seems the style for them to keep their eyes narrowed too, as if light, or perhaps reality, should be as shut out as possible. There is a general roar of talk, especially around the jukeboxes, but it is not deep and robust, as in the neighborhood pubs their elders go to.

Outsiders, people like innocent tourists or even locals desperately needing to make a telephone or natural call, can come in and through without a break in the mechanical support of the machines and the hissing of the monstrous coffeemakers, whereas in an old-fashioned bar almost any stranger will cause a moment or so of dead silence, before the natural decibels pick up again. The young men along the Quai du Port seem deliberately unaware of intrusion, at least momentarily, as if they were practicing to be cool 1930s gangsters, and they never laugh, or move their faces much when they talk. When they spit out or drop their cigarette butts, they never step on them, as if that were a kind of code or password, a *proof* of something.

It is foolish to bother to check such an unimportant fact as the number of espresso bars along the Quai in 1973 or 1976, as compared with 1970 when I was first aware of them, but there do seem to be at least twice as many, and this may be either the cause or the result of the current need for loud mechanized games in restless puzzled young men. It is noticeable in small towns in Provence, where thin boys drift into the small bars as soon as the older men go off to work after their morning coffee or nip, and stay there in seeming aimlessness until the places close at night. And of course if one holds to the theory that every great city is made up of a thousand villages, the arcades along the Vieux Port are surely as much a small community as Luynes or Sâlon or Les Arcs. The only real difference is that in Marseille the espresso joints seem to belong solely to the young. There is no risk of their ever smelling of the *pastis* that older men rely on for their refreshment and, some claim, their virility. There seems even less risk that the narrow-faced, narrow-hipped boys around the pinballs will someday work in the fishing fleet that beats like a gigantic heart across the sidewalk from the bars, on the ever-changing waters of the Vieux Port.

At best, they might become occasional salesmen of super-charged pleasure boats or secondhand sports cars, or perhaps qualify gradually as members of any number of fringe "clubs" of the big dope business there. But they are simply not built to work as the older men do: they are lighter and longer, and more prone to broken bones and chest pains. They seem to have enough money for one sharp suit, several espressos a day, slugs for the machines, and an occasional date. They look geared to a drop-out defeatism.

It is presumptuous to surmise, and such an opinion as this one is based rashly and solely on casual observation over a few years in small towns in Provence. Of course there have always been drifting do-less unemployed youths, uninterested in working at a trade or in more education than the law has forced them to accept. But lately, at least along the Quai du Port, the number seems greater, and therefore the demand for more places for them to huddle in has been satisfied with countless small noisy smoky bars. And the lodestone, the odor of civet and musk, the siren's song, seems to be the impersonal clashing tickle of the pinballs, a rhythm that sounds above the juke music and the steam from the espresso machine, and that reduces the human voice to a thin futile yell. It makes a security blanket, a womb.

Chapter 4

SOME OF THE WOMEN

I

Of course there are many kinds of women in Marseille, as everywhere, and they can fairly easily be bracketed according to their physical structures, their ways of living, their jobs, their accents. This soon becomes true in any settlement of people, whether it be a one-year-old subdivision "market-plaza" in Southern California, with its own post office and pharmacy and laundromat, or the quarters around the Vieux Port in a city twenty-six hundred times older.

I have never known the remaining aristocrats in Marseille, although I have read some of their books and probably seen them in a few restaurants and theatres. Their class never stays long in such a tough town: several kings and princes have been scared frantic by it, and the gaudy shows put on for their weddings and crownings and suchlike festivals were more cake than bread for the people's turbulent and often truculent hungers. The peers of the land are mostly transitory.

The upper class now seems based on how much soap was sold a hundred years ago, the famous oily *savon de Marseille,* and on how that much soap has made money enough to buy shares in gasoline companies around Martiques and the Etang de Berre, and now around Fos, the new industrial city promised by international tradesmen-in-commodities to relieve some of the pressure of the old and new ports of the ancient city, both in traffic and in population, as well as in hard cash.

The middle classes, if one can follow the old line of including people like lawyers, merchants, town officials, doctors, bankers (perhaps they should go up a notch financially?), live and eat well in Marseille, and are usually native-born and more or less devoted to the place . . . or at least more active about their public love for it. I saw many of them, over the past decades, on the streets and in the stylish and even low-class brasseries and cafés, and especially in the good restaurants, where they ate a lot at midday and turned pink, even under forty. The pinkest were the youngest, it seemed to me: they were trying hard to keep up with the hard-eyed city politicos they had been chosen to lunch with. They seemed to sweat a lot, discreetly. The older, more assured men were like affable stone.

In every class there were women, of course. Except for an occasional recognition of a beautifully cut suit, matched to the tiny Shih-Tzu dog worn like a fur on a lady's arm, I seldom saw the international *grandes dames,* and the well-established soapmakers kept their ladies either out of town or out of their habitats, except for a few overstuffed dutiful evening meals in the quieter restaurants. The professionally ambitious Marseillais never seemed to eat in the public with women until late at night, and then their ladies were either outrageously dashing in their getups or comparatively prim debutantes hoping to be engaged. Often I saw young men alternating these rendezvous, always looking fatigued, but still eating and drinking enough to become plump and important as soon as possible. If the women with them wore white makeup on eyelids and lips, and leopard pants edged with long sequin fringe, I knew they were from the hinterlands of Gstaad or Ischia and would soon move on, lean and alert. But if they looked like prospective brides, I knew that they would simply lose their figures, as Time and procreation and digestion wore on.

Somewhere in between them and the women I saw best and oftenest (the fishwives and waitresses and hawkers of sugared nuts around the Old Port), there were many females of all ages who are basically as strong and indeed invincible as their ancestors, no matter how many generations removed. The youngest start out in big department stores and brand-name shoe shops and pharmacies, and they are thin and usually lovely and as if bedazzled by life in general, and by their own loves. They behave in a haphazard way, fitting strange shoes, always the left foot on the right one at first, and always three sizes too short or four sizes too wide; they reach for aspirin on the shelf but bring down some tube of nonprescription antibiotic; they look constantly at the nearest clock, so as not to miss César or Patrice for a gobbled embrace and then a sandwich. . . . (They eat a lot, always hastily.)

Older girls, still seductive, wear stern but becoming white coats in pharmacies and delicatessens, and in little expensive shops lined with lotions and pomades. They are the few who have survived, it seems, and the native strain is beginning to show, no matter how darkened their eyelids or how subtly corseted their widening waists.

Then there are the few oddballs, the ones who stay aloof from their destinies and become night clerks in small respectable hotels, or managers of outlying branches of national banks. They are scrawny, and whether they manage a café or chandlery or a smart boutique along the Rue de Rome, they look wistful . . . discreetly tough . . . but wistful.

There are of course many trades for women in a place like Marseille, and since most of them have been practiced for centuries, there is real expertise. Competition is ruthless. I don't know what happens to the girls who fail, because of luck or health or other such hazards: probably they end in sanatoriums or cribs or gutters, or in proper warm houses filled with their own children.

But around the Vieux Port, where many of them were spawned, there are the mothers and aunts whose places they may one day seek out, the way ready salmon head upstream. They might be called "natives."

The native women of Marseille, the ones who are unmistakably of this place and no other that I have seen or read about, are short and trimly wide. As children they are thin wiry little monkeys, with large dark eyes. As girls they have a slim beauty that soon passes into what they will be for the rest of their lives, with breasts that stand up until marriage and then stay large after childbirth, without ever seeming to sag toward the ground in old age like those of taller softer females. They may develop paunches, the tidy kind that look made of steel, and among the lot of them there is never a snub nose, but instead the kind that grows stronger and beakier with time. Their arms and legs stay shapely enough, thanks surely to hard work, and their skins become like well-soaped leather, thanks perhaps to good olive oil and garlic and an occasional *pastis*, all taken by mouth in daily doses. (Tomatoes are also thanked for continuing their female vigor, according to many of their mates. . . .)

In all, the Marseillaises seem almost a part of their craggy land, like the thick trunks of the most ancient olive trees on the hills behind the city. And still they are from the sea, so that they smell of salt, and of what they eat and what they work with, but never of old sweat.

When they walk down a street, they cleave its air like small solid wooden ships driven by a mysterious inner combustion. Their men walk close alongside, often with an arm around the woman's waist or over her broad solid shoulders, pilot-fish escorting a trusted shark.

There is always the same kind of man with them, once they are mature: as short or shorter, often as stocky or else as thin as an eel. They seem to know each other as if they were born from the same egg, but there is obvious sexual enjoyment in their familiarity, and they look necessary to each other and are mutually respectful. The woman seems the more enduring of most pairs, and walks a half-step ahead, and makes decisions about things like where to sit down at what café for how long, and what to drink, and when to walk away alone so that the man can stay with other men for a time, and charge his batteries with a round of cards.

There is certainly nothing humble or timid or placating about the men. They are as male in their short strong bodies as their women are female. But they are as if pulled along in life by the dominant magnetism of their partners. They are necessary to each other, equal in their hard work, but it is plain that the woman can and often does survive several of the men whose arms lie trustingly over her shoulders as they walk together, and it is rare to see an old fisherman alone, while there are many ageless women, even shorter and broader than before, who stump strongly about, and sell fish with voices that are only a little more commanding than they were thirty years ago.

The voice of any female born and raised around the Vieux Port from countless parents of the same stock, the short dark strong breed that is a mixture of every Mediterranean race that ever touched foot there, that voice is unforgettable, once heard. It is harsh, but not hoarse, and rough and deep without being in any sense masculine. It is like the woman, built close to the earth and as strong as stone. Probably it can be soft and beautiful, in love or motherhood, but it seems bred to direct its own fate, over the sounds of storm and battle and even modern traffic. Without any doubt, a healthy fish-wife could call easily from one side of the Vieux Port to the other on a busy day, and I know one Marseillaise who sells flowers instead of fish because she lost a leg during the Occupation, whose voice (and with a fine lilt to it) carries more than a block during the worst noontime bustle. (People buy flowers in Marseille much as they buy fresh sardines or bread, and noon is the time to snatch up a posy along with the loaves and fishes. . . .) Voices like hers and all her sisters' are never a shriek or shout: they are simply a part of the whole amazing strength of their bodies, basically indestructible.

All this is not to say that the mature women of Marseille can be called beautiful, at least in our Western vocabulary, spoken if not felt. They have a toughness in all their attributes that is past beguilement and gentle allure. Still, they remain completely female, and therefore feminine, and while they often both outwork and outlive their partners, they seem always to be treated with a special kind of courtesy, no matter with what apparently rough bonhomie.

I have no firsthand knowledge of the private life of

heterosexual couples in the lower social and economic levels in Marseille, any more than I do that of other more affluent or notorious citizens, but in public there exists a patent and perhaps strange equality among the native working class. I have watched it for a long time, in public, along the Canebière and all around the Vieux Port.

Of course on the Quai du Port most of the females are young. They are the chicks of the Pinball Boys, waiting impassively to grow out of their sleazy modish clothes, and the figures that demand them, for the uniform of the thickened strong bodies of the mothers, who six days a week sell fish on the Quai des Belges and on Sundays and holidays may double there, behind the fuming pots of sugared nuts or the little ice-cream wagons.

On that Quai, in front of the stylish restaurants and brasseries, there are always other professional females, but they are seldom natives. They have longer legs, and seem in flight between the Riviera and Paris, in tourist class. I have watched them change plumage and makeup for a long time, but they are still for sale. In 1937, for instance, they wore the already outdated dark suits and silver-fox scarves and petulant lips that three or four years before were uniform in front of the Café de la Paix in the capital, and in 1973 they were windblown, without makeup, striding along the sidewalk in high boots, flinging themselves onto *terrasse* chairs as if they had just come from the ski runs at St. Moritz. They were the same girls. Their older sisters, who stayed longer and, as they tired, worked mostly around the Opera, were no more native than they, and seemed unaware of the pert young Marseillaises hurrying along the wide sidewalks at noon and after work, or of the mothers calling the price of sardines and mussels resonantly on the waterfront.

Farther around the Port, on the Rive Neuve, it is more the

men's territory, although there is at least one powerful old woman there who runs her own small wholesale fish market. And I met another one, hard as basalt, who ran a café next to the Criée Publique, the wholesale auction house, a huge cave of a building, hosed out and dead-empty from perhaps nine in the morning until three or so the next, and then a wild babel of screaming buyers and sellers of the last catch, as well as of countless truckloads of fish sent fresh from Normandy and Calais and Bordeaux. (This monumental market is soon to be moved northward along the coast, toward Fos, because of the traffic problems of all the buyers and sellers on wheels. What can be the future of the ugly-beautiful structure, whose tall glassed front looks from the Port somewhat like an early railroad terminal? Empty, it echoes. Filled with yelling fish merchants it pulsates like a gigantic heart. . . .)

I had been told that the husband of the café owner next to the Criée owned a concession there, a prime position on the Port, like having a seat on the New York Stock Exchange. His wife looked powerful too, a short tough woman with that flamingly purple-red hair. When I went into their café, the boss and three men were playing cards, and she leaned over a shoulder to watch the game. There was sudden silence, neither rude nor suspicious but complete. I refused to seem abashed by it, and when the woman strolled behind the bar where I stood, I used my most acceptable accent and after the ritual exchange of *Sorry to bother—Not at all*, I asked for her help. (This is a practical beginner for all kinds of adventure, of course, and should be done with a good imitation of candor and innocence.) I was, I said truthfully, trying to find someone qualified to tell me a few facts about the fishing industry in Marseille . . . the number of commercial boats, all that.

The four men had stopped playing. I went on dauntlessly making my pitch, about how important the whole story ap-

peared to me. The woman kept a straight face, swabbed at
the impeccable zinc bar, and then asked one of the men,
plainly her husband, what Madame should do. He seemed to
reflect a long time in the soundless room, and finally suggested, through her, and never looking at me, that I go
toward town a few doors, and ask at the ship chandler's.
Another man said, his eyes firmly on his cards, "Why not
the chief at the Criée?" The husband said with a mischievous
grin, "This little lady would have to be there between three
and six in the morning, when we work . . ." as if I never
went anywhere but to Mass or bed that early. The others
permitted themselves to laugh with their shoulders, in a con-
strained way, and looked down at their hands intently.

The woman said with some compassion, perhaps, but not
smiling, "I still suggest the chandler," and I made the usual
politenesses, and the minute I turned toward the door she
was leaning her wildly dyed hair over her husband's shoulder
and there was a healthy burst of talk and of cards slapping.
It seemed to me that although she had chosen the café life,
she could within an hour's notice of death or bankruptcy be
back behind her piles of the day's catch, a couple of rickety
folding tables away from her mother's on the Quai des
Belges, and perhaps right next to her great-aunt's.

During the market hours there, men sold their catches, too,
but it was the women who dominated, at least in decibels.
The men simply stood behind their piles of gleaming
sardines, slithery small octupi, long eels trying to get back
into the dirty Port water, greyish-pink shrimps hopping within
their pyramids of myriad brothers. They smiled and chatted
in a detached way as they scooped the catch into newspaper
cones, or whacked something into immobility for its last
ride toward the kitchen, but they seemed poised for escape
from all the selling end of their game. That was for the

women. Once the fish got to shore, the men were set to head
out to sea again . . . *les pescadous.*

Nobody seemed to protest this division of labor. The men
took care of their boats, and provided as much catch as the
weather and tides allowed, and sold it when their wives were
birthing or grieving; the women sold what was brought in,
and over the centuries had built up their own definite mannerisms of general jollity, no matter how impersonal, with
now and then a clownish harsh teasing or a shouted insult,
depending upon the human courtesy of the people buying
their fish. In the early seventies a good gambit to amuse a circle
of listeners was to tease somebody about using "Paris" or "old"
francs: to an outsider accustomed to paying four francs for
a batch of sardines in Bordeaux or even Aix, it was scary to
have some hard-faced old biddy start screaming that she
wanted four hundred, and then bawl him out, grinning all
the time but ferociously, while everyone tittered a little and
then drifted on along the Quai. . . .

Honorine was the typical loud canny lovable fishwife
deified by Marcel Pagnol, and I have watched her for a long
time. She can be mean or kind, and all the time she is shovel-
ing the fish into newspapers, and her eyes are laughing at an
inner joke. Once an Honorine sold me two Greek amphora
tips that were dislodged by stormy weather from the coastal
reefs, and it was the first time I ever felt that I was more
than a passing gull, in every sense of the word. She was
pleased that I wanted those shards, and I went off trembling
with awed pleasure . . . their agelessness, hers. . . .

Around from the Quai des Belges on the Rive Neuve, for
the first couple of blocks, there are some elderly tourist boats
for the extra seasonal trips to the Château d'If, and a bait
shack and then a lot of working fish-boats, before the dazzling yachts loom up. Land-side, there is a diminishing row of

restaurants, good to pitiful and gradually being abandoned or replaced by Oriental bistros, but still rapaciously, classically, traditionally, skillfully pulling in the pedestrians. Anyone who ever planned to walk along that sidewalk, at least when I knew it from '29 to '76, was on his own, and must be strong enough to cope with what I have always called the She-Wolves, those female barkers who have for decades or perhaps centuries scared off innocents like our British visitors.

They are no doubt an offshoot of Honorine and her brood, and possibly rejects or refugees from the low-class brothels of the sea town, very typical of Marseille women in their build and their cruel ability to whisper in a harsh hiss that everybody for half a block can hear and smile about. (There is such a helpless feeling, when one of these women grabs control, that everyone within earshot of the victim feels an hysterical relief that it is not he, but another . . . so he laughs, and slides by, if he is fast on his feet.)

One or two of the Rive Neuve fishhouses in 1973 were run by darling young men who flitted around as if they were back in their hair salons, but there were still some fronted by short sardonic women, who stomped along the wet sidewalks in cheap boots in winter and half bared their firm broad bodies in summer, and performed everything but a half-Nelson to grab a client before he reached the next restaurant.

"Come in, honey, come in *here*," they would command roughly, with ancient practiced blackmail and all the evil seduction of bad tides and rough weather in their voices. They would mutter in a hoarse provocative voice as loud as a shout, "Take a look, sweetheart! One look at that display, and you'll bring your little darling right in! Look at that lobster, a female busting with eggs! Look at those pink shrimps standing straight up! Hey, now, don't miss this chance!"

A lot of people were so dazed and embarrassed by this attack that they shuffled into the dens like helpless sheep. Some simply knew where they were going and ignored or smiled at the tireless hustlers, and sailed past. A few listened seriously, peered in at what the customers were gobbling, read the posted menus again, and either went in under their own steam or did not.

My sister Norah and I soon got to know where we wanted to eat, and how to cope with the vocal hazards of getting there, and the She-Wolves recognized this with forgiving fatalism and a friendly shrug.

There was one small older one, with frankly greying hair instead of the usual purple-red and with an oddly school-marmish air about her. Perhaps I liked her for this, and perhaps because she worked in front of an obviously second-rate place and had almost none of the brashness of her colleagues. Once Norah said to me with some disapproval or surprise, "You patted her on the shoulder when you said 'No,'" and I said, "But the last time she patted *me*! On the arm! That time I said, 'Not *tonight*.' And it went off all right. It seemed like a logical answer."

That grey-haired one was the She-Wolf I had promised to return to, never having gone to her place at all. For vague reasons I had felt shy and awkward at her advances, as if she were my second-grade teacher, and "I swear we'll come," I said, smiling, raising a hand solemnly. She remembered, and would give me a private twinkle, the next time I'd say, before she could begin her pitch, "It's still a promise. . . ." Then one night we took some visitors along the quay and headed right for her place, to keep my word at last, but in a pure funk went to the restaurant just before hers, because the array of harridans out soliciting for patrons of bouillabaisse on that weekend was too unnerving for our present guests.

When we came out, several bowls and bottles later, the smaller thinner older woman was a few paces down the block, still conning possible customers, and she gave me a sad look, and we never really touched each other again. She knew where we had been, and perhaps why, but she remembered the pact. . . .

Some people think these are bad women, whores. Certainly they are an embarrassment to proper Anglo-Saxons who have never before been so openly and noisily offered wares which in this case are gastronomical instead of sexual, and perhaps many of them spend their few free hours in much their accustomed rhythm, horizontally instead of on their sturdy feet. But, wolves that they have become or may always have been, I feel an almost affectionate admiration for them.

(A typical American appraisal I thus am happy to contradict is a nationally syndicated newspaper "feature": ". . . old women stand like prostitutes in front of the area's numerous restaurants, hustling customers for seafood of dubious quality.")

It certainly *looks* as if these Fallen Women solicit, although I have never been so blatantly treated by the many whores I have met on the sidewalks of my life. But along the seafood street in Marseille they are not really old. Of course they are not built like California carhops or International Bunnies, because they seem to have been born and bred for more than two thousand years around the Vieux Port, but mostly they are very vital and female, looking exactly as they have looked for all that time, short and a little thick, with faces carved from olivewood. It is hard to judge women chronologically when history itself is involved, in Marseille as in Peking, but I would put the average age of the procuresses along Bouillabaisse Row at about forty-four.

While I am protecting them from something they would never even bother to sniff at, their image in Western eyes, I must protest again: the seafood offered along their two or three blocks of the Rive Neuve should not be classed as "dubious." It is often mediocre, but that is the fault of the kitchen rather than of the fish, which cannot be anything but fresh, because the wretched pantries behind the dining rooms have little modern equipment for chilling or freezing. A whiff of spoiled fish on the Rive Neuve would kill the reputation of even a poor place in ten minutes, because most of the people who eat along there are natives, in spite of the seeming predominance of tourists. Some of the small restaurants have excellent chefs, or chefs skilled in soups or deep-fries or a dozen other adjuncts of fish cookery itself, and the Marseillais know about that, and the tourist is simply lucky. Some places have tired cooks, or even tired fry-kettles, but never tired fish. . . .

As I have said before, a few people (mostly Saxon) are not used to being stared at as they sit in a bare bright window sucking at shells and claws, while on the other side of the glass people stroll past them on the Rive Neuve and look at what is left on their plates, and then at the menu posted at the door, to see if it seems worth the price, and then either shrug off the She-Wolves or a little sheepishly come into the place they like the looks of. Americans are fascinated and rather tittery about this direct approach. English people find it too embarrassing for real comfort. Swiss, Germans, Scandinavians seem to like it, because it is "foreign" and relaxed. Italians find it "natural"; where there is fresh fish there is good food.

No doubt there are bad days, in any of the understaffed badly housed seafood restaurants along the Rive Neuve, just as there may be some "bad women" in the assortment of sidewalk touts and harpies. But who needs to eat an expensive touristic bouillabaisse when there are a dozen kinds of shellfish lying on green weeds waiting to be shelled, all gently breathing in and out, and several kinds of swimmers doomed to the poach pan or the skillet?

In one window of every fishhouse along the quay there is a tilted display, fresh once and sometimes twice a day, of the prettiest catch. The former hairdressers make the most whimsical, but in the plainest little restaurant there may be a curled fish balancing a giant shrimp on his nose, in a bed of silver sardines, with one lobster waving a feeler feebly behind him, to prove the possible class of the place. Norah and I liked to walk into town early, or at least by ten in the morning, to go to the Flower Market at the top of the Canebière, and we would see bleary waiters and some of the She-Wolves fabricating these fishy set pieces. The "girls" might be in curlers or with old sweaters over their nightgowns. The "boys" would be black-chinned and tousled. All their foreheads were wrinkled with concentration, and their lips pursed, as they tried the purple of a pile of sea urchins against the hideous fangy grey-pink of a *rascasse*, and then shook their heads and moved onto the set a majestic goblet hung with pink prawns. . . . Now and then we would be spotted, and there was always a smile and nod, and of course a beckoning suggestive leer from the females to get us back for lunch or dinner. . . .

There were many other fish places in Marseille, more elgant and often much better. But none of them had those fantastic women. They were not the same: they seemed tamer. The truth is, I suspect, that no man in the world would ever have the gall to behave as those females did and do along the Rive Neuve. Inside their dens, their caves, there were male waiters, of course, and men to help open the endless orders of shellfish from a banked dripping table or a great counter, but it was the other sex that dominated. I admit to being cowed by them at times, and to skulking along on the other side of the quay with my head turned away from their stern beady eyes, but at the same time I can still feed on an intrinsic courage that emanated from them, and may do so forever.

I I

Like every other *cours* in Provence, and like every such gathering place in most towns there around the Mediterranean, but especially in Marseille, the Cours Belsunce is unique. There can be no other like it, just as there can be no other Piazza di San Marco, although there are other formidably beautiful "squares" in Italy.

Belsunce is a wide street, tree-shaded in summer on the east side; the western side toward the sea was fairly thoroughly destroyed in the bombardment of May 27, 1944, and is now being filled in with high-rise 'scrapers. A few good old houses still stand, back of Belsunce, to prove its former dignity, and to the north it teems with life that can never be alien to a place like Marseille, although it is by now an "Arab Quarter," and has always had a shabby reputation among the more comfortably housed citizens of this ancient cosmopolis.

It was built in 1666 because the citizens were jealous of the beautiful Cours Mirabeau in Aix, their purportedly cultural and political rival. It was the style then to *stroll*, now a lost art: rich people showing their latest fashions at certain

hours, and nodding chattily to their favored peers; poorer
people doing what poor people did in those and any days,
shoving and eating and laughing, and showing their various
inward and outer sores and joys, like all the others.

Belsunce, called *Cours de Marseille* in proud defiance of
the promenade in Aix, was opened in 1670, by decree of
Louis XIV. First it was planted with a tree whose name I
cannot find, *micocouliers.* I assume it was fast-growing, since
the Cours was an immediate center of the town, and had only
been a-building for four years. Then there were mulberry
trees, those marvels of cool shade and messy pathways. In
1750, though, the *allées* along both sides of the Cours were
replanted with elms, and some ninety years later with plane
trees, many of which still stand nobly along the wide meeting-
street, as they do on the envied Cours Mirabeau in Aix, even
more beautifully.

Plane trees need a lot of root water (in Aix they are said to
survive on the buried canal that once flowed where the Cours
now stands) and there was plenty on the Cours de Marseille.
Halfway up it from what is now the Canebière there was a
great fountain, the Medusa, spouting from fifty mouths, and
in 1726 two more fine drinking troughs were built for man
and beast, with two more Medusas spitting out unfailing
streams of cool water to both sides.

These Medusas made a division, more aesthetic than some,
between the high and low classes of the town. On the north
side of the biggest fountain, life was rough, and inevitably
its verities spilled down toward the richer world, so that the
art of pocket-picking gave the whole Cours a bad reputation
by 1722, and few of the elegants dared set foot on it after
dark. It was still called "the loveliest spot in Europe," though,
just as the rival Cours Mirabeau is still called "the most
beautiful Main Street in the world." And while toward the

north the common people teemed and roistered, south of the Medusa, always spouting "a prodigious quantity of water," according to current chronicles, the Cours Belsunce was "elegant and animated . . . the rendez-vous of handsome personnages in embroidered clothes, their opera hats folded under one arm, their swords flapping against their haunches . . . the ladies made a fashion-show of their newest gowns, following every inconsistency of the changing styles, and the god of Vanity received there on the Grand Cours his most expensive compliments."

Aix has managed to hold on to its five lively fountains along the middle of its lovely street, in spite of wars, traffic, and other disasters. In contrast, in Marseille the great central fountain was knocked down before many years because it was believed to hinder the horse-drawn circulation to and from Aix and points north! The two smaller Medusas continued to fill the marble watering troughs, however, until 1841, when they were judged to be "too countrified," and were replaced by ugly cast-iron watering basins. (One of these was found in a pit in 1955, and is now exhibited in the Borély Museum, to hell-and-gone south of the city. It is a monument to Progress, at least . . . but hardly an archaeological treasure.)

In 1853 a bronze statue of Monseigneur François Xavier de Belsunce de Castelmoron, former bishop and one of the most devoted workers in Marseille during the horrible plague of 1720, was formally if belatedly erected at the top of the wide promenade, which from then on has been named for him, instead of being simply another small-town Provençal "cours." And once more traffic got the best of civic pride, and the noble old man was moved to the front of the Bishop's Palace, now Police Headquarters. During the last active war the statue somehow escaped being melted down for German armaments, and made another move, to stand in front of the

Cathedral, La Major, which is perhaps less lasting in its hideous neo-Byzantine bulk than the innate elegance of the warrior who fought to save his city from death by the pox. It is hard to conceive that the traffic of cars-buses-trucks will push him once more off his pedestal, as it did the Medusas finally, but an expression of clear resignation is intrinsic to the good bishop's face.

Traffic itself is as intrinsic, of course, to the Cours Belsunce today. But the sidewalk, at least on the east side, is as wide as it once was, and in summer the generous plane trees still shade it. And people drift along it in the special and very intense fashion true to any such place, from the Galería in Milan to the Plaza in Chapala. They are going someplace, maybe, and maybe coming from someplace, at a special speed that cannot be judged by its apparent indolence. Perhaps they do not really know the wheres and whences, much less the whys, but there is a latent purposefulness in the way they move, and in the looks they give to the foodstuffs in the sidewalk stands, to the windows of the little shops, to the other people sitting in the cafés, waiting for them or for somebody like them.

Did the hard division between two social worlds happen when the great spouting fountain went down? Was it really demolished to make the rich safer from the street thieves who lived on the wrong side of the Medusa watering troughs, rather than to ease traffic onto the long road to Aix? (One contemporary wrote that the whole Cours had "a very bad reputation, complete with exotic bazaars and 'Levantines'!") Whatever the reasons, Belsunce is by now a conglomerate, a puzzle, which can possibly be called, if not solved, a potential melting pot. There are few visible signs, except for an occasional doorway or cornice, of the affluent politicians and noblemen who once showed off their silks and their sweethearts and even built their townhouses on the "right" side of the fountain, and the commoners who used to stay up toward the Porte d'Aix now own the whole wide street, off the Canebière. And the minute anyone steps onto the Cours, a special lifebeat starts, that has been there, shunned sometimes, feared sometimes, for a few hundred years, through various historical throes and spasms and cultural and architectural upheavals, all felt instinctively but perhaps unremembered except for the bombardments of 1944, whose scars still show.

Cafés sprawl onto the wide east sidewalk, always looking half-filled with slender dark men hunched over tiny cups of coffee or glasses of pale tea or violently orange soda. They talk in groups of two or three, never loudly, or sit alone with an expectant patience. Shapeless ageless women hurry up to the narrow streets of the Arab quarter with heavy string bags of provisions from the main open market on the other side of the Canebière. There are dogs, and children, and surprisingly few identifiable whores. ("Arabs" have their own prides and prejudices.) The dogs and the children seem to know what they are there for: to wait for their masters or, on Sundays, to work in the booths, according to the number of legs they may be endowed with.

Along that east side of Belsunce there are all kinds of stands: food mostly, hot-cold-spiced-sweet, and then souvenirs of Marseille to send back to North Africa; cheap small rugs made in USA; trays of watches and ballpoint pens and bright jeweled combs. The smells are good, in the ever-fresh air under the plane trees. There is very little jukebox din, as on the Quai du Port on weekends, but there seems no wish or need to play the Levantine or Algerian music that would be expected from the looks of most of the people on the Cours, and that is wailed out elsewhere in Marseille, even a block or two northward, off the Rue d'Aix.

When I have been in town, I have always gone to Belsunce, and have retained to a probably unflattering degree my invisibility. Women are nonexistent there, as such, except for the ancient drudges with their market bags and their soft long shapeless dresses and one tattoo between the downcast eyes. They are as shadowy as I, to the quiet throngs of men who move idly, like tidal waters, along the Cours and then off narrow streets like Présentines, Ste. Barbe, Chapeliers. Eastward, on the Grands Rue, little open shops spill piles of clothes onto the sidewalks, and more clothes hang like flocks of garish birds on high hangers, and the merchants lounge against mounds of rugs and bolted yardage, or squat philosophically on piles of repossessed overcoats and work clothes. As everywhere in Marseille, rich or poor, an astonishing number of shoes are for sale, cheap or costly and obviously expendable. In the Arab Quarter they are cheap, and as available as a glass of tea. If there is any of the haggling that Westerners expect in Eastern bazaars, it is low-keyed, and the voices are more a steady murmur than anything excited, except perhaps during a period of anger or political revolt. I would not know except from the daily papers, because I have always walked these streets in times of seeming easiness, and in daylight.

Even the poorest shops in this quarter have a few traditional robes and coverings hanging in them, to beautify young girls and brides and I assume all women, except the oldest ones with string bags. Up past the Cours on the Rue d'Aix there are a few comparatively elegant stores, with windows filled with exotic exquisite long coats, and swatches of gold-shot silk, and jeweled slippers.

Nowhere are there women. Even the ancient biddies disappear, once they have crossed the Canebière and gone silently up Belsunce. The men, then, must be the ones who buy such beauty for their brides, their nubile daughters. . . .

Once only, though, I saw an amazing female in the Quarter.

At the top of the Cours there is a junky-looking store, like many in San Francisco's Chinatown: one knows instinctively that at the back, behind all the gaudy trash, there will be some rare porcelain, yellowed ivory, an amber hairpin. . . . I was considering an embroidered collar of gold thread and bits of turquoise, and to cool my greedy wits before a definite and perhaps predestined extravagance I went eastward for a few paces, on the Rue St. Jean, I think. The shopkeeper looked fatalistically after me, sure I would return to his bait.

The woman coming toward me cut through the tide of men like a shining blade. They fell back from her with a discreet but obvious awareness, quite different from their acceptance of my invisibility. They did not seem to look at her, or at each other behind her, but they *saw* her. Perhaps they knew her, or what she was.

She was unusually tall, surely a German or Swede, with a pale broad face. It had either seven or nine symmetrically designed tattoos or perhaps paintings on it, in a pale blue that was clearly outlined on the white skin, even though her whole face looked as if dusted with powder or flour. Her blue eyes were narrowed, fixed on an inner goal and looking only toward it. She wore a kind of pillbox on her head, with straight blond hair pulled tightly up into it, and pale blue gauzy veils fell from it, over all of her long and perhaps slender body except her impassive face.

She glanced fleetingly at me, or rather her eyes touched me as if I were one more object within her immediate view, and then she sailed past, with the silks fluttering in her wake.

I was astounded by her, and wondered almost fearfully why she was abroad, on a bright crowded Sunday, when all the other women of the quarter remained hidden behind tight shutters. She seemed to be walking straight toward something, and while nobody stepped aside, it was a ridiculous impossibility that anyone could or would be in her way.

I went back to the corner shop almost unsteadily, my eyes still on the strange blue markings of that exalted.face, on the implacable progress of that tall body through the crowds of quiet dark men. The collar of gold thread and turquoise looked vulgar to me, and it cost too much, and the shopkeeper shrugged smilingly and said he would see me again some day, which he did.

And I walked down the Cours Belsunce, past all the little cafés and foodstalls and snack bars with windows full of unbelievably sweet oily cookies painted in wild pinks and yellows, and my mind was full of puzzlement. What kind of woman had I seen? She was regally beyond evil, and perhaps good. She could have controlled all the prostitution or heroin market in the Mediterranean world, or she could have been the adaptive and charitable refugee wife of a local Arab peddler, but she was perhaps the most impassive *force* I had ever seen in a female, and the most mysterious, even in Marseille. She must have existed long before the Cours was built, long before the Phoceans came; A.D. 1670, 600 B.C., such trivia fade fast when someone, something like that, walks along its own private path.

I I I

There is an iron staircase, a steep long footbridge that goes straight down to the Rive Neuve of the Old Port in Marseille, from very high up, near the ancient Abbey of St. Victor. It spans what used to be the Canal de Rive Neuve, that bypassed the Port and hopefully drained off not only some of the shipping but much of the pollution that a couple of hundred years ago made the city one of the world's prime stinkholes. The canal is now dry, and used mostly to store construction equipment for the gradual rebuilding of some of the quays. It is ugly to look down upon, but sometimes one does, especially on the upward climb of the stairs. I usually did, to catch my breath, and, once I was sure of the drabness below me, I looked instead at the old church, or into the star-shaped ramparts of the Fort St. Nicolas beyond it. They calmed my lurking vertigo.

One day I had stopped halfway up the hideous resounding stairs, and then started on the second half of the climb, when an elderly lady, very nicely dressed in the discreet well-cut black clothes and artful "toque" that are worn only by French women of her age and station (She is on the Ladies' Board of St. Victor, I said to myself, and is a member of the musical committee for the Bach concerts . . .), started down the top steps and then faltered when she saw me.

Lady, I said to myself, this is no place to hesitate . . . either keep moving, or sit down until you feel better. I kept on climbing slowly, and she came down, holding onto the cold metal rail. When she got about five steps from me, she smiled archly and said in a fluty voice, the kind ladies of her age and station reserve for waitresses in tea shops or their own grandchildren, "It is so difficult, in fact it is impossible, to know whether one is walking toward a man or a woman these days!" She laughed musically. We both stopped going down and up, after this strange unsolicited comment, and finally I said, with some stiffness I suppose, "I assure you, Madame, that in spite of my pants suit I am a female."

The whole thing suddenly seemed almost unbelievable, out of control, a dream, as we stood there on the ugly iron footbridge with the dead canal far below us and piles of gravel and rusting cement mixers, and the clean air blowing in from the sea. She laughed, this time with a little less musical certainty, and said with some confusion, "Things do seem mixed up, don't they? Girls act like men, and it is rumored that men even act like . . . well, not like real men . . . sometimes. Here in Marseille all kinds of strange things seem to happen, like seeing a man come up the stairs and then it is not a man at all. But of course I know you don't mean to look like a man. That is—"

I interrupted her, and I knew that soon I would regret being rude, but for the moment I *felt* rude. I felt affronted by this silly ladylike simpering relic, tottering toward me down the dreadful iron stairs. "No, Madame," I said very distinctly, "I do not mean to look like a man. I am not a man. I am a traveller, and I find a pants suit excellent on trains and buses and planes and even iron footbridges."

She looked increasingly flustered, as for a moment or two I really wanted her to, because I was temporarily past pity or empathy. I thought her first simpering remark was un-called for, especially on a hideous high arch that, at best, is some kind of atavistic challenge to my steadiness and cour-age. "You are a foreigner," she said triumphantly, as if she had found a toehold in our encounter.

"Yes, I am. I am from California," I said to beat her to asking me.

"Ah, what an enormous country," she exclaimed exactly as I knew she would, loosing her gloved grip on the rail long enough to put her hand over her heart.

"Yes," I said, and then I cruelly went on in the ritual I had learned too well from many of her counterparts over the teacups in Dijon and points south, east, and north in France for the past forty years. "The United States are much too large and enormous, and we are a very young nation, still feeling growing pains, not knowing our strength, making all kinds of blunders that must be blamed on a spiritual adolescence. We are a mixture of the most daring refugees from every oldest country of the world. We are an amalgam. Our thinking and even our everyday manners are impulsive, and often crude."

She blinked at me, and then said with new firmness, "But you speak quite coherently." She sounded polite but astonished, and this made me even more impatient, mostly because I hated to stand there on that bridge, far above the cruel sand of the old canal, with the wind nudging us. I bowed and said, "Thank you."

She smiled in a flustered way, and said, "Well, I must say goodbye. You are wearing a costume that I cannot accustom myself to, but one can tell that you are obviously nicely brought up. Goodbye, goodbye."

I bowed again to her, and listened to her careful steps down to the bottom of the footbridge. Then I went stamping up to the top of the iron stairs, and almost immediately felt swamped with remorse at having been rude, and to an older woman. How could I have sounded so cold and basically so irritated by this harmless sweetfaced lady? On the other hand, how had she dared simply announce to me that she could not tell whether I was male or female? What business was it of hers? But perhaps she had just been given a mood changer, a tranquilizer of some kind? Perhaps her daughter had just died of cancer and she had been to St. Victor to pray? Certainly she had quit her accustomed role as a well-bred aging lady to whinny to me, as I panted up the iron steps toward her. Had it been because she needed to talk to another human being? Then why had she said such a strange thing? And after all, what business *was* it of hers? I had said nothing about her peculiarly traditional black costume with the little toque and the smooth kid gloves, and the handbag for her rosary.

I tried not to think of her faded face with the small good bones underneath the skin, and her puzzled eyes. I felt acutely, painfully, ashamed of myself for a few more minutes, and now and then I still do, and probably always will, for not having recognized a call, perhaps a call for help, from another dizzied human.

Chapter 5

ONE OF THE
MEN

In 1973, while my sister Norah was wandering through the dusty stacks of small but famous Marseille libraries, public and private, on the trail of Mary Magdalen's lesser-known apocrypha, I spent most of my time absorbing the general aspect of the Old Port, either from our two big windows above the Rive Neuve or down on the waterfront. I was largely silent. Opening a conversation there can be either provocative or impolitic, depending upon where it is done, and I chose to remain inaudible and thus somewhat unseen. I have been fairly conditioned, though, to love to talk, perhaps especially in French, and that is why it was good for me to meet the doctor down our street.

Norah disliked him immediately, for several reasons including the fact that he had something like fourteen children, and was therefore a selfish Catholic (she occasionally sounds oddly like her Irish grandmother!), and also because sometimes I would go to report to him on basic matters such as how one of his pills was performing, and instead of being back at the apartment in half an hour, I would come in three hours later, my head humming with his well-educated volubility. I was tiddly on his good talk, like a child drunk on fruit juice after too long a thirst.

My sister, naturally more anxious about why a pill was necessary than what possible effect it might have, took out her uneasiness by being coldly disapproving of my lackadaisical manner, and indirectly of my sparkle. I told her Dr. Gabillaud was talkative. "Plain gabby!" she said. And he is still Gabby Gabillaud, high on my list of therapeutic spellbinders. I would like to see him again. I feel averse, though, to taking up a doctor's time unless I need his trained help, and three years after I swallowed the man's capsules in Marseille, when I returned there, I could neither cough nor creak commendably enough to ring his doorbell.

I think often of him, as I do of a few other medicos in France and Switzerland and England, and it both interests and saddens me that with them I feel a stronger bond than I do with their peers in my own country. This is not because I was a foreigner, thus calling out their extra compassion, their fleeting amiability. On the contrary, I was probably an interruption in their familiar rounds of office and house calls, and obviously a transient and unprofitable investment in the kind of energy that a good doctor spends beyond his professional obligations.

And Gabby Gabillaud and some of those other Europeans did spend it on me. It was more valuable to my adrenalin supply, my loyally pumping heart, my occasional aches and quakes, than any injections or suppositories yet devised. When they had finished their explorations, both verbal and manual, and scribbled their lingua franca prescriptions for what may or may not have ailed me, they would sit back with a small sigh, look at me as if I had suddenly come into focus as a

person and not a problem, and begin to talk, about Paul
Valéry, or German-Swiss dumplings, or a former student of
Maillol who had just fallen off her unfinished statue of a
ninety-foot phallus. I would respond like the proverbial old
firehorse to the whiff of conversational smoke. I would feel
younger, more like a human being. And when the unknown
man sitting with apparent enjoyment behind his desk looked
suddenly at his watch, I would stand up as if I must leave a
good dinner before its end, and walk out in a heady cloud of
silly jokes and puns, epigrams, criticisms, all playing like
firelight over *language*, language used as it should be used:
a prime means of communication.

Gabby talked that way. Sometimes I wondered cynically
if he really did, or if he merely sounded fine because I was
so hungry for French from somebody besides a Marseille
waiter or cabdriver, but by now I know that he was an intelligent, well-educated man, and that *he* needed to talk to *me*.
What is more, he let me talk too, and I heard my rusty accent
grow smoother, and felt my mind stretch. I asked him questions, sensing that he wanted me to. He would rise like a
wily old trout, recognizing my bait, and knowing how to
escape it with a flick and a neat flash.

Once I heard someone come into his untended waiting room
and begin to walk around, sigh, drop a magazine. I finally
said something polite about not staying. He glanced at his
schedule on his big flat desk, said, "That's old Fantoni. He's
in for his shot. He'll be all right for a while," and went
right on about the need for men in high office to have their
own escape hatches. He told me graphically about a schoolmate of his, now a famous political leader, who since puberty
has hidden at regular times to listen day and night to recorded
music. "It's like periodic alcoholism," I said. "Yes, but this
is restorative, not destructive," Gabby said. "And by now, it

is a double game with him. It works up his glands to fool the journalists, who link him with international starlets, secret rendezvous with nuclear-physicists. Even his wife believes that he has at least one mistress. He comes back from the three days of Baroque music, or 1930s jazz, a renewed man."

In the waiting room, Fantoni banged open a window, and groaned a little. I stood up again. "Doctor, do you wish to see me next week?" He looked as if he was trying to remember why I was there, and then permitted himself a small grin as he bowed perfunctorily to me. "Of course," he said. "Monday at eleven, when the office is not so crowded."

Old Fantoni, the only other soul around, looked crosswise at me, and held his stomach gently with one hand. I felt sheepish but exhilarated; Norah would be chilly with me, and nobody would notice how much better my French sounded, and I wondered why this did not happen at home. Why could not my wits, if not my American accent, be sharpened by my monthly visit to a trusted friend's office? Why would I come out feeling as dull as when I went in? I would have an impression of the doctor's real fatigue, of being rushed through a hideously crowded schedule, of needing more than the routine checks of pulse, blood pressure, respiration. I needed to have more than my prescriptions renewed. And what was perhaps most tonic of all in my visits to Gabby and his French peers was that in some ways I felt that I too had been good medicine. . . .

Maybe our doctors at home, I thought as I headed for the apartment above the Vieux Port, are so overcrowded and harried that they cannot permit themselves to be more than healers to their patients. They choose, in self-survival, to have little sustained contact with the sick, in their training and then in the clinics and huge hospitals and busy groups they graduate to. Now and then a handful will break away, to try in an idealistic fashion to recapture the old spirit of "the country doctor" in a rural community. They must learn to make house calls, and to drive into the hills in storms to deliver babies. They must think about their own children's chancy schooling and about their frustrated bored wives. They must make annual contact with "the outside," at some exhausting medical conference, and try not to listen to their classmates wondering how to cope with income taxes, nor to the blandishments of great pharmaceutical laboratories, nor to their in-laws suggesting they give up this person-to-person nonsense and specialize in ophthalmology or psychopodiatry, in an affluent suburb where they will, first thing, put in swimming pool and tennis court. . . .

I wondered how French or English or Swiss G.P.s found the nerve to avoid all this pressure. How did they raise fourteen children? How did they keep their wives? The first time I saw Gabby, for instance, he came to our lower-class, shabby flat at almost ten at night, after his rounds. He had been called at perhaps five o'clock by our concierge, who "went" to him for some female trouble but knew he would cure my wild coughing. He looked like a tired, quiet, middle-aged businessman. He listened to my story, gave me about six prescriptions to be filled the next day, did nothing about immediate relief of what I felt was a cosmic whoop, and stood up as if he would like to dust off his trousers. When I asked him his fee, he said, "Two thousand francs." I was horrified until I realized that he was pre-de Gaulle and meant twenty, and he put the bills, worth about four dollars, into his coat pocket, and asked me to see him in three days.

I cannot remember any late house calls before in my lives in Europe, nor do I remember paying money to a doctor. They would send a bill annually, after I had forgotten that on August 4 the younger girl had thrown up after a bee sting and that on November 29 the older had gashed her leg in an awkward slalom. . . . But Gabillaud lived in a blue-collar part of the quarter, and perhaps it was easier that way. Certainly the fee did not seem to interest him one way or another. I thought he was a cold fish, and felt peevish that he had not left some magical pill to make me stop coughing.

Three days and two shots later (given by a licensed nurse sent from the neighborhood pharmacy where I had all the prescriptions filled), I went a couple of blocks down our ugly street to his apartment house. His office was on the ground floor, and he lived on the one above, according to the mailboxes. The waiting room was grim and dark, perhaps a former mean, measly dining room. There was an inadequate but elegant desk in the little hallway, with a telephone, and I learned later that one or another of the doctor's attractive daughters occasionally marked appointments there. A half-open door showed the former kitchen, now with an examination table crowded into it. Then Gabby opened the final door, and I went into a room that in a flash reminded me of other forgotten doctors' offices: London, Berne, Dijon, all completely different from the professional cubbyholes at home, so antiseptic and impersonal.

It was big, once the *salon* of the apartment, with tall windows opening onto a neglected green garden, shabby and tranquil. There were good armchairs and a chaise longue and plenty of books and reading lights, and there was a general feeling that the family used the room whenever it was not a hospice for the dying and the sickly. It felt clean, healthy, and receptive. I sank into a fine chair upholstered in worn silk, and forgot to cough.

The doctor looked freshly shaved, and almost dapper, compared with the rumpled man of the night call. I deduced, early in our game, that he was hipped on allergies: he started out by tracing my chronic bronchial cough to a life-long predilection for living near the sea, the ocean, even lakes and ponds. His logical questions proved him right, at least to himself. Then he used his own case to strengthen mine, and bared his weak defenses in unwitting betrayal.

His whole career, his life in Algeria as head surgeon in a big civil hospital after years of study and practice in Bordeaux and Paris, had ended abruptly, tragically: he told me that in 1961, during the Mutiny, he had developed a violent reaction to *rubber*. "Had this ever happened before?" I asked with guileful innocence, thinking of that time of wild revolt and of the thousands of people fleeing Algeria and of all the scandal and anguish there and in France. "No," he said, almost serenely. "Within a few days it became obvious that never again could I wear rubber gloves. And that meant giving up surgery forever. It meant leaving a country I loved, abandoning my patients, uprooting my children from their schools. An allergy, Madame . . . a simple twist in the metabolic pattern, the body chemistry of a mature man! I was finished!"

He tried to use this sad story as a proof that once back in California I must undergo a long series of tests to decide what it was about sea air that made me cough. I pretended to consider all this seriously for the next few months, but his apparent unwillingness to track down his own sudden inability to tolerate rubber gloves seemed quizzical to me, and I sniffed out what I could of his neurotic nature.

I noticed that his hands were strong and firm-skinned, but that he held a pen as if it hurt him. He touched doorknobs with care. He never shook hands, as so many people do in southern France. Once he decided to examine some of my orifices in the converted kitchen. To do it he rinsed his hands from a bottle and put on mittens of thin clear plastic; afterward he washed his hands very gently with two kinds of soap, powdered them, and ran a sterilized orangewood stick under his nails and around the cuticle, in a slow preoccupied way. When he saw me watching him, he asked me curtly to wait for him in his office, but when he came in he did not seem anything but bland and interested in me-the-patient.

Over the next weeks I asked him questions that were so obvious as to make me feel ridiculous: were allergic conditions slow in building; was there any proven connection between them and emotional stress; could they be cured or merely alleviated, with the possible causes and cures dictated by chemistry or by circumstance? The doctor never seemed aware of my game: I was a "case" to him, and he himself was *not*. He was an extraordinary example of the quirkiness of Fate, or Providence, or perhaps God. People like me could have series of injections in their bottoms, or move to a new climate, or stop eating eggs. He was a surgeon cut down in his prime, a victim of the sudden curse of wearing rubber gloves. There was no remedy for any punishment as unique as his. He shrugged, laid his strong, somewhat hairy hands on his desk as if they were made of porcelain, and went into another casual story about his famous schoolmate who played records instead of having a mistress, or about a former patient who raised cheetahs (Gabby was given one every New Year, and sent it to the Longchamps zoo), or the rise in heroin addiction in Western Europe. . . .

He talked with somewhat the same self-enjoyment, somewhat the sensuality he showed in cleaning his nails, but with more animation. We both enjoyed it. I talked too (another vocal voluptuary!), and he seemed to enjoy what I asked and occasionally stated. Once he lost his usual ironical detachment, when we were talking about the way young people, his in Marseille and mine in Pittsburgh or Berkeley, young people anywhere, can be pushed into drug abuse. He turned very pale, and said, "I have spent my life learning how to save lives, and I am ready to die to oppose capital punishment, but I am also ready to kill anyone who sells drugs. *Kill!*" He forgot his hands, and raised them to make a violent gesture of pressing them unto death around a throat. . . .

And only once did he permit himself to touch me except professionally. That was the day after I fell on my face, when he put one hand for a minute on my shoulder, as if in his concern he must silently pat me, commend me, encourage me.

And that was the Monday after Palm Sunday, which is a special holiday in France and perhaps most so in Marseille. It is almost the end of Lent, almost spring. People swarm out of their nests like lustful bees, helpless lemmings, and walk or ride into the countryside. If they own cars, they throw grandparents and children into the back, and drive as fast as they can along the nearest and preferably the most crowded highways. They head, afoot or on wheels, for good food and open air, preferably with a view thrown in.

My sister and I felt the fever of Palm Sunday along with countless other Marseillais, and after a remarkably good lunch up on the Rue des Catalans we started the interminable trek on the curving Corniche J. F. Kennedy, which is very wide, very ugly, built along the wild coast outside the city. To our left were six lanes of cars full of people going anywhere as fast as possible. To our right was the Mediterranean, looking pale blue except on the surly rocks below the high

cement curve of the roadway. We began to trudge instead
of walk. Finally we sighted a little café across the way, and
far from coincidentally it was located by one of the rare
stop-and-go lights. We decided to cross and sit down.

We grabbed a green light, ran to the pedestrian island
just as the yellow went on, and unlike us in every way except
on Palm Sunday, 1973, we decided to run for the curb before
the red went on.

The island was shaped somewhat like a badly designed
throat lozenge, larger at one end, and sloping on the six-inch
sides, and I misjudged by about an inch, and instead of taking one hurried step across the little raised platform, I
plunged off it, straight forward, five feet and seven-plus
inches, into the path of the nearest of three lanes of happy
carefree well-fed celebrants getting up speed again as fast
as possible with their green light.

I heard Norah cry *"Oh!"* and felt her pull me back onto
the soft warm welcoming asphalt of the pedestrian island,
where I would have liked to take a long nap. But there was
a general screech of brakes, and a dozen people slowed and
called out, "Can we help? Do you need help? Can we take
her to a doctor?" "No, no, thank you," Norah called back,
and she began to look at my face, while the motorists gathered new speed. Then two young men ran from the sea edge
of the Corniche, and bent over me. They were interns at Ste.
Marguerite, they said to my sister, and one picked up my
face from its lovely cushion and said, "Hospital. Now," and
the other ran back (Norah said he simply waltzed between the
long lanes of traffic), and wheeled their car around toward
the café we'd been heading for.

"Can she walk?" "Yes, she can," and I was mopping off my
face with wet paper towels the barman brought me in the

toilet. People looked compassionately at me as I drifted in and out of the café, but there was no disgust at my ugliness, my bloodied clothes.

Outside, the two young men folded me into the back of a ratty old *deux-cheveaux* with its cloth top down. The older more decisive one sat beside me looking as wary as a pointing setter, with one hand on my wrist. I said, reorganizing my mind and mouth to be polite or at least conscious, "This is a boring way for you to celebrate Palm Sunday," and he said, "Oh, we were just cruising. Nice sun today."

We drove a long time, I thought, and then were in a huge collection of grubby old buildings and half-finished sidewalks, and I was in Emergency Surgery while Norah thanked the two young men and tried vainly to pay for their gas, endow a new clinic, send them to the Shah of Iran, anything to thank them.

The emergency room was cluttered. I felt cozy. A table covered with bloody sheets stood waiting for attention. On another table a long black man, with a towel over his genitals and a crushed leg lying crookedly down from his live body, smiled at me. I sat on a stool while a tiny nurse with enormous black eyes swabbed efficiently at my face. She was alluring, and passionately skillful. A young doctor poked and cut at the dead black leg on the table, and the man laughed softly.

"Does it hurt?" I asked while the nurse got more supplies. "Not on your life," he said in an amused way. "Second time I've done this. My old leg between a stone wall and my motorbike. Then *toubibs* fix me so I don't hurt a-tall."

"Shut up, now," the tiny nurse said, and started to pin my forehead together. "Last time you had a tetanus shot?" I could not remember, so nodded when she shook my shoulder a little and snapped, "Within two years?" She gave me a booster anyway. Two men came in to take me across the hall for X-rays, and as I went out, the Black said laughingly to me, while his *toubib* sliced out a piece of useless old flesh, "Don't worry, Sister!"

There was a lot happening. In my quick trip to the X-ray room, perhaps fifteen feet from the bloody one, I saw two corpses, a child heaving under a sheet on a gurney, several dazed battered people like me. There was no more confusion than there was any effort at all to make the place quiet, attractive, reassuring, as it would be in my country. No potted plants stood in niches, and in the waiting room where my sister sat, there were not enough chairs and children leaned silently against the walls.

I got a quick look at three or four X-rays before they were rushed across the hall to Emergency Surgery: yes, my nose had snapped very neatly; no need to set it; there would be swelling. No concussion.

In Emergency, another young man was clipping the former leg into some semblance of such, and the long Black had snoozed off. The ferocious little nurse was talking with some passion about stitches. "Use plastic clips," the intern said. "Scar," she said, and when he said *clips* again, she came over to me and with a few keen looks into my eyes, onto my face, she dutifully clipped shut the long vertical gash on my forehead. Now and then she felt my wrist. The man with the chopped-up leg was snoring. "Doctor, look here," she said in a peculiar blend of business and sex. He looked, said warmly, "Superb, magnificent!" and went on with his own chore, stitch-snip-stitch. I felt happy that they might sleep together later.

So, on instruction from a tired desk orderly in the huge old hideous hospital, I went the next morning to Dr. Gabillaud, I could barely see his door, much less read the information on it, and did not realize until later that it was not his "office day."

I rang the apartment several times, and heard girls calling, "Papa! Papa!" Finally he opened the downstairs door, looking fussily scrubbed, in a natty suit and with a dot of shaving soap in one ear.

"My God," he said. "What has happened to you?"

He put his hand to my shoulder, as he steered me into the pleasant big room, and when he looked appraisingly at me I knew, for the first time really, that I was a mess. A three-inch square of gauze and tape covered most of my forehead, and another held my nose in place. Both my eyes were squinty and puffed, with dark bruise marks halfway down my cheeks: two shiners. My lips were swollen. I smiled carefully at him.

"Well," he said, "at least you have all your teeth! Were you mugged? Did you fall out of a window?"

So I told him, and increasingly I wondered at the unhesitating kindness of Frenchmen in a dozen cars, out for a yearly holiday ritual, who stopped or slowed down on the hectic Corniche to ask if they could help. There I lay on the pedestrian island, I told Gabby, bloody and dazed, my sister bending over me, people in cars sounding concerned-generous-helpful. There we were, on a festive day. And there were the two young interns, out for some sunshine. . . .

"Of course. Why not?" The doctor sounded testy. I told him that at home people seemed afraid of becoming involved, scared of lawsuits, of malpractice. "Heathen," he said. I said that forty citizens could stand watching a woman be raped and murdered, and not lift a finger to help. "Barbaric," he said. "In France we have lived with the law for so long that we know how and when to make use of it. We are not afraid of it. In your country you are still so inexperienced, that you are in awe of it. The law is your stern parent, like God, and you fear its punishment. Here we respect it, but only if we respect ourselves more. We use it when we need it."

"But those two young men—they looked thin and poor. They needed a rest. They spent half their free afternoon helping us."

Gabby brushed that away with a surprisingly relaxed gesture of his immaculate hands. "It's their job," he said. "They've already spent years with sick, injured, dying people. In the United States—" and he was off on what became weeks of talk between us, mostly a dialogue about medical problems in our two countries. French students started active patient-care before they opened their first textbooks, he said, and were in the *home* the minute they enrolled in a school. In my country an ambitious intelligent young medical aspirant worked in abstractions, in theories, before he ever delivered a baby or set a bone. By the time an American did his internship he had already decided what branch of medicine he would follow, and by then he might well be wooed by money and power into advanced research. . . .

"We'll never have a Nobel for medicine," Gabby said with some bitterness. "By the time a Frenchman qualifies as a doctor, he has spent a lot of his creative energy on day-and-night care of the sick and is too poor to stop work for further study. Professionally we are a breed of superb-to-piddling country doctors, enslaved by poverty and plain exhaustion."

Gabillaud had two sons and several French protégés in Canada, all medical students. There they would be freer to choose their paths in medicine: they could go from Toronto into the northern wilds of Ontario if some instinctive urge forced them to be frontier bonesetters, and if they wanted the excitements and fat salaries of laboratory research they could head for Detroit, Dallas . . . "In France," he said, "nine out of ten young doctors like the ones you met on Palm Sunday will end up in poor country districts, killing themselves to keep a few ignorant peasants alive."

"But what about those interns and residents at the hospital? They were handsome, skillful, experienced, so young," I said, and he interrupted me. "*Ah,*" he said triumphantly. "They were the pick of the crop! You just happened, my dear friend, to be rescued by two kids doing their last year with Jacques Tatin, one of the finest doctors in Marseille—in France! That was his own pavilion they took you to."

"But it was in a big municipal—"

"*Ah!* Here, aside from having private clinics, very expensive and stylish, many doctors as renowned as my highly respected colleague have their own pavilions in public hospitals, where they train their most promising students from the university school of medicine. The Tatin pavilion is uniquely emergency, to sound out the interns. *All* famous doctors in a town like Marseille, or Paris or Bordeaux, consider it part of their duties to teach on the local faculty. In your case, by neat coincidence, your rescuers happened to be studying under my friend Tatin. He is still fairly young, and brilliant, and he grooms a stable of the most promising colts in French medicine, including his own son. Of course he has his private clinic—no need for Junior to head for Toronto! Tatin is a magnificent kidney man—"

"But my nose," I said. "And the young doctor working on that leg! Urology?"

"Precisely!" Gabby said. "Men who can intern with Tatin have already spent several years, perhaps their best ones, working in every branch of the art of medicine. Half of them

will never go much further than their own practices in provincial towns. A special few will end by being rich, covered
with decorations, safe with their own famous patients in their
own elegant clinics. A few will be like me, or rather the way
I *was*, head surgeons in big hospitals and still with their own
practices. I'm now a gynecologist, you know from my little
sign. But I can recognize an allergic bronchial cough when
I hear it. And I am very good at stitchery, thanks to two years
in an emergency pavilion in Bordeaux, much like Tatin's.
And I wish that young rascal had not put clips on your
forehead. I could have made that scar as unimportant as a
wrinkle. Now it's a scowl. But of course I'd have to charge
you."

By then this was a quiet joke with us, well along in our
dialogue. His first fee, the night he came to the apartment,
had so plainly startled me that from then on he somewhat
sardonically translated every sum for me, in "old francs"
and then "de Gaulle." The day he stared from across his
desk at my poor crumpled face, he waived any fee. The
others were all unpredictable: about two dollars when he
wrote prescriptions, a dollar now and then, once about eight
when I had to undress and go into the converted kitchen for
probings. (This was when housewives of low means did not
blink at paying five or six dollars a pound for the Sunday
roast.) I suppose that in almost five months, while I grate-
fully renewed some contact with the French language, I
spent about thirty dollars.

Prescriptions were costlier. The corner pharmacist continued his first disapproval of me, when I firmly paid cold cash
for his magic elixirs, potions, pastilles. I tried to explain to
him that I did not feel entitled to French Medicare, since I
was a transient foreigner and paid almost no taxes. "It's
there, Madame," he said reprovingly. "Take it. Make the

most of a good thing," and every time that I did not, he shrugged as if with fatalistic disapproval of my stupidity. And to my continuing astonishment there seemed to be almost none of the maze of paperwork (*paperasserie*, which sounds funnier in English than in French) that is accepted as a necessary and routine evil at home—and of course in some branches of French officialdom like the postal service.

When I went to Emergency at the big public hospital in Marseille, the desk orderly asked for my name and address as I left. The sexy wee surgical nurse had already told me to return at once if I felt feverish, and in ten days if not, and had dismissed me fiercely as another bloody body was rolled into her room. When I went back, the second Wednesday after Palm Sunday, she spotted me at once in the hall and said angrily, "Oh, *you!* This is not your day! Oh, yes—it is!" She stood on tiptoe to rip the old tired bandage off my head, nodded with a dazzling smile, and pushed me into her room, which was gorier than before, but empty.

I sat again on the low stool, and she swabbed at me as fast as a bird pecking for grain. It hurt a little, but I knew that she was in no way careless or ignorant. She stood back to take a long satisfied look. "Superb! Magnificent," she murmured, since the handsome intern was not there to say it. "Now *out!* Don't come back!" And I was in the hall before I could even try to thank her. I thought, she is like a delicious Provençal olive, firm, small, succulent, with a forthright bite to her flavor. . . .

The desk orderly asked, "Dismissed? Name, address?" He gave me an indecipherable written description of my outpatient care noted by l'Assistance Publique de Marseille, number CICH 1428, and asked me to sign it, so that my social insurance could pay the bill. He looked with frank astonishment at me when I explained that since I was a temporary resident, and a foreigner, I myself wanted to pay. Finally he said, "You mean you are a *tourist?*" He shrugged as if I were therefore mad. "The bill [you poor benighted nitwit, his voice added without words], Madame, is forty-four hundred ninety francs!" Thanks to Dr. Gabillaud, and a few fish-women on the Quai des Belges who liked to startle visitors with the "Old and New," I did not even blink, and handed out forty-four francs and ninety centimes, and he signed my receipt and bowed sadly at me from his chair.

I had thus rashly paid about nine dollars for two visits to Emergency, a booster shot against tetanus, a lot of bandage and tape, and several X-rays and six clips. When I told Gabby all this, he smiled and said casually, "You are obviously either idealistic or merely stubborn. But here in the office, my poor lady, you must pay and pay! I milk the rich tourists, to treat for nothing a handful of penniless *pieds noirs* from Algeria. . . ."

And not long ago, on the radio in California, I heard a newscast by a bedazzled young reporter who told of having broken his leg in Marseille. He was hospitalized for two nights, in a cast, and then allowed to hop around until the bone was correctly healed, with several visits to the municipal clinic where it had been set. Finally he was discharged, and apologetically required to pay an extra sum of almost four dollars for a special metal brace the doctors had put into the plaster with his permission, so that he could go back to his work sooner. That was all, he reported dreamily, and I smiled with complicity and thought of all the American doctors who must be tut-tutting his subversive socialistic message. . . .

This report of mine could be a chatty incident about the avaricious cold scheming cheating lying Frenchman so often described by us tourists, but it is really about what happened to me on Palm Sunday, 1973, on the Corniche Kennedy. Or perhaps is it more truly about how I managed subconsciously to prolong my official visits to a doctor who spoke beautiful gabby French?

By the time my sister and I had to leave Marseille, she was philosophical about my lengthy visits to Gabillaud, and by now she feels as I do, that we've all met before, in Simenon's stories about Commissioner Maigret. Maigret's best friend has always been Dr. Pardon. The Maigrets and the Pardons dine together once a week or so, and know exactly what favorite dishes to serve each other, and when the two men can find an evening free from murders and childbirths, they talk and talk . . . about puzzling cases, even about themselves. And we listen, delighted Peeping Toms. . . .

Yes, Gabby is another Pardon, a true "neighborhood doctor," after all his less constricted years. He is concerned about his patients, and deliberately involved in what is happening to them, what will happen next, why, where. I would like to see him again, but there is no excuse to. I still scowl, and always shall. But I still have all my teeth, and could smile at him. And then we could slide into a delicious little Gabby-fest about the authenticity of Rodin's head of Cézanne on the fountain in Aix, or about the increasing ambiguity of the AMA toward socialized medicine, or or or. . . .

Chapter 6

THE
GAMBLERS

I

Sometimes I wonder if I sound a little tetched about cab-drivers in Marseille . . . if I choose them on purpose, if I have some compulsion about savoring their unpredictably raffish behavior.

The truth is that while I lived there with my sister Norah in 1973 and later, I spoke with few people except waiters, shopkeepers, and cabbies and myself. Norah was thoroughly involved in research and was gone all or much of most days, while her accent improved in the company of elderly librarians, eccentric scholars, and fellow-delvers. I, on the other hand, spoke an increasingly creaky and careless French, still better than that of many of the people I used it with but not challenging, so that by the time we were packing to return to California, and my professor from the University of Dijon (1929–31!) came to bid us a quick return, he held his hands over his ears in disgust.

I said, "I can't help it. I've met perhaps two educated Frenchmen in five months. I talk . . . communicate . . . simplistically with people who are as alien here as I am: waiters from Iran or Egypt, cabbies from Sicily and Algiers and God knows where. . . ." But when I told him a little of what they talked about, he shrugged forgivingly and said, "You'll be all right."

Of course it is one thing to sit in a café and read *Le Meridional* and *Le Monde* and sip a vermouth-gin until Nórah shows up after a morning at the City Library in the Bourse, and another to entrust one's life to a taxi driver. The latter experience has, perforce, more intensity; it is more memorable, whether or not it should be. In a café, one can get up and walk away. In a cab, the set of the driver's shoulders, his smell, the frightening instant of meeting his eyes in the rear-view mirror (what kind, bloodshot or jaundiced or drug-dazed color): all that is a vital challenge, and often as pungent as ether.

Norah may meet me at our apartment with the jaunty news that while Artemis, the Greek goddess who protected Protis in his surprising nuptials in Massilia in 600 B.C., had eighteen breasts, the Christian saint Mary Magdalen in perhaps A.D. 60 had only two . . . BUT . . . they are said by the local devout near her shrine today to have flowed with copious (and of course holy) milk when she was a very old saint indeed. That's fine, that's great, I say to the avid scholar. Then I tell her about my latest cabdriver.

Today, for instance, there were no taxis in the stand at the Place de Gaulle, opposite the Bourse, but I did not feel like walking home and knew I need only wait. It was not raining. One came sliding into its place up the curb toward the Opera, and I noticed without really noticing that a young couple with some bags or suitcases stopped it and that it then came down toward me, where passengers were supposed to wait. I got in, and told the driver my address. He was a heavyset man of perhaps sixty, with longish grey-white hair and the broad rubbery face of a former clown or vaudevillian.

As we started, the young woman ran up to the taxi and rapped on the window and asked why he had passed her by, and he said loud and firm, "Because you stink," and drove off.

I decided that I was once more in the weapon of a maniac, helpless bullet in gun, so I sat back and asked mildly, "Why did you say that?" He could either answer me in the same manner, in a reasonable way, or he could explode, and since I was trapped anyway, it did not much matter to me. He chose the first path, and said, "Because she does."

"How do you know, with the window closed?"

"I know by her face," he said flatly. "She's a Gypsy, and Gypsies stink."

I started to say, always in the mild and nonreproachful way, "But after all she is a—" and he interrupted me. "Don't tell me, lady, that she's a human being, which I knew you were going to say, because Gypsies are not human. They do not qualify. And they have a terrible smell, because they are damned."

I asked what the smell was like, and he said, always in a matter-of-fact way, not as if he were humoring me or playing a rehearsed scene, "It is purely and simply *le suint. Le suint gitan.*" (I thought I knew that it was something about old sour sweat on dirty bodies, but I looked it up when I got back to the apartment and it meant a kind of greasy ooze.) I said something like "Oh," and he manipulated a couple of neat cornerings.

He was a relaxed sure driver, which is the only way to be in Marseille and probably everywhere. Then he said in an almost fatherly way, "I doubt that you have ever lived with them." I said that I had known a few and observed them whenever I could, and he said, "Yes, but you've never lived with them, *lived*. I have. And they stink."

This seemed the natural end to the conversation on that subject, and in a few blocks we went on to how many pleasure boats as opposed to fishing boats there were in the Old Port. He told a lot I had been spending several days trying to dig out of officials for my own satisfaction, and the rest of the ride was informative and pleasant, and I was glad that I had grown up enough not to be upset by varied prejudices, at least to the point of jumping out of a cab, which I did once on Union Square in San Francisco.

That time I knew that I could not listen to one more word from the driver, who was a proud Midwestern member of the John Birch Society and currently loudmouthed about the subversive hippies floating amiably over the lawns and into the bushes of the public park. He was intolerable. But the chauffeur in Marseille was quiet, reasonable, and absolutely fixed in his loathing of the Gypsy smell, and I felt interested in both his deliberate hatred of a whole race because of perhaps a few examples (or even one), and his dispassionate candor. He used words well, without affectation, and there was no feeling at all that he was trying to make me know that he was not a taxi driver for want of anything better, which often happens with the talkative ones, nor that he was trying to teach me something . . . set me right.

I was glad that I had not sounded outraged or preachy to him, in my first resignation about being caught once more in a rapidly moving vehicle with a madman at the controls. He had his own dignity, which included the belief, for no matter what private reasons, that Gypsies have a special ghastly smell, which proves that they are damned and not quite human, or perhaps that they are not human at all and therefore *must* smell that way. What business was it of mine? I had asked him as a professional driver to take me home, not to explain his raison d'être, and he managed to do both in an expert and unaggressive way.

I remain basically affronted by what he said so firmly, because it is against my hopeful human yearnings, but since he did not affront anything else, I listened that day and perhaps even learned something, if not about Gypsies or him, about myself.

At least he did not make direct or sly chitchat about "Arabs," the current hate-objects in Marseille. I would have turned mute, not trusting myself, and he might have driven with petulance or ferocity, neither of which is enjoyable to the captive passenger.

This interchange did nothing, of course, for my accent, and not much more for my sister's interest in my currently peculiar life style, and/but I am probably relieved that it went off amiably. We all survived, in most ways.

I I

This is not so much about a young man in Marseille in 1973 as it is about people of any age, anywhere, I suppose. He was perhaps twenty-five, short, with the beautiful silver-copper skin of some Algerians, and soft black hair down to his shoulders, in studied waves and strands. He was a taxi driver.

I had to wait for several minutes at the official taxi stand on the Place de Gaulle, because it was shortly before noon and raining hard, after a few springlike but faintly ominous hours of darkening skies. This kind of weather will drive

to shelter the natives of Marseille almost as firmly as do
the occasional gusty winds, which whether they come from
the Swiss Alps or Italy or across from Spain, or even
correctly down the Rhône Valley, are generally called "le
mistral." This word is always said with a fatalistic shrug,
part affection and part resignation, as if to condone and
accept human patience in the face of natural forces, and
indeed it has long been held that if a *crime passionel* can be
proved to have been committed while the mistral blew, the
criminal is exonerated. Such is not the case with the *other*
wind, the tramontane, which according to several sources
blows from anywhere except down the Rhône but actually is
a cold northeast wind from near the Italian border. Some
natives say the weather is deliciously clear and sparkling while
it blows, and to others it is vicious enough to fill the air with
flying roof tiles. One fisherman told me that the only trouble
he ever had was when the mistral and the tramontane were
blowing at the same time. "Then the boat dances a little,"
he said. Other fishermen have told me that the two winds
can never happen at the same time. How would I know? All
I know about the day I met the young man is that I myself
would say that there was no real mistral, no real tramontane,
but only a good March rainstorm. . . .

As I worked my way down the line of people waiting for
taxis, one harassed-looking lawyer or broker invited me under
his umbrella, and I was so taken aback by his storm-bound
casualness, knowing he would never do such a thing without
formal introductions in fairer weather, that I spoke unusually
bad French, which took him aback too, if only temporarily.
When his cab rolled up he hopped in without another word
and I was left in the downpour, resolving never to speak such
vile stuttering syllables again, even to myself.

My cab came next, and I dove into it and said good

morning. Usually taxi drivers respond, if they have not said it first and often with embellishments, but I looked with some slight speculation at the young silky-haired hack, and said in the most impeccable enunciation I could call up from the courses in diction I took at the University of Dijon in 1929 and on, something like "Please take me to 41 avenue de la Corse." I did it well, as if to prove that my linguistic blur under the stranger's umbrella had been a passing aberration.

The young man said "O.K.," and then buried his head between the palms of his well-shaped hands, and I could hear the rain on the roof of the car. I knew that there was pressure on the cabbies because of the rain, and that it was almost noon rush hour, and also that sometimes people have to withdraw from the world and start over again. I have a fairly clear empathy with taxi drivers, and I felt that I should let this beautiful young man gather his forces after God knows what ordeal, professional or otherwise.

The chauffeurs in line behind him were sounding their horns, and finally his hands dropped to the wheel, and he sighed deeply, perhaps with resignation. I said, always with a clear and well-planned pattern of the requisite phrases, fully believing that he, like several other drivers since the west end of La Corderie has been renamed La Corse, would wonder where in Hell my address was, "Generally, if one so wishes, one can reach my address by taking either the Rue Sainte or going out on the Rive Neuve."

He shot off, but at the first traffic wait he said fiercely, never turning around, that drivers don't need directions and that they know where they are going and a few other such statements. I had heard them before, from amateurs anyway, and never as ferociously, and I agreed with him (the docile captive, the trapped rat . . .).

He drove skillfully, coldly. When we got near my place,

which is on the opposite side of the street from his direction,
I said something like, "The number I gave you is on the left
side, but I'll get out across from it, here . . ." and he slammed
to a halt. I started to open the door, and he said, "Just a
minute!" and I thought again of people who feel angry for
reasons other people don't know, and of all the puzzlement
of trying to function and even exist in this climate, this
climate of puzzlement. I closed the door again, to listen
to him.

He continued, with his eyes straight forward, "We drivers
are all licensed, in Marseille. We don't accept directions from
passengers. In order to get a license we must learn every
street in the city and the environs. We know how to get
anywhere at any time, and we do not need the advice of
casual pickups . . . of officious passengers who think they
can tell us where to go and how to get there, in their schoolteacher prissy foreign accents."

He stayed low-voiced but explosive. "I'll explain to you,"
he said with a mad patience, "that it costs every one of us
plenty to get a license, because we have to know the right
people and keep them happy. So certainly, with my legal hard-
won papers, I do not need your free instructions. My qualifi-
cations are as good as anybody's, and I refuse to submit to
being told like a schoolboy, as for instance right this minute,
to go out to the Corniche in order to turn around to a third-
rate hotel door."

I not only had never mentioned going out to the Corniche
but it had not occurred to me to, as he whirled in a U-turn to
stop in front of the door. What is more, I had not told him
I was going to a hotel at all. But I looked at the back of his
furious young head, covered with carefully arranged lock-
lets, and I thought a little about being in a huge high-
powered sprawl like Marseille, within a so-called minority

circle, and the tough routine of getting a license through every possible pipeline that fed through that circle, and then of having personal gnawings and woes. And I simply paid him with the usual tip and got out, into a wide rushing gutter and a heavy rain.

I thanked him impersonally, and he did not respond, which is unusual in Marseille, and I felt that he was far off again, and might well have to bury his face in his hands. I did not look back, in case this was so.

I I I

Like many people who find themselves spectator sports in most of the current games, I consider taxi drivers a good gamble, and I bet on them every time.

I manage to let most of them feel that I not only trust them with life and limb, but that I think they must be interesting and have something to tell me, something nobody else could. This maneuver brings out the best, nine times in ten, and is conducive to excellent driving through the dirtiest parts of New York, down the worst hills in San Francisco, around the most horrendous carrefours in Paris and Marseille. And in return for the attention the drivers pay to road and me, in that order, I am genuinely grateful for their personal as well as professional reactions to my guile, and I think they enjoy this too.

Mostly.

Once in New York and once in Paris I knew I was captive of a dangerously insane driver, and was ready in a few seconds of acceptance for either hospital or merciful death. Often, too, I have been conscious of overfatigue or personal stress in the man in front of me. Mostly, though, I have been

able with not too much effort to settle into a relaxed confinement with a normally mad cabbie, and assume that he will
indeed take me to X Street and the corner of Z, and tell me
a few titbits on the way.

Sometimes taxi drivers are new to their cabs, or to the
hiring company or even the town. But once I got one who was
simply *new*. The only recognizable and reassuring thing
about him was the cloud of *pastis* that moved into the cab
with him: I knew that I was still in Marseille, even if he
did not.

He looked as if he had lived well. He was finely tailored,
in an almost stockbroker style, barely balding, a trim man
just touching successful middle age. He came out of a little
bar across from the taxi stand on the Place de Gaulle,
where I had been waiting by a row of blandly empty cabs.
I was ready to stamp away, frustrated by the plain fact
that drivers have to relieve themselves now and then, and
even drink and eat and gossip a little. I was surprised to see
this man walk straight toward me and the front cab and
then get in it, for certainly he was not a real part of the bar,
of the Place, of the cab itself.

He smiled a little at me, and with my intrinsic willingness
to gamble one more time I got in too, and gave him the
address I hoped to reach. He smiled more, and suddenly I
realized that he was scared almost silly. I wondered if he
was stealing the cab. He fumbled with key, ignition, all that,
and plainly had never been at such a wheel before. His
shoulders in their handsome suit looked vaguely defeated.

"Do you know where to go?" I asked bluntly, as if to slap
him awake, and it was the beginning of a lengthy dialogue,
while we moved uncertainly from lane to lane through two
of the worst intersections in Marseille, and went east on two
westbound-only streets, and in general learned a lot. He did,

anyway, for it was indeed the first time he had ever driven a taxi, as well as the first time he ever saw the city. We both saw more than believable, because of the traffic lanes. What can you do if only the left lane turns up by St. Victor and you are in the right one, except head helplessly through the tunnel, on and on, and then try to double back . . . ?

He could see or feel that I was almost catatonically un-rattled, and I saw and felt at once that he knew how to drive, as such, so we simply cruised through a large part of the Rive Neuve area while he told me in upper-class Parisian that he had dropped into the cabbies' bar on the Place and accepted a bet one of the men had made, after several rounds offered by the big-city toff, to handle his hack for one fare. The man said that he was looking for local color, and we both laughed comfortably about the notorious sense of humor of the Mar-seillais as he wobbled into another wrong turn.

He was sweating a little, but was collected. I felt at ease, in my familiar taxi-mood of fatalism. We finally got to my door, and I gave him the usual tip in spite of his tailoring, and he bowed, thanked me, and said, "Never again, Ma-dame." I hoped he would find his way back to the café, but did not say so.

One thing he had said was that he could never have done such a crazy thing if he had been cold sober, but this did not bother me. Sobriety is a rare and dubious virtue, if that at all, with people under heavy stress like cabbies, cooks, and even politicians. It is often an improvement, for them and for us, to be able to disregard every bothersome detail of survival except the immediacy of the business, and to stay clear in the center of a blur. This nirvana is of course unattainable to most thirsty people, and its pursuit is hard on the human liver as well as human lives. Occasionally, though, alcohol is a godsend, and I feel that several *pastis* drunk in an unfamiliar town got one driver and me through a potentially dreadful dare.

My sister and I discussed this highly debatable theory, as well as my miraculous arrival at the right address, and hoped that the lost Parisian was safely home again, a wiser man. We began making little jokes about him in comparison with other drivers we had met during the months in Marseille. Most of the time there, we walked, but in heavy rains or moments of unexpected weariness we headed for two or three stands we had spotted, and revived ourselves with the heady excitement of the real gambler before Chance itself. And it added an extra zip, to know that at least we would not be the temporary captives of my own gambling driver. "Let's blow ourselves to a taxi," we'd say after a morning in the Flower Market. "Our favorite tourist is gone, so we'll make it home. . . ."

About two months after my boozy encounter, we had to go through some hours of unexpected hassling with the French Railway System, to send several cartons of stuff-junk-rubble back to California. And right there in the office we had to rewrap everything, retie it, retape it, and then rewrite three labels and three other papers for each carton, and although the two young men who took care of us were nicer than anyone could be in this whole wide world, and were polite and jolly and in all ways superbly compassionate and gentle, my sister and I found ourselves thoroughly shaken when we finally got out of the local branch of the Société Nationale des Chemins de Fer.

I said flatly that I did not know if I could walk to the nearest café chair: I was trembly in my marrow . . . and why, when the young men had been so nice? My sister said that she felt very odd too. We decided, as we headed for the Quai des Belges and the dimmest quietest corner of a bar that had one, that we were organically, psychosomatically, hopelessly at war with bureaucracy itself. Furthermore, we were fighting repressed pique or anger or plain disgust because all our first laborious wrappings and labelings had been torn off before our eyes. By the time we had either revived or else numbed our nerves with a drink, and got this settled, we felt better, and strong enough to walk toward the Place de Gaulle and its taxi stand. We could even joke a little, and say that today of all days it was lucky that we did not have to cope with my pal from Paris.

Of course it was he who came out of the little café as we waited by the head cab. We both knew him without a word between us. He was as trimly tailored as before, but needed a shave. He wore the familiar cloud of *pastis*, like an invisible toga. He did not look at us as he slid into his seat.

I gave him the same address, and he glanced at me in his rear-view mirror, but I knew then as I know now that he did not remember either my accent or what it had once said.

He was at home, this time, with the key, the switch, the wheel. But he got out a map and looked quickly at it, before he started a smooth expert drive to our place. None of us said anything, for various reasons. Once there, he manipulated a fancy U-turn on the wide busy street, and leaned over to open the door for us. He smiled a little, thanked us for his tip, and then burst out, "I've been here exactly two months, and tomorrow I take my taxi-license tests!" He sounded jaunty and excited. We congratulated him, and he drove neatly away, and we felt Full Circle as we went silently to our apartment.

Chapter 7

THE FOOD OF ARTEMIS

It has been said, and rightly, that a tomato of Provence tastes different from that grown from the same seed in another soil and air. It will have a pungency, an earthy savor, and a smell that are robust but not coarse. It makes understandable at once, without words, why the men of the South of France know that the reason their women ("strong, wild, fertile," they have been called) are more lastingly seductive than others is that they are fed from the cradle on the local love apples.

These fruits, sliced fresh from the gardens, cooked into every conceivable dish, made into thick pastes for winter sustenance; alone or with a little olive oil; stewed-baked-grilled in countless ways: tomatoes in Marseille stand alone or blend happily with eggs, fish, meats. They are true kitchen stalwarts, like the human females who feed on them.

This same salty vitality is everywhere else in Provence, as far as I can see. Women, tomatoes, children and men, herbs and trees . . . and sheep and the small black fighting bulls: they all have it. The rice of the Camarque, for instance: it was almost unknown until after the fall of Dien Bien Phu, when France's Oriental supplies were cut off and the desperate government drained miles of salt marshes in the Rhône delta and made paddies. These produced, almost violently, one of the most unusual and delicious grains I ever tasted, hard and strongly salted. It soon became sought out, first to surprise people used to the comparatively delicate rices of Indo-China, and then to satisfy a real craving for its noisy personality. It was a match for the Provençal tomato, and indeed it was a perfect foil for the whole cuisine of the area.

Suddenly, and while the fame of Camarquais rice was spreading fast, politics and an international thirst for light modest wines helped the government rip out most of the flourishing paddies, drain them, and prepare the salty old silt of the delta for miles and miles of vineyards. Quick-growing, undistinguished grape stock was planted with a speed that made serious vintners of the "North" (really any of them, North, East, or West of the "Côtes du Rhône" and Lyon) shake their heads in somewhat sardonic disbelief.

The first crops were pressed and blended and bottled with shocking speed, and then bought with unheard-of local enthusiasm in small shops, huge supermarkets. The wines, light and mostly as undistinguished as their roots, were adequate for drinking, easy on the palate and the pocketbook, and pleasant everyday companions to Provençal food. They were candid in their origins, and they continue to sell phenomenally well in their own region, produced as they are by both the large cooperatives and the smaller growers, for quick consumption. And they have a dryness that makes them truly "sand wines," sprung up almost as fast as the rice before them, and the marsh grasses before the rice, on the edge of the Mediterranean.

All this durable strength, this mysterious saltiness, is what gives the food as well as the wine of Marseille a zest that I have never known anywhere else.

Of course there can be dreadful dishes there, just as there can be infamous bottles. Every kitchen and winery has its own share of idiots, rascals, and wretches. But in general, and over a period of more than forty years, I honestly think I have had an almost untarnished succession of exciting, amusing meals in Marseille. As a stranger, I have never eaten in a private home there, although once I was invited to an alfresco luncheon in the country near the Mont Ste.-Victoire, by some Marseillais I wish I still knew. It was one of the most delicious meals I ever ate, and the conversation was so light and witty that I can still smile about it.

As an almost professional ghost, however, I have developed a fairly dependable nose for good public eating places, from the most stylish-but-honest to the lowliest-but-honorable. I know that nearly all French towns can boast of one kind or the other, and that the big cities are filled with them, but for me Marseille remains the chosen magical mysterious One. And I think it is because of the peculiar liveliness of what grows behind it on the ancient soil, and especially what swims and creeps and slithers at its watery gates. There is no doubt about it: freshly caught fish, scaly or in the shell, have a different flavor and texture and *smell* there than in any other port in the world. The flavor is intense and assertive, no matter how delicate: a *loup*, for instance, will remain its own self even when it is grilled over dry fennel leaves and then flamed with an extra douse of Pernod. Texture is fine or coarse or succulent or crisp, depending on whether one eats a fresh sardine, a fillet of tuna, a raw mussel. And the smell is so pure that it is as heady as the first breath from a dark winery cellar just hosed down—or from a silent printing-pressroom if one reacts as I do to good ink and paper.

Any reputable open-front fish shop in Provence will smell this way, but the best place there, and perhaps in the whole world, is the old Criée on the Rive Neuve in Marseille. This great airy vaulted room is the public wholesale auction place for the area, and opens after midnight, and is closed again by five in the morning, except for swabbers in hip boots washing every spot, every trestle and board and crate and ladder, with stiff brushes and fierce jets of water from their long hoses. In another hour or so the place is locked, silent, but while the night's bidding went on, it was one of the noisiest places ever dreamed of, somewhat like the "capital pit" of a great stock exchange but with an utterly different vibration to its screaming roar. This is perhaps because there are always many women there, with the harsh strident voices of classical fishwives, often gruff and bellowing but always female.

And at La Criée, at its wildest peak of trading and out-bidding, with dealers and fishmongers and agents shoving and shouting around the trestle tables heaped with the finest of the available catch, there is never any smell of sweat, or garlic, or anything but exquisitely fresh clean briny *fish*.

Outside along the Rive Neuve the real activity starts a few hours before La Criée opens, with countless huge refrigerated trucks rolling in from Normandy, Brittany, the Gironde. Their lobsters and Channel soles and herrings, their several kinds of oysters, are packed in special white styrofoam boxes, tightly closed, but even so, a mist of pure *fish* manages to escape from them as they are rushed into other trucks and headed for Lyon or Switzerland or ships in the Port, or are trundled into the cool dim vault of La Criée to be ready for its violent predawn awakening.

It is foolhardy to try to pick one's way at night along that part of the Rive Neuve, landside, when the trucks are coming and going. Men unload the white crates with deft speed, and see only what they must do. But when Norah and I lived above the end of the Quai, we often walked home from "town" at the most hectic moments, and never once tripped or got bumped into, or even cursed at. We could have been two moths.

Probably we would have been kicked away, if we'd been cats. (It is odd to realize that I have never seen a cat near the Criée, nor the morning fish boats along the Quai des Belges at the end of the Port, nor the many fish restaurants all around. Is the smell too fresh and saline for them? Is there too much cold water in the harbor, on the floors, sloshing everywhere? Have centuries of being unwelcome given Marseille's cat-world an inborn sense of what places to avoid? Or do cats really like fish as much as they are supposed to?)

Most of the nearby restaurants, from fine to humble, display their daily fish in front of or near their doors, so that clients must pass them and be lured by the gleam and glow of color, the fragile smell. On the hotter days a coolness hovers over the ice-packed slanted counters, and iodine and salt waver up almost tangibly from the beds of seaweeds the fish lie on. Often, in a window opening onto the street, as crown of the display inside, there will be a kind of *pièce montée*, a Dali or Carême sculpture of one stunningly graceful *loup*, posed for an endless second with a great pink shrimp in its mouth, as it leaps from a high wave of smaller red and blue and silver fishes over the piles of oysters, mussels, urchins, clams. . . .

Once I saw such a fantasy in an elegant restaurant window on the Quai des Belges: a ring of small lobsters dancing on their tails, holding claws in a circle around a great humped black fish with glaring eyes. On his back were two big lobsters, side-saddle, holding his reins in their own claws. The pavement was of hundreds of fresh sardines laid in patterns bordered with purple sea urchins, and a hidden electric fan made all the lobsters' delicate feelers wave in rhythm. The whole thing was a past/present dream, subtly nightmarish but hilarious. It was extravagant, and meant to last a few hours at best, and I still see it, and smell its airy salt.

I do not remember anything at all about eating fish the first time I was in Marseille in 1929, although the strong-voiced women selling their husbands' catch from the stern of each little boat backed up to the Quai des Belges seemed to have chosen an enviably sane job to me, a refugee from the dank academic walls of Dijon. (By now the catch is unloaded in a flash onto little trestle tables set up on the Quai, and usually the wives are there to sell, while the boats head out to sea again, or dawdle until the tables can be folded and stored on deck for the next day. As one hefty old woman said to me in about 1970, "For the first time in my life, I don't have a stiff neck, from yelling up at all you nitwits on the Quai—")

The next time I went to the Old Port I felt infinitely removed from the shy tongue-bound bride of some three years before. Dijon was behind. I knew what I was hearing and saying, and how to eat and drink better than thus far in my life. For our last meal in the country we loved so surely, my husband and younger sister Norah and I went to the Mont Ventoux. I have since watched it grow elegant and then decline, but on that bright May Day in 1932 or so, it was simple and very welcoming to us, and to celebrate (not leaving, but the return, any time, no matter how or how soon!), we ate a majestic bouillabaisse, and drank amply of a bone-dry white wine from the bone-dry white country a little farther down the coast. Perhaps the fish stew was especially good, as it can be. Perhaps it was "one more bouillabaisse," as is generally the case. Certainly it did not make me a passionate devotee of the local attraction, and I think that since that far day I may have eaten it only four or five times. But then it was a perfect dish to help us say Until Soon Again. It was rich and fumy, of course, with warmth for the belly and sustenance for the spirit, and we were ready for whatever might be ahead when M. Sicard pushed us gently into a taxi, after one last glass of the family *marc* with him. "Drive fast," he called after us. "Until soon," we called back.

But it was a few years and several new lives before the next meal in that upstairs dining room. M. Sicard had retired to his vineyards. The restaurant had lost its stairway down to the Quai, and was hushed and elegant, with an entrance onto the Canebière, and a delicately fragrant oyster stand in the downstairs hall, all lemons and wet seaweed and breathing shellfish. I was with somewhat hushed elegant people too. We stopped and chose the oysters we would eat, and went on up to the new room, glass on two sides, with the whole Port below us. It was lovely, and as different from the old place as I was different from the young student-wife.

That restaurant was excellent, and stayed so for perhaps thirty more years, a record in such a chancy game. Affluent important locals liked it, and shared it with their foreign friends and victims, and well-heeled worldly travellers knew about it, and I saw some of the most beautifully dressed women of my life there. The first time I ate by one of its twinkling window-walls, I embarrassed my severely correct hostess by ordering a dozen Belons for the first course, and another dozen for the second. They were as perfect as they had smelled, on the way past them up the stairs, and I like to think that my discreet but obvious enjoyment softened the social shocks that continued to fall on my proud old lady.

For a long time I returned almost compulsively to that upstairs room on the Quai des Belges, always for lunch and always with great satisfaction of many senses: the glitter or sullen storminess of the Vieux Port; the good waiters and the maître d'hôtel and the cloakroom matron, most of them greeting me as if I had been there the past week and not several years before; the smell of the waiting shellfish going up the stairs with us.

But in 1971 the oyster stand was gone. I felt apprehensive. The headwaiter told me that the "new clientele" ignored it, so that the shell-opener had nothing to do downstairs that a kitchen apprentice could not do less expensively upstairs. He shrugged. He looked dismal, with well-trained remoteness.

In about 1973, I think, I got a whiff of real disillusion, when the staircase and even the tables wore advertisements of somebody like JoJo and his Magical Electric Organ, playing every night during dinner, any tune from any country. Goodbye, part of me said painfully.

Three years later I went back to the old corner. There was a high wooden wall around it, so that the entrance was blocked off. At night there were dim lights upstairs, but no signs of waiters or diners, and in the quick-order-café-brasserie on the street level were notices pointing to an inside stairway to "Our Deluxe Dining Room." I ate in the brasserie once, because it was a night for soup and a salad after some high days of downing shellfish in every logical guise as well as straight from the shell . . . and nobody ever went upstairs. I shrugged. I felt disconsolate, or much worse, and although fairly well trained, I was unable to be remote about my innate sense of loss. Something had gone, and it was too late to do anything but realize how good it had been, while it had seemed a natural part of my life, something always to head back to.

Now, when I return to Marseille, how can that restaurant *not* be there? I have been betrayed, and I know this must happen again and more than once before I too stop.

The Two Sisters, for instance: they cannot possibly live forever on the Rive Neuve! Every time I see them, and all the indefatigable nieces, lovers, husbands, cousins, who work in their small fishhouse, they look younger, or at least in good fettle. They serve at a mad dauntless speed, and with such apparent enthusiasm and delight that it is tonic to be near them.

There are, of course, a lot of other such restaurants along that quay, and some of them are, or can be, very good. One or two are always bad enough to fail, day after tomorrow, or are rebuilding from past errors. A lot of their clients are Marseillais, supersensitive to fish and its perfections, but they are also tourist lures, complete with tough teasing women who stand in the doorways and almost blackmail the passersby to come in—eat the best bouillabaisse ever made. . . .

This technique, as I well know, is painful to many blond blue-eyed visitors. The *entraîneuse* is out there raucously taunting people on the sidewalks, who amble along looking with mild curiosity for a good meal, and it is an embarrassing circus to the tender-skinned Northerners who accidentally find themselves on the Rive Neuve. If they are extravagant or cowed enough to order lobster, the harridan will stand on the sidewalk right by their table, and point through the window at everything on their plates, loudly drawing a small crowd to gape and envy and perhaps push on into the restaurant. Italians and even Germans can take this noisy exposure in stride, but the English turn as red as their fine fare, and wish they were anywhere but in Marsales, "that most sordid and filthy hole," as one of their compatriots called it in about 1800.

I think that I have eaten once or even many times in every fishhouse on that side of the Vieux Port, over the last forty-odd years. They change, of course, and occasionally die, or linger pitifully past their prime, half-empty. For several years now, a small Chinese restaurant has survived where a good fish place used to be. It smells all right, but of soy sauce and mushrooms rather than, more properly, of seaweed and shimmering cold fishes and plump shells. One or two of the places are stylishly decorated: modern "rustic" furniture, copper pans and Camarquais cattle-prods on the walls, flowers towering over the whimsical displays of fish or strawberry tarts. There are a few plainer places with paper tablecloths and napkins, ample servings of fish soup, unlabeled rosé in liter bottles. Every class of restaurant is crowded, all year round, as long as its fish is of today's catch and is treated with respect.

The Two Sisters' place is in between, aesthetically at least. It has a small glassed terrace with five or six tables pinched into it, a little restaurant, an upstairs room for celebrations along with a window display of fish and a few proud lobsters languidly waving their feelers, and a steeply banked stand of shellfish with an elderly relative opening them with feverish skill as customers order trays of whatever they want and can afford. The trays are put on the tables on wire legs about ten inches high, and the diners pick what is nearest to them if they are polite . . . or reach for what looks plumpest on the far side. People in the money, though, trying to impress a girl-friend or the boss, or ignorant of the current value of the franc in dollars, pounds, lire, marks, will usually eat oysters:

expensive, so fresh that the delicate dark flanges recoil a little at the touch. They are for special treats.

One good way to taste two or three of them, not the costliest Belons of course, but tangy lesser breeds, is to order a *panaché*, a mixed platter of every shellfish on hand. It is pretty, and fun. Like all other such platters, the open shells lie on a bed of cold seaweed, sometimes laid over cracked ice in warm weather, with halved lemons in the center. There will be one or two kinds of mussels: small darkish ones cultivated at Bouziques, very pungent; large fat ones with pale or orange-colored flesh, from the rocks along the coast. There will be a few urchins, and at the Two Sisters', the shell man snips out a bigger hole than their mouth, or whatever it is, and they are rather gritty. Then there will be a few clams, fat and crisp, and several of their little cousins, the *clovisses*. (When I am eating these sweet clams, I wonder why I think they are more delicious than any oyster . . . until I taste an oyster again!) There will be some *violets* in the *panaché*, unless one asks otherwise, and if I am alone I ask exactly that, for they are the one real disaster in the whole orderly chaos of Mediterranean sea life, for me at least. They seem like a mistake, somewhere along the path of natural creation. They are misshapen lumps of dun-colored spongy stuff, not shell, not skin, and inside they have a yellowish flesh, not sticky, not solid, not runny. People like them, and break open a *violet* and spoon or suck out the insides and smile. Like egg yolk but subtler, they say, and reach for another. I give away my share, if we are eating a *panaché* together, and slyly accept a clam or mussel in exchange. . . .

At most of the fish restaurants, there are little dingy shakers of vinegar for people who like it on shellfish, but I have never once seen anyone use it. In fact, most of the cut lemons on the shellfish seem to go back unsqueezed. Perhaps this is because the fish themselves are so succulent and cool and generally revivifying that nothing can make them better. They seem to breathe pure sea smell into the air, and to melt something of this same purity into their shells, to be drunk slowly, one long sip, after the meat has slid down our hot hungry gullets. It would be a pity to rush through such a salubrious inner bath as a platter of just-opened shellfish can give two-legged people, and a *panaché* needs a good half-hour of spaced concentration. Fortunately there are dozens of places in Marseille where this somewhat ritualistic enjoyment can be found and I know a lot of them, and by choice I would return without question to the Two Sisters', forever, or as long as they were there.

Once the two women are gone, the restaurant cannot possibly be the same, no matter how hard and well they have trained their relatives. They are as forceful as any females I have ever seen in a town well known for its ferociously strong ones, and I can well imagine them as young fish peddlers along the Quai des Belges, braying their strident quips to draw idlers and customers to their trays of the morning's catch. Possibly they worked along the sidewalk of the Rive Neuve, before they acquired the restaurant itself; they seem basically tough enough, even in their later years, to have stood up to the *entraîneuses'* dubious art of dragging clients into no matter how shoddy a fishhouse.

By the time I met them, more than twenty years ago, they looked as they still do: the younger one with dark hair and mocking but kind eyes, the older with grey-white hair and the almost benign face of a reliable client of Central Casting, always ready to play a gentle old granny, a saintlike elderly nun. Of the two women, I feel certain she is the tougher. Both of them seemed fed on tiger milk, and rubbed with a potent salve made by Artemis herself, of equal parts of olive oil, garlic, tomato paste, and rosé wine, blended with enough flesh of new sea urchins to make a thick paste. (When I have eaten with them, I feel as if some of it had been rubbed off on me. . . .) I can see them in bed making love and birthing children as easily as I can see them zipping through the restaurant from back kitchen to front glass door, watching every table, talking constantly.

There are always some waitresses and waiters to watch and supervise, or a *loup* to grill and flame, or a steaming bouillabaisse to serve in a storm of ladles-spoons-plates. People need to be seated, need more wine, need an extra pastry or a feast-day glass of cognac. The oyster man disappears into the back room for fresh supplies, and one of the Sisters opens mussels and clams twice as fast as he, while the other pulls a big lobster from the pile on top of the stand and holds it up triumphantly beside a table. "Look at its fat load of roe," she commands in a modified shriek, so that all the surrounding tables will fall silent to stare in awe. "What a superb female," she cries, whacking its belly casually, as if its claw were not reaching for any part of her to pinch, and then she runs toward the kitchen with it. Another group of clients stands up, and there is a rush for their coats, with both Sisters helping tuck them on like nannies with sated children. "Come back soon, come back," they call out onto the sidewalk, without losing a step in their routine dance.

And this goes on twice a day, six days a week. What we see is the top of the iceberg, as in any good restaurant. Beneath it is the real organization: the staff, both seen and invisible; the provisions, constantly checked and renewed; the upkeep of the whole small tight place, with all its linens, glasses, table fittings, and its essential fresh cleanliness. Above all, there is the skilled synthesis of fast and slow *people*, that they will work together on bad days and hectic festivals, through heat waves and the worst mistrals. (There is one niece or perhaps friend who is somewhat simple-minded, and who has been there as long as I can remember. She is unfailingly sweetfaced and attentive, and is very slow. One or the other of the Two Sisters is always nearby, watching to see if she needs a deft hand with the serving, never telling her to hurry. . . .) Such an operation lives or dies with the control of its leaders, in this case two women, and every time I return to its welcome hum and buzz, I know before even seeing them that both of them are there. I doubt that one could carry on without the other . . . run the joint so joyously, except perhaps by plain momentum for a time. When that wears off, weariness will settle like dust on the absorbed bright faces of all the relatives, and perhaps younger people will buy the restaurant, and perhaps it will stay a good one. Even in Marseille, though, the secret of Artemis' salve is not known to everyone, and the Two Sisters, changeless as they may seem, cannot live much longer than the rest of us. Selfishly, I hope it will be longer than I do. . . .

The Mediterranean has fed us for so long that it is unlikely even current human stupidities of pollution and destruction will stop its generosity. As we learn respect instead of carelessness, its fish will swim more healthily than ever, and its shells will form closer to the shorelines again, and the salt-sweet weeds will wave lushly for the picking. And meanwhile there will probably be places, as now, where we can smell the tonic freshness of a stand of mollusks on their cool grass, and choose a fish to be poached or broiled while we pick wee snails with a sharp pin from their shells. Even strangers in a port like Marseille will let their noses guide them to such pleasures, and I can think of at least four restaurants there, besides the comparatively "plain" fishhouse on the Rive Neuve, where I would gladly go tonight, tomorrow noon, this minute.

Two are very near the Two Sisters. The New York, on the Quai des Belges, is currently the most stylish- place in town, and perhaps the most expensive, and its small but irresistible oyster stand (with a stalwart young sheller in fisherman's togs, of course) serves impeccably fresh Belons and even lesser breeds. They are fat, cool, and as crisp as lettuce. The mussels match them, and all the clams, and a *panaché* at the New York is impressively delicious and worth a leisurely period of serious demolition, as is any other dish there.

Then up from the Rive Neuve on an ugly little square is L'Oursin, a far cry in elegance from the New York's four forks and one star, and in fact not even noted in Michelin. It is primarily a shellfish store, with open crates out on the sidewalk and a long counter of them on one wall of the corridor toward the back, with a few small tables facing it. Busboys run in from nearby bars, and neighbor children come with plates to be covered with open juicy shells, and the oyster man is a busy fellow long after the day's stuff is delivered from La Criée.

The back of the store, past a table with an incongruous display of excellent fruit tarts, widens into a dark room that is still small, with a tiny bar in one corner and "rustic" checked cloths on the crowd of tables. There are three or four healthy young waiters and the elderly owner, all related to him and the oyster man and Madame the Cashier at her desk right by the door, and all in tight striped skivvies. They are quick and skillful, and concerned about whether the wine is right, the dish a success. The last time I was at L'Oursin I really did not like some mishmash of clams and mussels in a vaguely Espagnole sauce that the chef recommended, and when the waiter saw that I had abandoned it for part of my sister's *petite friture,* he was plainly upset. "It was well made," I said ambiguously, "but not to my taste." He frowned and sighed. "A pity," he said. "You should have told me sooner. . . ." (What would he have done but sigh sooner? It was I who had ordered the dish. . . .)

Most of the clients seem familiar to the place and the staff, and they eat gustily and talk and laugh. There is usually one solitary young man, never the same but always very well tailored, who eats and drinks with finicky savoir-faire and seems to be thinking about what to say later that afternoon to his divorce lawyer. Once one cried silently, without a sob or hiccup, through oysters, stuffed grilled *rouget,* and fresh strawberries, with a large bottle of the house's best Savoy wine, a coffee, and then a cognac. He never wiped his cheeks with his gleaming white handkerchief, or blew his nose. When he left, there were several dark stains on his pale grey flannel lapels, and I hoped they would not dry before he kept his appointment.

The smell of shells and breathing fish and seaweed is of course stronger at L'Oursin than at the New York, but it has the same vitality in small or large doses, and is probably best, sharpest, strongest, at a big serious fishhouse called Au Pescadou, out on the Place de Castellane where all the main banks seem to be.

The Pescadou is run by a very successful firm of wholesalers whose little refrigerator trucks supply fresh mollusks and fish to good restaurants and markets all over town. It is not cheap, and is well located to please people used to fine food and wines . . . mostly important-looking men at noon, with a few well-fed elderly women from the neighborhood's stylish apartment houses. The restaurant is big and functional, with no balderdash about cut flowers and so on. One enters it through a large dim cave, open from the street and lined with an astonishing display of all kinds of fish, some still flapping or scrabbling or writhing according to their build. This cave is a market as well as a heady invitation to the restaurant, and people study what to buy for lunch or dinner, and maids run in for three dozen oysters to be opened. There are piles of beautiful lemons. The oyster man works like lightning. Four bankers pick out a *loup*, and a busboy rushes it back to the kitchen.

Once inside the Pescadou, there seems to be an almost religious hush, unlike the buzz and laughter of any other big restaurant I know. The noise of the insane traffic around the carrefour of the Place de Castellane is muffled by the deep cave of the fish store, and the diners talk quietly, perhaps of great financial dealings, but more probably of the best way to poach a fish of over four pounds. Many people eat by themselves, looking pleasurably thoughtful but not sad, not crying. Of course there are shellfish on their seaweed or cooked in a dozen ways, but most people seem to eat fish there, very simply cooked, served with austere concentration by skillful waiters who seldom smile.

Almost as different from the Pescadou as L'Oursin is from the New York is a fourth Marseille fish place I would go to in a flash, Michel's out at the beginning of the J. F. Kennedy Corniche, along the wild coast toward Cassis and Toulon. It is always crowded, I think. The shellfish and all the dishes are excellent. Like the Pescadou, it is somewhat less expensive than the New York, much more so than L'Oursin or the Two Sisters. (All of them cost a lot, lately, anyway. . . .) Michel's is also called the Brasserie des Catalans, and has three forks and a star in Michelin, although it does not seem "elegant" to me. There is a well-stocked stand of fish and mollusks facing the corner door, and the bright narrow restaurant branches off to left and right of it. The décor, aside from the alternately snarling or twinkling sea outside, tends toward fishnets and their stuffed glaring catch, and incredible shells. The waiters are experienced, and in a reserved way kindly. People take the main course seriously at Michel's, and poke and finger the fish they will choose to be cooked, but there is certainly no hush there, and everyone talks and laughs a lot. As usual, the wines are well chosen for what they are drunk with, and they are drunk generously, as if something nice must be celebrated.

It is ridiculous to imply that the restaurants I myself would gladly go back to in Marseille, any time at all and the sooner the better, are preferable to a dozen, a hundred, others that anyone else might name and know. I happen to like some very much, to be eager to find their peers or even better, and to feel apprehensive about a couple that may disappear . . . and to be actively sad about several whose doors can never open again, for me or other strangers or, saddest of all, for the Marseillais who have known them.

Of course it is possible, although improbable, that the old restaurant at the corner of the Canebière on the Quai des Belges will rise from its present dismal ashes. Certainly the air there, always moving, forever braced with its own strange chemistry of salt, sea water, fish, wet shells opening and shutting, could make a phoenix out of any once-sensate thing. But there was one place on the Rive Neuve, in air almost as restorative, that died *dead* a few years ago. It was Surcouf, between the Criée and the strip of noisy little fishhouses, an oasis of elegance looking out blandly at the sleek yachts and sloops around their clubhouse. Affluent elderly Marseillais went there, and smartly dressed Parisians on their way to Cannes and Monaco, and stylish young men and girls taking prospective relatives to a "correct" place to impress them. The food was among the best of my life, and best served. It seemed to leap from the sea to the plate, with one quick pause in midair over the chef's enchanted kitchen. The *patronne* was a very large soft woman, the antithesis of locals like the Two Sisters. She was nice, in a *grande dame* way that tagged her at once as from Bordeaux or Lyon or one of those almost foreign places, and she liked my two little girls.

Another person at Surcouf who liked Anne and Mary was the charming elderly barman, a White Russian left over from Paris in the twenties. The first time we met him, the girls were carrying two small dolls made by a Russian noblewoman, that had been given to them by a rich friend when they left California, and that acted as security blankets until they understood the words flying all around them. The little dolls were exquisitely dressed, that day in correct street clothes no doubt, and the Russian recognized them at once as creations of the Countess So-and-so. Anne and Mary became fairy creatures in return, bearing secret messages to him from the past. It was delightful, and the dream went on for almost two years. The girls continued to take the magic dolls to Surcouf long after they felt silly about such childish things, and I sipped dry champagne with the barman and then watched my thriving daughters learn the difference between a superb *bourride* and a merely excellent one. . . .

In about 1961 we found the restaurant closed. Madame had died. Surcouf would open again in two weeks. We felt reluctant to go back, and it was months later when we telephoned for a table for four, for dinner, to celebrate a dear friend's birthday. The place seemed dimmer, although it was promisingly crowded. A new man was behind the bar, and our Russian friend was headwaiter. He looked haggard, and overdid his proprietary manners toward Anne and Mary, no longer children. He seemed to want to impress the young ill-trained waiters, who were openly mocking of him and muttering rude things at his lordly ways. He almost frantically insisted that we order a *loup* grilled over fennel twigs, saying loudly that we had always loved it so much. The girls glanced at me: we had never once eaten it at Surcouf. That night we did, and we could rightly tell the Russian that it was supremely delicious. But we left in a quiet depression, feeling the desperate moist handclasp of our friend, trying not to hear the brash young waiters giggling behind his back.

I remembered a chill I had felt one day when I was waiting for the children to join me for lunch. Over a drink with Madame, I asked her why she had opened the front of the Surcouf onto the sidewalk to make a *café-terrasse*. It had been a disaster, she said. It attracted the wrong kind of people, low-class sightseers who wanted a beer and a view of the Port and no more. "But we must move with the times," she sighed. I felt upset and contradictory.

The next time we went to Marseille we could still see the vertical electric sign saying *Surcouf* from our hotel windows, but it hung over a nightclub called something like Le Wisky Boom Boom. By now the club is empty, and the sign is gone, as is Madame, as probably is the Russian, as are the Countess's little dolls. . . .

There were other places, far from phoenixlike. One was almost too sophisticated, the Campa. We went there now and then, for its beautiful service and stuffed mussels, pastries that sent the children into trance, and the walls covered with fragments of very old mirror, freckled, blotched, that made the dim room and all its elegant clientele into drifted attenuated sea plants in a deep pool. Then one night we led two hungry travellers to it, and not a soul was there except the crew of waiters standing like mummies inside the door. Most of the lights had been turned low. The headwaiter swam in from the kitchen before we turned tail, and implored us to come in, and flicked on lights.

We saw ourselves in countless dull blotched twisted mirrors. Two waiters revived, and almost overwhelmed us with their hysterical spate of vitality. Wine was brought in two silver buckets, the old-fashioned kind in rococo carved wooden stands. If there had been a small stringed orchestra asleep somewhere in a pantry, it would have been dusted off and propped up to play for us. We were served stuffed mussels, of course, and other local oddities like the dried roe called *poutargue*, and more that I've forgotten, all better than ever before. The evening turned to gold. We laughed and talked, and the maître d'hôtel and the young waiters grew pink and danced around us, and nobody else even opened the restaurant door. When we finally went happily away we knew it had been a special evening, and not long after that the girls and I went back and there were ugly boards crisscrossed over the door: "Permanently closed." Why? How had it been so impeccably organized for so long? Did someone die, or flee with the funds? Were all the worldly eaters extras in a film, or had we dreamed the whole thing?

Sometimes everything I remember so keenly about the old Mont Ventoux on the corner of the Canebière seems as unreal, now that I know it is gone or changed. I am almost afraid to find out if it will actually break out again from behind its present corset of high boards. I wonder if I'll ever be there, once more, to look down on the Old Port, and drain the shell of every oyster on my plate, and then perhaps eat a piece of orange tart. I wonder if I want to. It is tiring, sometimes, to play the phoenix . . . even in that salt-sweet air. Artemis, help me!

Chapter 8

THE
OPEN EYES

I

There are many people like me who believe firmly if somewhat incoherently that pockets on this planet are filled with what humans have left behind them, both good and evil, and that any such spiritual accumulation can stay there forever, past definition of such a stern word.

For some of us, it exists strongly in Stonehenge, for instance, and can be a bad or good experience, depending upon one's ability to accept non-Christian logic. Almost as puzzling as Stonehenge, once in my life, were the front steps of a small doleful cathedral in central France, where I soon knew that it would be best for me to leave, rather than try to locate my uneasiness of spirit.

Then there are kindlier and even restorative places, which like the bad or merely disturbing ones influence people whether or not they are aware of their vulnerability before such old forces. The half-ruined garden in the Misión de

San Juan Capistrano in Southern California, as I knew it more than fifty years ago, was such a spot, in spite of its comparative youth, and I suspect that it still gives even casual tourists an extra gift of serenity, no matter how unexpected or unrecognized . . . and that the Franciscans may well have planted it there on ground that had been loved by the Indians long before.

But to counteract such good, there is another pocket of ageless influences that can affect most human beings dangerously, if they let it and even if they do not: the wild white crag of bauxite in southern France called Les Baux. It is clearly a menace to us because of the accumulation of vicious brutality that has gone on there from the first greedy prehistoric Baussenques, who lived only for money, to Wise Man Balthazar's ruthless descendants, who lived only for power won through the graces of his holy star with its sixteen rays.

There have always been sorceresses and female prophets in Les Baux, whether from Rome or Romany. The treacherous grottoes carved by wind and human greed are peopled by millions of bats, called the mosquitoes of Hell, and there are remote black antechambers for nightmares and exorcism, and long dangerous tunnels leading to the Phantoms' Cave, and finally the Place of the Black Beast Himself. There is a buried Moorish treasure, deep somewhere, too horrible to dare search out. A Golden Goat guards its keys, and often runs noisily through the narrow crooked paths of the fortress, kicking down obscene sexual symbols that crop up ceaselessly on the immense stones.

The Church has tried for several hundred years to dissipate this gathering of evil spirits in Les Baux, and in the end has got rid of all but one of its pagan ceremonies, so that the famous enactment on Christmas Eve of Christ's birth is a controlled gentle version fit for family viewing, complete with watered-down pre-Christian symbols, and pretty with traditional tunes from costumed piper and drummer.

And up on the wide meadow, so high above the Valley of the Rhône that often the sea is visible, near to the steep cliffs from which live captives used to be pitched by the descendants of St. Balthazar, there is a great cross, completely useless if it is meant to quell the incredible evil of the place, whose force has built up until now one wonders how it would be possible to live on that mighty rock, even as a guide or postcard seller . . . why the gentle little lamb (Lamb of God, in his cage blazing with lighted candles for the sacrifice), and the flower-hung powerful ram pulling him toward the altar to the tune of fife and drum . . . why they don't wither and die, each Christmas Eve. What would happen if the Church let them march straight out to the cross near the deadly cliffs, instead of only up the short nave of the chapel? Would the bats sing? Would the grottoes glow with their own answer to the holy candles?

Possibly not even an atomic bomb could unsettle, for very long, the collection of such an ancient mysterious mecca of damned souls. But of course not all the souls that have stayed in Les Baux have been damned, any more than all the people who built Stonehenge were filled with an awesome knowledge of celestial logic, or than the captive Indians who built San Juan Capistrano for their priestly invaders were filled with gratitude and joy. Both good and evil rimmed these receptacles perforce. Evil and good have been yeasts, bacilli, and one or the other has taken over, the way cancer or syphilis can either gain control of a human body or lurk in the shadows, held at bay by natural, spiritual, and even scientific forces.

The ancient port-city of Marseille, some fifty miles south of Les Baux, has a reputation for wickedness that is certainly wider spread than almost any other's in the world, partly because so many millions have passed through there and found what they were looking for, but unlike Les Baux, it seems to remain basically healthy. However, if one subscribes to the theory that some places collect curses or blessings as if they were pockets to be filled, buckets, vases, then it would be easy to blame the bad reputation of Marseille on some such thing as its three hundred years of building and servicing the galleys there and keeping them filled with slaves and criminals, most of them sending out great stinking auras of hatred.

The first galley made in France was toward the end of the fourteenth century in the Vieux Port, and it served as one of numberless fighting vessels built and docked in Marseille's shipyards. In 1385 the local fishermen outfitted one to protect their boats from pirates, and as the Church grew in strength, archbishops had their own escorts of slave-powered galleys, and carved saints rode every prow, from Michael to the Holy Sinner Magdalen. In 1533, for the marriage of Catherine de Médicis with the Duke of Orléans, there were eighteen royal galleys in port, and by 1696 Louis XIV kept forty-two galleys in Marseille waters, all outfitted and ready to fight.

The galleys designed and built in the great yards of the Vieux Port were called Marsilians, and were known wherever men rode the waves, for their two rudders and their catlike maneuverability. They could turn this way and that, and sneak up silently on any foe, for any prey.

These cats were manned by human beings who, if they were kept in good condition by their owners, could row six knots an hour through any tide or weather. And from an edict signed in 1564 by King Charles IX, they were either Frenchmen condemned to forced labor, or Mussulmen captured in war or bought as slaves, all called Turks but made up of real Levantines, or Senegalese Blacks, or North African barbarians. Their average price was high, around four hundred pounds, and they were bartered for, and traded, exactly as if they were precious silk or jute.

The Turks in Marseille were given their own mosque and cemetery. To keep things decent, captured French slaves in Constantinople also had a special chapel built for them. Everything was fair and square, and the bills of lading read like:

Bought at Mallorca by order of Lord Beaufort:

For 9 Turks:	6,453	pounds
For Customs Duty:	645	"
For Purchasing Agent:	32	"
For Boarding-Vessel:	16	"
	7,146	pounds

Signed: Séguin, Consul

There was hateful rivalry between the costly Turks and the cost-free French galley slaves, used cannily by their captains, of course, but little chance to express it. Mostly the men lived and died on their benches, chained by one leg, and wearing a gag around the neck that was ready to pop into the mouth on order, to prevent talk and make the ears more alert for commands. For a time all the slaves wore red caps like a brand, but later they had none at all against the sun and the sleet. Their officers were armed with a stick, a whip, and a lash. . . .

If a man became patently useless at his oar, he could be bought off: a Frenchman cost one high-placed purchase and replacement, but a Turk needed two backers and then two more Turks in his place. Madame de Sévigné more than once finagled galley spots for troublesome young countrymen in the seventeenth century . . . much as reputable Americans bought positions for their unwanted siblings or enemies in both sides of the Civil War. This exchange solved unwelcome political, domestic, and perhaps financial problems, and the risk of a resentful or even murderous revenge was slight.

The galleys of Marseille were from the first a tourist attraction, and perhaps it was there and then that pocket-picking became an art that still thrives, I am told, in broad daylight along the Canebière, on the Cours Belsunce, in murkier corners. It is said, for instance, that one bishop went on board a new galley to give it and the slaves his official blessing, and announced that he defied any man there to take his wallet, but when he left he found that he was without the heavy gold episcopal cross worn around his neck.

Once in port, often three or four thousand slaves at a time were housed in enormous barracks at the southeast end of the little harbor, used also for shipbuilding, sword sharpening, and the countless parties so dear to the city: the men would shout huzzahs like trained seals at a given signal, raise their oars in forty galleys at a time before the City Hall for some visiting admiral or prince, and sit helplessly under thousands of paper lanterns on the brightened water, while people danced and bands played.

Louis XIV loved to make war, or at least to have a good force behind him in case things came to that point, and by the end of the seventeenth century Marseille was the hub of his fighting navy, for building, arming, and maintaining an astonishing fleet of the subtle, sneaky, Marsilian galleys. A new Arsenal was built, an engineering marvel, from its prison barracks and ironworks and road factories to the elegant Commanders' House, hung with Gobelin tapestries, a fine place for celebrating everything from the King's recovery from a head cold to the overnight stay of one of his grandchildren. Three balls could go on there at once, complete with specially written operas and great suppers.

There was a real hospital for the condemned men, however, in those grand days: six big wards for the Turks to one for the French. This practical as well as merciful provision came from a gentleman of Provence named Gaspard de Simiane-la-Coste, apparently the only such benefactor without a statue in that country given to their erection in any and every little park or cranny. Above the hospital wards was the armory, rising up in four galleries around a covered hall, and known to house the most beautiful war implements in the world. It was a sight to behold, and countless travellers did so, and there were grand parties, at which living tableaux were given to martial music, with symbolic representations of Louis XIV's might, ringed by kneeling Turks hung with golden chains that were exchanged for their own irons as soon as the shows were over.

The Arsenal was, well before 1700, a city in itself, and employed free men along with its forced labor. Some of the slaves were allowed to go outside, and gradually they built shacks across the Vieux Port where under constant guard they could carry on their old trades as tailors, toymakers, and weavers. Many more men were used as domestics by the officers and rich citizens. They were returned to the Arsenal at night, and any Marseillais who let one escape was fined the price of a new Turk.

Once, during the dreadful Plague of 1720, Marseille ran out of gravediggers, and on August 8, twenty-six Turks were put into service, with the promise of their liberty. Two days later, however, they were all dead. Fifty-three more, then eighty, then a hundred and another hundred men were sent into the nightmare around the Port. The job was to pick up the bodies, pile them onto carts, and dump them into the great ditches dug hastily for them. Twelve hundred people a day were dying, and on September 16 a brave gentleman named Roze commandeered enough galley slaves to clear a thousand cadavers off one of the quays, where they had lain for some three weeks, in less than half an hour. A commemorative plaque and a bust were erected to him. And back at the Arsenal, while only four men survived this forced service, the air was kept "perfumed" and most of the galleys were moved out of the Old Port, and of ten thousand slaves only about seven hundred died.

By the middle of the eighteenth century there were only eleven galleys left in Marseille, thanks largely to the fact that naval activities had been moved on down to Toulon and that slavery was beginning to seem "un-Christian." By 1784 the Arsenal had been sold by the King to outside speculators, since Marseille did not want to buy it, and only two galleys were left to be viewed by the tourists and then carted off. One of them, *La Patience*, served in the invasion of Egypt from Toulon in 1784, and was manned by free volunteers and then scrapped.

And by now nothing is left of the Arsenal . . . except that some people sense a pool of spiritual agony there where for hundreds of years men who had been ripped from their homelands by force, war, politics, must live and die chained to their oars or in their prison barracks. Up around the Opera, where the Hospital and Armory once stood, there are countless shady little hotels with their listless women waiting outside, and behind them rooms for shadier pleasures. Along the Rive Neuve, above the fish-bistros, there are "clubs" of varied repute, offering even more varied diversions to their members. Farther down toward the wholesale fish market, La Criée, and back of the waterfront, there are gathering places called names like the Galley Slave and the One-Eyed Pirate, where loops of tiny lightbulbs twinkle at odd hours, and sounds of bad dance-music seep up from the sidewalk, and some of the toughest girls I have ever seen lead young men toward the dark.

All of this is part of what was left by countless slaves who sweated blood and hatred and lust there. It will continue. A mysterious thing about Marseille, though, is that its collective evil is balanced by a wonderful healthiness. This too is what the galley slaves have left: the children they sowed in the sturdy stock of the Massilians, the children of Greek sailors from Phocea, and of wandering hardy tribes behind them, the prehistoric salt gatherers.

The reason, perhaps, for this balance of evil and good influences on the people of any such place is that it can be, as in Marseille, deeply religious.

It is "Christian" now, in the sense that this form of worship is the last manifestation of its ageless need for altars, altars behind altars, idols behind idols. It needs something to shout to and to dance around, to curse and to beseech, and because it is a natural gathering place on the globe for such human necessities, saints and sinners have collected there around the Vieux Port as irrevocably as water runs downhill.

When young Protis found himself married to the king's daughter and ruler of half the port-land, all in a few hours, he accepted the whole startling situation as a direct command of Artemis, the protector of sailors and therefore his own goddess. As soon as possible he built a temple to her, on the high northern hill above the city, and brought from Ephesus in Greece a handsome statue of her in her mummy-like wrappings covered with symbols and then her magnificent torso with its eighteen breasts in two vertical lines. She was accompanied by a famous priestess. A much simpler temple was built to Apollo, somewhat lower toward the sea, with its face looking out for mariners, but Artemis must face inland, to watch ferociously the creatures of the hunt, and to frighten off barbarians.

I I

There is a saying, conveniently ascribed to the Chinese, that a temple should be built on a high breezy hill, within sound of water, and with a twisting path to dizzy and baffle evil spirits trying to assault it. Marseille's first two Grecian altars qualified in every way, and probably were built on other older worship grounds, because this rule is truly ancient. And since then Diana, the goddess of the hunt, took over from Mother Artemis, the fierce forest virgin, and after Diana came early Christian saints like Martha who survived the trip from Gethsemane to tame the great monster of Tarascon (somewhat after her natural time of death but legendary and therefore past chronology, and how else argue than historically with the great fire-breathing dragons that apparently peopled pre-Christian Provence?), and of course Mary Magdalen.

She was Artemisian, in her ability to survive the rigors of cave life in the bleak mountains east of Marseille, after she and Martha, and of course black Sarah, and dozens more saints, drifted to the local shores in a small rowboat piloted, some believe, by Joseph of Arimathaea, all nourished by one pot of chickpeas. The Holy Sinner, as she is now affectionately referred to, survived as well as Artemis could have in her dank cave, and baptized secret Christians for anywhere from twelve to forty years before she succumbed to what has been diagnosed by medical skeptics as chronic bronchitis.

As far as is known, she had only the normal allotment of breasts, but she nourished an uncommon lot of legends, and is still one of the leading and most subtly powerful citizens of Marseille and its environs.

And gradually statues of the Holy Mother Mary pushed out the earlier images of the huntress-goddesses, but usually on or near the same high airy sites. She grew softer, kinder, more gracious, as the Catholic Church changed God from cruel to loving, and the priestesses from avenging females of frightening power to innocent maidens.

And I became a friend of one, the little brown Virgin of the Abbey of St. Victor, below our apartment on the Rive Neuve side of the Vieux Port. I saw her often, because it was easy and easing to stop there on my way toward the Canebière or wherever.

She sat, about as big as a ten-year-old girl, in the catacombs that are constantly being excavated and opened under the massive fortlike church. She is made of walnut wood that has darkened since the end of the thirteenth century, when she was probably carved, and I do not know how or why she is there. There are ugly little replicas of her for sale at the bakery near St. Victor, which is famous locally for the *navettes* it makes all year round instead of only for her special week of celebration of Candlemas, La Chandeleur, on February 2.

That is when I first saw the little statue, enthroned to the left of the altar in the great abbey, almost hidden by layers of rich brocades and cloth of gold and gauzes of jeweled silver, her small head crowned with heavy flaming gems. The nave was filled with people, the whole place humming like a hive around its queen, all gently, all carrying slender green or green-and-white tapers. Hundreds were lighted, and there was a fine glow of them around Our-Lady-of-the-

Renewed-Flame, but most of the people bought them at the door to take home for a time of illness or disaster. Later I learned that the little brown Virgin is called on for help in times of trouble, and that she was brought out, for instance, in 1849, during an outbreak of cholera, and sat for some time beside the altar, offering whatever it was that she was being asked for. (I also learned that people who felt guilty about something used to go to the big door where the candles were sold during La Chandeleur, to smash their fingers under its heavy knocker as penance to her. . . .)

My own first meeting during the lighted celebration in 1973 passed without any requests from either of us, as far as I can tell. I did not buy a candle, although their slender fresh green pleased me. I stood here and there in the soft murmuring glow of the beautiful abbey, and liked the way people seemed somewhat shy but happy, and admired the jeweled doll.

During the next months, I ate a lot of *navettes*, little boat-shaped cookies, tough dough tasting vaguely of orange peel, smelling better than they are. They are supposed to symbolize the miraculous vessel Magdalen and all the other saints piloted to safety near Marseille. I did not much like the little pastries, but the bakery was run by some interesting ex-vaudevillians, and in one window were two sizes of the ugly plaster copy of the brown Virgin. I deliberated for almost four months about buying the small one to give to a Christian friend, but I never did. Now I am sorry. But it was too ugly, when I could go down into the grotto chapel and look at her: no jewels, no glittering capes, no glowing green candles, but still a steadfast emanation of health and simplicity flowing from the small wooden image.

It is difficult to understand *why* this goddess has been a solace to the Marseillais in bad times, but there is no doubt that she possesses an ageless serenity, and sends out a balm of renewal. The abbey where she stays, named St. Victor for the city's prime Christian martyr, was first built in about A.D. 400 on the site of the old Greek cemetery, across the Port from the beautiful temples where life was worshiped instead of death. When, and why, did the new small idol come to this gathering place of earthly sorrows to give help?

III

It is often hard to admit to the awareness of what is mysterious. I found it painful, when I went back alone to Marseille in about 1970, to acknowledge that I felt an almost physical dislike of Notre Dame de la Garde, the Old Gold Lady up on the hill, the Good Mother of all navigators. I returned to her church many times, to try to understand what had happened to my respect and acceptance of her as intrinsic to the religious sanity of Marseille, and in 1976, riding on a bus toward the Vieux Port from Aix, I suddenly understood it very clearly.

There is one point on the route where for a flash the distant unreal golden statue can be as sharp and in a strange way as heart-lifting as the sound of a trumpet. In the fifties and sixties, my children and I would wait for it, stop talk, fix our eyes on the special spot in time and space. And there she would be. And we would know we were almost on the Vieux Port again. We felt safe.

There was another small moment of excitement, of fulfillment, from the train, whether we took the local from Aix or rode the Mistral down from Paris or Dijon. We knew when to wait for it, prepare ourselves, and then suddenly *see* that gleaming Lady, tiny as a pinprick but mighty, towering over the town. We were almost on the Vieux Port again. We felt safe . . . *again!*

Soon, that day, certainly before we went back again to Aix, we would go up to the church. We walked, or now and then took a cab, to the peculiar hydraulic elevator that has since been condemned. It ran by water which gushed dramatically at the bottom as the wobbly little cage rose slowly to the top of its slightly slanting tower, and most of the passengers were plainly frightened by the strange ascent, no matter how often they had made it. My older girl always closed her eyes until we jolted to a halt, and while I never felt anything but a fatalistic curiosity about the little flight, it was good to step out of the cage onto the long high bridge that connected the elevator tower to the mountain itself. Far below us were rooftops and then, on down to portside, the crowded quarters of the Rive Neuve. It seemed as if we could see forever, but we always hurried, because we knew that once we were on the mountain, once we had climbed the hundreds of stairs up to the church, the puny bridge and its little views would lose all their first excitement by comparison with what we had there.

We could walk clear around the huge ugly basilica, and look in every direction of the compass, from its great terraces and ramparts. Sometimes we held on to each other, to feel safer when the wind blew. Usually we climbed up to the east bastion of the fortress that the church is built on, where it juts out like a gigantic stone ship's prow. A flat round table, set with a map in mosaic, told us what we were seeing: city, Vieux Port, the Mediterranean, all the islands . . . we never tired of looking at it, and never felt dizzy, because the fortress was so mighty and so safe.

All this, though, was simply a ritual, almost dutifully performed before the real reason for our countless visits to the mountain: the *inside*, inside, first the low dim crypt, then the light-blazing basilica above it.

It sounds sacrilegious, perhaps, to say that it was an enchanted palace, part of fairyland, but in the best sense that was so. The outside of Notre Dame de la Garde is awesome, with its drawbridge, its bastions, but it is also stark, and in a controlled way, savage. There are still pits in its walls from its last bloody siege, when the Germans held it before it was freed in August of 1944 by the Third African Division of the French Army. But underneath those new scars, for hundreds of years, are the ghosts of revolutions and mutinies and imprisonments and treacheries, and it can never be anything but frightening, even in the blazing sunlight of Provence.

The crypt, then, is like a low dark cave at first. It is enormous, the size of the church above it, but with a womb-like reassurance, and gradually the soft lights in the little side chapels, and the glow of candles, make it come into focus like a murmurous dream. There have always been people there when we were, kneeling, wandering quietly from one chapel to another to look at the countless votive pictures and tablets and medals and miraculously useless crutches. Everything praises the miraculous, of course: the watchful defense of sailors first, then all travellers, and then the sick and otherwise endangered, by Our Lady of Protection, who in one form or another has stood on that steep rock for thousands of years, to guide and reassure.

It is impossible not to feel, there, something strong and trusting about the human spirit, and my girls and I accepted it wordlessly as we looked at crude little paintings of shipwrecks, and read quaint impressive poems of gratitude from sailors or their families whose prayers had been answered.

I think there is an elevator inside the church, probably for infirm visitors, but we were neither hobbled nor newcomers to the place, and it was fine to leave the softly dim crypt and walk up the great outer stairs to the basilica itself. We knew what would happen. It always did. Once inside, the place seemed to explode with light and color and rich crazy beauty. It scintillated. It was gay and lightsome. We gasped, and entered with a familiar feeling of delight.

The walls are made of many colors of stone, brought from wherever marble turns rosy or yellow, wherever any rock can be quarried that is green or blue or red, veined or pure. The ceilings of all the side chapels, of the dome above the main altar, of the nave, are mosaics brightly paved with gold. Their arches are supported by angels and archangels. The floor too is a brilliant mosaic carpet. The windows are like crystal, to make all the surfaces glint and gleam.

Above the altar there is the tall Virgin and Child in silver, sometimes crowned with gold and diamonds. They used to be carried in pilgrimages through the town, and once after the Revolution in the eighteenth century she wore a tricolor scarf on her head and the Child a little Phrygian cap, I have been told. . . . There is a lot of lapis lazuli, as I remember, and above the altar are two astonishing lamps of silver. It is all heartwarmingly, generously vulgar.

And the best part, of course, is what countless Christians have brought to Notre Dame, to recall their gratefulness. Their *ex votos* hang from the high vault of the nave on cords or perhaps wires that are almost invisible, but that are symbolical of the connection between earth and heaven, and they twirl a little sometimes, very slowly, if there are crowds beneath, or if the mistral is strong outside. There are little whittled rowboats once brightly painted, and dimestore battleships; there are life rafts and plastic toy submarines and a few streetcars and many airplanes. There is at least one World War II tank, I remember, and a toy ambulance, and my younger daughter swears there is a very small baby buggy.

A lot of the side chapels are dedicated to martial miracles: sailors, regiments, generals, admirals. There are little marble plaques from famous soldiers, dedicated to Our Lady for saving them from long-forgotten battles on such-and-such a date. There are a lot of medals and epaulettes and swords.

The fine excitement of the whole place, though, comes from the hundreds of subtly moving votive images on their long strings, tiny in the dazzling rich colors of the church, all there because men prayed and were saved to live a little longer. The odor of thanksgiving is strong, from all these devout emotional symbols, and it is extremely innocent and direct.

My children and I always absorbed it as simply as we breathed the heady salt air of Marseille, and almost romped down the old winding path past the oratories where pilgrims could stop to pray and catch their breath, with a new feeling of life. Once back on the Rive Neuve we took the little ferry across to the Quai du Port, and stood in front of the lovely Town Hall and looked across at Our Guardian Lady. There she was, straight as a flame on the high belltower above the church, above the old fortress, on the sharp mountain above the town and the port and the sea. We were safe.

There were the requisites of the Chinese dictum: temple on high hill, winding path to baffle evil spirits, sound of water . . . if not the rush of the old hydraulic elevator, the plash of *l'eau bénite* in generous basins for the believers . . . so, what happened to make me feel sour and resentful a few years later?

I went back automatically, and things seemed drab and cold. There were busloads of tired lumpy tourists. There were gift shops and snack bars. Worst of all, there were printed signs everywhere, telling me in four languages not to do this, to do that, to keep quiet, to be respectful, to remember that I was in a holy place, and most of all that this holy place did not in *any* way belong to the city of Marseille but to the Church in *every* way, at *all* times. . . .

The signs were what turned the trick. They were even inside the entrance to the crypt and the nave: Pray! Silence! Be Reverent! . . . and they still were there when I went back in 1976 to see if what I discovered on the bus was true. It was: I had lost the innocence, the feeling of mystery that was so strong when I was with my children.

I was alone. I felt everything as a weary cynical observer, not as a delighted excited new soul. The beautiful mosaics looked coarse. The silver lamps and Mother and Child were vulgar. The votive ships and submarines and tanks seemed foolish and dusty. And the signs . . . they were insulting, and I felt trouble in them: someday the Marseillais would take things into their own hands, as they had done before, and heads would roll, and the drawbridge would be pulled up in another siege . . . and the reason I was so dour, I saw in a flash as I looked automatically at the precise point in the bus trip across to the far flash of Notre Dame de la Garde, was that I had let myself lose the innocence my little girls had loaned to me. I felt ashamed and sad.

So I went to stand in front of the Town Hall. And there she was! Across the crowded waters of the Vieux Port, high as the sky, golden in the sunlight, the colossal statue seemed to ride the basilica, the fortress, the crag, the city itself, as if she were the figurehead of a ship forever safe from danger. I knew that at night she would be lighted, a symbol to tired travellers and the ships at sea, and that the grave sound of her mighty bell would ring for them, for me.

I knew many other things; the statue is more than forty feet tall, made of an alloy of copper and zinc in four hollow sections, with a circular staircase inside so that there is a bird's view of Marseille through the eyes of her somewhat pudgy face. She was put into place in 1870, and the deep-toned bell was christened Marie-Joséphine and first rung in 1845. It was made in Lyon, shipped down the Rhône to Avignon, dragged by relays of Percheron horse teams toward the mountain, and then up. I know about some of the countless pagan-Christian pilgrimages, and royal luncheon parties after Mass, and desperate prayers during the Plague of 1720 and the cholera epidemic in the nineteenth century. The first gift to the church was a little sack of coins from Gilbert des Baux, one of the descendants of Wise Man Balthazar . . . but the second was a liter of olive oil from a nameless work-man. Then pearls and gold flowed in. . . .

I knew, too, that after Julius Caesar crossed the Rubicon in 49 B.C. and destroyed Marseille to spite Pompey, he built a temple to Vesta or perhaps Ceres on the mountain, to show his gratitude for being so powerful. And before that, the Phoenicians worshiped Baal Milkarth there. And of course the Phoceans had a temple to Artemis there as well as across the Port, where later Diana and Apollo were worshiped on the gentler hills. I knew how the high peak has for unknown centuries been a watchtower, a chapel, a fort, sometimes all together. And the garish richness inside, the ugly striped architecture outside, the cruel ramparts and staircases with their insolent signs, became completely unimportant as I took a new long look. They were almost as evanescent in Time as I myself was, but they had, through the innocence of my children, taught me how to be aware of man's trust, even if my own seemed occasionally to weaken and falter.

Albert Einstein wrote, "The most beautiful thing we can

experience is the mysterious . . . the source of all true art and science. He to whom this emotion is a stranger, who can no longer pause to wonder and stand rapt in awe, is as good as dead; his eyes are closed. To know that what is impenetrable to us really exists . . . this knowledge, this feeling, is the center of true religiousness."

Marseille is not a stranger to this awe, and its eyes have never closed.

Chapter 9

SOME
DIFFERENCES

The differences between a *fête* and a *foire*, in Marseille, are cold and clear, but the two are as apart-alike as breathing in and then out, in a healthy body.

A *fête* is a celebration of something. It can be a public holiday ordered by Church or State and printed on calendars: Christmas, July 14, All Saints' Day. It can be a family anniversary, a birthday, printed in private memories. It can be like the day in February when people walk to St. Victor to buy a green taper for Candlemas, either to light bemusedly in the murmurous abbey or to carry home for possible succor in case of death or rheumatism.

A *fête* can be solemn and quiet or unbelievably noisy, but a *foire* is noisy perforce, and often garish or giddy as well as commercial in one way or another. It is a big organized carnival, no matter how decorous its motives. People will come to it from everywhere, in summer yachts or winter caravans, and sailors to it will sleep in their chosen ways all around the Vieux Port, as will artisans and their wives during the Foire aux Santons up along the Allées at the top of the Canebière . . . and then the garlic merchants, and the nursery garden growers, and the land developers. . . .

Kings, bishops, the Chamber of Commerce, and other representatives of earthly power have officially organized fairs in Marseille since August 19, 1318, when Robert of Provence authorized a three-day celebration in honor of his dead brother, St. Louis of Anjou. Louis, who had been Bishop of Toulouse, was buried in the Franciscan Convent in Marseille, and for reasons best known to King Robert and probably his astrologers, it seemed a judicious time to give the populace a little diversion . . . dancing, free food for the lucky, pomp and paradings.

Fairs are far from coincidental, politically or otherwise, with the conjunction of stars and human yearnings. Long before Rome, it has been a truism that if subjects seem to be growing fractious, hot-blooded, or otherwise lunatic, a good circus is indicated. If garlic, onions, and herbs are ready to be used, let people flock to town to buy them and then spend money in the public houses as well as the crowded merry streets lined with booths. If the sun is high, let amateur sailors be invited to crowd the bright blue port with their pretty barks, and then fill all the quays with their tanned thirsty gaiety. And if the future looks grim, no matter how short it may be (Lent used to be a good example of this limited period of self-denial), let there be a good carnival first, to ease the body and give due cause for remorse (with the primeval rewards of springtime after the dark days . . .).

When Protis sailed into the Vieux Port to buy salt some twenty-six hundred years ago, he unwittingly crashed a party that some observers feel has never really stopped. The King's daughter chose him in marriage that first night, by raising her wine glass to the young Greek captain, and wine is still as much a part of life there as is water, or the celebration of turning one into the other, although there is little drunkenness in this ageless miracle, among the natives.

The first Massilia, now one of the world's richest, most devil-ridden and exciting ports, seems to live in and for a constant calendar of festivities and rites, and a full enjoyment of whatever they offer. Except for the slight inconvenience of having to get back to work on Monday morning when the whistle blows, Sunday night is as long and lovely as Saturday. Weekends as well as fairs and all such celebrations are made for pleasure and relaxation, and it is a poor stick of a Puritan from Dijon or Paris, or even Chicago or Munich, who cuts short the obvious delights of a pleasant evening simply because tomorrow means work.

The same is true of any holiday in Marseille. It lasts longer, is noisier, and in general seems like more fun than in any place else in the world. New Year's Eve, for instance: in my own experience, it starts about two hours before midnight on December 31, on the Vieux Port anyway, and lasts until the last feeble toot of a taxi horn at three the next afternoon.

It begins with horns, too, and increasingly they include happy-sounding cornets, trombones, even saxophones, and all kinds of whistles, blown from the windows of every moving car, and from ambling groups on all the sidewalks. At midnight, of course, there is a splendid ritual of sound, and all the bells ring above the burst of noise from ground level, with the grave tone from Notre Dame de la Garde holding them together. Guns and other explosives crackle, and there are wild yells and screams, and sirens. And the most astonishing thing about this deliberate abandon is that its conventional salute to the New Year does not cease with the pealing bells and the singing of "Auld Lang Syne," but is as savage at three and then five and even eight in the morning as it was at midnight.

I listened to it once from the top floor of the Hotel Beauvau, and although I never slept a minute of that night, I felt afterward as if I had been cleansed and refreshed by the virile strength of the sound, which seemed as if it would never stop, and rose in a subtly wavering roar to my windows. Now and then I would look down at the Quai des Belges, bright as day under the elaborate civic decorations of great dolphins and starfish made of colored lights, and cars would be moving with slow skill, sometimes with somebody like a white-haired man alone on the top playing a trumpet, other times bursting with wild-eyed girls in vivid silks, singing. I would go back to my bed again, rocked in a more pagan rhythm than ever before or since.

By nightfall of that New Year's Day, Marseille was as quiet as a church. An occasional empty bus moved along the silent streets. Most of the restaurants and cafés were closed, or kept dimly lighted by one semiconscious waiter who complied with the unwritten law about maintaining refuge for weary travellers. . . . All the stores were dark. It was eerie to walk along the Canebière and not meet even a dog. There was no sign of the sixteen hours or so of celebrating: no broken glass or dirty confetti, no vomit against a wall. The Marseillais had greeted the new year as they felt it to be fitting, drunk on their own love of any excuse for a party, and strong enough to make it perforce the noisiest, longest one ever given, at least since the year before. There was no citywide hangover, as would seem indicated after such a rout, but only an innocent need for sleep and silence.

By the next morning the fishwives were sharp-eyed behind their trays of flopping catch along the Quai des Belges, the shops everywhere were bustling, the banks were sedately busy. . . .

There are, of course, official holidays besides New Year's Day, such as Christmas, May the 1st, Bastille Day. This somewhat rigidly dictated list does not daunt the Marseillais, however, for there are always the *foires*. There is a Spring Fair, complete with day-and-night displays and contests for everything from swimming to hairdressing, and from judo-for-ladies to the filleting of fresh sardines. Somewhere along in here comes the International Sailing Week, when the Vieux Port is filled with elegant vessels of every size, and the pubs hum with bronzed, hungry yachtsmen and their ladies, all speaking twenty tongues.

Easter is in the *fête-foire* pattern too, in a city that has fought fiercely for Christianity since its first martyrs, after Mary Magdalen preached there on the porch of the temple of Athena (and left her brother Lazarus to be the town's first Bishop), a city that is willing to accept its present Communism for any good excuse to decorate the altars, and then dance to the gods and goddesses that were behind them first: Apollo, Artemis . . . further back.

In midsummer, there is the Garlic Fair, which until lately, when it was moved to a nearby area, was held at the top of the Canebière, around the handsome old bandstand and down the shady Allées where, two days a week in almost every weather, is one of the most beautiful flower markets in the world. The air is as heavy as ozone there, on Tuesdays and Saturdays, and so purified by the thousands of potted and cut blossoms that it seems improbable any odor could attack it, from the gassy vehicles pouring up and down the wide street . . . except in midsummer, of course, when over that whole part of the city there floats from the Fair the scent of freshly gathered garlic.

It hangs in short braids, or loops in long heavy cables from all the stands that spring up in a few hours. It spills from the backs of parked trucks and wagons. It lies in piles on canvas spread on the sidewalks, and there are nutlike sacks of it as tall as a man. Housewives pinch and sniff and fill their baskets for storage; buyers for big hotels and restaurants in Provence sample freely as they make out their orders; wholesalers from half of Europe compare lots and bargain with the farmers. It is exciting, and a handsome scene, with the silky glistening garlic everywhere, to look at and to breathe. Some men in Provence say their women are beautiful because of garlic, and some women say their babies are healthy because of it, and their men stronger than other men.

There is another International Fair in September, complete with exhibits, contests, booths, flags, the general commercialized hoopla. But the next time the real stands go up, at the top of the flowery Allées, the trees are bare, and will stay that way until the last stall is empty, and then well past that. The famous Foire aux Santons begins on the first Sunday in December, and with luck, or perhaps the contrary, a few booths will still be open in mid-January, shielding what is left of the stock of little clay figures piled on the rickety counters, half-priced, with the boss or his indomitable wife sleeping on a cot behind a flap of canvas as nightwatchers of the leftover crumbs.

At the start of the Fair, it is a different picture. The Allées are lined on both sides with dozens of booths, brightly painted and as brightly lighted in the quick wintry twilights and then the chill nights, and the wide sidewalk between them is jammed with people, pushing and gaping and joking with the vitality that I believe is peculiar to Marseille. It is like the midway of a carnival but more intense, less fragmented, of course with loudspeakers blaring above the human sounds in this age. There is a general air of animal enjoyment, and cafés do a land-office business, and it is all (at least for now) because thousands of painted figurines can be looked at and compared, and bought, to depict the birth of Jesus Christ.

The images, not all of little saints as their name would imply, come in several heights, set rigidly by the Guild of Santonmakers, with the tiniest called "fleas," and the biggest perhaps a meter high, and in spite of personal quirks of the artists who produce them, they are endearingly alike.

How could the story be changed? Everybody in Provence knows that the Baby was born in a stable, so there is a Provençal cowshed, with straw laid on the floor for a bed. Sometimes the straw is real, for an expensively large image, and sometimes it is a tiny blob of yellow plaster for one of the minute crèches that are fitted into halved walnut shells and still sold by the less famous *santonniers*, the ones with wives and small children willing to help paint them when the season is slack. The Baby always wears a decorous white shirt, and is pink in the face. His Mother and Father never change either. How could they dare to? She wears blue and looks beatific, and he wears a brown cape and looks bewildered.

There are the Ox, the Ass, and the Three Wise Men. And then there are the other people who came to worship, that night in the village in Provence: the Shepherds who saw Balthazar's star, the Fisherman and his catch, the Laundress with her basket of clean linens, the Mayor and his Wife, the Miller with a sack of flour, the evil Gypsy, and all dressed in the village clothes and country capes and boots of the early nineteenth century, when the play that tells about this great event first took shape. In one form or another, it is always called *La Pastorale*, and it still plays all through the region, well past Christmas itself: a cast of dozens of local people and animals, held more or less in line by two or three roving professionals: very broad humor, good fife-and-drum music, hearty dancing, local jokes, everything sung and spoken in Provençale. The audience knows every line, and often has a child or newborn lamb in the cast, and the women wear old family costumes oftener than stylish holiday clothes. The show is hours long, with a merciful break half through it.

The story is about a quarrelsome village, miraculously united by the birth of a little stranger in a cowshed, and it is even more familiar than our Red Riding Hood or Mickey Mouse, and the *santons* repeat its simple legend meticulously, to a knowing and basically pagan audience. The Mayor must wear his black silk top hat and the Fishwife carry her brass scales, and the Virgin be in blue, no matter what hands (Gypsy? Communist? Muslim?) have shaped and painted the little figures.

Tradition steps aside for the extras, though: hens and their chicks, and Provençal windmills and cypress trees and a bridge for the boy angler, and dogs and lambs and a donkey to help the woodcutter. They are irresistible, and the tinier they are, the more the fairgoers seem to want them, to put in their pockets and take home for a family Nativity.

The first time I saw the Foire aux Santons it was at its peak of excitement, the second Sunday in December. Thousands of people joined the slow march up and down the Allées, gaping, stopping to buy, eating hot sugared peanuts from the little stoves that smoked here and there into the cold air. The last time was well after the holidays, and most of the stalls were gone or boarded up. Two or three stayed open to sell their remainders, the chipped or misshapen or mismated *santons* that nobody had wanted: a six-centimeter

Mary and a two-centimeter Joseph, a Baby with one arm gone.

It was a *foire* I went to, then and often in Marseille. It was as commercial as the Summer Regattas I looked down to in the Vieux Port, when it was a solid flicker of bright sails heading for the open sea. All the fairs were planned, perhaps contrived by both stars and men, to bring people together when the planets gave them the right indications of harvest, high sun, rebirth. So it may be that they were *fêtes* too, ageless celebrations of life.

Chapter 10

MAY DAY,
1932 – 73

May Day is taken seriously in Marseille, a solid Socialist-Communist stronghold. It is firmly and almost solemnly a breather for the hard workers: stevedores, shipbuilders, construction men . . . and few women are seen in the cafés and on the quays of the Vieux Port, even if they are breadwinners in their own right.

Some of the better-class restaurants close, ostensibly to give their staffs a free day but really because the people amiably monopolizing the sidewalks would never set foot over an elegant threshold, for both financial and ideological reasons. On the other hand, the pubs and bistros are open and crowded from early on the Great Day until the last dog dies. Usually the weather is benign, and little round tables push almost over the curbs.

The older men look shaved and rather formal under their Sunday hats as they saunter along, their eyes out for old pals, fellow welders or carpenters they may not have seen since that big job in '54 or '62. They meet, greet, sit talking for a time, and then roam on, drinking sagely in the face of a hundred other such encounters before nightfall. The younger men, more casually dressed but as carefully, are hatless. They make a formless parade of parental dignity and pride, with one or two small children wearing their starched and frilly best, tiny girls riding their fathers' shoulders, boys old enough to walk keeping step, three to one, alongside. There is not a pram or baby-pusher in sight: plainly a woman's symbol, and not manly enough for this annual display of virility and fatherly tenderness. There is much handshaking and comparing of progeny, on the wide sidewalks, and hundreds of children peck politely at their tenth or twentieth ice cream or orange soda while their fathers talk shop over their small glasses of *pastis*.

The sounds are good, from thousands of male voices laughing and gabbling in the sunny air. The traffic is not heavy, since a lot of the buses are laid off and there are few taxis. The port looks strange without its rickrack in the wakes of the two little ferries, firmly tied up for the Day at their berth on the Rive Neuve. The fishhouses on that side do a long steady business, of course, mostly for groups of three or more men eating oysters to prove that at least once or twice a year money means nothing to them, or ordering a magisterial bouillabaisse to prove that they are genuine citizens of the town. The young fathers wander up the Canebière to the Place St. Louis or the Cours Belsunce, where they buy snacks for the children from the open booths and sit under the softly leafing plane trees with a few buddies, before they head home for the special meal the wives have made during their "free" day without all the kids underfoot.

There is a haunting air about the First of May, aside of course from the obvious ceremonies that have been carried out rather summarily in various working quarters and big meeting places: oratory, discreet police surveillance, a flourish of trumpets now and then. All that must of course be got through, a token, a symbol. But what the men wait for is to wander in the sunlight, once their comradely duty has been done, and be free, free for a day that without the Revolution would mean routine work. They want to show off their little children, and encounter hit-or-miss their peers, and drink a few *pastis* without pressure from either women or clocks. There are no bosses, in other words, on May Day. It is the workers' own, hard fought for and hard won and to be savored to the hilt, by men who may never have tasted revolution itself, but who know why it has occasionally been indicated as necessary to the laboring masses.

On May 2 the dream will be over. On May 1 it is something to hang on to, and in the dancing sunlight around the Vieux Port, that is easy. Toward evening the little children sleep in their fathers' arms, or on benches anywhere, and gradually the young men gather them up and walk slowly toward their flats, while the older ones sit longer with a few friends and start a lazy game of cards. In the outskirts of the big city the day-long click of the *boule* balls grows still, and lights go off early everywhere, if men must be up for the first shift at the yards, the depots, the high-rise construction going on near the new university. Sidewalk snack wagons and the little restaurants around the Vieux Port put up their shutters, and gradually the fishing boats ready themselves for whatever will be needed to assault whatever schools of fish may swim on May 2.

So . . . May Day can be peaceable, as it seemed in Marseille in 1973 and may still stay, far removed from its bloody beginnings and from the social convulsions of the past decades. The workers of the world, at least in that old southern port, arise and after dutiful meetings to prove their unity they wander with proud but relaxed freedom through the suddenly quiet streets of their town.

When I was first in Marseille on a May Day, in 1932, I think, things were more tense, and less firmly controlled by the people. The streets were almost silent, not filled with relaxed roamers as I saw them forty years later, but with occasional small groups of truculent-looking men who slid off when the cops, always in twos, came into view. Of course banks, post offices, schools, and most stores were tightly closed, and then as in 1973 the only things kept open seemed to be the cafés and the emergency rooms at the Hôtel Dieu and some outlying hospitals . . . and of course the police stations.

My husband and young sister Norah and I were there to board an Italian freighter for San Pedro in California. It seemed strange then and by now even stranger that the tub would sail that special day, and that we three would be there on time, drifting around the Vieux Port in a contained anguish at having to leave the country, the language. We were subtly catatonic, each in our own way, perhaps a little drunk on white wine and regret.

As I remember it, our favorite hotel, called the Good Old Beauvau in our private vocabulary then as now, housed a restaurant on the corner of the Canebière and the Quai des Belges, called the Mont Ventoux or perhaps the Beauvau–Mont Ventoux. And as I remember it, there was an upstairs dining room, above the sidewalk brasserie, with an open balcony. And one went up to it from the Quai instead, as later, by a plushy stairway leading off the main street. I even think that I remember vines or green leaves shading the balcony tables, but this may be the influence of old postcards and novels and research volumes bought but seldom consulted. According to a 1939 Michelin it was run by M. Sicard then, and probably was a few years before, when he almost threw me out of his restaurant.

We had done the best we could about seeing that our big wicker trunks were properly at the right dock, and had gone into one open record shop along the silent Canebière and one circumspect pharmacy on a side street, and after a drink in the kind of bar that fell quiet when we came in, we sagged disconsolate but undaunted toward the stairs of the Mont Ventoux.

Halfway up, the owner came hurrying down to us. Plainly he was tense and alerted to possible May Day difficulties, and over my shoulder I wore a small accordion that I had bought to fill the hours in a hotel room while my husband (in the University of Strasbourg's quieter library) changed a comma to a semicolon and then back again in his doctor's thesis. And M. Sicard said, with forceful clarity, *"Out! No beggars or street musicians! OUT!"*

What we did next apparently melted his heart, for we stood there like children to confess that we were sailing from Marseille in about two hours and that the accordion was for the long voyage, but that we *must* eat one more good meal on the Vieux Port. His eyes in a trained flicker appraised our shoes and hair, and with a cautious bow he led us to exactly the table we wanted, next to the balcony on the corner of the Quai and the Canebière. (Was there really such a balcony then? Was there a velvet hand in a steel glove named Sicard? Were we there at all?) We spent more than three hours eating and drinking, and knew tacitly that we were like people hoping vainly to be snowbound in a snug mountain cabin. Perhaps the freighter had already sailed . . . the snow would be too deep for a rescue. . . .

As we broke from the dream and started sheepishly to push back our chairs, the dragon-boss came toward us with a big dusty bottle and four balloon glasses, poured a family elixir distilled somewhere behind Cassis, and sat down firmly to share it. He was full of gallant chuckles about mistaking me for a street musician. We told him all kinds of winy nothings about being students in cold northern hinterlands like Dijon and Strasbourg, which he recognized to be French but plainly felt were as dismissable as Kanchatka or Popocatepetl. He told us of his farm and vineyard and family. We exchanged addresses. We told him about finding an open record shop, and he said it was a dangerous day, and then we said we hated violently to leave France and Marseille and the Mont Ventoux and him.

Suddenly he became alarmed, and with drastic assistance from what staff he could drum up at that hour he located a friend of a friend of a waiter who grudgingly agreed to drive a crony's cab to the Joliette docks. "It will cost somewhat more today," our new friend murmured, and then shouted impressively, "All speed! This is a life-and-death matter! Goodbye, goodbye. . . ."

It was May Day, the driver's day, and he hated capitalists, especially American tycoons who travelled selfishly on luxury liners and knew nothing of the hell working people lived in to serve them like slaves. He was a small rat of a man, filled with phrases, and as steeped in his own libations as we were numbed by the mysterious brew from behind Cassis, and his colossal grouch seemed both logical and familiar to us, headed as we were toward farther shores. We agreed to all of it, fatly fed and wined, as we bumped furiously and erratically toward our pier and one of the most evil little ships of my long life with and on them. (We three were one-third of the passengers, all neurotics, and the officers were more off focus than any of us, despairing rejects of the military system in their country. Their pathetic little Italian vessel was later to be sunk as the first one tagged by the British in World War II . . . a quasi-noble if overly delayed demise.)

On the way to this climax or dénouement or whatever it proved to be in our high lonely day in Marseille on May 1, 1932, we sat for a timeless time in the steaming taxi while a surprising number of armed cops on the dock and up on deck blew whistles and yelled wildly at each other, and the skinny little driver moaned hopeless epithets. He hunched down behind the wheel, and kept his engine going in high and in gear, longing to take off, but plainly more compassionate to us as fellow victims of Society after one look at the rusty little freighter.

Cranes were hoisting big crates and trunks, mostly wicker, toward the two open hatches. We stared, because three of them were ours, and it was baffling to see them swing up and over the hatch and then come down ponderously again to the dock. The police looked wildly at colored papers, and the driver became more and more nervous, and gunned his motor hysterically. He was frantic, but was too decent to dump us there with all our bundles and packages and the accordion. Probably, we felt, he had left his brood of small rat-faces and some half-sloshed buddies to do this crazy favor for a brother-in-law. . . .

Finally my husband talked to one of the excited police, who laughed shortly when asked if the ship would sail that day, and said in a cryptic manner that he would guarantee it, but without some of its cargo. We could wait right there on the dock, he said in a mocking way, and watch the fun.

Our driver, who looked more and more like a trapped animal wanting to be anywhere on earth but there, helped us feverishly to unload all the foolish packages of books and cigarettes and toothpaste for a month's chancy living, and shot off down the nearest alley without even a look at the money we had paid him.

His fraternal hopes for a better world had apparently not extended to the police, and neither, during the rest of the afternoon, did ours, as we stood in the thick air and watched a crew of uniformed men run long steel needles into every bundle and through every wicker crate and trunk on the dock. There was something doggedly vicious about it, and as the sweet fire of the Sicard liquor dimmed and vanished, we felt like three shocked ghosts, expelled from Heaven to an unknown level in Limbo; atonement in reverse. We were lost souls, wracked with puzzlements and vague horrors.

When the searchers got to our trunks and plunged their lethal wands through the woven sides, they hit something hard in one, and gathered around it, yelling and stabbing futilely. A pale ship's officer ran down the gangplank, looking wild and Italian. He talked for a minute with the police and then hurried toward us, calling out our names. Automatically we had our passports and tickets ready, and he apologized in a hysterical staccato and asked only if we had the trunk keys with us.

"Why?" my husband asked in a cold way I had never heard before but knew was based on the last fumes from Cassis. "That trunk contains scholastic material."

"And all our winter shoes," I added.

The young man cried impatiently, "The keys, please! Every ship in Marseille is being searched, sir. Three of the most dangerous murderers in the history of this decadent country are trying to escape to America, haven of criminals! They are perhaps on our vessel, because it is May Day and the criminal elements of this depraved Communistic serpents' nest are aiding them. They are typical Marseille toughs, pimps, murderers, arsonists, drug traffickers. So the *keys*! We are five hours late in sailing, for God's sake!"

He ran back madly to the police, brandishing our keys as if he had just won some kind of polemical battle at least. The uniformed men still kept trying to plunge their hideous needles at every angle in the book trunk. My husband moaned that his papers would be ruined forever. My sister Norah, as sardonic at fourteen as she is now, said grimly, "No blood, no murder, dummies." I said, "Dog eat dog." We felt old and sad.

The suspicious trunk flew open, and the books and the shoes were indeed in a sorry state, and the policemen hurried off the dock without more than a cursory salute to the ship's officer. They were the first and I think the last truly rude people I ever met in Marseille, on or off duty, if of course one accepts and forgives certain stresses of an occupational nature. Or perhaps it was those slim wands that prejudiced me. . . .

"This has been a nightmare, a catastrophe," the sweating officer told us in a belated bid for our numbed sympathy. "The ship has been invaded since noon, while every inch was searched. Then all the passengers' and officers' baggage had to be taken off. Never dock at Marseille," he suddenly shouted. "Never, ever! But especially on May Day! It is a pesthole. It is anti-Christ. The dinner gong will be in ten minutes, one hour and fifty-two minutes late!"

He dashed up the gangplank, leaving us silent on the dock, three people thinking of dappled sunlight on the balcony above the quiet Vieux Port, and the good meal, the wines slowly drunk, the potent liqueur and the nice proprietor. I should have offered to play him a little tune, I thought, once the clients had cleared out. Mostly, though, we thought about how sharp and fast those police needles were, thrusting thirstily into the bowels of every basket, looking for the bowels of every hidden wretch.

Once we were on board the miserable little hulk, our feelings about the ex-brigands who scuttled over it to keep us more or less fed and bedded for the next thirty-six days were more mixed than they might have been: had these wild-eyed human wrecks plotted to harbor three desperate fellow travellers along with us innocents heading toward the Land of the Free? We ate at the one mess table with the officers, and grew easy enough with them, but no word was ever said about our delayed sailing. Well after we landed in Paydro, though, we learned that according to the newspapers one of a suspected three Sicilian gangsters had indeed tried to join our ship in Marseille. He was hidden in a wicker trunk, which was carried into a small shed on the dock; some thirty bullets were jammed into it while our driver kept the cab's motor roaring and all the cops shouted louder than ever, to drown the unequivocal sounds.

I have travelled knowingly with many people in flight from one thing and another, and probably with many more I have not recognized. Of all of them, I feel sorriest for the man hopelessly folded into an airy creaking box, trying to get onto that filthy little ship on May Day. What difference could it have made to justice, to Marseille, to the total criminal population anywhere, if he had been able to emerge, once past Gibraltar, and then vanish through the Pacific Coast port authorities toward Chicago?

Years later I told my mother about this strange departure, and she said that once in about 1902 she was on a night train in Eastern Europe, and border police burst into her sleeping compartment with their swords drawn, and thrust them in a wide flash under both the berths, under the mattresses on which she and her companion lay, then into the racks above, where ladies in those days put their hats and such like. It happened in less than a minute, without a word said, and it was a breathless unforgettable adventure. Ours was actually more tedious. . . .

At home, there was the parcel of Paris-jazz-hot records we had left tipsily at the Mont Ventoux, with a scribble from the boss inviting us to come soon again. We did, but too late: he had vanished, although his restaurant still exists. And there are no more wicker trunks: the Gypsies have stopped making them, to the sorrow of provincial theatre troupes and impoverished students. They are fine for storing blankets, as well as for hiding a man or killing him invisibly, once neatly packed inside.

Chapter 11

THE GOOD OLD
BEAUVAU

I

The little street called Beauvau, for the prince who was governor of Provence in 1782, is the first to the right as one goes up the Canebière from the Vieux Port, and it ends three short blocks later at the Place de l'Opéra. By now it is a narrow subtly nervous place, disliked by drivers of anything on wheels, but in 1785 when the old quarter of the Arsenal of Galleys was rebuilt, it was an elegant but impressive thoroughfare with a fine perspective toward the beautiful theatre, and with the first real sidewalks in Marseille, made of bricks and with occasional stone posts to warn horsemen to stay where they belonged, in the unpaved roadway.

One of the first buildings on the new street housed the offices of the Post Master M. Barrochin, and the diligences stopped there, so that travellers could ask for mail that might have come on ahead. Stendhal was one of them, in

1805, when he came to Marseille to study with a famous local actress for his future book on love.

The Post Master moved, and by the time George Sand stayed there in 1839, the fine building had become a reputable and even stylish hotel, well known to travellers because of its cleanliness and its nearness to the Port. The Hotel Beauvau was a double refuge for Sand, who moved there from a hotel farther from the stench of the harbor, because the Marseillais were making plain to her their disapproval of her living openly with her lover Frédéric Chopin and her two children. (She had been once before in the town, six years earlier, with Alfred de Musset. . . .) She hated the town, full of smells and snubs, but stood it because Chopin was desperately ill and there was a famous lung specialist in the town who was somewhat scornfully rumored to be as attentive to the writer as he was to the musician. His skills did not succeed in getting George Sand into Marseille society, but Chopin revived enough to give an organ concert at Notre Dame, for a famous singer's funeral.

Another guest at the Hotel Beauvau was the poet Lamartine, who stayed there in 1832 before he set sail for the Orient. In spite of an open lack of enthusiasm among the townspeople for romantic effusions, a solemn reception was given for him, at which he read a lengthy, mellifluous ode to Marseille. In it he promised to return, which he did several times, accompanied once by his wife, and oftener by other ladies. And Prosper Mérimée stayed at the Good Old Beauvau in 1839, before embarking for Corsica. . . .

And my family and my friends and I have been staying there since our first magical lunch in its little restaurant in 1932. Since that May Day, when we too had to embark for Panama and California, knowing in bones and heart that we would return, the hotel has felt curiously like home. We

seldom talk much about it to anyone who might hate it, as
Mme. Sand did, but for different reasons. (The Port smells
fine by now; Marseille society is fortunately not essential to
us; compared with the ailing and exhausted travellers of the
last century, we are eminently free from wanting or needing
handsome medicos nearby. . . .)

The place has had sharp ups and downs in the past one
hundred and fifty years, like most of us, and although it is
currently immaculate and even somewhat elegant, I never
suggest that people stay there without being certain-sure
that they are right for it. For one thing, it could, like many
another monument of seeming impregnability, become in seven
days a shoddy dump, overrun by rats both two- and four-
legged. For another, it is very noisy, if one stays on the
water side, looking out over the whole exciting Old Port and
down onto the long Quai des Belges, ugly in 1976 with upheavals for the new Métro, but soon (What is soon in that
ancient place? A year? A century?) to be grassy and almost
prim again, with at each end a familiar bronze child, piping
and dancing. Yes, even on the top floor of the Beauvau, the
noise is not for finicky ears. It lasts most of each twenty-
four hours, what with ambulances and paddy wagons screaming in the night, and the small putt-putt of fishing boats
before dawn. . . . Another (and perhaps the main) reason I am
careful about suggesting that people go to the Beauvau, no
matter how much I love them, is that it is where it is, in the
heart of one of the greatest and therefore most wicked ports
in the world.

The first time I ever did more than eat in the hotel I was
with a fine old lady from Delaware who was discreetly terrified by this plain fact. At first I thought her unresponsive
chilliness toward everything we did or ate was connected
with the foreign drinking water, one of those touristic hazards

never mentioned but deeply respected by people of her generation. Then I realized that in spite of the air of gentility then evident in the hotel, she was acutely miserable. A maid turned down her bed and pulled the heavy velvet curtains over the noise, the beautiful view. But then my normally dignified old friend put a chair under the window handles in case some thug lurked outside on her fifth-floor balcony, and she overlapped the thick curtains with safety pins as high as she could reach, to foil Peeping Toms. She did not eat, being afraid of Mediterranean fish and repelled by both garlic and olive oil. We walked only on the Canebière, where the sidewalks were wide enough to eliminate pickpockets and jostlers. And of course we moved by the second night to a proper Anglo-American hotel near the St. Charles railroad station where, within a few hours, we took the first fast train to Cannes. It was a good lesson for me, in my study of People-and-Places.

I ignore most of the rules when I feel that the gamble may be worth it, but I have half-lost the throw a few times, and occasionally think I should quit my far-from-academic playing. Once, about ten years after the Liberation, I invited an old family counselor to stay at the Beauvau with us. We were used to very shabby furnishings in post-war Aix, and although we knew that the Good Old Beauvau had not been decently refurbished since it was used by the Occupiers during the Occupation, we were never aware of the stained carpets with holes in them, the faded dingy curtains with a few rings rattling loose on the bent rods, the cracked tiles in the 1910 bathrooms, until we saw the shock and patient disapproval of our dear friend.

He found a good chair with its springs intact, and spent most of his days there sitting with his back to the Vieux Port, reading London and New York papers and occasionally pulling out long green silk threads from the tattered upholstery. He left the hotel room only to go to luncheon and dinner, and fortunately there were some excellent restaurants to which, also fortunately, because he believed Marseille too dangerous a city to walk in, there were available taxis. When we were going less than two blocks from the Beauvau, I murmured to the driver to circulate for ten minutes . . . and although our friend spoke excellent French, he was apparently too apprehensive to pay attention to what was said to the cutthroat at the wheel. (There was also a dark corridor on the second floor, which led directly to the corner restaurant, and which I used for rainy nights and often found useful for visitors like our otherwise fearless old lawyer.)

Another time, in 1973, I ignored my unwritten game-rules too carelessly, and literally scared off our lifelong friends from Britain. As I have said, they came for a week with my sister Norah and me in Marseille and left in three days, so fast we could hardly enjoy more than their dust. Everything went wrong while they were with us, in the hotel or out: windy weather; extra noise from one of the celebrations that roar beneficently through the old town every few weeks; a touch of gut trouble blamed on garlic or olive oil or else a broody oyster (it could not have been the local water, since they carefully primed all that with drams of bedroom Scotch . . .); a general feel of apprehension and uneasiness. But by 1975 or so, both Time and Space had smoothed their mysterious salves over all of us, and letters between California and Aberdeenshire recovered their old innocent affection.

Never again, though, will I gamble with the Good Old Beauvau as *pawn*. It is too precious to be tarnished, bruised, not in its own awareness but in mine.

At first there was a tall, boxlike piece of furniture to the left as one entered the lobby, with a stool in it. The Concierge sat there in front of his books, and registered guests and answered questions and supervised every come-and-go, every strange intruder, every honored resident, as if we were unruly children in the cloister of a strict convent school. We tiptoed. People who sat across the elegant shabby lobby from him, behind the imposing vase of fresh flowers that was always there, whispered or stayed silent, and tried not to rattle their papers.

The Concierge was a tall, boxlike piece of furniture, too. He had one of the most disapproving, sneering, dour faces I ever saw, and his taciturn coldness could make me shake with frustration and almost weep, but in some forty years I came to think of him not only as honest and dedicated to his profession, but as a human being who knew and remembered me over long blank periods and who approved as warmly as he could permit himself of my children and even me.

Once I telephoned from Aix (a project in itself, involving over a half-hour of maneuverings in the nearest public booth, several blocks from our house), to ask him if he could get us tickets for the benefit vaudeville show at the Opera on Christmas Eve. He was icy with scorn and disapproval. Was I planning to expose my *children* to this exhibition of magic and lewdness? Should he ask for half-fare for the innocents? I was reduced to protesting that we had seen the show before, that it was like an English pantomime, that it was to help old vaudevillians. Why should I excuse myself? But I cringed before his grey sour face at the other end of the telephone, at the tall ornately carved desk in the Beauvau. "The children love it," I cried. "The tickets will be here when you arrive on Friday," he said curtly, and I stumbled out of the booth, ready to sob at such presumptuous hardness.

It was impossible to enter or leave the Beauvau without

passing his pulpit and his cold hateful stare, and I invented reasons to make him smile, but never succeeded. Will you please tell me when a good train leaves for Bologna? Is fresh cod in season now? Is the library at the Chamber of Commerce in the old Stock Exchange open on Mondays? He had every answer, in countless books around his legs, invisible to us circulating idiots who were not he, not the Concierge.

I came to think of him as unflinching, eternal, like Gibraltar but a little nicer. About thirty-five years after I met him, when the pulpit had been hauled away and he stood behind the Reception Desk, flanked by lissome young assistants in Pierre Cardin suits and backed by nearsighted kind girls at typewriters, I told him that I was snowbound in Marseille and that if I could not leave within three days for Paris I would be there for some time and flat broke. He shrugged disdainfully, with an impatient gesture, and said in a cold voice, "Please forget it. Stay as long as you want. We are not disquieted." Since "they" were not, neither was I.

Another time I invited an English family to stay a week at the hotel, while my sister and I lived out farther on the Vieux Port, and the morning I brought flowers for their room and their arrival, I told the Concierge that because the International Stock Exchange had closed that day, I might not be able to pay the bill until . . . "Please," he said disagreeably. "Do not discuss it further. We know you." I said no more.

Once he *almost* smiled, when I asked him if he could recommend some places around the Vieux Port for a few months of residence. He pulled out a real-estate list and crossed off at least twenty places with a murmured description of strangely lurid pastimes available in each. He made a neat list of two. "These may possibly be suitable," he said, and as I left the lobby I knew he was watching me with overt pity but perhaps, *perhaps* a tinge of warmth.

When my sister and I got the apartment we had always had in our subconscious wishes, we bought a big bunch of Transvaal daisies at the Flower Market, and left them at the old Beauvau. It was the Concierge's day off, but later one of the nice girls in glasses said he wished us to be thanked for our courteous attention. He himself never mentioned the silly posy, in several more meetings, and stayed as icy as ever, in spite of his almost familial involvement in our various lives.

I do not know his name; he has always been referred to as He, or *M. le Concierge*. By 1976 he had retired, I was told. If he is still alive, I am sure he is as nasty as ever, and I know I like him, and miss his sour gloom in the lobby.

There is one other person I miss there, who left when the Concierge did: a dark-browed man with cowlike eyes. He was the size of a midget, but heavy-shouldered, and he carried suitcases from the sidewalk to the rooms, up, down, out, in. He grew bald while we knew him, and spoke with the fruitiest Provençal accent I ever heard. The last time I saw him, squeezed into the two-person elevator with several bags and me, he asked very shyly if I remembered him, and then, "How are the little girls?" I told him they had children of their own. He looked unbelieving, but said nothing until he left me in my room, when he muttered something almost unintelligible about how Time passes, eh, Madame? He had tears in his dumb brown eyes, and ran out the door.

Now dapper, frail boys stagger under the airplane luggage, and elegantly dressed and coiffed oldsters of perhaps twenty-three man Reception, still backed by nearsighted typists and telephone girls. The flowers are gone from the little cluster of tables and chairs in the lobby, and if one doesn't know of a delightful low sitting room between the ground floor and the next official one, where flowers always bloom for the aficionados of the Good Old Beauvau, the place looks un-inviting, even without the Concierge.

At the time he sneered down on us all from his high pulpit, there were curved glass cases on the lobby walls, to display perfumes and scarves and other touristic fancies. Gradually they emptied and grew haphazard, if not openly neglected: a few rolls of Kodak film, two flyspecked *santons*, a hand-painted scarf saying "Souvenir du Château d'If." Since about 1971 they have been taken down, to nobody's chagrin.

But until about then, there was a direct path, indicated by deliberately unreadable signs, up strange stairs and down corridors, to the hotel restaurant. The route was dank and smelly. One went past the kitchens, sure of being lost or unwelcome, and suddenly there was a lovely room, glass on two sides, sparkling with silver and goblets and stiff linens. It never seemed anything but good to me, although of course I had eaten meals there that my friends did not find as special as I. The service was not only excellent but *concerned*, so that it seemed to matter to everyone if the salad dressing was correct, or the orange tart crisp. This temple of welcome has gone, like the Concierge and the midget porter and countless other permanencies. But it may rise again, and I hope it will once more have a secret upstairs tunnel from the hotel, for rainy nights and wary strangers.

Meanwhile, outside the hotel door on the Rue Beauvau, is a small well-incised plaque, high enough above the sidewalk to stay free of graffiti:

> Alphonse de Lamartine   en 1832
> Frédéric Chopin   en 1839
> George Sand
> séjournèrent en cet hôtel

and I smile at the sight and the thought of it, because underneath, there is another smaller notice, invisible of course except to a chosen few:

We too, in 1932 and on—

I I

By now I have spent all four seasons of the year on or near the Vieux Port, although it has taken me a long time to do it. I know the look and smell of the place at its best and perhaps its worst, as far as wind and weather can go, and of course I have been very uncomfortable there. Once in late July I looked up the Canebière and wondered if I could walk to the next bit of awning shade without falling down in the white-hot glare. Once I thought my hour had come, in a small boat trying to return from the New Port, La Joliette, around the small stretch of open wild tossing Mediterranean into the Old Port. And of course there have been times of whims and megrims . . . stars and planets pulling all of us this way and that, willy-nilly, tidal waves in small ponds and teapots. But what remains is good. It always has been. And the old hotel on the Quai des Belges has mysteriously been its core.

It seems strange that I have spent several Christmases in Marseille. They are like glass-headed pins on a map, fixing Time into a conditioned focus: it is clearer to think of December 25 than of March 22, or even July 4, I suppose, in any given year of a lifetime.

It may be even stranger that several of those holidays on my inner calendar were located in the Good Old Beauvau, as many other times have been. Again one wonders what pin holds hard to the physical and spiritual map a certain locality. Why that place? But that place it was, without argument.

One of the times, when I was living in Aix in the 1950s with my little girls, we went with instinctive directness to the Beauvau, and what happened there made me remember a jingle I once knew, by Thackeray, I think:

> Christmas is here:
> Winds whistle shrill,
> Icy and chill.
> Little care we;
> Little we fear
> Weather without,
> Sheltered about
> The Mahogany Tree.

I dreaded for the children the sudden awareness of being in a far country that can engulf Occidental travellers at Christmas more probably than any other time. If I had never actually felt it myself, I knew it lurked like a sad sickness, an almost invisible malaise, for many people. I reflected often, as the season approached, about what best to do to keep my girls happy and warm and gay when they would be light-miles from everything they had always known at home.

Friends were kind to us, in the face of the truism that Noël to Frenchmen means doors locked against the world, tight family ritual. I refused their solicitude and made one of those arbitrary, almost brutal decisions familiar to guardians and other duly appointed dictators, and on December 24 we took the bus into Marseille, to the edge of the Old Port and the small hotel we knew happily, from other such private flights—the Good Old Beauvau.

There is nothing much grimmer, I have heard too often, than Christmas in a hotel bedroom. I felt quite free from bravado, but I was bent upon disproving this for the three of us, somewhat as if staring the obvious in the eye would be more of a real diversion than peering obliquely at it from the friendly courtesies of Madame Lanes or the Aubergy family. We were thousands of miles from home, in a shabby old building in a dubious port-town . . . and we reacted to my deliberate dare like healthy firehorses at the sound of the bell: never had I seen my girls more sparkling and alive, nor myself felt surer.

The two rooms were familiar to us. First thing, we pulled back the once-elegant curtains as usual, to see all we could of the Quai below, and the Vieux Port, packed with fishing boats and a few big yachts docked for the winter and one American Navy craft, nosed in right at our feet, by the stone that marks where the first sailors may have landed more than two thousand years ago.

When Anne and Mary asked where we were going to open the secrets that we had all been wrapping furtively in Aix for Christmas morning, I suddenly knew what had been bothering my subconscious. "We'll grow a tree for them," I said. "Oh, of course," the children said. And there in front of the tall bright windows, as if a magic seed had been planted in the stained old carpet, grew the hatrack from the little hallway.

It was even taller than I, made of Victorian mahogany, shaped into a slender trunk, a sudden curling of branches at the top like a wildly functional palm tree, for gentlemen's hats and coats, with at the bottom convenient shorter curls to put our secret bundles in. It was perfect.

We left it there in the light, an earnest for the future, bare but ready.

Outside the air was cold and exciting. People rushed this way and that, clutching parcels and scarves and hats, gathering in knots and then melting back, around old men playing trick instruments that sounded now like guitars and now horns or drums, and two women with a troupe of trained mice shivering in the wind, and a fat man lying on a worn rug, while a boy, paper-thin, did somersaults and pirouettes on the upstretched massive feet. . . .

First we went along the edge of the Old Port to the ferry crossing, a part of our Marseille pattern, like pulling back the curtains. If we had ever felt in danger in that tiny harbor, we knew we were safe on Christmas Eve, for in the middle of the stuffy little flat boat was a crêche, shivering gently to the pound of the engine below it.

There was a Holy Family, perhaps two inches high, with the Baby Jesus in his cradle, and there were the shepherds, and even three tiny sheep following the Wise Men. The *santons* were everywhere in Provence at Christmastime in those far days, and Anne and Mary approved happily and pointed out characters they already knew from the dozens of them in *La Pastorale*, a version of the Nativity, as much of the Midi as garlic and *pastis*. Before the five-minute voyage ended with a good bump against the opposite quay, we had each added some coins to the conveniently large shell by the Manger, for the crew of our doughty little ship. . . .

We passed judgment on a few more crêches that afternoon, in spite of our hurry: a favorite bar, a good restaurant, stores, bank windows. The *santons* were usually bigger, often more beautiful, dressed in rich silks and jewels sometimes, but we liked best the tiny figures standing in sand and seaweed on the ferryboat.

The crowds grew denser as the light greyed. There was still much we must do, to make the Mahogany Tree thrive, and I felt that I should keep everything more than life-size, however I dared, to hold us firmly in Marseille, not drifting toward California.

That is why I let the little girls go off alone, for the first time in that town, with some money and some directions. "Buy shiny little bonbons," I said nonchalantly. "And stay on the Canebière. And don't go up it more than three blocks. And always cross with a lot of other people. And come straight back to the hotel." And I hurried away from them, not daring to look past the sight of Mary's hand in Anne's. My heart lurched. I felt one flash of horror at what I had done, to send my children alone into the jungle.

When I dashed into the lobby with a bag from the pastry shop, and two bundles of Christmas Roses I had bought from a streetseller, and some caviar and champagne and a ball of red string, Anne and Mary sat primly behind the high carved desk of the Concierge, like two small trunks to be delivered to our rooms. Their laps were piled with many more paper bags and packages than I had given them money for.

Upstairs, we went through their loot. Storekeepers had insisted, they told me solemnly, that they take a few samples of things along with what they actually bought: pipe cleaners to make into strange shapes, a bag of gold-covered chocolate coins to hang from the wooden branches, handfuls of brightly wrapped bonbons, a surprising mesh bag filled with little plastic airplanes and tanks and racing cars, "half-price to us because we are so far from home," I was told blandly.

Anne invented a way to coil red string up the tree trunk and hang things from it. Mary fitted our secret packages around the bottom. I did the tall work. All the time, below us and out to the Fort St. Nicolas, the Old Port lay black and heaving, covered with boats glinting in the lights from the bright quays, the two dogged little ferries crisscrossing, and cars and buses blowing their whistles into the crowds of heedless excited people, and above everything, perhaps more sacred than profanely pagan, the steady golden radiance of the great statue of Notre Dame de la Garde, to guide us to safety from the farthest wave.

Our tree was beautiful, too. We turned off the lights, and let the Vieux Port glow behind it. The little candies and toys swung slowly on their long strings from the topknot of branches, and beneath them the Christmas secrets waited.

We ate a small slow meal in a little restaurant where the family *santons*, carved from olivewood and dressed in ancient woven costumes, made one more crêche for us, and the cook, already gently illuminated by his own Christmas spirits, sang the children a long Provençal carol about the shepherds watching their flocks by night. Back at the Beauvau, Mary took a nap, and Anne and I sat silently in a big chair by our Mahogany Tree, watching the Port. While we were at dinner the Navy craft had turned on long strings of flickering colored lights, and lanterns moved slowly up and down on the small boats in the windy night, and all the cafés along the Quai du Port and the fishhouses of the Rive Neuve were bright . . .

. . . and suddenly the bells were ringing everywhere . . .

. . . and we pushed coat and mittens onto Mary, and ran out into the town again. We were late: it was just midnight. We moved with other laughing, hurrying people along the Quai des Belges toward the old church that is sinking back into the marshes of the Lacydon. Inside, we could not go faster than inches toward where we knew the altar was. We heard the faint chanting of the Mass. Even so far back, the air was shimmering from all the candles, and smelled of incense and beeswax, garlic and holiday libations. The organ thundered wheezily over our heads in the choirloft, and boys sang like birds, and more people surged in against us from the windy street.

I held onto my girls, invisible in the mass of heavily wrapped, panting, shoving Marseillais, and then as well as I could I worked us back to the big door and *out*. We stood for a moment, getting used to the secular air. I bought candles from a piteous woman on the steps. Mary, still half asleep, asked sadly why she had not been there when the new Baby Jesus was born, and I gave her the candles as promise that we would come back early in the morning to find Him there.

At home, our tree gleamed for us in the light from below, and its richly colored fruits glinted in the air we had set moving. Ah, it is beautiful, we agreed, and went straight into sleep, instead of sitting up wickedly, gaily, as we had long planned, carousing gently in the French custom for Noël.

Before daybreak, the bells burst into their Christmas song again, all over town, a thousand different exultant tones, always with the grave sound of Notre Dame de la Garde dominating. We hurried toward the church with our candles, and the nave, almost empty, was still filled with the glowing light from all the pyramids of them blazing and burning. We went slowly up to the crêche beside the great altar, where life-size *santons* stood regally or knelt with awe before the manger . . . but there, to Mary's repressed astonishment, mixed with deep dismay, were *two* cradles, with a Baby Jesus in each one! She behaved like a true Christian, ready to accept any miracle at its appointed moment, but later explanations and native logic did little to allay her basic confusion, and even Time has not quite wiped out that first chagrin. Her child's faith doubtless suffered more than my wearier acceptance could. But even I felt a clinical distaste for the newer of the two Babes.

The first was the "right" one: a faded, scratched doll of papier-mâché and wax, grossly fat like all such images of two hundred years ago, to denote well-being and contentment.

It was dressed in yellowed linen trimmed sparingly with crude lace, and one finger was gone from its pudgy raised pink hand. It lay on real straw, and around the old cradle, which looked as if it had rocked many human babies, were bowls of green and black olives, some loaves of fresh bread, a few bottles of wine, and one small cheese on a cotton napkin.

The other Christ Child lay on an ornate rayon pillow in its polished crib, so that no lowly straw might show, and it was a modern doll with luxuriant blond curls, and a ruffled christening robe intertwined with ribbons and frothing with nylon lace. Its half-closed eyes were languorous behind long lashes, and its mouth was pursed over white even teeth, ready to say *Maman*. I cannot remember that any gifts had been brought to it.

We lit candles here and there in the echoing church, and then gave coins to the piteous vendor still dozing outside, waved to a familiar bus driver at the Aix-stop on the Quai, and hurried home to our tree, with all the bells still pealing.

The sun was up. The ripe fruits twinkled and twirled on their long stems. We flipped our beds into shape, pushed a little table next to the Tree, telephoned for pots of hot milk and coffee and extra plates. I brought in last night's untouched feast from the balcony.

There was a new young waiter, whose lonesome face lit up when he saw our celebration. We picked some of our fruit for him, and he took a few sips of champagne and went off almost gaily, with tacit approval.

Then we ate one of the strangest Christmas breakfasts of our combined lives: caviar on hot rolls, big cups of frothy café au lait for Anne and Mary and the cool dry wine for me, and finally, thick ceremonious slices, so far past our slaked hunger that they became pure sensuality, from the *Bûche de Noël* I had bought. It was the smallest Christmas

Log in all Marseille, probably, but even so its rich chocolate bark, its inner trunk of whipped cream and delicate dark sponge cake, its leaves from the dainty sprigs of holly shaped in almond paste, almost made us reel in our chairs. We sat back like Roman banqueters, stunned, waiting half comatose in the bright sunlight for digestion to rescue us.

Anne suddenly produced three tiny bottles made of chocolate wrapped in silver foil. They were, she assured me unblinkingly, filled with a nonalcoholic digestive, highly recommended to her by a charming man in a wine shop she had dropped into during her Christmas marketing. Mary added firmly, as a future medico of the family, that they were indeed indicated for just such an emergency as our present one, and that they had not cost a sou, because of the seasonal jollity. . . . Pure flim-flam, I decided with some maternal satisfaction, and smiled at my innocents.

We bit off the chocolate corks of the dwarf-size potions, and solemnly toasted each other and California and the world in general, with some drops of what may well have been a digestive, and gradually we revived, and the shabby old bedroom took on its final triumphant look of Christmas, with drifts of tissue paper from our secret packages piled on the stained red carpet. The air hummed with cries and murmurs of pleasure, above the sound of all Marseille hurrying to late Mass, early lunch at Aunt Mary-Martha's, a holiday *pastis* at Mario's Bar-Grill. Below our windows the Old Port lifted and fell gently after yesterday's small wind. Over it all, us, the Port, the whole wonderful old town, rose our Mahogany Tree, hanging rich and generous with its harvest of bright fruits.

I thought of singing. Then I remembered how far away we might still feel from home. I began to tell Anne and Mary about Old Joseph of Arimethaea, and of how he wandered far from Jerusalem, perhaps with a Holy Grail under his arm. When he got to Glastonbury in England, I told them as we sat under our Tree, he stuck his dry hawthorn staff into the ground, and it burst into leaves and blossoms to celebrate Christ's birth. Twigs from that staff still bloom, at Christmastime . . . just as we knew that other dead stalks in other lands east, south, west, north, could bring forth their own blossoms and sweet berries, and for the same reasons.

We felt safe and trusting—*home*.

A CONCLUSION

Yes.

Like Mme. de Sévigné, I am giddied by "the whole atmosphere . . . the sea, the fortresses, the mountains. . . ." And I would *be* there, past, present, future. I would be near the Vieux Port, within sight and feel of it.

One day I found the Harbor Master. It took me some time, partly because I did not know his correct title of Port Captain. I asked at the big Criée on the Rive Neuve, and was referred to a couple of small cafés and a chandlery.

The cafés were the kind that fell silent when I went in, first because I was a female foreigner who obviously did not know where she was, and second because I asked a question the people preferred not to answer: Where was the Harbor Master? (Later I learned from him that the owners and workers at the public fish auctions were at odds with him, choosing to stay right where they were on the Rive Neuve when he wanted to move them up the coast.) The chandlery was run, hopefully for a short time, by a bewildered beautiful young drifter from Rouen or someplace far north, and he fluttered helplessly and then suggested I go across the street to the most important of the yacht clubs, which I did.

It was covered with signs warning me not to set foot in it, but I went up the elegant gangplank and read a dramatic map of the moorings available to the members and a delicious menu for that night's dinner, before I was ushered in and then out of a busy little man's office: he could do nothing for me and knew nothing at all about anything I hoped to learn. (Later I suspected that he too preferred not to recall the Harbor Master, whose proletarian opinion that the valuable privately controlled moorings along the quays really belonged to the city of Marseille, for fair taxation anyway, was unpalatable.)

I went off the Rive Neuve, up to the Rue Sainte, which used to be the road that led Greeks and then Romans to their cemeteries high on the hill where St. Victor was later built. On one of the old buildings I found a grimy brass plate saying something like Reunion Society of Pleasure Boat-Owners, and went into a dark smelly hallway and halfway up the first flight of some rotting narrow stairs before I heard myself telling me to turn around and leave, get out, forget the reason for being in such a foul sinister deserted building. Victorian words like *malodorous, invidious*, were in my head, and when I got back onto the Rue Sainte, I felt a childish relief that nobody had heard my steps or run after me, scrabbling ratlike . . . twisted little legs . . . one ear under a straggle of grey hair . . . "Madame, Madame! Come back! Come smile at me. . . ."

I walked firmly down to the Rive Neuve again, and banged on a couple of locked doors in the bright sunlight, small neat clubhouses for the Bargemen's Union, the Jolly Syndicate of

Oars and Anchors. Finally a man in the bait shack at the bend of the Rive Neuve into the Quai des Belges sent me, correctly enough, to Number Three on the Quai du Port.

It was easy, too easy after my various frustrations, right off the far end of the Quai opposite the little bait shop, and I felt encouraged. But Number Three was a small souvenir store run by an attractive plump woman who explained compassionately to me that the Quai du Port *naturally* started at both ends and stopped at the Town Hall in the middle, or something like that. I would find the Harbor Master at Number Three at the other end, she said.

The day was hot and by then I was footweary and there was tomorrow, so I waited for it behind a cool glass of rosé. And in some twenty hours I was at the sea end of the Quai, a place familiar to me for many years because of the fine small buildings there, which I never even dreamed were oc-cupied by the elusive Captain and his crew. I felt shy about simply walking through the gate by the first of the two matching Italianate pavilions and asking to see the boss, but there had been no apparent way to telephone for an appoint-ment. I pretended I was a young, eager, beautiful girl-reporter in a TV serial. . . .

The buildings are lovely, especially from across the Port: low, graceful. The first was built in 1719, to house the officials of the Health and Sanitation works, and its twin sister was added in the nineteenth century. There is a famous statue of St. Roch over the gateway, erected to protect Marseille against the Plague, "Scourge of Provence." It is perhaps more a symbol of blind faith than of terror by now, but well repaired after an American corvette knocked it down while maneuver-ing up to the Quai for a medical inspection in 1839. There used to be important carvings and paintings inside, mostly about health and sanitation, of course (i.e., disease and sewage . . .), but they have been moved to better housing, and by 1973 when I went to meet the Harbor Master, the large light rooms were sparsely furnished, very clean, with a few bright posters and blown-up photographs of the Vieux Port on their walls, and the tall graceful windows wide open. (In 1976 all the business was located on a large square floating dock, while the fine old pavilions underwent restoration as valuable historical architecture.)

At first I thought nobody worked there. It was as quiet as a country garden-house. Then a lone young man spotted my obvious confusion about where to find the Captain behind one of the unmarked open doors, and when I told him why I was there he conferred somewhere. The hall I was in was bare and airy, and a bee buzzed in and then out onto the waterfront. I could hear a typewriter somewhere, tapped hesitantly. The clerk beckoned to me, and I went into a big, almost naked office where he introduced me to Captain Agostelli and then left.

The Harbor Master was a tall, square man, more like a Northerner than a Marseillais except for his dark eyes. He was courteous in a gruff way, and reminded me of Inspector Maigret, which I finally told him. That seemed to please him very much. I soon stopped trying to be a bright, scared news-hen and felt like myself, always comfortable with an attractive person across from me.

Captain Agostelli was talkative, in the easy way of a man who has nothing in the world to do but chat about his main interest in life. It seemed impossible that he watched over the whole Port, like an eagle, like a beagle, like Maigret himself, as we sat there in the fresh salty air and he told me of what was happening that day, that minute, outside the window.

In April of 1973, the Captain estimated, there were about

2,600 boats of all categories there: 1,696 pleasure craft, mostly sail; 250 motorcraft in the small marinas of the Lacydon off the Rive Neuve; 372 fishing boats, of which 115 were more than 12 meters long; 373 yachts in passage of ten days or less. Of these last, 163 were French, 107 English, 18 American, 27 Panamanian (American), 22 Belgian, 8 Dutch, 7 German and 7 Spanish, 5 Italian, and the rest Austrian, Portuguese, Bermudan, Canadian, Argentinian, Puerto Rican, and so on.

Most of the yachts, he said, were very rich, into port for fuel on their way to more stylish moorings, where their owners would meet them by plane. Their crews were highly skilled in every possible way, he said noncommittally.

On all the trawlers in port, the *chalutiers*, of more than twelve meters and often with deep draft, there was a large floating population of foreign fishermen, with two or three Frenchmen as owner-captains. Their papers were kept firmly in order, and for a stay of more than one or two days, the crewmen had to report with their *permis de séjour* to the Marseille Police Headquarters. The men were mostly Portuguese in 1973, with Arabs next, and then a scattering of every other nation, and all of them wanted to bring their families to Marseille.

The low-cost housing problem, Captain Agostelli said, was tight for these people. Local fishermen made as many as a couple of short sorties a day, but the trawlers often went out for three or more, for tuna, and sometimes for several weeks. The women and children needed decent quarters, and HLM was obviously the answer to the worldwide and age-old question, Who will pay? (HLM, which in French sounds like an exotic Moslem word, Ash-el-Emm, is often mentioned in Provence and probably everywhere in France, and stands for *Habitations à Loyer Modéré*. . . .) Of course the families wanted to be near the Port, not out in the suburbs. This meant demolition, high-rise, more non-French. . . . He shrugged hopelessly.

Another current problem was the relocation of the public fish auctions, the big Criée and the two or three smaller ones. They were destined to be moved from the Rive Neuve to a new port designed especially for the collection and distribution of the catch, at Somaty, between the big harbor of La Joliette and l'Estaque, where Cézanne once painted. Everything was (and still is) ready: conveyor belts, proper loading zones for the fleets of trucks from all over Europe, a quick-freeze installation, railroad tracks. But the *criées* could not come to terms, to the exasperation of the Port authorities and especially of the Captain.

Still another thing that plainly made him fret and perhaps lose sleep was that nobody ever seemed to know who was responsible for harbor improvements. This had been going on for centuries, he growled. In 1784, for instance, when the lands belonging to the Grand Arsenal of Galleys were sold, a majestic plan to enlarge the Port was proposed. The government, of course, would have nothing to do with it. It seems that the Port had belonged to the city since the thirteenth century, and anyway it had never been made clear who owned the water itself and the quays. Furthermore, nobody was willing to claim possession of anything at all, because of the proposed expenses for improvement! And the citizens were pleased with things as they were; in spite of the infamous stench they had pleasant views, an agreeable promenade along the Quai du Port, a safe harbor for storm-bound vessels. . . .

I asked the Captain about the Chamber of Commerce. He

threw up his hands, and muttered that it was the same in those days as today: independent, implacable, impossible. Occasionally, as in 1838 when the town refused to widen the Quai du Port, the Chamber put up some 800,000 francs, mostly to thwart the Municipal Council by forcing it to let some of the nice old buildings be demolished. In the same finagling way, a new port for the dangerously flammable job of caulking ships was installed just under St. Victor on the Rive Neuve, with the city bowing out and the government taking charge and, of course, the Chamber of Commerce contributing 600,000 francs. . . .

"And now?" It was plain to me that the Captain was whipping a favorite nag.

"Now," he said almost ominously, "I must sit here and watch a slow rape of this fine old Port. In New York, where I worked with the Port Authority for more than a year, learning, learning, every inch dockside is privately owned and paid for. Therefore rents and taxes are completely controlled. Here in Marseille everything is now in the hands of the city, and supposedly the people, and is therefore corrupt and ill-managed."

I felt almost uneasy at his candid vehemence, for posters from the last elections were still peeling off the town walls, and I knew who owned the local newspapers and a little of what the town fathers were promising. He was indiscreet.

"Do you know the Société Nautique du Lacydon?" he asked, thumping his desk the way an impatient bull will paw the ground when nobody is looking. His face was red.

I told him that I looked down on it from where I lived above St. Victor: a neat small port filled with pleasure boats. He snorted. "That was an enormous job, all footed by the City of Marseille, with no repayment of any kind demanded for the first three years, and with memberships in what amounts to a rich private club selling for huge sums that go into the club itself! Who owns it? Is the city collecting any taxes? And who paid for it? It cost us millions, I tell you!"

He stood up and loosened his collar and sat down again. "I learned a lot in New York," he said mildly. "And what do you think of our sewage? This was once the foulest port in the Western world."

I told him that it smelled fairly clean to me . . . compared, for instance, to the East River around the docks in New York. Of course, I said cautiously, there were always bits of rubbish brushing against the Quai des Belges before the garbage-sweep sucked them up . . . especially after a holiday. . . .

He said, "There again! The government! The town! In 1837 several studies were made of how to swill out this bucket, after the City had organized a futile system of pontoons with scoops and so on, but the State declined to mix in what it called 'a local problem.' And here we are, known worldwide as the filthiest, most stinking port in the world! We had one little scow that went around, called *Marie-Salope*, Mary the Slut. By 1857 the Port was so filled with silt that even she could not navigate well, and the pollution was incredible. We were getting about 150 liters of filthy water a second, to flush out a Port with an overall water surface of some 27,000 square meters! Then in 1850 Longchamps brought us the clean water of the Durance, a steady flow of more than a thousand liters a second." He stood up again, tightened his tie, and said, "We still have *Marie-Salope* on duty. The open pipes are connected to a main one that dumps away from shore, and the household garbage is carted off to Le Crau, but . . . no doubt New York has its problems too."

"No doubt," I said. He sat down just before I stood up to

thank him and go. He looked strong and unruffled. "There is always something interesting going on here," he said chattily. "Perhaps you could help me with a little problem. . . ."

I could not keep from laughing, and it was then that I told him he reminded me very much of Simenon's Inspector Maigret. He looked enormously pleased, and almost smirked as he leaned back and said, "I should be puffing at a pipe! Well, the come-and-go of yachts here is really much too casual for my own comfort, and I have one sticky little situation on my hands right now that involves one of your countrymen. You know that when a skipper comes in, he shows me his passport, but no note is made of it here?"

"We have to in hotels," I interrupted, and he said, "Yes, but not in ports. It is careless, all right, but it's a French tradition. And an American with an odd name, something like Hirsh Guinafrom, from some little town in perhaps New Jersey, docked here about ten months ago, complete with a crew of one beautiful dame, and showed me a passport which I returned to him, and then he disappeared. He and the woman simply vanished.

"In about six months I began to get a lot of complaints from other boat owners about the dangerous condition of the abandoned yacht, and I wrote to the town in America. Answer: 'Person Unknown.'"

I felt as if I were reading the last book off the Presses de la Cité, with Maigret across the desk from me instead of his Marseille sibling. I suggested in a rather ambiguous way that the local American Consul would probably be able to verify the name and address if such a passport still existed, or even if it did not. The name did not sound quite right, I said.

Agostelli sighed as if he were tired, weary, exhausted. "Perhaps it will have to come to that," he muttered. But I could see that he much preferred to let the unwelcome de-

serted boat rot or burn or sink, or break loose and drift out
to sea. . . .

We looked appreciatively at each other, he because I had
told him he reminded me of a mutual hero, and I because he
was a pleasant person, and after my thanks I left the bright,
salty air of his office with regret. I was glad I had tracked
him down.

On the way home, around the three sides of the Vieux
Port, I felt at ease, perhaps more than ever before. There
were things I missed: the jugglers at Christmastime in the
fifties; my children then; the man I called Bacchus who for
a while in the sixties sold shells marked "Coastal," "Local,"
"Exotic," while he looked peacefully at the Port and drank
five or six liters a day of dark red wine; the strangest beggar
of my whole life in the doorway of the old church sinking
into the marshes of the Lacydon.

He was perhaps the last of the great army of professional
mendicants who once almost ruled the town of Marseille,
and occupied the Vieille Charité and directed the funerals
and weddings of the helpless citizens with their threats and
payments. He lay motionless and soundless, comatose, in rain
and blazing heat, one leg cut off, hardly a living thing except
for a small trickle of urine that now and then seeped out.
Someone must have come at night to pile him onto a cart
and take him away until the next morning, and dump a few
coins out of the old mariner's cap that lay by him all day.
It was hard to look at him, except as a once-man, until the
day when I made myself see past his bloated face, past his
one leg, past his thin red hair, and he opened his bright pale
blue eyes and gazed straight at me, and I knew who he was.

Twenty years and fifteen years before, he had been the
strong bold Gypsy-boy in Aix, a jaunty gimpy with a crutch
and blazing hair, and red-haired, blue-eyed babies by every

little skinny Gypsy-girl in town. He had swung boldly up and down the Cours Mirabeau, never begging, but watching his girl-women at their trades. I had seen him since he was perhaps fourteen, when he already had one small girl pregnant and proud.

He looked fully at me, and I at him, because he knew exactly who I was. I felt shaken. The recognition was ageless. Then his eyes closed, and he was a bag of rotted rags and bones, and I went down the quay past the bus stop to Aix, knowing that I had touched Time on the sleeve.

Perhaps that is what makes it essential that I be in Marseille, to stay in active contact with immortality now and then. It is not necessary to have a dead man look into my eyes, any more than it is to talk with a fine healthy Port Captain or watch my children skip carefully between the long nets laid out to be mended, tomorrow or twenty years ago. But how can I know, otherwise?